Growth of Constantine's

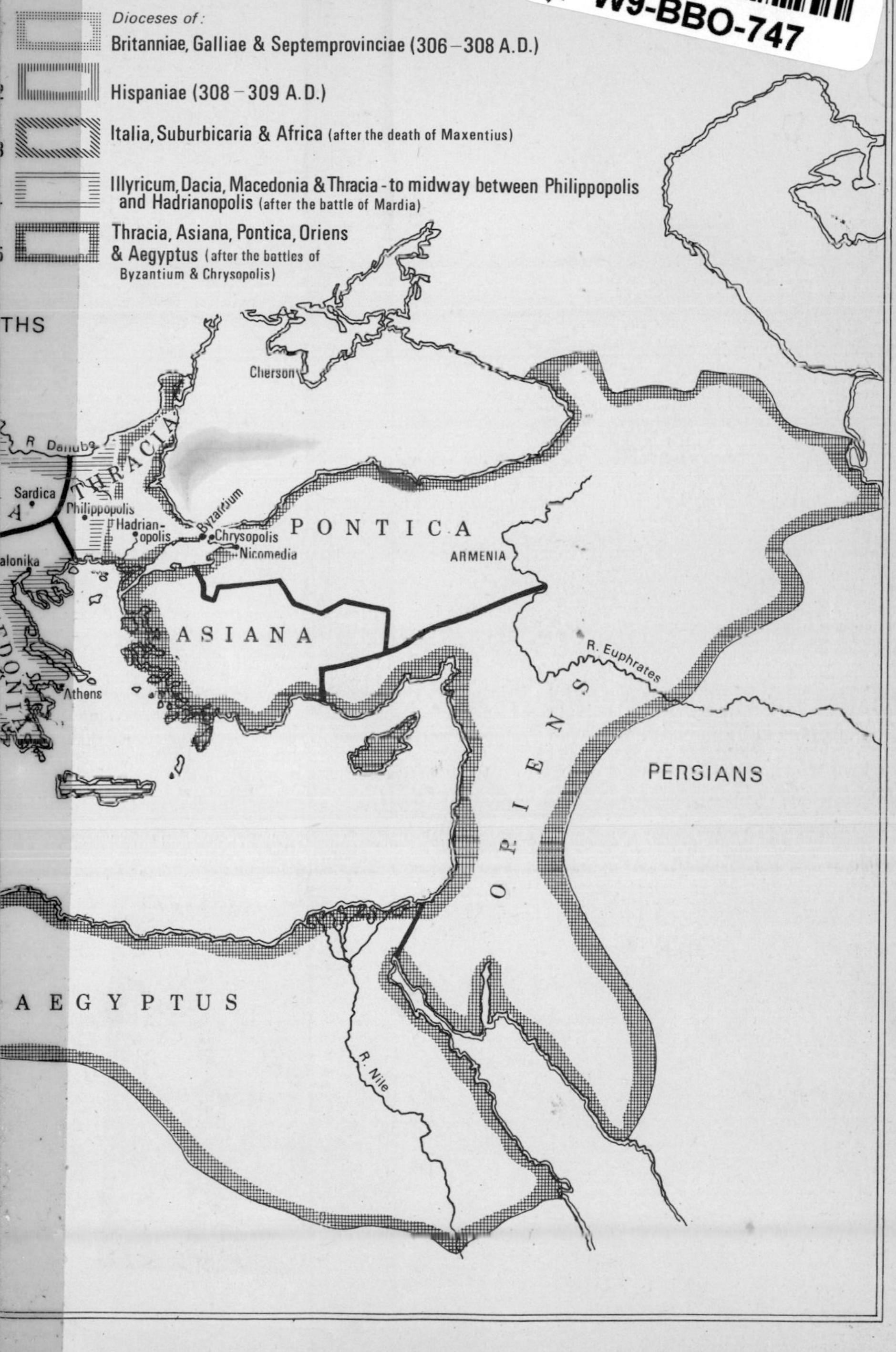
Dioceses of:
Britanniae, Galliae & Septemprovinciae (306–308 A.D.)
Hispaniae (308–309 A.D.)
Italia, Suburbicaria & Africa (after the death of Maxentius)
Illyricum, Dacia, Macedonia & Thracia - to midway between Philippopolis and Hadrianopolis (after the battle of Mardia)
Thracia, Asiana, Pontica, Oriens & Aegyptus (after the battles of Byzantium & Chrysopolis)
THS
Cherson
R Danube
THRACIA
Sardica
A
Philippopolis
Hadrian-opolis
Byzantium
Chrysopolis
Nicomedia
PONTICA
ARMENIA
alonika
ASIANA
Athens
R. Euphrates
ORIENS
PERSIANS
AEGYPTUS
R. Nile

CONSTANTINE THE GREAT

By the same Author

THE GREAT SCHISM 1378:
THE DISINTEGRATION OF THE PAPACY

Colossal marble head of the Emperor Constantine.
Roman, fourth century

Photo: Metropolitan Museum of Art, New York

CONSTANTIN
THE GREAT

JOHN HOLLAND SMITH

CHARLES SCRIBNER'S SONS
NEW YORK

B
Constantine

A-1-71 (I)

Printed in Great Britain

SBN 684-12391-6

Library of Congress Catalog Card Number 77-143935

For my father and mother

ACKNOWLEDGEMENT

I am greatly indebted to the Librarian and Staff of the Royal University of Malta.

JOHN HOLLAND SMITH

CONTENTS

LIST OF ILLUSTRATIONS

Maps

(Drawn by Patrick Leeson)

CHAPTER ONE

THE FAMILY

FLAVIUS Valerius Constantinus, known to later ages as Constantine the Great, celebrated his birthday on February 27[1], but unfortunately never disclosed how old he was in any given year, even if he knew it himself. The Christian historian Eusebius, the Bishop of Caesarea, who preached his funeral oration and was his first biographer, said that he lived twice as long as Alexander the Great, and that his life-span was double that of his reign. He was emperor for thirty-one years, in terms of the Christian era from A.D. 306 to 337; Alexander was thirty-two when he died. By Eusebius's account, then, Constantine lived between sixty-two and sixty-four years, and was born in the reign of the Emperor Aurelian, between 273 and 275[2].

This date is nowhere absolutely contradicted, but there are several small yet significant indications that he may in fact have been born several years later than the traditional 274, and have seized power when little more than twenty years old. Most significant, perhaps, is a chance remark of his own, to the effect that, at the time of the outbreak of the Great Persecution of the Christians in 303, he was 'little more than a child'[3]. Again, there is once said to have existed at the Emperor Maximian's villa at Aquileia a family portrait which, unless it was a work of pure imagination, must have been made between 289 and 293, showing Constantine as a little boy. Moreover, the panegyrist at Constantine's wedding feast in March 307 spoke of him as 'the adolescent emperor'[4]. The panegyrist was out to flatter, and it is easy for a man looking back on great events to think 'How young I was in those days!', but few men would consider themselves children at the age of thirty, and to call an emperor of thirty-two or -three 'adolescent' would be to carry flattery to the point of insult. So although it is commonly said that

Constantine was born in the year 274, and for convenience's sake that date will be used here, it may well be that he was not actually born until five years later, and was aged about twenty-five when he became Caesar in the West in 306. His birth can scarcely have occurred at any date later than 280, because he was already known for his courage and fine bearing in the mid-nineties, and it is hard to imagine a man showing such soldierly qualities before the age of fifteen.

His father was Flavius Valerius Constantius, known to later Byzantine historians as the Emperor Constantius I, 'Chlorus', 'the Pale'. His mother was Helena, later called Saint Helena, and remembered for her alleged discovery at Jerusalem of the cross on which Christ was crucified. At the time of their son's birth, if that event in fact occurred in the seventies of the third century, Constantius was still only at the beginning of a brilliant military career. Eulogising Constantine five years after his accession to imperial authority, the panegyrist Eumenius hinted that the Flavians were of the most noble descent and deserved power on that account, one of their ancestors having been the Emperor Claudius II, Gothicus (268–70)[5]. The story is of very doubtful provenance. It was probably inspired by Constantine himself, to give the family some respectability, and dissociate it from its immediate imperial predecessors. Like most legends, it underwent development with the passage of time. At various stages, it claimed that Constantius Chlorus was the earlier emperor's bastard, his nephew and his great-nephew. When it was firmly established, imperial propaganda maintained that 'Claudius [Gothicus], Quintillus and Crispus were brothers; Claudia was Crispus' daughter, and Constantius Caesar was born of her and Eutropius, a most noble man of the Dardanian race'[6]. The real name of Claudius, the Conqueror of the Goths [Gothicus], was probably Marcus Aurelius Claudius, but he was also called in official inscriptions Flavius Claudius Valerius Aurelius; the Flavian legend assumes that when 'the most noble Eutropius', whoever he really was, married the emperor's niece Claudia, he adopted the family name 'Valerius' and the imperial forename 'Flavius', styling himself Flavius Valerius

Eutropius to claim connections through his wife's people with two of the oldest Roman families: the plebeian Flavians, whose history could be traced back to the days of the Republic, and the patrician Valerians, whose founder was a Sabine immigrant into Rome before the expulsion of the kings.

Constantius Chlorus's father may have been a Dardanian named Eutropius, but otherwise the story is most unlikely. If the truth were known, he probably started from nowhere. Aurelius Victor, the historian and gossip, claimed to know that he was the son of a peasant from a backward corner of the empire[7]. Victor was probably right, but the point was unimportant. As far as that was concerned, Claudius 'the Goth', whom Constantine acclaimed as his forebear and founder of the Neo-Flavian line, would have found it hard to prove his descent from the most important of the old Flavians, Titus Flavius Petro of Rieti, a centurion in the army of Pompey the Great, who, honourably discharged after the Battle of Pharsalus, became a tax-collector. His son Sabinus followed him in this career with such singular probity that he was immortalised with statues 'to the honest taxman', although his grandsons deserted it, the one, Sabinus, to become Rome's City Prefect, the other the Emperor Vespasian. Surviving references to Constantius 'the Pale' suggest that he was an outwardly calm but inwardly tense man, whose white face was a symptom of the intense energy which he put into the struggle for survival and self-advancement during bloody years when the empire was threatened not only by foreign enemies but also by revolution and civil war. Although in later years Constantine tried, for political reasons, to impress on his contemporaries the nobility of his father's descent, in the years of Constantius' rise to power nobility counted for little beside ability, a forceful character and reliable friends.

The Roman world was very different from what it had been in the days of Augustus and Tiberius. It had little interior stability, its finances were overstrained, its population anxious, and its future uncertain. Emperors seized and held power by virtue of their control of Rome's largely non-Italian armies –

and so, in the last resort, by strength of character. Of the emperors who bickered over power or shared it in the forty-four years between the death of Claudius the Goth and his putative great-grand-nephew Constantine's establishment of himself as sole emperor in 324 – Aurelian, Tacitus, Probus, Carus, Carinus, Numerian, Diocletian, Maximian, Galerius, Constantius, Maximum Daia, Severus and Licinius – only the least effectual, the brothers Carinus and Numerian, actually inherited power from their father; the others owed their success not to their birth but to their grasp of the existing situation. Coming mostly from Illyria (modern Yugoslavia) or the Danube area, the majority were little better than bandits whose terrorism had been legalised by the grant of military commissions and whose survival depended on their forcefulness, not their blood. Constantius Chlorus was not unlike them, despite his reputation for gravity and respect for learning. If he had been essentially different he would not have lived to rule till overtaken by a natural death.

An inscription fixes Constantius's birthday as March 31[8], but the year of his birth is unknown. He is said to have been 'first a Protector [imperial bodyguard], then tribune, and afterwards governor of Dalmatians (*praeses Dalmatianorum*)'[9] – enough in itself, it would seem, to constitute a highly successful career for a peasant's son. This was, however, only the beginning. During his son's childhood, his rise was meteoric. The key year was 284, when, a few months after the death of the Emperor Carus and the division of the empire between his sons Carinus and Numerian, the Eastern emperor, Numerian, died in mysterious circumstances; and a revolutionary officers' council elected Diocles, the commander of the imperial bodyguard, to overthrow the dead man's brother Carinus, emperor in the West, and build a renewed empire out of the chaos left by fifty years of near-anarchy. Whether Constantius played an active role in the revolution is not known, but he quickly gained the confidence of the new administration. Diocles – now calling himself Diocletian – defeated and killed Carinus in 286 at Margus, a town only a few miles from the frontiers of

Constantius' province of Dalmatia. Constantius had obviously chosen the winning side before the battle, for within little more than a year he was in Gaul, commanding troops for the new emperor in bitter campaigns against the *bagaudae*, marauding bands of starving peasants and disgruntled veterans who hoped that, by taking advantage of the military confusion and divided loyalties left by Carinus' defeat, they could throw off imperial rule and make Gaul independent.

Diocletian's commander-in-chief in this Gallic war was an old comrade-in-arms named Maximian[10]. To give him the authority he needed, Diocletian shared some part of the imperial power with him, calling him the Caesar Maximian. His appointment as Caesar, sharing the divine powers wielded by Diocletian 'the August Emperor', gave him a title and office usually granted only to a ruling emperor's son, when it was equivalent to Crown Prince and Heir Apparent.

However, for the time being, Diocletian kept ultimate power in his own hands. He alone used the title Imperator Augustus. The rank 'Augustus', always reserved for those in supreme authority, had first been used in 27 B.C., when the Senate granted it to Julius Caesar's nephew Octavian, after he had made himself the first Roman emperor, but could not decide what to call himself. According to Munatius Placus, who first proposed it, 'august' places were those consecrated by the augurs as especially holy, so an 'august' man would be one filled with the genius of authority poured out on rulers by the gods. When Diocletian made Maximian his Caesar in 286, he reserved this Genius of Authority for himself, but adopted him as his heir, in imitation of Julius Caesar's adoption of his nephew Octavian into the *gens* Julia during the Civil Wars. The requirements of the political and military situation were the only officially admitted explanation of the promotion, but his choice of Maximian was perhaps governed by concerns more personal than mere statecraft. By elevating Maximian to the status of junior emperor, with tacit right to succession, he was not only giving special authority to a proven leader in a difficult area, but also binding a potential rival more firmly to himself.

Marcus Aurelius Valerius Maximianus was a soldier from the Danube provinces. Of obscure origins, like so many in Constantine's story, his ruthlessness and undeniable ability had brought him rapid promotion in the Persian Wars under Aurelian and Probus. By all reports, he was an ignorant and brutal man; it was said that his rule was iron while, by comparison, the more merciful Diocletian's was golden. However, he ruled an iron territory, from Hadrian's Wall and the Atlas Mountains to the Rhine and the Adriatic. While the *bagaudae* roamed his provinces, he could not have afforded clemency, even if it had been in his character to exercise it.

Constantius Chlorus served him in Gaul as his Praetorian Prefect, the general officer commanding both the military and politico-judicial arms of the state. By the year 289, continual success had so firmly established him in favour (or, perhaps, made him so potentially dangerous a rival), that Maximian betrothed him to his adopted daughter Flavia Maximiana Theodora, so as to bring him into the family; and a medal was struck commemorating the event. After further victorious campaigns against the Frankish Alemanni from east of the Rhine and rebels in Britain, he himself was raised to the purple in 293, when Constantine was nineteen, being named as Caesar to Maximian, who now became Diocletian's fellow-Augustus, supreme ruler in the western half of the empire. He was made consul on January 1, 294, and was granted that honour again in 296, 300, 302, 305 and 306.

The early years of Diocletian's reign are insufficiently well documented for it to be possible to determine the precise chronology of the steps in Constantius Chlorus' promotion and correlate them with the stages in the reconstruction of the empire undertaken by Diocletian in fulfilment of his promises to the Officers' Council of 284. It had certainly not proceeded very far by March 1, 293, when, probably at Milan, Maximian put the purple cloak symbolising imperial authority around his shoulders and presented him to the bodyguard as their new Caesar Imperator. Diocletian's first nine years of power had not been easy ones. The campaigns in the West during which

Constantius had won such respect were matched by wars along the Danube frontier with the Gothic and Sarmatian tribes, in Syria with the Saracens, and in Egypt against Roman rebels backed by dissident nationalists. It was these continuing troubles which led Diocletian to proclaim Maximian first as his Caesar, then as his fellow-Augustus, simultaneously appointing Constantius as deputy and another Illyrian soldier, a brutal, ignorant but efficient general named Galerius, as Caesar and so heir to himself in the East[11]. There were, however, other factors weighing with the First Emperor at this time, preponderant among them the need to establish a dynasty if a stable reform was to be effected, and the empire saved from renewed chaos when he himself disappeared from the centre of the scene.

The Romans of the old Republic and early Empire would have called Diocletian and his fellow-emperors barbarians, not only because of their non-Roman origins, but also because of their behaviour. They were lacking in real gravity and much given to display. They built themselves vast palaces, and dressed in gold and jewels. They were the first emperors to permit themselves to be called 'Lord' (*dominus*) in Latin, and 'King' (*basileus*) in Greek. This last development was of the highest significance. It was a visible sign, clear to all able to read an inscription, that the domination of the emperors over all the institutions of the Republic was at last complete. Two hundred and fifty years earlier, when Tiberius had once been called 'Lord and Master' he had claimed that he was being deliberately insulted. Now these titles of once-hated kingship had become respectable – or had at least to be publicly respected. Only a few years later, no one raised serious objection when Constantine assumed the diadem of gold and pearls as a symbol of his authority, although when Caligula had worn it, the world had laughed openly at him.

The person of the First Emperor was naturally held to be especially sacred, and his quasi-divine authority was continually emphasized, not least in the titles used for offices in the reformed administration. So, for instance, the Council, later simply called *consilium*, was entitled under Diocletian the *consilia sacra*, the 'sacred committee'. When Diocletian appeared in public, his jewelled shoes and gold-and-purple cloak set him apart from ordinary mortals. In his own court, he could be approached only through a complicated system of security checks and with a ceremonial ending in a ritual act of adoration, the *proskynesis*, which, when Alexander the Great had introduced it into his court from Persia six centuries earlier, had almost provoked a revolution. However, these Illyrian and Danubian soldiers knew what impressed ordinary people, and their aim was to glorify and protect themselves by making their imperial office and authority sacrosanct. They succeeded, in as much as they all escaped that common fate of emperors, assassination.

Further to emphasize his holiness and quasi-divine role in the state, Diocletian began to call himself 'Jovius', signifying that he was the spiritual son and temporal manifestation of Jupiter, the father of the Roman gods, the ultimate source of all authority both in heaven and on earth; and announced that Maximian would be called 'Herculius', the son and reflection of Hercules, hero of brave men and performer of impossible tasks at Jupiter's behest. When the emperor Commodus had called himself Hercules at the end of the second century, it had been with that self-deceiving egotism which so often made insecure emperors look ridiculous. When Diocletian and Maximian called themselves Jovius and Herculius, they were not deceiving themselves. They may have hoped to deceive some of the more credulous of their subjects, but their real aim was more practical. They knew that they were in fact usurpers, although they had snatched supreme power from men with little better title to it than themselves, and had been confirmed in office by a cowed senate. Now they were trying to give stability to their regime by cementing themselves and their chosen associates, Constantius and Galerius, firmly into the structure of the reformed empire. They must have known that in their lifetimes most people would be continually aware of the artificiality of the system. But the two Augusti were men building for the future, and they could reasonably hope that if they could create twin dynasties and set their families firmly in control of the empire, later generations would accept their descendants as genuine emperors with good title to the power they wielded. With this long-term end in view, as well as with the intention of binding the Caesars to the Augusti, Diocletian offered his own daughter Valeria in marriage to the Caesar Galerius, in order to establish a Jovian line in the East, while Maximian confirmed his step-daughter Theodora as Constantius' wife, to continue the Herculian line in the West.

The scheme was politically sound. It united four strong men, while planting the imperial power in four different corners of the empire, so facilitating the close supervision of affairs and making revolution seemingly impossible. With Diocletian in Asia Minor, controlling the vast area from Thrace through Mesopotamia to Egypt and Libya, Galerius ruling the Balkans and Central Europe, Maximian holding power in Italy, North-West Africa and Spain, and Constantius supreme in Gaul, co-ordination of a plot against the emperors became quite impractical, while every potential trouble-spot had a man with imperial authority within a few days' hard riding.

Except geographically, the empire they ruled had little in common with that of Augustus and his immediate successors. Diocletian had fallen heir to a cumbersome relic, operating ever less efficiently as successive adventurers grasped at supreme power. In the course of the years, the powers of the Roman senate, once the sole source of authority under the gods, had been so often ignored that they had gradually withered, and the orientalization of religion and morals, so deplored in its first manifestations by far-sighted senators in Republican times, had progressed to a point where the only logical next step was that which Constantine ultimately took, the transfer of the actual capital to the East. During just three centuries of imperial rule, in the course of which some fifty emperors had more or less briefly clung to power, the ultimate source of authority had passed first from the senate to the emperor, then from the emperor to the army, and especially to the Praetorian Guard.

When the Guard had first been formed and its first Prefect appointed, in the reign of Augustus, it had consisted of about

12,000 hand-picked Romans and Italians, charged with safeguarding the person of the emperor. Wisely, Augustus himself had allowed only three cohorts, about 1,500 men, to serve at any one time in the city of Rome itself, and had refused the Guard a barracks, billeting it in lodging houses scattered around the city, so that it would be difficult for the soldiers to combine and take co-ordinated action without detection. His successor Tiberius made the mistake of bringing the whole force together in a fortified camp under the city walls, and so made the Praetorian Prefect potentially the most powerful man in the state. The Guard first showed its teeth when two of its tribunes assassinated Caligula in A.D. 41, and Claudius, realizing that his life was in the balance, offered its men 15,000 sesterces a head to cheer his accession. From that day on for many decades, the Praetorians were the final arbiters in any struggle to control Rome. They often demonstrated absolute contempt for the law. Their irresponsibility reached its nadir in A.D. 192–3, when they ran riot in Rome and, after murdering the Emperor Pertinax, sold the *imperium* to the highest bidder, a businessman named Didius Julianus. The reign of the Emperor Julianus lasted only until the Pannonian legions heard of his election, whereupon they proclaimed Septimus Severus as Augustus and marched on Rome. Once firmly established in the city, Severus disbanded the Guard, but soon found it necessary for his own safety to revive it with increased manpower. By the end of his reign, it numbered some 50,000 men, drawn not from Italy, but from the fighting tribes of the Danube area and the far West. Severus was allowed to die of natural causes, but time after time during the century till Diocletian's accession, the survival or disappearance of a ruler depended on his generosity to the Guard paid to protect him. Praetorian Prefects like Asclepiodotus, the first to hold the post under Diocletian, controlled not only the army, but also the imperial post, food supplies and the administration of justice. To a man of Diocletian's stamp, the situation was intolerable. He determined to end it, and all similar threats to imperial authority. The appointment of Maximian as Caesar in the West, and the doubling of all essential offices in order to provide him with an administration, in effect halved the power, and thus the menace, of the Praetorian Prefects, and made it much more than doubly difficult for a plot to succeed. Maximian's first Prefect, Theodora's actual father, Hannibalianus, although still a terrifying figure to the average man, had in reality an authority much less extensive than any prefect before him. Maximian's advancement to the rank of Augustus, and the creation of the two new Caesars, led to a further reduplication of offices. The system proved expensive, but was for a time effective: once there were four emperors, working from widely-scattered capitals, each served by a Praetorian Prefect and a team of subordinate administrators, a successful palace coup became impossible. As Constantine was to demonstrate, the system could be beaten—but only at the terrible risk of piecemeal subversion and open warfare.

The constant need for watchfulness on the frontiers made Diocletian's army large and difficult to maintain[12]. Years of haphazard government had left the imperial finances in confusion. However, taxes had to be collected and the men on the frontiers fed. The attempts Diocletian and his fellow emperors made to bring financial and administrative affairs under central control after half-a-century of near chaos have recently been the subject of intensive study, and much new evidence has emerged, all showing how efficient an executive Diocletian was.

The four emperors ruled from four capitals: Diocletian himself from Nicomedia in Asia Minor, Maximian from Milan in northern Italy, Galerius usually from Sirmium (now Mitrovica) in Pannonia on the River Save south of the Danube, and Constantius from Augusta Treverorum (Trier) in Belgica. Their overburdened Praetorian Prefects were assisted in their duties by vice-prefects (vicarii, 'vicars') each of whom administered one of the thirteen major districts, known as 'dioceses', into which the whole empire was divided. So, for most practical purposes, by the year 300, the hundred provinces were ruled by four Prefects and their thirteen assistants.

Diocletian's Prefect of the East (*praefectus orientalis*) controlled the vast area from Thrace, eastwards to the River Euphrates and south and west to Egypt, with the assistance of five senior officials: the Count of the East, the Augustal Prefect of Egypt, and *vicarii* in the dioceses of Thrace, Asiana and Pontica (now eastern Greece and Turkey). Galerius' Prefect of Illyria (*praefectus illyrici*) ruled the Danube and Hellenic provinces, through diocesan vicars of Pannonia, Dacia and Macedonia. Constantius' Prefect of the Gauls (*praefectus galliarum*) operated through vicars of Gaul (northern France and Belgium), Britain, and Vienne (southern France). Maximian's Prefect of Italy (*praefectus italianae*) administered the diocese of Italy through one vicar, Africa through another, and Spain through a third.

Only Rome stood outside the system. She was ruled by a City Prefect, whose authority extended to the hundredth milestone, and so was both honoured and cut off from the common life of the empire. Diocletian seems deliberately to have isolated the ancient capital. There is no doubt that he despised the city as effete, yet still regarded it as potentially dangerous. He seems to have visited it only once, for the celebration of his *vicennalia*, the twentieth anniversary of his accession, and even then stayed as short a time as possible. The wealth former emperors would have poured out on Rome, he lavished on his capital Nicomedia, beautifying it with baths and theatres, colonnaded streets and fine basilicas, until it became a worthy home for his authority and divine genius. Rome languished in a backwater, and was ultimately to revolt, but the power of the empire to which she had given her name revived and continued to grow.

Unfortunately for Diocletian's complete success, the needs of that empire were greater than its utilizable resources, and the administration was under constant strain to provide the money needed to keep the machinery moving. Economic and fiscal policies were no more exact sciences then than they are today. Inflation had bedevilled the currency for more than a century, and Diocletian failed to bring it under control. In the year 301, an edict was issued attempting to fix prices of essential commodities throughout the empire[13]; but the results of years of instability, coupled with the increase in the number of civil servants and soldiers, the cost of imperial building programmes, the strain of maintaining four palaces and administrations, and the evil effects of the free circulation of millions of copper coins used as small change but unacceptable to the government in payment of taxes, were too malevolent quickly to be overcome. New taxes in money were raised, and the exaction of taxes in kind, the hated *annonae*, hitherto an occasional charge on areas where the legions needing support were actually stationed, was put on a permanent and rational basis. For this purpose, accurate censuses were carried out and an elaborate system of assessment was evolved – all of which, of course, led to a further increase in the number of administrators, and the accretion of more authority to those senior officials responsible for seeing that taxation was equitable, the Praetorian Prefects and provincial governors. It is a measure of their achievement that for the first time in sixty years, gold became plentiful enough for gold coins to be struck, of standard weight and content throughout the empire, at first seventy, then sixty to the Roman pound. The value of a pound of pure silver was fixed at one-fifteenth that of fine gold, and new silver coins were introduced, weighing one ninety-sixth of a pound and worth one twenty-fourth of a gold *aureus*. The monetary system was completed with small coins of plain copper and copper washed with silver. It was their instability which brought chaos to what should have become a stable economy. The plain copper *nummus* was said to be worth two of the *denarii* which, although they had long gone out of circulation, were still used as a standard by bankers and traders[14]. The silver-washed coin, introduced by Diocletian in 295, was valued at five nominal *denarii*. If the *denarius* had stood firm at its official figure of 600 to the *aureus*, all would have been well, but in fact it drifted continually downwards. In 299, the salary of the newly-appointed teacher of rhetoric at Autun was fixed at 600,000 *nummi* a year – an impossibly large figure, if the *nummus* had been stable, equivalent to not less than 2,000 *aurei*, at a time when a soldier could be clothed, fed, housed and armed for about four *aurei* a year. Inflation had already eroded the value of the new *nummus*. Its fall was a process which neither Diocletian's reform nor even Constantine's administrative genius could reverse. Diocletian's edict fixing prices merely led to the disappearance of the goods named in it from the shops and markets until the new law was forgotten. Within a third of a century, as hoarding against inflation removed gold and silver coins from circulation, Diocletian's *aureus* was to be quoted not at six hundred *denarii*, but at a quarter of a million, and even more.

Diocletian's government has often been described as top-heavy and over-centralized. But he believed in close government, and in its interests according to Lactantius, 'sliced the provinces up small'[15], increasing their number from around fifty to about a hundred. This reform both made combination for rebellion more difficult and facilitated the administration of imperial judicial and financial policy. Expenses were greater, but control was tighter. When Constantine ruled, he would pull the reins tighter still, and by doing so, make himself sole ruler until his death. The empire was not a modern state, organized for the welfare and comfort of its citizens, but rather a private estate, run for the benefit of its tenant under the gods, the Augustus, and his family. Seen in this light – the light in which Constantine saw it – the empire could never be over-centralized or too closely administered. Or, to change the metaphor for one which Diocletian himself might have preferred, the whole empire was an army, at the command and disposal of its general officer commanding, its August Lord, the *basileus*. One of the primary duties of the Praetorian and City Prefects was to ensure that the emperors were always instantly informed of any change in the temper of the people, and an army of clerks assisted them in this and other, essentially allied, tasks. The word 'army' is a just one in this context. The clerks of the new empire were called soldiers and paid as such. Until almost the end of Diocletian's reign, when military *duces* ('leaders') took over control of the forces in some frontier areas, both prefects and provincial governors were still expected to command troops as well as administer justice and collect taxes. The departments into which the clerks were organized were still called *scrinia* (chests), as they had been in the days when Diocletian's records were kept by army clerks in military chests which could be moved from place to place on mules whenever the commander of the guard struck camp. When the time came for Constantine to bid for power, the empire had moved a long way from the days of the Revolutionary Officers' Council which had made Diocletian great, but it was still a general's dream-world, full of high-sounding titles, flint-hard regulations and sharp words of command. Although Constantine could and did pull down the artificial dynasties of the Jovians and Herculians, he succeeded only in streamlining the essentially military machine, not replacing it with something better. But then he was a soldier himself, and would have recognized nothing as better.

In 293, however, when his father became Maximian's Caesar, Constantine was still twelve years from power, and his chances of ever achieving it appeared very small indeed. His father's promotion may have fired his ambition, but he was actually placed in a perilous position by his father's marriage to Theodora. The establishment of a legally-recognized Herculian dynasty in the West threatened disaster to those already close to the emperor. He was one of the three people in greatest danger. The other two were his mother Helena and Maximian's own son Maxentius.

Constantius's promotion and marriage blighted Maxentius' hopes of inheriting his father's power and uniting East and West under himself by marriage to Diocletian's daughter. He was later to show his resentment by rebellion at Rome.

They also ended for thirty years Helena's involvement in imperial affairs. She was, perhaps, fortunate to escape with her life, but that life probably seemed of little value to her on the day when, after many years of marriage, Constantius repudiated her to ally himself with Maximian's daughter.

Helena was a remarkable woman, one whose story, as Hakluyt said in the sixteenth century, made her 'famous in all the world'. Although the mediaeval British historian, Geoffrey of Monmouth, claims to have heard somewhere that she was daughter of King Coel, the eponymous founder of Colchester and allegedly the hero of the nursery rhyme 'Old King Cole', her origins are in fact as obscure as Constantius' own; and Constantine was, as the Byzantine historian Eutropius delicately expressed it, the son of 'a marriage of the more obscure kind'[16]. Even those writers most anxious to glorify the neo-Flavians admitted that Helena's father had been a provincial innkeeper, and the pagans Zosimus[17] and Orosius[18] claimed that she had helped him in his trade by prostituting herself to his customers. If this charge is true (and it may not be: the historians who made it were propagandists, concerned to denigrate the Christian empress), Helena would seem to have been uncommonly fortunate in acquiring so steady a man as Constantius for a husband, whether or not she succeeded in persuading him legally to marry her. Throughout his life, his reputation was that of a pious and restrained man, reverencing the old Roman virtues of dignity and respect for the laws and institutions of the commonwealth. Recording the period after 293, when he was one of the four emperors reigning simultaneously, the compiler of the flattering *History of the Caesars* describes them as 'the four fitting princes of the world: wise, benign and fittingly liberal, with one mind in public affairs, reverent towards the senate, moderate, friends of the people, solemn, grave, religious and proper princes'[19]. If any word of this eulogy is true, it is because two of the four were Diocletian and Constantius—and if Constantius was really as grave, religious and proper a prince as the *History* maintains, Helena, the innkeeper's daughter, was lucky to catch him and could scarcely have hoped to hold him.

The claim has frequently been made that Constantius and Helena were not truly married, and that in fact she lived with him in legal concubinage, rather more than a mistress but much less than a wife. It has also been suggested that the fiction of a legal marriage between them was invented by her enemies late in her life, so that the story of Constantius' having divorced her in order to marry Theodora could be used to denigrate both her and Constantine in Christian eyes. However, rejection by one's husband was no sin, whereas to the Christians prostitution and concubinage were. The attack would have been more telling if it could have been argued that Constantine was the illegitimate son of an immoral woman. The fact that this charge was not made is a strong argument for the validity of the marriage. On the other hand, there is no documentary proof that the marriage ever took place, although Victor writes of Constantius 'taking as his wife Theodora, the step-daughter of Herculius Maximianus, divorcing his first wife', using the legal terms usually reserved for legitimate marriages in both instances[20]. The balance of the evidence is so evenly struck that the question of Constantine's legitimacy would seem insoluble. However, his father always treated him as his true son and heir, while he himself showed his mother the greatest respect.

One fact which seems never to have been disputed is that he was Helena's only child. Where he was born is not known. The names of three places have been proposed: Colchester in Britain, Drepanum, a city on the shores of the Gulf of Nicomedia on the southern coast of the Bosphorus, and the town of Naissus, now Nish, in the province of Dacia, in the Balkans. None of them can certainly be excluded, but Colchester is the least likely of the three.

The legend of Constantine's birth at Colchester seems to depend on the equally unproven story that his grandfather was King Coel. There is no evidence that Constantius visited Britain before he became Praetorian Prefect to Maximian in 286 or 287. He may have done so, and those who argue for Constantine's birth within King Coel's frontiers must maintain that in fact he did, or that Constantine was not born until about 290—in which case, Diocletian made him a colonel at the age of six, and he proclaimed himself emperor at the age of sixteen. Gibbon suggests that Geoffrey of Monmouth himself invented the story of Constantine's British origins, and certainly no earlier evidence for them now exists. Whoever the British patriot was who fabricated it, he had probably misunderstood the panegyrist who, when Constantine was emperor, somewhat fulsomely told him 'you ennobled the Britains by arising there'[21]. The rising, *oriendo*, referred to here was not that of Constantine's birth, but of his accession to the glory of the principate, which occurred at York with his acclamation as Augustus, the embodiment of the sun-god, when he was a little over thirty years old. The panegyrist was saying in effect that on the day of Constantine's accession, the sun rose in the far west of the empire, bringing the glory of its light first to the Britons. Later, Constantine used a somewhat similar image in one of his own rambling speeches. However, apart from the older stories claiming that he was born elsewhere, there is nothing to show that his parents were not in Britain between 274 and 280, and Geoffrey of Monmouth's tale cannot be categorically denied.

The evidence for his birth at Drepanum in northern Asia Minor is not much more convincing. It stands mainly on the facts that he renamed the city Helenopolis and its province Helenopontus in his mother's honour, and that the emperor Justinian beautified the city because his illustrious predecessor had been born there. Justinian's act of piety was, however, performed two hundred years after Constantine's death and can scarcely be taken to prove anything. It is more likely that Helena herself was born at Drepanum, and that is why Constantine renamed it 'Helena's City'.

The weight of the evidence, such as it is, favours Naissus as Constantine's native town. His contemporary, Julius Firmicius, who, as a student of astrology, had a specialist interest in such matters, affirms it absolutely, and it is confirmed by the unnamed author quoted by Ammianus late in the fourth century[22]. Few would doubt Naissus's claim to be the birthplace, were it not for the fact that it was the site of Claudius the Goth's famous victory over the Gothic federation, and so from the propagandists' point of view an eminently suitable choice for the advent into this world of the real founder of the Neo-Flavian line. The coincidence, however, would not be as unlikely as it might appear at first sight. Naissus was an important city, and it would not be really remarkable that both Claudius should valiantly defend it and Constantius Chlorus' son be born there.

It would help to fix the date and place of Constantine's birth if there were hard evidence pointing to where Helena's father kept his inn, when Constantius began his service in the south

Danubian area, and how long after the start of Helena's association with him her only son was born. It is tempting to speculate that the inn was at or near Naissus, that Constantius met Helena while serving 'Gothicus' in the Gothic campaign, and that Constantine was born within a few miles of the site of his alleged imperial relation's greatest victory. It is, however, impossible to be dogmatic on any point relating to Constantine's origins. If only his father's name were unknown, he would perfectly fit the pattern of the oracular hero of classical antiquity: born in a strange country, going through difficulties in his youth, but coming home in his prime to the capital of his people to lead them to glory.

Helena is still remembered as the Christian empress, the benefactress of bishops and discoverer of the True Cross at Jerusalem. There is, however, nothing to support the assertion sometimes made, that she was already baptised before Constantine's birth and her early influence ultimately brought him to Christianity. Such facts about her life as are known would suggest the contrary – although no more than indicate it. Eusebius of Caesarea, whose pro-Christian tract *On the Life of Constantine*[23] is one of the few contemporary accounts of the emperor's career, declares that Constantine in fact converted his mother. Eusebius was in a position to know the truth, but his *Life* is propaganda for the Flavians and the Church, and as such must be regarded with some suspicion. There are, however, other indications that Helena was not a Christian during her son's early years, though taken altogether they do not add up to certainty.

If she was a native of western Asia Minor, where Christians were actually in the majority, at least in the cities, by the middle of the third century, she may have been baptised in infancy; if, however, like so many of the characters in Constantine's story, she was born in the Danube Valley, somewhere near Naissus, her baptism as a child was much less likely. There were few Christian communities in the area before Constantine began to favour Christianity.

Then again, if Helena's father really was an inn-keeper and

she herself a prostitute when she met Constantius Chlorus, she was certainly not a practising Christian and it is unlikely that she had been baptised. Although, owing at least in part to the growing number of conversions, some relaxation of early Christian discipline had already been noticed in the second half of the third century, tolerance never went so far as to welcome inn-keepers, let alone their morally lax daughters, into the Christian ranks, unless they abandoned their profession before reception into the church.

The most powerful argument against the supposition that Helena had been baptized even as late as the beginning of the fourth century, however, is the fact that both she and her son survived the Great Persecution unscathed. She would not have gone unharmed if she had, as the fourth-century Christian historian Theodoret claimed, already been baptized before 303, or even if she had merely been suspected of Christian sympathies. In the first days of the terror, Diocletian executed trusted palace officials because they were Christians, and ordered his wife Prisca and daughter Valeria to burn incense in the prescribed form on the bare suspicion, never confirmed, that they were secretly nursing thoughts of conversion. A fear going so deep could scarcely have overlooked those more likely plotters against the state, a disgraced former consort of the Caesar Constantius and her forceful son. After her divorce, Helena and Constantine must have been under constant suspicion of being disaffected persons. She disappeared from history for thirty years, but he was kept in the eastern provinces under supervision until believing that his life was in danger for political reasons, he took energetic steps to escape in 305. He was given high honours, but he was not trusted. Living with the Eastern imperial court, he was usually more than two thousand miles from Constantius' protection, but surrounded by the Christians' most perfervid enemies. Constantius himself came under attack because he refused to persecute rigorously and his court was known to shelter many Christians holding positions of authority in the state. If there had been any doubts about the religious convictions of either Constantine or his mother, they would surely have been early victims of the oppressive legislation. If the sacrifice to the Genius of Empire which was the test of loyalty was ever demanded of them, they must have offered it unhesitatingly, otherwise Eusebius would have written not the *Life of Constantine* but the *Acts of Constantine the Martyr*.

At what date Helena did embrace Christianity remains a mystery. Nor can anyone say with certainty what gods she worshipped during her son's childhood. Intellectually, she may have tended towards the fashionable monotheistic worship of the Supreme God, *Summus Deus*, manifested primarily as Apollo, the sun-god – the religion, not unrelated to Mithraism, of Claudius the Goth and many other soldiers, probably including Constantius Chlorus himself. It is unlikely, however, that her religion was untinged by superstition and the observance of omens. Her son was certainly a superstitious man, and the accounts of the procedures she herself went through as late as 327–8 in the quest for the True Cross and the sites of various episodes in the life of Christ make it plain that even in Christian old age she was not averse to a little magic-making when the occasion seemed to require it. Yet, insofar as she was permitted to make herself responsible for her son's education, she probably taught him to honour his father, that coming man, and respect the gods of the state as aspects and reflections of the Supreme God, manifested as the Unconquered Sun and the authority of the emperor. Certainly, when Constantine was himself engaged in the struggle for supreme power, these were the gods he actually served.

Helena's separation from Constantius drove her into obscurity and left Constantine, aged around nineteen and about to embark on a military career, exposed to any calumny and an obvious risk in the eyes of the secret police of the recently-established *schola agentium in rebus*, 'corps of agents in [political] affairs'. A year later, his position was partly restored by his betrothal to Fausta, Maximian's daughter. It was, however, only a partial restoration. A future marriage would depend on his good behaviour. Unfortunately, the surviving evidence is insufficient to show whether this promise of honours to come was a sign of special favour on Maximian's part, an act of imperial policy forced by Diocletian on a perhaps unwilling fellow-Augustus, or the result of a bargain struck between Constantius Chlorus and his chief. There is the feeling of something very mercenary and inhuman about the whole transaction. Most probably, the betrothal was the outcome of both political and personal pressures, but while its political importance is obvious, its human results have not been chronicled. There is no record of Constantine's feelings about Fausta at this time, any more than there is of Helena's personal reaction to her dismissal. They must both have been anxious about the future. However, all that is certain is that Constantius and Theodora were married, Constantine was betrothed to Fausta, and both Constantine and Helena were called to the East, far from Constantius Chlorus' seat of government and beyond his help. It looks as though Constantine were both being held hostage for his father's loyalty, and trained to succeed him if the first attempt to establish an Herculian dynasty should fail. He was, according to one author, *literis minus instructus*, 'less than well educated'[24]. That is not surprising. Having spent his childhood either in military establishments in Gaul during a period of war and revolution, or at his mother's provincial home, he probably had next to no education before he went to the Senior Augustus' court. (If this was so, his background was precisely that of the Eastern Caesar Galerius, whose character was reflected in his by-name Armentarius, 'the Drover'.) Neither his ignorance nor his parentage was allowed to block his career. When we next hear of him, at the age of twenty-two, he was a young officer in Diocletian's suite, travelling with him in the province of Syria – and, there can be no doubt from the skill with which he later manipulated the administration and the men running it, closely observing the steps taken to reform the empire and learning something every day about the machinery of power. Intelligence and determination compensated for his lack of the formal arts taught by Roman schoolmasters.

CHAPTER TWO

THE OBSCURE YEARS

CONSTANTINE spent the twelve years A.D. 293–305 at the courts of the emperors of the East. Neither the edicts and rescripts of the emperors Diocletian and Galerius, nor any contemporary inscription on stone or coins, make any reference to him during these years, until just before their end, when he appears on an Egyptian coin as 'the Caesar Constantine'[1]. His later biographers told stories but recorded few hard facts about them. A great deal is known about the empire, and something of the doings of the emperors themselves during the period, but how events touched Constantine and influenced his attitudes and actions remains largely a matter for conjecture.

The fourth-century historian and propagandist for Christianity Lactantius, whom Constantine later engaged as tutor to his eldest son, bluntly declares that Constantine was called to the East as a hostage for his father's loyalty, but the historian Paraxagoras claims that Diocletian summoned Constantine to court so that he might be educated[2]. Both these statements probably contain elements of truth. Constantius Chlorus' loyalty was a matter of concern to Diocletian, and Constantine was notoriously 'less than well educated'.

If Constantine was born in A.D. 274, he was eighteen or nineteen when he joined Diocletian's retinue in winter quarters at Sirmium on the River Save, and he was probably drafted immediately into the army by a direct mandate from the senior Augustus attaching him to the imperial guard. If he was not yet eighteen, he may have been put under a schoolmaster for a time before beginning his military career, but any such period of education was brief and ineffective: so much is clear from the turgid style of his later speeches, edicts and letters.

In the army, his first ranking appointment may well have

been as a *protector*, an officer cadet, in the ranks of a unit known collectively as 'the Protectors', one of the formations permanently attached to the sacred *comitatus*, the emperor's bodyguard and mobile defence force. Diocletian himself had commanded the Protectors at the moment of his election to the principate in 284. Some of its senior officers were on permanent or long-term appointments, but it was largely composed of soldiers of some years' seniority, the quality of whose early service, first in the legions on general duties, then, often, in the ranks of one of the cohorts on detachment with the sacred *comitatus*, had led to their being singled out for promotion to commissioned rank. Successful service with the Protectors opened the way to higher command. Constantius Chlorus was a protector before becoming Governor of Dalmatia and afterwards Praetorian Prefect to Maximian. Galerius' nephew, Maximin Daia (or Daza), who was named Jovian Caesar in 305, reached the principate through the same unit, although according to Lactantius, out of respect for his uncle's imperial status, he was excused early service in an ordinary legion. Before joining the army, he was a shepherd. On enlistment, he was posted directly to the Shieldsman, the *Scola Scutariarum*, of the sacred *comitatus*, 'then was made a Protector, shortly afterwards a tribune, and the day after that, Caesar'[3].

There is no evidence to show whether Constantine was compelled to serve, however briefly, with either the Shieldsmen or the Lancers (the third principal unit of the *comitatus*) before being honoured by Diocletian with letters of appointment as a cadet. On the analogy of Maximin Daia's career, he probably was. He and Daia were contemporaries and rivals in very similar circumstances. Both were related to Caesars, but neither had a direct claim to the purple under the Jovian and Herculian dynastic system. Diocletian was anxious to preserve unity among his fellow emperors. He would not have made the mistake of forcing Galerius' nephew to prove himself in a way not required of Constantius' son. If, however, he did serve with them, before appointment to the Protectors or to equestrian rank, his service was probably no longer than Daia's. Outraged reaction from

Constantius was immediate when, in 305, Maximin Daia was made Caesar and Constantine passed over. There is no reason to believe that he would have been any less touchy for his honour twelve years earlier, had his son been kept long in the ranks – even the chosen ranks of the Shieldsmen or Lancers of the Guard.

Frankly, however, all this is speculation. Nothing resembling a record of service covering Constantine's induction and early military career has survived, and only a novelist could pretend to describe the stir created among the agents of the secret police by his arrival at court, or the acrimonious conferences between those set to watch him and his senior officers in the *comitatus* which must have preceded every step in his promotion. However, whatever traps were laid for him, he survived them and was ultimately given an imperial honour as a Tribune First Class (the equivalent of a modern colonel), although with which formation is not known.

He served both the Augustus Diocletian and the Caesar Galerius as a tribune of the bodyguard.

At this period, Diocletian's court was rarely stationary for long. It spent the early summer of 293 making a tour through what is now the Balkan Peninsula and Northern Turkey. On April 2, it was at Byzantium, and Constantine probably had his first glimpse at this time of the city he was later to make his capital. By the end of June, Diocletian was back at Sirmium ready, no doubt, to meet any threat from the barbarians during the campaign season after the harvest. In fact, there was no serious trouble on the frontier that year, although Constantine may have seen active service in border skirmishes. His Christian biographers claim that during his early years with the army, he won great personal acclaim for his courage in wars against the Sarmatian tribes in the region of the middle Danube.

In September 294, Diocletian once more left Sirmium, to visit towns in the Danube Valley and Thrace before crossing the Bosphorus to spend the winter at Nicomedia, his official residence. The following spring, he went south into Syria, to quell unrest among the Saracen tribesmen of the semi-desert

2

area beyond Damascus. Constantine was certainly on his staff at this time, for it was during that summer that he was first seen by the Christian who was to become one of his chief religious advisers, preach at his funeral and write the earliest account of his career, Eusebius of Caesarea.

In the year 295, Eusebius was a layman, in his thirties, working at the famous Library of Pamphilus at Caesarea, although later, after being imprisoned twice for his faith, once in Syria and again in Egypt, he was to be ordained and ultimately be made bishop of his native city. His impressions of the young tribune – if his memory forty busy years after the event is to be trusted – was wholly favourable. In his *Life of Constantine*, he wrote:

> [Constantine had been] with his father's imperial colleagues, spending his life with them, as we have said, like God's prophet of old [that is, like Moses in exile among the Egyptians: to Eusebius, the conversion of Empire to Christianity was a New Exodus, and Constantine its prophet]. And even in his earliest youth, they judged him worthy of the highest honour. We ourselves were eyewitnesses to an instance of this, when he passed through Syria with the Augustus, and stood at his right hand, and commanded the admiration of all who saw him, by the tokens of imperial greatness obvious in him. For he was matched by none in grace and beauty of form, or in tallness, and so surpassed his contemporaries in personal strength that he struck terror into them. However, he was even more conspicuous for the pre-eminence of his spiritual qualities [or 'mental powers': the Greek reads 'psychic endowments'] than for his physical gifts; being endowed firstly with sound judgement, and then also having gathered the harvest of a liberal education. He was, moreover, distinguished above the ordinary both by his natural wit and his God-given wisdom. The ruling emperors, noting his virile and vigorous appearance and enquiring mind, were moved to jealousy and fear, and they carefully watched for an opportunity to inflict a damaging wound on his character.[4]

There is, of course, a contradiction here. The emperors cannot have judged 'worthy of the highest honour' a man of whose loyalty they were so doubtful that they thought it worthwhile to watch 'carefully' for a chance to injure his reputation.

Eusebius both overpraises Constantine and underestimates the difficulties of his position. There can, however, be little doubt that in early manhood he was physically an impressive figure. Later in life, he put on weight and may have suffered from a goitre. His nickname among the people was 'bull-neck'[5]. The statue of him in the Campidoglio at Rome, although it depicts him in early middle age, and perhaps as much as fifty pounds overweight, nevertheless offers remarkable corroboration of Eusebius' description, showing a man of exceptionally fine build, with strongly marked features, heavy eyebrow ridges and a strong chin[6].

Accurate though Eusebius may have been, however, in his description of Constantine's personal appearance, he exaggerated both his intellectual and moral gifts, and his personal popularity. Until late in life he may have been virile and vigorous, but he was also frightening, because his strength went with a temper that rested on a knife-edge and anger brought out a streak of cruelty in him. Ten years or so after Eusebius first saw him, he came under attack for condemning prisoners to mortal combat with wild beasts in the amphitheatres of Trier and Colmar; five years after that, he attempted to wipe out all opposition in North Africa by ruthless annihilation of all dissidents, and early in his reign as sole emperor, in 326–7, he executed his eldest son, his own second wife, his favourite sister's husband and, in the words of one chronicler 'many others', on a variety of doubtfully proven charges. He was, as Eusebius claims, naturally intelligent, but such wisdom as he displayed in personal relationships at any rate had little of the divine in it. He was in fact an overbearing man, egotistical and self-righteous, ruthless in gaining his ends, dangerous to oppose, generally alert, but susceptible to flattery, although not as open to it as many weaker emperors had been.

When Eusebius saw him in 296, birth and ability had taken him to a place at the Augustus' right hand during the imperial visit to Caesarea, and standing there, in his trappings of bronze and gold, silver and scarlet, overtopping all his companions, he probably did command 'the admiration of all who saw him' –

the admiration, that is, of all those who stood with the insignificant librarian in the crowd, asking one another who the tall young man might be. The truth about his companions' and superiors' reactions to his powers and abilities is perhaps reflected more accurately, however, in Eusebius' choice of the words 'terror', 'jealousy' and 'fear' to describe them. A man of the capabilities of the Caesar Constantius' son appeared to pose a continual threat to the positions of many at court. The Augustus could call him to his right hand: he had nothing to fear from him; but to those nearer his own age he would obviously be a life-long rival. They intrigued against him, brought him unfavourably to the notice of the Caesar Galerius, and finally all but engineered his death.

Despite Eusebius' claims, the harvest Constantine gleaned from his liberal education was, by the standards of the best schools of the age, a very poor one. Later in life, he tried his skill at everything from preaching sermons and defining the nature of God to planning cities and constitutional reform. In general, his administration was much sounder than his argumentation, although by that time he had enjoyed years of constant contact with the subtlest minds of the time. He was a genius in man-management and the mechanics of power, not in intellectual or even spiritual achievement.

The East through which he travelled with Diocletian was a fascinating and varied territory. Although the ancient Egypt of the Pharaohs was lost in the dead centuries and most of the peoples of the Bible had long since vanished, the lands from Libya to the Euphrates were once again the heartlands of civilization, intellectually and spiritually inspiring the world. Great schools still existed at Athens and Rome, Diocletian built and restored the roads and fortresses, baths, basilicas and palaces which provided for physical defence and made possible everywhere life on the 'Roman' pattern (although there was little of the old Rome left in it), but it was to the thinkers of the East that men turned when they sought the meaning of life.

The East pulsated with life, whereas the West seemed slowly to be dying of blood and revolution. In the course of the first three Christian centuries, it had given the rest of the Roman world a multitude of philosophers and sophists, and no less than three competing world-religions, all offering salvation, Christianity, Mithraism and Manicheeism.

Not that the East was peaceful. Where religions compete, there is always bloody conflict. Moreover, while permanent inflation was depressing the living standards of the poor and leading to internal unrest, the armies had constantly to be enlarged, because none of the frontiers was secure: the Danube and Black Sea areas were under continual pressure from the Sarmatians and Goths; the senior Augustus himself was compelled to lead troops to put down rebellion in eastern Syria; the Augustal Province of Egypt was notoriously restless; and the eastern frontier, the Euphrates River, was under pressure from the Persians.

In 226, the once-powerful Persian kingdom had been restored by Ardeshir, the first prince of a new dynasty, the Sassanids. The old kingdom had given the world Mithraism, the religion of the sun-youth who saved through the ritual use of bull's blood. The renewed kingdom offered it a new religion, syncretist by nature, non-Persian in origin but built up largely on Persian dualism, contrasting life and death, light and darkness, truth and the lie. It was the invention of a man named Mani[7], who counted himself among the great prophets of the world and persuaded many to accept him at his own valuation. Led by the Sassanids, and inspired by Mani to believe that their new religion could save the world, the Persians were soon strong enough to upset the balance of power in the Middle East, by engineering the assassination of Rome's ally King Chosroes of Armenia, whose kingdom had been a buffer state between the easternmost provinces of the empire and Rome's traditional enemies still further east. Chosroes' infant heir, Tiridates, was smuggled out of the country, and his kingdom became a Persian satrapy. Trying and failing to restore the situation, the Emperor Valerian (*c.* 260) had suffered a long train of humiliations at the hands of the Persian King Sapor, whose forces had ultimately captured the emperor himself and smashed their way through to Syria and the Mediterranean coast, carrying with them the teachings of Mani, their prophet, as the Arabs were to carry Islam a little over three centuries later. They met stubborn resistance only twice during the first western campaign, from the devotees of Elagabalus, the sun-god of Emesa, and from Odenathus, the Governor of Palmyra.

Elagabalus' followers did not delay the Persians long, but Odenathus, having appealed in vain for help to Gallienus, Valerian's son and successor, threw them back with the forces at his immediate disposal, and forthwith declared Palmyra's independence from the empire. Free Palmyra, joined in rebellion by Egypt, was finally brought back to her allegiance by the Emperor Aurelian at about the time of Constantine's birth, but the years of near anarchy left a lasting scar, and unrest in Egypt and Syria continued into Diocletian's reign.

In 292, serious rebellion broke out again in Egypt, and, although quickly suppressed, it was probably the final stimulus to the appointment of the two Caesars to be the 'helpers', as Diocletian put it, of the Augusti. With the east and south temporarily pacified, Diocletian was free in 293–4 to make the progresses through the north-east during the first of which Constantine joined his court. What his helper Galerius was doing at this time is not known, but in 295 he fought off the Danubian Carpi, while Diocletian was in Syria, showing the flag of his imperial presence, as it were, among the Saracens, and incidentally giving Eusebius his first glimpse of Constantine. Meanwhile, trouble was simmering again in Egypt, and in 296 it boiled over in open revolt. A certain Domitius Domitianus had himself proclaimed emperor, as Firmus had done twenty-four years earlier, and ably guided by his *Corrector*, one Aurelius Achilleus, managed to seize control of the whole Augustal Province. Diocletian demonstrated that ten years as an emperor had not blunted his military talents by smashing the rebellion in one brief campaign in 296–7; but investigations revealed an intolerable state of affairs in Egypt and Libya, where neglect had brought all minorities to the point of disgust with Roman rule and allowed the roads and forts to fall into such disrepair that it had become impossible for the Augustal Prefect to deal quickly and decisively with troublemakers. Diocletian decided that the situation could be saved only by a complete overhaul of administration of the provinces of the north-east coast of Africa, and immediately began preparations for this work.

However, while his attention was fixed on Egypt and Libya, and Galerius was fighting on the banks of the Danube, the Persians under their King Narses expelled Tiridates from Armenia and re-established their hegemony there. Diocletian ordered Galerius to the Euphrates. In 297, while the Augustus was mopping up final traces of resistance in Alexandria, Galerius marched into Persia and was soundly beaten. He spent the winter of 297–8 regrouping, calling in reinforcements from his Danube armies. Presumably, he had so far not taken the Persians seriously enough, for when in the following year he mounted a full-scale attack, Persian resistance crumbled rapidly and he was able to force an adverse treaty on Narses, restoring Tiridates to Armenia, bringing seven satrapies in the Upper Tigris Valley as new provinces into the empire, and binding Narses and his successors to keep the peace for forty years.

The forty years' peace so won was of the utmost importance: it secured the eastern frontier for the whole of Constantine's remaining years of life.

The indications are that Constantine played a part, as Tribune First Class, in this Persian campaign, and proved himself as a leader. Certainly, at some time in these closing years of the third century he was brought to Galerius' notice in a significant way. Lactantius claims that Galerius tried to engineer the young tribune's death during the fighting, by ordering him into the most dangerous situations[8]. An anonymous author copied by Ammianus in the late fourth century relates that, knowing Constantine's pride in his own prowess, Galerius matched him in single combat against a Sarmatian prisoner-of-war, who was warned that he was fighting for his life[9]. Elsewhere, it is said that he was jeered into taking on a lion single-handed, and defeated it[10]. These stories have a legendary quality: the young Constantine, our Samson-like hero, the sun-god in person, living among the 'Philistines' of Galerius' court, overcomes the lion of envy, the spearmen of the devil, the ambuscades of evil, by the power of God and in the fullness of his own strength. But they do link Constantine with Galerius (who certainly later opposed him), and there may be a touch of truth in them somewhere. Galerius the Drover was a frontiersman by birth and profession, commanding picked soldiers supposedly in a state of instant readiness. His officers had to be willing to lead their men into appalling danger – and probably also to take on lions or Sarmatians, or any other living creature, if ordered to do so. Among such picked men, under such a leader, it is not unknown even today for young officers to indulge in horseplay, daring one another to undertake feats of courage or endurance which to pacific civilians might well look like invitations to commit suicide. Moreover, Eusebius' reference to Constantine's having struck 'terror' into his contemporaries, although it might be a mere rhetorical flourish, would naturally mean that he was a bully, always ready to 'throw his weight about', taking advantage of his long reach and fine physique to establish physical ascendency over his group. Such a man may be admired, but he is rarely liked. Galerius, anxious to promote the fortunes of his nephew Maximin the Shepherd and others of his favourites among the young men, may well have taken advantage of Constantine's boastfulness and arrogance to push him into situations from which he might emerge covered with ignominy, or might not emerge at all. It would, however, seem inherently more likely that Constantine was matched against prisoners or animals for wagers and in the hope of seeing him 'cut down to size'. If Galerius had seriously wanted the young tribune's death, he could have arranged it much more efficiently than by clumsy attempts to induce Constantine to bring it upon himself. After all, death was his trade.

While Diocletian and Galerius were fighting for peace and stability in the East, and Constantine scrambling for position there, Constantius Chlorus was busy in the far West. The Egyptian revolt of 292 was preceded by peasant risings in Gaul of a different character, but springing from fundamentally similar causes. The suppression of the chief bands of *bagaudae* in 287 did not end the troubles. The wars inside Gaul provided the Franks and Saxons of northern Germany with a fine opportunity to renew their attacks along the coasts of the provinces of Germania, Belgica and Lugdunensis Secunda (later, Normandy and Brittany). To protect the shore-folk against them, Maximian ordered his Praetorian Prefect Constantius (as he then still was) to oversee the building of a fleet and the fortification of a suitable port to act as a naval base. The actual work was entrusted to a Menapian from Belgica, whose hitherto unsuspected ability had been revealed in the early months of the recent war, a sea-captain named Mausso Carausius[11]. At first it looked as though the choice of Carausius was a good one. In the winter of 286–7, he built a fleet at Gestoriacum (Boulogne) which, the following summer, swept the pirates from the seas. He was, however, too efficient, and his success aroused envy and suspicion. After a triumphant return to base, he was accused of concealing part of the plunder taken from captured ships, and of having made illegal agreements with some of the pirates. Rather than wait for trial and possible execution, he had himself acclaimed as the Caesar Carausius and led his fleet to Britain. He must have been a remarkable man, for not only did his ships follow him but when he landed units of the fourth, seventh, ninth, twentieth and thirtieth legions all declared for him, falling on and annihilating auxiliary squadrons loyal to their paymaster Maximian. To replace them, Carausius pressed Gallic traders into his legions and hired mercenaries, ready for the coming confrontation with the Augustus. At the same time, he tried to act like a true emperor himself, garrisoning the northern frontier against the Picts, and instituting a currency reform, striking *aurei* as heavy as Diocletian's, at sixty to the Roman pound.

In 287–8, Maximian's forces under Constantius were too fully committed in Gaul and on the Rhenish frontier for him to act against Carausius, but in the winter of 288–9, Constantius directed the construction of a new fleet at Gestoriacum. A panegyric delivered before Maximian on April 1, 289 by Eumenius, a favourite of Constantius and a civil servant who on his retirement was to become a professional orator and teacher of rhetoric at Autun, mentions this fleet as being ready to put to sea. It sailed shortly afterwards, but was destroyed by a storm in the Channel. Convinced by this demonstration of divine favour towards Carausius that he was destined to rule the West, much of Germania Secunda, Belgica Secunda and Lugdunensis Secunda (western Belgium and Holland, and north-western France) declared for him. After this setback, Maximian decided that Carausius was in fact doing little harm in Britain and came to terms with him, granting him recognition in Britain and north-west Gaul on condition that he kept the seas free from pirates. He began calling himself Marcus Aurelius Carausius, apparently to link himself with the imperial family by identifying himself with Maximian's brother Marcus Aurelius; elected himself consul, and struck an *aureus* showing himself with Diocletian and Maximian, bearing the inscription 'Carausius and his brothers/Augustan peace'. He ruled his provinces unmolested for four years, until Constantius' appointment as Herculian Caesar with responsibility for Britain and Gaul.

On his appointment, Constantius naturally made it his first concern to win complete control of the territory allotted to him. He laid siege to Gestoriacum, closing the harbour with a mole, to cut Gaul off from Britain, and started building a fleet in the Seine. When Gestoriacum fell, so too did Carausius. His Praetorian Prefect Allectus murdered him and had himself proclaimed Caesar Augustus in Britain. Constantius made haste slowly. In 294, his preparations to invade Britain and restore Roman normality there were interrupted by a rebellion among the Moors of north-west Africa. While Maximian went to Africa to quell their revolt, Constantius took control of the whole administration in the West, working from Maximian's capital at Milan, where the civil service had its headquarters, and from where he could rapidly mount a counter-attack if the Augustus' expedition ran into difficulties. By the winter of that year, however, he had returned to the north, and was busy directing his ship-builders and overseeing the resettlement in Germania and Eastern Belgica, around Trier, of the Batavians, one of the Frankish tribes, defeated that year by his Praetorian Prefect Asclepiodorus. It was 296 before he was ready to move directly against Allectus, but when the moment came his plans, typically, were perfectly practical and skilfully executed. It was known that Allectus had stationed a fleet off the Isle of Wight, to oppose landings in the Solent or along the south coast of Britain. Constantius had no confidence in his ability to win a sea-battle, so to avoid having to fight one he divided his fleet. Asclepiodorus, with most of the ships under his command, sailed west from the Seine estuary, to effect a successful landing somewhere in St George's Channel, while he himself went east and north, towards the Thames estuary. A thick mist hid these manoeuvres from Allectus' patrol boats, and Asclepiodorus' landing went entirely according to plan. He burned his boats on the shore, probably not only to prevent a retreat, but also because he had insufficient forces both to guard them and to fight away from the coast; converted his sailors into legionaries, and struck eastwards through Britain. Allectus hurried to meet him, only to be defeated and killed in a battle somewhere in northern Hampshire. When, a little later, Constantius landed near London, he found the whole province ready to acclaim him as 'Restorer of the Eternal Light'.

Britain had, however, prospered under Carausius and Allectus, and Constantius now had to prove to the people of the province that they were not mistaken to put their confidence in their true emperors. He first restored the defences, both along the coasts and at Hadrian's Wall, then instituted a policy of vigorous reconstruction, introducing into Britain the kind of reforms which Diocletian was fostering in the East. Public buildings and roads were improved and the city of Verulamium largely rebuilt. Following Diocletian's directives, he 'sliced the province up small' for the sake of better government, dividing it into four parts, each under its own president (*praeses*) and with its own civil and judicial services, the whole in future being known as the Diocese of the Britains, and ruled for the emperor of the north-west by a *vicarius*. The campaign against Allectus and the reconstruction following it were not, perhaps, stamped with the imprint of genius, but they were efficient and thorough, and confirm the overall picture of Constantius as a dedicated, careful man, respectful of imperial traditions and determined to see them respected by others.

Constantius spent rather less than two years in Britain after the defeat of Allectus. The resettlement of the Batavians inside the imperial frontiers had not made the Rhenish frontier permanently safe. The Alemanni were still restless. By 298, they had found a strong leader in King Gennuboudes and when the campaign season opened that year, they swept into the provinces of Belgica and Germania. In the course of the war against them, Constantius himself had a very narrow escape at 'the City of the Lingones'. Trapped there with only a small garrison and no hope of relief unless the main body of his forces could be alerted to the danger, he had himself let down on a rope from the city wall, made his way through the enemy lines and so came to the main camp of the legions, to lead the army back to the city and raise the siege. The war ended with Gennuboudes captured in the ensuing battle. Constantius did not execute his enemy – as Constantine was later to execute leading Frankish prisoners – but bound him to the empire with a treaty of friendship and restored him as king over his people. Gennuboudes was later to betray his trust, but there were soon to be reliable Frankish auxiliaries from beyond the Rhine serving with the legions[12].

The immediate result of these victories in Britain and Gaul was that for the first time in many years the frontiers were at peace and it became possible to press ahead in earnest with the reconstruction planned by Diocletian since his accession fourteen years earlier. As most of the work was in the administrative sphere, few traces of it survive. Courts were set up and city councils organized, censuses taken and tax-assessments made; the whole complex system of imperial bureaucracy was set in motion, so that Augustan peace might rule and the huge standing army protecting that peace might be fed, clothed and armed. Roads were repaired, the post reorganized and water supplies secured by building aqueducts. In the cities, public buildings destroyed by the *bagaudae* and the barbarians were rebuilt on a grander scale than before. A panegyric delivered in the presence of Constantius by Eumenius in 299 at Autun, where Constantius had appointed him schoolmaster on his own petition after his retirement from the civil service, reveals how much work was involved in planning and co-ordinating the rehabilitation of just this one city, in providing finance, approving plans and supplying labour. For this essential work, men were not only seconded from the legions, but also recruited from as far away as Britain[13].

Amid all this activity, Constantius probably had little time for family affairs. However, if the number of his children can be taken as a yardstick, his marriage to Theodora was a success. They had three sons and three daughters: Delmatius, Julius Constantius and Hannibalianus; Constantia, Anastasia and Eutropia. Hannibalianus died in infancy, but the others lived to play important roles in Constantine's empire. They were the legitimate imperial family, the third generation of Herculians, but when Constantine seized power, none of them showed him any hostility. The signs are that Constantius himself favoured Constantine, and demanded regular reports on his promotion and prospects. Generally, they must have satisfied him, but it is a pity that neither the report that his son had married and produced an heir, nor his comment on it, has survived. Constantine was still officially betrothed to Maximian's daughter, and his marriage could have been politically disastrous, while the birth of his child meant that the dynastic situation was growing very complicated.

Constantine's first wife was one of only four women whose names figure prominently in his life-story. The others were his mother Helena, his half-sister Constantia, and his second wife Fausta, Maximian's daughter. Something is known of these other three, but Minervina is one of the enigmas of history. Where she came from, where she disappeared to, what she looked like, to what race she belonged – none of these questions has an answer. Surprisingly, not even Constantine's bitterest pagan enemies tried to make capital out of his association with her, so she must have been a most unexceptionable person. They attacked both through his mother Helena, whom he adored, and his second wife Fausta, whom he murdered, but they ignored Minervina as completely as though she had never existed.

Her name meant 'household slave of the goddess Minerva' but, at this late date, this would not necessarily imply either that Minervina herself was a pagan, or that she was a barbarian slave. Over the centuries, so many slave families and barbarian prisoners had been admitted to citizenship, and so many pagans converted to Christianity, that names from the third and fourth centuries reveal little unless they can be linked with particular families or situations – as when, for example, Mausso Carausius began calling himself Marcus Aurelius Carausius, or Constantius Chlorus changed his name from Flavius Valerius Constantius to Gaius Marcus Constantius on his elevation to the purple, adopting the forenames of Diocletian and Maximian, his 'fathers' the Augusti, as an act of flattery and token of dynastic loyalty. Minervina may have been a barbarian, was possibly a slave by birth or capture and was almost certainly a pagan; but she may have been none of these. All that is certain is that she bore Constantine a son, Flavius Valerius Crispus, whose paternity he never denied, and that later he divorced her for dynastic reasons – just as his father had divorced his mother. The year of the marriage must have been about 299, because Crispus was approaching manhood when, in 317, his father, by then sole ruler of the western half of the empire, named him Caesar; two campaign seasons later he served with distinction against the Alemanni on the Rhine, and was soon afterwards adult enough successfully to take command of his father's fleet.

Constantine seems actually to have married the singularly self-effacing Minervina in legal form, despite the difficulties that must have made with Maximian, to whose daughter he had already been betrothed for some years. He was said to be a man of 'proper morality' (*probis moralibus*) and although it was Lactantius, one of his hero-worshippers, who made this claim, it appears to be borne out by the facts, at least until his last years[14]. Although he could have been convicted of vanity, cruelty and judical murder, he was never accused until late middle age of sexual immorality or the other excesses which so often accompanied it in the lives of the emperors, luxury and greed. He was not given to orgies. He was too dedicated to power.

The only references to a legal bond between Constantine and Minervina, however, occur in panegyrics delivered before Constantine in later years. That at his marriage to Fausta, delivered in 307, spoke of his divorce from Minervina. Another, eleven years later, claimed that Constantine had 'shown a continence greater than' Constantius', because when attracted by Minervina 'you immediately surrendered to the laws of matrimony... You may be said to have been wedded to chastity'[15].

Arguments from silence are dangerous, but the lack of attacks from Constantine's enemies, his legendary chastity and the evidence of these panegyrics combine to suggest that his marriage to Minervina was a true one under the law – especially as his enemies' silence remained unbroken when, later in his reign, he passed laws forbidding concubinage, the prostitution of inn servants (was Helena in his mind?) and the seduction of slaves[16]. Constantine was a puritan of sorts. Maybe the excessive virility which Eusebius sensed in him was only a superficial thing, and his thrusting for dominance sprang from a subconscious urge to prove his manhood . . . but these are deep waters, and there are few facts from which to construct a raft to sail safely over them. The one certain thing is that in bearing Crispus, Minervina provided an acceptable fourth-generation Herculian, should one be required, little over twenty years after the founding of the dynasty, and before the baby's grandfather Constantius had stopped fathering children of his own.

CHAPTER THREE

THE CAESAR CONSTANTINE

THE great persecution of the Christians, the effects of which coloured events throughout Constantine's reign as emperor, did not actually begin until February 303. Diocletian was, however, moving towards persecution at least five years earlier, driven to it by his concern at the growing number of conversions to non-Roman religions and the danger to the state which, in his honestly-held opinion, these faiths constituted.

To anyone convinced, as Diocletian was, that religion was an indispensable part of the national life, and that the gods upheld the state, the empire at the end of the third Christian century must have looked in imminent danger of collapse. The philosophers and preachers of alien faiths had deeply undermined the old religion. Under pressure from syncretistic ideas originating in Egypt and the East, the identity of the old gods had crumbled, and for many they had become at best aspects of the Supreme God, the *Summus Deus*, architect of the universe. The manifestations of the Supreme God were held to be innumerable. His cult could be adapted to almost every taste. It appealed especially to the philosophers, and to men of action – soldiers such as Constantius Chlorus. At the time of Aurelian, the Supreme God, identified with *Sol invictus* (the Unconquered Sun), the real hero of the Persian cult of Mithras so popular in the army, had also been the god of the emperor and the empire, and the official cult of Jupiter and his pantheon had suffered all but total eclipse. However, worship of the unconquered sun, or even of Mithras – whose cult was declining, mainly because initiation into its more arcane mysteries had become too expensive for most purses – was not utterly inimical to the official religion of the empire, in the sense that the other religions based on the concept of salvation, Christianity and Manicheeism, were.

Nor did it threaten total syncretism, swallowing up the personality of the gods and of the Supreme God alike in a universal pantheism, as Neoplatonism, this generation's other contribution to religio-philosophical thought, seemed to do.

When Christian fourth-century historians asked themselves why the terror of the Great Persecution fell on the church, they found no difficulty in discovering an answer satisfying to their sense of religion and history. According to them, its cause was a decision on God's part to punish the Christians for their dissensions. The method He chose was to permit evil spirits to inspire the emperors, and especially Galerius, with a frenzy against His unworthy adherents. So, for instance, Eusebius of Caesarea ascribed all the ills of his times to God's disgust with the Christians. He accused them of arrogance, sloth, envy, recrimination, hypocrisy and dissimulation[1]. However, he carefully avoided mentioning by name both the crime for which they were first punished under Diocletian, military insubordination, and that for which most martyrs in fact suffered, sedition against the imperial state.

The reality of Diocletian's fear of the 'saving' religions is most clearly shown by another fact generally ignored by the Christians – the fact that he published an edict 'Against Malefactors and Manichees' in 296, two years before he first took steps to eradicate Christians from the army. The edict's terms were ferocious: it made death by burning mandatory for convicted Manichees[2].

The religion of Mani is interesting both in itself and for the light it throws on the nature of the religious syncretism which Diocletian so hated. Mani had travelled in India; he had some knowledge of Buddhism, probably also of Christianity (if only in its gnostic forms), and certainly of the dualism taught by his sun-worshipping fellow-Persian Zoroaster. From all these elements and his own genius, he created a synthetic religion which he himself claimed would replace all others. His introduction to his own 'bible', the *Kepheleia*, reveals something of the yearning of those from Persia to the Far West who, in this century, were seeking a single faith combining the best elements from all religions. It also reveals something of his supreme egotism.

> The writings, the wisdom, the revelations, the parables, the psalms of all earlier religions, gathered from every region, flow together in my religion, in the wisdom which I have revealed. As one stream mingles with another to form a single great river, so the ancient books are brought together in my writings and a single great wisdom comes into being, one in no way comparable to what earlier generations have preached. No one has ever written, no one has ever revealed, books like these written by me.

Mani recognized only three forerunners worthy of some measure of comparison with himself, Jesus, Zoroaster and the Buddha. He said that he was 'an apostle of Jesus Christ' filled with the Holy Spirit of Truth. He promised salvation to those who chose the light, the truth, the good principle; damnation to those who rejected them and himself.

King Bahram of Persia rejected him totally in A.D. 272, crucifying him to save the nation, but his faith lived on, to be carried into the Roman Empire by travellers and merchants as well as the fanatical armies of Sapor. It had a very wide appeal. The high-flown fancifulness of its allegories and the esoteric imagery in which its dogmas were cast attracted the half-educated and credulous, while many intellectuals welcomed the new insights it appeared to offer into the nature of the Supreme God. It found special favour with those attracted by the kind of theorizing fashionable among gnostics, both Christian and non-Christian, a speculative theology about the origins and ends of things, resting on the presuppositions that all knowable phenomena are emanations at several stages removed from the Unknowable Godhead; that the creation is the work of an evil godling, the demiurge, who trapped a spark of goodness in matter; and that there is a perpetual war for the redemption of the divine spark in every man from the darkness of the evil, visible universe[3].

The third great challenge to Diocletian's restored worship of the old Roman gods, Neoplatonism, offered other paths towards spiritual satisfaction to those for whom such speculation held no attraction. Unlike Christianity and Manicheeism, the New Platonism of Plotinus[4] did not offer salvation from the world and the flesh, either through the intervention of God or by personal striving for purification, but rather promised identification with the world by the path of understanding.

When towards the middle of the third century, Plotinus, an Egyptian who had encountered the greatest Christian speculative theologians at Alexandria and may have travelled in Persia in pursuit of wisdom, opened a school at Rome, it soon became apparent that in him the Supreme God had found the most subtle and able of champions. Plotinus was unwilling to join with the gnostics in calling the created universe evil, or even with the Christians who considered it corrupt. He said that the whole universe is manifestly infused with intelligence and goodness; yet although from his point of view to deny the sun's intellect is ridiculous and 'the souls of the stars have much more goodness and intelligence, and much closer contact with the Intelligences [beyond the visible universe] than do our own', nevertheless 'there are people [the Christians], who, while they do not revolt from calling even the most evil of men their brethren, will not condescend to give this name to the sun and the heavenly bodies, or even to the spirit of this world'. Like his master Plato, Plotinus taught a Stoic ethic and a doctrine of transmigration of souls. He welcomed an intelligent acceptance of polytheism, through which, he wrote, 'the Great Ruler of Intelligent Beings bears witness to his own greatness'. He accused Christians of arrogance, on the grounds that they both rejected the gods yet claimed to know the Supreme God, and that they declared that they knew all about morality without ever having explored true moral courage and virtue. Trusting that if they had faith, they would be given salvation from outside themselves, they seemed to him to have freed themselves from the burden of having to struggle to achieve virtue through intellectual efforts to understand the pleasures and pains of life. They had, therefore, never developed real moral strength of character (*virtus*), and so had no real knowledge of God.

'Without real moral strength,' he wrote '*God* is only a word.' His pupil, Porphyry[5], found Christians guilty of fundamental atheism and total lack of knowledge concerning the divine nature; and – encouraged perhaps by Aurelian's dedication of a new temple on the Quirinal Hill to the Supreme God manifested as the Unconquered Sun – gave new intellectual respectability to demonology and augury by his skilful defence, in fifteen books *Against the Christians*, of oracular shrines, astrology and divination through omens and dreams.

From the point of view of imperial authoritarians like Diocletian, the essential difference between such religions as Christianity and Manicheeism on the one hand, and Neoplatonist metaphysics and the Sun cults on the other, was that while the latter appeared to be compatible with the religion of the state, the former took pride in proclaiming that they were not. Christianity called Christ its Lord and king, promising eternal punishment to anyone worshipping gods other than Him and His Father. Mani had claimed openly that 'my religion is superior to all other religions' and expected it to replace them. Christians had been intermittently in conflict with the empire ever since Christ's own execution. The first to rally the people to fight Manicheeism in the empire was the 'established' High Priest of the Sun at Emesa. The edict of 296 'Against Malefactors and Manichees' was logically followed by action against the Christians two years later – and equally logically, from Diocletian's point of view, Neoplatonists and similar teachers were left undisturbed.

The troubles of the Christians under Diocletian began with a military purge in 298. Describing this first step towards persecution, Eusebius wrote, 'At last, while our congregations were still well filled, divine judgement began . . . with the Christians in the army . . . the Master of the Soldiers [Veturius] permitting them the choice: either to obey orders and retain their present ranks, or to be stripped of them if they disobeyed the edict. A great many of the soldiers belonging to Christ's kingdom chose to confess him. . . .'[6]

Unfortunately, neither Eusebius nor anyone else records the

substance of the edict which Galerius' Master of the Soldiers tried to enforce in 298. Eusebius appears to suggest that it was a general order demanding obedience and discipline, but this is unlikely. There is no hint in other histories of great unrest among the soldiers. The 'edict' may have been the order, known to have been issued around this time, requiring the ceremonial performance of the oriental rite of *adoratio*, genuflexion to the emperor or the emblems of his authority, on enlistment, first appointment, promotion or re-deployment. Or again, it may have been an ordinance with a somewhat wider scope, intended to restore the allegiance of the soldiers to the Roman gods, and so bind them more closely to the state as Diocletian envisaged it. Diocletian's rehabilitation of Jupiter and Hercules by the creation of the Jovian and Herculian dynasties and recruiting of Jovian and Herculian legions may have had as little religious significance as has sometimes been claimed, but seems pointless unless it reflected a real desire on his part to see the restoration of the gods and heroes, at least as a stabilizing element in the reconstruction he had promised at his election.

Whether it was the *adoratio* or some other quasi-religious ceremony that the Christians had refused to perform which provoked the edict, their objections to it were very strong. Many of them preferred ignominious discharge from the service to obedience. If the rite was the *adoratio*, their objection is understandable. Christians bent the knee in worship only to Christ and the relics of the martyrs. To offer that honour to the emperor would be to offer it, through him, to the pagan gods – an act of idolatry. As 'soldiers in Christ's kingdom', Christians were by religious profession enemies of the Roman state as it was then constituted. Their worship had been tolerated since the time of Gallienus (260–8), but the edicts of earlier emperors making Christianity a proscribed religion and the profession of it rebellion had never been completely withdrawn.

Veturius' attempt to enforce the edict in the Danubian provinces proves nothing about his own attitude, either as an individual or as Master of the Soldiers. In seeing that the order was carried out, he was merely enforcing discipline, as any good general has always been bound to do. Galerius' role in the purge was a more basic one – but not as obvious as has sometimes been claimed. According to his most bitter opponent, Lactantius, in his book *On the Deaths of the Persecutors*, the whole affair was inspired by his mother Romula. She was 'a transdanubian, a priestess of the mountain gods – a very superstitious woman, who gave religious feasts almost every day. . . . The Christians stayed away, devoting themselves to fasting and prayers for her and those who feasted with her. So she came to hate them, and persuaded her no less superstitious son' to adopt her view that their religion was a pernicious danger to the state[7].

Galerius may have shared his mother's particular 'superstition' – which was probably faith in the Great Mother and her son, the god of vegetation and fecundity – and was certainly in a position to influence the direction of events after his resounding victory over the Persians in 297; but Lactantius' account of the origins of the purge is too highly coloured to carry conviction. No doubt Romula did hate the Christians, but the army was purged not to accommodate her, but to reinforce the official cult which had always played so large a part in Roman military discipline, and, by the restoration of that discipline and the old values, to please Diocletian himself. In enforcing the purge through Veturius, Galerius was fulfilling his role as 'helper' of the Augustus. Paralleling as it did the action against the Manichees, Veturius' purge was part of a co-ordinated attempt to bring the disaffected back to pure 'Roman' ways. It was doomed to failure from the beginning, for 'Roman' ways were a thing of the past. The very rites by which Christian soldiers were expected to show their allegiance to their 'Roman' emperors from the Danube Valley had originated in Persia.

Many officers appear to have resigned their commissions and many soldiers to have accepted ignominious discharge rather than obey Veturius' orders. There are, however, few trustworthy records of the execution of Christians at this time, and those which did take place have generally been ascribed rather to the injudicious action of over-zealous local commanders and magistrates than to imperial policy. Five soldiers of the armies of the Danube – the martyrs Pansecratius, Valentian, Heschyias, Marcion and Nicandor – together with one retired veteran, Julius, died in Moesia; Maximilian, a conscientious objector against the form of oath he was expected to take on enlistment, was executed for insubordination at Tebessa; Marcellus, a centurion who refused to renew his oath of service, was beheaded at Tangiers; Tipasius, a veteran on the reserve who ignored his recall papers for a campaign against the Moors, was executed in Africa: if these men had belonged to any other army but Christ's, history would have dismissed them as troublemakers deserving to suffer the full penalties of the law[8]. On the basis of their records, Veturius' purge was justifiable in law. It seems to have been effective everywhere, except in the dioceses ruled by Constantius Chlorus. Probably himself a worshipper of the Supreme God, he had great sympathy for his Christian subjects. There are no reliable records of executions in his provinces, and when persecution was extended to all Christians, the complaint was made that his court and army were full of them, and continued to be so. Was Constantius himself ever attracted by Christ? The possibility exists. It must have been at about this time that he named one of his daughters Anastasia or 'Resurrection'.

After the army had been purged, the Christians were left in peace for about four years. Full persecution began at Syrian Antioch in A.D. 303, and there is little doubt that it was largely inspired by pagan fears of being overwhelmed by Christianity. The story as Lactantius tells it hints at a successful plot arranged by Diocletian's Chief Haruspex, Tagis. He says that it all started one day when Diocletian, in his role as chief pontiff, was offering sacrifice in the presence of Galerius and his officers:

> While he was in the East, fear drove him to seek to probe the future, and he sacrificed cattle and sought future events in their livers. And some of those servants who knew the Lord were present at the sacrifice and put their immortal sign [of the Cross] on the pieces. This being done, the devils fled and so the sacrifices were spoiled. The haruspices were filled with fear, for they could see no signs in the entrails at all, and it was as if they had offered unacceptable sacrifices. Offering fresh victims, again and

> again they saw nothing. Whereupon their chief, the Haruspex Tagis said, whether on suspicion or because of something he had seen, that the sacrifices were giving no response because sacrilegious men were taking part in sacred things, and he [Diocletian] became so furiously angry that he ordered that not only those who had attended the sacrifices but all those in the palace should offer sacrifice, and that those who fought shy of it should be beaten with rods.

He also ordered Galerius to purge the armies of Asia[9].

On the basis of this command to Galerius it had sometimes been argued that the alleged failure of the omens (whether by the magic of the sign of the cross, or because Tagis had decided that the time had come for a show-down with the Christians) actually occurred in 298 and was the occasion of Veturius' purge. It seems more likely, however, that this was a second purge, undertaken because there were still Christians in the forces, ordered in a fit of rage engendered by superstitious fear, and restricted to the eastern armies. Diocletian's sudden loss of self-control was a symptom of his state of mind. He was growing tired by 303 of trying to bring order to an unruly empire. Two years later, he was to suffer a nervous breakdown and abdicate. When his anger had cooled, he might well have rescinded his orders before the purge of the palace and the army had developed into a general persecution, if he had not been under continuing pressure from such men as the Chief Haruspex and other pagan priests, as well as from his own increasing mental tiredness and confusion. As it was, he called a conference of leading military and civil officials, and, as many of his predecessors had done in moments of difficulty, sent an appeal for divine help to the shrine of the sun-god Apollo at Didyma, near Miletus. What makes it seem certain that either a plot against the Christians already existed, or one was now rapidly being formulated, is that Apollo's reply was far less ambiguous than his utterances usually were and was precisely parallel to Tagis' original explanation of the failure of the omens. Lactantius says that the oracle was consulted on the Feast of Terminus, the seventh day before the calends of March – February 23 by our calendar. According to Constantine, who was at court when the message from Didyma arrived, 'Apollo declared . . . that he was prevented from speaking the truth by the just upon earth, and that this was why oracles from his tripod were lies. His priestess lamented this evil among men . . .' Diocletian claimed not to know who 'the just upon earth' were and 'one of the priests in attendance replied, "The Christians, naturally" '[10].

Lactantius uses the presence at Diocletian's winter conference of 302–3 of a pupil of Porphyry's named Hierocles as a prop for his argument that the persecution was planned by the arch-persecutor Galerius with the pagan high priests, and that Diocletian had to be browbeaten by the members of the conference into issuing the edict which was published on February 24[11]. If this is true, it did not take long to break the emperor's resistance to the idea of persecution. The edict must in fact have been ready for signature when Didymean Apollo's reply reached the imperial court. The oracle was consulted one day and persecution began the next: it looks very much as though only a flat refusal by Apollo to countenance persecution could have spared the Christians. The truth is probably that Diocletian himself decided that persecution alone could save the empire, and consulted the generals and magistrates of the East to test their reactions and pick their brains about the form the edict should take. Hierocles' presence at the conference cannot be used to prove a pagan plot to which Diocletian was not privy. It is true that, later in 303, he was to circulate a vicious pamphlet against the Christians entitled 'The Friend of Truth', but as well as being a pagan propagandist, he was also a high official of the empire, the Governor of Bithynia, in north Asia Minor, and therefore a natural person for Diocletian to consult on policy matters. The idea of a conference probably grew out of the news of fresh rumblings of discontent, traced by rumour to the Christians. Eusebius' mention of 'great dissensions', and therefore unrest, among them is echoed, as Burkhardt has pointed out, in Galerius' Edict of Toleration promulgated in 311, where he complains of the Christians 'neither giving the gods the worship they owed to them, nor honouring the god of the Christians'. It is echoed again in the call for a second purge of the army, and once more by Eusebius in his somewhat tangled account of the persecution itself, when he writes of 'attempts being made to attack the empire' by threatened Christians at Melitene on the Armenian frontier, and 'all over Syria'[12]. There had been rebellion in Syria in 294, spearheaded by the Saracens. It had been put down easily enough, but a new revolt, inspired by the Christians, who belonged to no distinctive tribe and who, although traditionally recognized as enemies of the state, yet had many agents among the officials of the palace, would not have been so easy to suppress. The presence of men like Governor Hierocles at the conference in Nicomedia may well indicate the first counter-measures of the administration not against the Christians as such, but against a conspiracy headed (or credibly said by the pagans to be headed) by Christian revolutionaries. Naturally, once in the imperial presence, committed enemies of the Christians would make the most of their opportunities. The failure of the auspices, an anguished imperial appeal first to the rod, then to a politico-religious shrine as well known as the Didymean oracle, hints of unrest among the Christians: the situation developed in a way that their enemies could scarcely fail to exploit successfully.

The first edict of persecution was posted in public places in Nicomedia 'in the nineteenth year of Diocletian, in the month Dystrus', on February 24, 303. In fact, action against the Christians of the capital had started during the night of the 23rd–24th – within hours, if Lactantius is to be believed, of the reply at Apollo's shrine, and before copies of an edict prepared only on the 23rd at Antioch could have reached the city. The first anti-Christian move made by the pagans was to dismantle the newly completed Cathedral Church of Nicomedia, standing provocatively opposite the palace gates. All its copies of the scriptures and sacred vessels were destroyed[13].

The texts of the first edict of persecution, and the second, which followed it within hours, have not survived. From action taken on the basis of them, and from Eusebius' garbled account, it seems that the first ordered the suspension of worship, the destruction of church buildings, the confiscation of church property and the surrender of the scriptures, while the other dismissed Christians from all posts of authority, made suspects liable to torture if they would not sacrifice to demonstrate their loyalty, denied Christians access to the courts of justice, and reduced imperial freedmen who professed Christianity to their former slave status.

According to their enemies, the Christians struck back. And according to Constantine, speaking of this time much later to a conference of Christian bishops, so too did God.

At Nicomedia, a Christian fanatic tore down a copy of the edict and was executed the same day. Then the imperial palace caught fire, not once, but twice, and the murmurs of sedition already noticed arose from Syria and Melitene. After the second fire at the palace, Galerius ostentatiously removed himself from the city, saying that he had no intention of waiting there to be burned alive. Diocletian, convinced now that if he did not smash Christianity, the Christians would destroy him, promulgated a third edict, ordering the arrest of Christian leaders and their imprisonment until they had shown their loyalty by sacrifice. The Christians claimed that their enemies had laid the fires and then put the blame on them. Diocletian ordered that all the inhabitants of the palace should be made to sacrifice and watched the ceremonies himself, even directing Prisca, his own wife, and Valeria, Galerius' wife, to offer incense. He was badly frightened. The second fire at the palace had raged through the Sacred Bedchamber itself. In his *Oration to the Saints*, Constantine said that in fact it was caused neither by the Christians nor by Galerius, but by heaven-sent lightning, and that it drove Diocletian to abdication and retirement from fear:

> Diocletian, however, after displaying the relentless cruelty of a persecutor, evinced an awareness of his own guilt and, owing to the affliction of a disordered mind, endured the confinement of a mean and remote dwelling. What, then, did he gain from his active hostility against our God? Simply this, I believe: that he passed the rest of his life in dread of lightning. Nicomedia attests the fact; eyewitnesses—of whom I myself am one—declare it. The palace, the adjoining private chamber, were destroyed, consumed by lightning, devoured by the fire of heaven . . .[14]

Precisely in the manner of the Old Testament, the emperor here ignores the interval of two years between the commencement of the persecution and Diocletian's abdication, because to have admitted it would have spoiled his effect. Bringing together three unrelated events – the persecution, the lightning and the abdication – he asserts a causal relation between them. In his times, this method of argument was commonly accepted. Constantine saw the lightning which destroyed the palace as an act of the Christians' god. So too did Diocletian, whether that god was working directly, or through his Christian servants, whether the fire was caused by lightning or arson.

In the terror which followed, three eunuchs on the staff of the Sacred Bedchamber including the Great Chamberlain himself, were executed. Another who died was Anthimus, the Bishop of Nicomedia. Persecution became general throughout the territories of the two Augusti and the Caesar Galerius. At Rome, churches, scriptures and archives were all destroyed. Pope Marcellinus surrendered the scriptures to imperial officers on demand and was stigmatized by his fellow Christians as one of the lapsed. Bishops were arrested throughout North Africa. The prisons of Egypt and the Orient were filled to capacity.

Constantius Chlorus, however, still held his hand, satisfying his critics by destroying a few church buildings. He seems not even to have demanded the surrender of the scriptures – with the result that, when persecution ended, there was no bitterness among Christians in his dioceses between 'confessors', who had suffered for their faith, and 'those who handed over', the *traditores*, whose loyalty to the empire and fear for their own safety had overcome their Christian scruples. Constantius, it would appear, found Christians useful and loyal, and so continued to trust and employ them.

Constantine's role in the persecution was minimal. In later years, he spoke of it with horror, but there is nothing to show that at the time he did anything but stand by and watch. He was still learning. The fanaticism of those who suffered and died, and the expediency of those who gave up their sacred books, offered a pinch of incense, and lived, must have confirmed a good deal of what he already suspected about human nature.

In the summer of 303, the whole court moved to Italy for the celebration at Rome of the twentieth anniversary of Diocletian's accession, his *vicennalia*. He had probably never set foot in the capital of Caesar and Augustus until he was welcomed there by the City Prefect and the senate as the Caesar Augustus. He actually entered his twentieth year as emperor on September 17, and that day he proclaimed a general amnesty, under which imprisoned Christians were permitted to go free, along with the rest of the criminal population, as long as they showed themselves willing to keep the law in future. But precisely at this moment (or possibly even a little earlier – to catch Christians at the prison gates, as it were) he had promulgated a third edict, ordering all Christians to offer sacrifice, and making refusal to do so a capital offence. Many, having tasted imprisonment or torture themselves, or seen its effects on others, accepted the amnesty. Others died, but not many, and none in the dioceses ruled by Maximian and Constantius Chlorus[15].

In his edict against 'Malefactors and Manichees', Diocletian had written, 'It is the greatest of crimes to reverse what has once been established and defined by those of old and is still capable of continuing.' At Rome that autumn, he and his court – Constantine among them – could see for the first time the reality of the past which he had inherited. It ought to have been an inspiring experience, but he found it distasteful and perhaps unnerving. It had been arranged, for reasons which remain obscure, that his accession day should be celebrated not on the anniversary itself, but on November 20. That day's festivities were to be followed by a month and a half of celebrations, culminating on January 1 with the solemn ceremonies accompanying the conferment on him of the office of consul. It would be his ninth consulate, but the first he had accepted in person from the senate. However, the earlier celebrations proved too much for the ageing emperor. He accepted the honour of a triumph glorifying all his victories, but obviously took no pleasure in the gruelling round of banquets and games. He complained that Rome was corrupt and effete. On December 18, he abruptly left the city, dragging his court away before the licentious feast of Saturnalia began. On January 1, 304, he was clothed with the dignity of his ninth consulship at Ravenna, and a few weeks later was refreshing himself in the more congenial atmosphere of the Danube frontier. But, according to Lactantius, the winter was one of 'bitter cold and rains' and he developed a chronic and debilitating fever, which even the coming of spring did not relieve. Perhaps this illness impaired his judgement; he failed to recognize that he had lost the struggle with the Christians, and reached the conclusion that to be effective, persecution must be total. From Pannonia, he issued a fourth edict against them, re-enacting the legislation which had guided the magistrates under Decius, in 250, and ordering all citizens of the empire to appear before the courts and offer sacrifice. Fortunately for Western Christians, however, this edict seems to have been rigidly enforced only in those areas directly under the rule of Diocletian himself and Galerius.

Diocletian had begun the twentieth year of his reign at Romulus' city: he ended it at his own capital, Nicomedia, with the splendid ceremonies surrounding the dedication of a new race-track. The journey into Asia Minor cancelled out whatever good the spring and summer in the Danube Valley may have done to him, and he began to fail. From its mental effects, his illness may have been cerebral malaria, but it was more probably psychosomatic in origin. Eusebius says bluntly that he became mentally deranged[16]. It would, perhaps, not be surprising if after twenty years of ruling the empire he was simply too tired to know what he was doing. By mid-December, he was said to be dying, and the whole of that winter, it seemed that he could not long survive. It was even rumoured that he had already died, and been buried in secret. He made no public appearances until March 1, when, reviewing troops at Nicomedia, he looked on the point of death. He was, however, to free himself from the burden of government and live for a good many years yet. At the time of that military review, he was probably in correspondence with Maximian about the next step in their careers, their joint abdication[17].

It took effect two months later, on May 1, 305. Galerius became Augustus in the East; Constantius Chlorus in the West. The days when the news of the impending abdication leaked out must have been tense ones for Constantine. His admirers were convinced that he would be named Caesar, perhaps to his father, but more probably to Galerius.

That he had his admirers is unquestionable, but what he had done to deserve their admiration is not immediately obvious. He had taken part, years earlier, in the Danubian campaigns, and won some personal acclaim for his part in them. He had travelled with the emperors and been noticed for his fine physique. He had, however, never commanded an army or administered even a small city (otherwise surely one of his devoted biographers would have recorded the fact). Yet there was obviously a strong rumour, based perhaps on nothing but hope, that he would either be promoted by command of Diocletian, or would seize power for himself. The mint-master at Alexandria, maybe trying to push him into action, went so far as to strike an *aureus* inscribed CONSTANTINUS CAESAR[18], but at the end of the day when the names of the new Caesars were announced, Constantine still wore the scarlet and gold of a tribune first class.

Lactantius claims that Galerius blocked Constantine's promotion. In a passage of his *Deaths of the Persecutors* more entertaining than truthful, he purports to give the actual words of the conversation between the Augusti on the day the new Caesars were chosen. He says that the first name proposed was that of Maxentius, the son of Maximian, but he was a man 'of pernicious and evil mind, one moreover proud and contumacious, liked neither by his father nor by any of his relations'. Then Constantine's name came up. Diocletian said, 'Shall I appoint him?' Galerius replied, 'He is not a suitable person. If he is contemptuous of me now, while he is a private person, what will he do if he once gains power?'

'But he is a pleasant enough person, and should be given

power: it would give his father a better and juster opinion of us.'

'Appoint him, and I shall not be able to do as I like. I shall have to order those under my authority who are afraid of him to do nothing unless I command it personally.'

'Well, then, who shall we appoint?'

'Severus,' Galerius said.

'What – the dancer? That alcoholic, who turns night into day and day into night?'

'He is a suitable man – he has commanded the armies loyally. Shall I send him to Maximian, to be clothed with the purple?'

'All right. And who else would you give it to?'

'This man,' Galerius said, indicating the adolescent and still semi-barbarous Daia . . .

Diocletian asked, 'Who is this man you are proposing?'

'A relation of mine . . .'

Daia, or Daza, who had recently started to call himself Maximin – to point his relationship with Galerius, whose official name was Maximianus – was finally chosen, although Diocletian objected that he had not been trained in public life.

The new Caesars were presented to the armies on May 1, 305. How high the hopes of Constantine's supporters still ran that day is vividly conveyed by Lactantius in his account of the abdication:

> Diocletian and Galerius held a parade to publish the names of the Caesars. Everyone looked at Constantine, for no one doubted that the choice would fall on him. The troops present, as well as the commanding officers of the legions summoned to the ceremony, fixed their eyes on Constantine, rejoicing in the hope of his coming promotion, and busying themselves with prayers for his good fortune.
>
> Nearly three miles from Nicomedia, there is a hill, on the summit of which Galerius had received the purple: a pillar stood there, with a statue of Jupiter on it. It was to this place that the parade marched. The soldiers were called to order. Diocletian, in tears, harangued them, telling them that he had become infirm and needed rest from his labours and was going to resign the empire into stronger and abler hands, and at the same time would appoint new Caesars . . .

> Suddenly, he declared that the Caesars would be Severus and Maximin. There was universal amazement. Constantine stood nearby, in full view, and many asked one another whether his name too had been changed to Maximin, when, in the sight of everyone, Galerius, thrusting back his hand, pushed Constantine aside and drew Daia forward, and having stripped him of the clothes he wore as a private citizen, stood him in the most conspicuous place. Everyone wondered who he could be . . .
>
> Diocletian took off his purple robe, put it on Daia, and resumed his original name of Diocles . . .[19].

Maximin Daia was Galerius' nephew[20]. He was, in Lacantius' view, Galerius' creature entirely. Although Lactantius probably exaggerates the stir his promotion created, it is clear that his elevation to the purple was unexpected, and that at least some of the spectators were dismayed at the public insult to Constantine.

The other new Caesar, Severus, was an old comrade-in-arms of Galerius', who had served with him in the armies in Aurelian. He had a reputation for drunkenness and enjoying a party, but he was a distinguished soldier, and Constantius seems to have had no hesitation over adopting him into the Herculian dynasty as Flavius Valerius Severus[21]. Both Constantius Chlorus' son and Maximian's were probably passed over as a matter of policy: the Jovian and Herculian dynasties were to be perpetuated not by inheritance, but by the promotion of those alleged to be fittest to rule. In the long run, neither Constantine nor Marcus Valerius Maxentius was to acquiesce in the senior Augustus' ruling on this point.

The new appointments and promotions were followed by a redistribution of the dioceses. Pannonia, a province north of the Adriatic Sea, formerly part of the territories of the Eastern Caesar, was given to Severus, who had been born there. He ruled it together with Italy and Africa, but surrendered control of Spain to his Augustus, Constantius. Galerius kept the east-Danubian provinces of Moesia, together with Thrace, Asiana and Pontica (the east Balkans and modern Turkey), but gave the whole of the rest of the huge Eastern empire, from Libya to the Euphrates, to Maximin Daia.

Lactantius presents the abdication of Diocletian and the accession of Maximin Daia as the successful outcome of machinations on Galerius' part, suggesting that the overbearing Caesar browbeat the ailing Augustus into abdication. In fact, however, Diocletian wanted to retire. He left Nicomedia secretly on the day he laid aside the diadem, and withdrew to Salona, on the Adriatic coast of Dalmatia, where he supervised the construction of a palatial fortress as his new home – the 'mean and remote dwelling' of Constantine's *Oration* – and afterwards devoted himself to gardening. If there was any opposition to the change of regime, it came from Maximian, who later tried to snatch back the power which he had surrendered by abdicating, and from the champions of Constantine.

Constantine's position under the new administration was difficult and dangerous. It is true that his father had the dignity of being senior Augustus, but he was far away in western Gaul, preparing a campaign to defend the most remote of the empire's frontiers against the Picts, and could do little to protect or help his son. At Nicomedia, Constantine's enemy Galerius was now all-powerful, and in the newly-appointed Caesar Maximin Daia his father's friends the Christians had one of the most bitter opponents they were ever to encounter. He himself was suspected, not of Christianity, but of disaffection. His father, reading the signs of the times, wrote to Galerius, asking that his son should be sent to him. Galerius refused the request, not outright, but with delaying excuses. It was rumoured that Constantius was dying. Galerius feared that if Constantine were allowed to join his father, they would engineer a *coup d'état* before the senior Augustus' death. Constantius, for his part, was afraid that if he allowed Constantine to remain within Galerius' reach, he would suffer an accident that would end forever his chances of attaining empire. The situation was explosive. Lactantius claims – and it may well be true – that Constantine survived it only because Galerius was sometimes in a mellow mood after dinner. Approached one afternoon when he had eaten and drunk well, he good-humouredly signed a mandate permitting Constantine to leave the imperial palace and use the posting system to travel wherever he liked. The next day, awaking at mid-morning, he repented of his clemency, but Constantine had already left Nicomedia. Galerius ordered a warrant for his arrest to be made out, but when the posse sent in pursuit reached the first staging post, they found no change of horses available for them. Constantine and his party had taken what they needed and hamstrung the rest. When next heard of, Constantine was with his father at Gestoriacum[22].

This picaresque but unsupported tale leaves many questions unanswered, not least that of the sequel to the story of the posse. Lactantius generally loses no opportunity of demonstrating Galerius' despotic inhumanity, but there is no hint in his narrative of imperial retribution falling on either the leading agent for his failure to effect an arrest or on the master of the staging post for his inefficient protection of an essential imperial institution. His silence may mean nothing – but it may be a pointer to the fact that there was more to the story either than he knew or than he was willing to tell even years later. There are others. Although Galerius must have had signal stations on both shores of the Bosphorus, he apparently took no serious steps to prevent Constantine's landing in Thrace or have him pursued through Europe. It looks as though, when the Augustus' first anger cooled, he reflected either that Constantine's flight would benefit the East, or that his own position was too vulnerable for him safely to end or revenge it. The truth may be that Constantine fled to escape not (or not only) the enmity of Galerius and Maximin Daia, but involvement in a seditious movement which had chosen him as its figurehead – a movement which in his opinion was not powerful enough to succeed, but which with him as its leader could have given Galerius cause for concern. If such a plot did exist, its instigators can only have been the Christians. With persecution intensifying, some eastern Christians may well have tried to tempt Constantine, the son of the mighty protector of their co-religionists in the West, to lead a rebellion, promising him their support if he would end persecution on his accession to power. Admittedly, there is no hard evidence in support of this theory, but it would account for

Galerius' willingness to see Constantine vanish from Nicomedia at the minimal cost of temporary suspension of the post.

When Constantine reached Gestoriacum, he found his father almost ready to sail for Britain and the campaign to throw the Picts back beyond the Wall. Few details of this brief war are known, except that it was a success for the imperial army and its confederate allies, but fatal to Constantius Chlorus himself. He died at York on July 25, 306, after reigning as senior Augustus for only one year and a little under two months[23].

He was scarcely dead before his tributary ally, King Crocus of the Alemanni[24], commander of the auxiliary Frankish cavalry during the Pictish campaign, led his detachment in acclaiming Constantine as their new Augustus. The legions took up the cry and, whether after a show of reluctance or not – a panegyrist later said that he put spurs to his horse but was brought back to the camp[25] – Constantine was clothed in purple and hailed as Imperator, Caesar and Augustus. As news of his accession spread, province after province in Britain and Gaul declared for him. Of his father's old dominions, only Spain did not immediately prefer him to Severus, the legal heir to the Herculian Augustus. It was a victory as notable as any in war.

Eusebius suggests that Constantius had planned his son's acclamation, and, by doing so, had followed the Divine plan for the future of the empire. Constantius died, he wrote, 'after making his legitimate son Constantine Basileus and Augustus in his place'[26]. Lactantius, whose knowledge of events in the remote West at this time was scanty – he does not so much as mention the Pictish Wars – draws a touching picture of Constantius 'dying in peace and quiet' at his palace in York, after endowing his son by Helena with supreme authority[27]. The later pagan authors, Eutropius and Zosimus, both confirm that Constantius planned Constantine's seizure of power[28]. If he did in fact do so, it was a deliberate act of rebellion against the constitution of which which he himself was the guardian, at the end of a lifetime of devotion to legality. While it is not impossible that when he realized that his life was ending, he set himself as his last task on earth the securing of his eldest son's accession (especially if he was aware of the unsatisfactory nature of Galerius' appointments), it seems inherently more likely that King Crocus organized the acclamation of his old leader's son, perhaps after pondering on some chance remark of Constantius', or perhaps with some slight encouragement from the dying Augustus. The barbarian chief would naturally prefer a man whom he knew and whose father he had respected, to an unknown and untried leader to be sent, probably, from the far end of the world. The loyalty of Crocus and his men was not to the concept of empire but to the Emperor Constantius, who had defeated their tribe in battle, offered them clemency, settled them within his frontiers, and shown them good fighting in the North. On his death, what would seem more natural to them than that, following their own tribal custom, they should elect his son to rule them – especially as they knew that son's courage?

However, whether it was King Crocus, Constantius or Constantine who made the arrangements for the transfer of power, the acclamation was made and the die cast in favour of open rebellion. The claims of the Caesar Severus and of the young but indubitably legitimate Herculian sons of Constantius Chlorus were alike ignored. Once in power, however, Constantine was careful to try and give all his acts the veneer of legality.

He is known to have been impulsive, but if he had really been as hot-headed as has sometimes been suggested, he would surely have found the ease with which he acquired authority intoxicating, and gone on immediately to strike for supreme power, as so many usurpers had done before him. In fact, he acted coolly. He made no open attempt to subvert Spain, though his agents may have been at work there. He invaded neither Italy nor the Danube Valley. Instead of loudly challenging Galerius to destroy him or be destroyed, he quietly but unmistakably asked for the senior Augustus' acquiescence in his revolution by sending to Nicomedia, together with an official announcement of his father's death, a portrait of himself as the Augustus of the West, wreathed in imperial bay. Then he set to work to consolidate his position north and west of the Alps.

Galerius was not willing at that moment to face the prospect of war with the West – which seems to confirm that he was not sure of his own position in the East, fearing that Constantine had many supporters there, who might have risen if he had been attacked. (Only months later, when a similar rebellion occurred in Italy, Galerius did move against its leader, Maxentius the son of Maximian, who was unknown in the East.) Lactantius says that when Galerius received Constantine's portrait as emperor, the sight of it threw him into a paroxysm of rage: he burned the wreath, tore the picture up, and retired to bed for the rest of the day[29]. When he had taken stock of the situation, however, he did what he could to save his dignity, while tacitly admitting that he had been out-manoeuvred. Ignoring the fact that Constantine was technically a rebel, he rejected his claims with one breath and acknowledged them with the next, announcing that, in accordance with the constitution, he himself had succeeded to Constantius Chlorus as Senior Augustus, with Severus as his junior colleague in that rank, while Constantine should be recognized as the legitimate Caesar of the Herculian dynasty – and so the lowest-ranking of the four emperors, inferior even to Maximin Daia.

Caesarship of the Herculians was not what King Crocus had planned for Constantine, but for the time being the new Caesar was content. Among the peoples whom he actually ruled, he was recognized as his father's legitimate heir and so, whatever title he was given at Nicomedia, had effectively established a dynasty, the New Flavian; for in Northern eyes his own son Crispus was already a Caesar, his natural successor, just as he had been Constantius'. In the rest of the empire, he was accepted as the legal holder of his father's first imperial office, Caesar of the West, and was therefore well placed later to claim Augustan rank. Everything that had happened had been given the appearance of legality, boldness had been rewarded, and although he was still junior to Maximin Daia, some of the shame of having been passed over the previous year had been wiped out. The great Architect of the universe, the Supreme God whom Constantius had worshipped, was manifestly working for the Flavians.

Constantine ruled from the Wall to the Alps and the Pyrenees, while his father became 'Constantius the Divine', dwelling, as the court poet Optatianus put it, 'in a celestial abode at the heavens' very heart'[30]. His was one deification to which the Christians did not object. They agreed with Eusebius that Constantine had been 'a man of gentle and benevolent spirit towards his subjects', the only emperor in their day 'worthy of the name'[31].

Apart, of course, from their hero Constantine.

CHAPTER FOUR

THE ROMAN REVOLUTION

GALERIUS' acquiescence in Constantine's assumption of the purple, with the grant first of the rank of Caesar, then, shortly afterwards, of the title 'Son of the Emperors', relieved the new emperor of the fear of proscription and attack from Spain, Italy or the Danube; it set him free to concentrate on guarding the Rhenish frontier and continuing the work of consolidation and reconstruction begun by his father in Gaul. Gratifying though Galerius' recognition must have been to him, however, his success was humiliating to Marcus Valerius Maxentius, the legitimate son of the forcibly retired Augustus Maximian. If the normal rules of succession had applied at the abdication in 305, Maxentius would have become the Herculian Caesar, and on Constantius' death might have expected to be nominated Augustus in the West. By Diocletian's decree, however, blood was no longer the determining factor in the legal inheritance of power, and although Galerius had given his daughter Valeria to Maxentius in marriage, so apparently adopting him into the Jovian royal house, Maxentius – like Constantine – was passed over at the abdication. Now, in 306, Constantine had power, while he still had none. Chagrin and envy pushed him into rebellion.

In his boyhood, it had been confidently predicted that he would one day rule the world. Sixteen years before Constantine's usurpation, on April 21, 289, he had heard a panegyrist tell his father 'and when the right moment comes, a day will dawn when Rome will see you in triumph, and will quickly submit to your son's right hand'[1]. While Maximian ruled as Herculius and Constantine was an insignificant figure at the distant court of Diocletian, Maxentius seems to have been content to live very privately. He was more 'Roman' than any of the reigning emperors, actually residing within the area of jurisdiction of the City Prefect, at a property on the Via Labicana, a few miles outside the walls of Rome[2]. When he and Valeria Maximilla named their only son 'Romulus', it was probably in honour of the City as well as of the boy's great-grandmother, the pagan priestess Romula. He expressed no open objections when the Italian, African and Illyrian dioceses were given to 'that dancer', Severus. Perhaps he had received secret assurances of future favours from his father-in-law. As soon as the news of Constantine's succession and seizure of power was confirmed, however, he rebelled, making a bid for glory before it was too late. In the words of an anonymous author preserved by Valesius, 'After Constantius had died in Britain and Constantine his son had succeeded him, the Praetorian Soldiers made Maxentius, the son of Herculius, emperor.'[3] The date was October 28, 306, only three months and three days after Constantine's acclamation as Augustus at York.

The role played by the Praetorians in Maxentius' revolt was a key one, both for its temporary success, and in determining their own future disbandment. In crying for Maxentius' accession, they were playing their disruptive part in Roman history for the last time. For the time being, however, they played it as skilfully as ever.

Romans in general, and the Praetorians in particular, had good reason to feel that it was time for a change in Italy. Certainly since Diocletian's sudden departure from the City in December 305, if not from long before, the old capital had been uneasy in the minimal role it was expected to play in the world. Diocletian had condemned the Romans as at once both too outspoken and too frivolous, and had deeply offended them by accepting his ninth consulate at Ravenna; but in fact their city was by no means the decadent and rather pointless nonentity it is sometimes made out to have been. It was still the home of the empire's oldest and richest aristocracy and of its first ruling body, the Senate. It was also the site of its most hallowed temples and thriving schools. Under imperial displeasure, however, the City's future looked bleak.

The future of the Praetorians looked even less promising. In fact, they officially had none. From being the chief bodyguard of the emperor, they had been demoted by Diocletian to mere sentinel duties at Rome, tied permanently to the service of the City Prefect. Now Severus, acting under instructions from Galerius, had signed an order addressed to his Vicar in Italy, Abellius, requiring him to disarm and disband them. Abellius might have succeeded in this unenviable task with only a minimum of bloodshed if Rome itself had been amenable, but the City felt slighted by imperial indifference and was perturbed by the news that Severus had started a census intended ultimately to lead to the City Prefecture's assessment for taxation, in total disregard of ancient Italian privileges. In the circumstances, it needed only the slightest sign from Maxentius to bring the soldiers into the streets. The Praetorians, led by Lucinius, the officer in charge of the Pig Market, murdered Abellius and then, on the pretext of restoring order, purged the City of elements loyal to Severus, proclaiming Maxentius their emperor. Whether or not he had deliberately provoked the violence which led to his acclamation, he showed himself prepared to take immediate advantage of it, coming to power as many emperors had done before him, ringed with the swords of the Praetorians, actively supported perhaps by few apart from the soldiers, but effectively opposed by none once the riots were over. Anxious not to brand himself indelibly as a usurper before he was sure of the permanence of his success, he refused to call himself Augustus, but adopted the title, appealing to local patriotism, of 'Prince of the Romans', and appealed for support to his father, and to Constantine[4]. The newly recognized Caesar did nothing which Galerius might interpret as support for the revolution, but after only brief hesitation, Maximian joined his son at Rome. The Praetorians marched out beyond the boundaries of the City Prefecture and began the conquest of Italy in the name of their Prince. It proved an easy assignment. The south offered no resistance, and the north little except in the areas garrisoned by Severus' legionaries. Severus' plans for taxing the country had made him and the Senior Augustus Galerius universally unpopular. His army was steadily pushed back towards the frontiers of his native Illyria.

Maxentius' usurpation and conquests were an unforgivable insult to Galerius' supreme authority. He had been able, without too great loss of face, to accept Constantine's accession in the north and west, because there was no legally appointed Caesar ruling there at the time; but Maxentius' self-promotion was another matter entirely. Galerius had himself confirmed Diocletian's appointment of Severus to rule Italy, and for him to have accepted Maxentius' usurpation would have been tantamount to admitting that the machinery of government had broken down. Simultaneously underlining the difference in his eyes between Maxentius' position and Constantine's, and demonstrating that he still claimed sovereignty over the City, he named himself and the newly-legitimized Herculian Caesar consuls for the year 307, while calling upon his old drinking-companion Severus to exert himself and save the day in Italy. So within six months of technically rebelling against Galerius, Constantine became legally his collaborator in the two highest offices of the state, the imperial power and the consulate.

Meanwhile, at Rome, Maximian was taking stock of the situation, and did not like what he found. He had never really accepted the need for his retirement, and may have had a hand in his son's rebellion, but now he recognized the weakness of the Prince of the Romans' true position. Alarmed at the prospect of having to face the Danube armies reinforced from the Eastern legions and perhaps, if Constantine threw in his lot with Galerius, those of Gaul as well, with only his old command the Praetorians at his back, he appealed to Diocletian, justifying his 'rebellion' – if such his resumption of authority could be called – on the grounds of necessity, and pleading with his old comrade to come out of retirement and save the empire from distintegration[5]. Another man might have been tempted, but it seemed that Diocletian no longer cared whether the empire hung together or not. He had abdicated once and for all time. If the empire was to be saved, Galerius must effect its salvation, through Severus. Maximian knew that he and Maxentius could expect no mercy from Galerius, but just as the situation began to appear desperate, good news reached Rome: in the South and West, Africa and Spain had declared for the rebellion, accepting the rule of the Unconquered Prince, as Maxentius now called himself, 'the Unconquered Prince of the Romans, Marcus Aurelius Valerius Maxentius'[6].

As soon as the snows of 307 melted and the mountain roads were open again, Severus marched on Rome with those forces from Pannonia and northern Italy which still acknowledged him. Maximian marched to meet him. Lactantius tells the story:

> [Maxentius] sent the purple to his father, who since laying down imperial power had been living in Campania, and named him Augustus for the second time. But Severus marched under arms and came to the walls of the City. Then, however, the soldiers, having destroyed their insignia, deserted and gave themselves up to him against whom they had come. What remained for him they had deserted but to fly? But presently Maximian, having resumed authority, came up with him, when he had reached Ravenna. And he, when he realized what must happen – that he would be given up to Maximian – instead surrendered himself to him, giving the purple back to him from whom he had received it. And having done so, he begged nothing of him but an honourable death[7].

Maximian accepted his surrender, but refused his request for death, holding him in dishonouring captivity, probably at Tres Tabernae. Thanks to his father, the Unconquered Prince had won again.

As soon as Galerius learned of Severus' second defeat in Italy, he mounted an expedition from Thrace to stabilize the situation in Illyricum, reconquer Italy, and rescue his old comrade. Ultimately, he too reached Rome, but succeeded neither in recapturing the City nor in saving Severus. Whether Maximian's prisoner committed suicide before Galerius could find him, or Maximian had him murdered, is not clear from the surviving accounts of his death. The truth is probably that Maximian wanted to keep him alive to use as a bargaining-counter in dealings with Galerius, but that Severus succeeded in finding a way of killing himself rather than be used as a pawn in a situation where he had once been a king[8].

There were, however, many events of lasting significance between his surrender at Ravenna and his death at Tres Tabernae.

After their victory at Ravenna, both Maximian and Maxentius called themselves Augustus, so that four men then claimed to be senior emperors: Galerius, Severus, Maximian and Maxentius, in addition to the truly senior Augustus who claimed nothing for himself but peace, the ailing Diocletian, growing cabbages at Salona. There were also two legitimate Caesars, Maximin Daia in the East, and Constantine in the West.

When Maximian realized how popular his success against Severus had made him, he began to explore ways of cutting the number of senior emperors down to three, by eliminating his son Maxentius from the list. So far, however, the Unconquered Prince had proved a mild and tolerant ruler, respectful of the laws and the Senate. Only the Christians feared him: they had not yet dared to replace their Bishop Marcellinus, martyred under Severus' rule, nor were they to do so until the following year, 308. Maximian was not willing to make common cause with the Christians, nor would they have been strong enough for his purposes, even if they had been willing to unite under him; so biding his time, he announced that he had a new plan for strengthening his son's rule: he would go to Gaul, to subvert Constantine from his armed neutrality, thus uniting the West under himself, the original Herculius, to whom Constantius' son and legions would surely feel a certain loyalty.

Constantine had not wasted the first six months of his rule in Gaul, and they had not been easy. As soon as the harvest of 306 had been gathered, the Frankish tribes of the Chatti, Ampsivari and Bructeri, whom Constantius had permitted to settle on the west bank of the Rhine, had broken out from their villages to pillage and burn throughout Lower Germania and Belgica. Their rising was not only a challenge to Constantine's new authority, but also a betrayal of the treaties which his father had made with them. For him to have failed to react sharply would have entailed loss of all credit both among them and with his own soldiers. His counter-blows were swift and utterly crippling. Before winter had closed down on northern Europe, he had smashed the tribes, killing thousands and capturing thousands more – including two of the rebel leaders, Ascaric and Regaris. His prisoners paid with their lives in the amphitheatre at Augusta Treverorum for their temerity in having attacked him. A few months later a panegyrist said that so many of the Bructeri were killed in the course of the Victory Games that the beasts exhausted themselves with slaughter[9]. Such hyperbole was excusable. With a single brief campaign, Constantine had proved himself as a leader, making it common knowledge throughout the empire that his name was one to be reckoned with. Arriving in Gaul early in 307, Maximian found himself pleading for support not from a young man still uncertain of himself after a sudden rise to power, but from a successful general flushed with victory. Obviously, he could not hope to buy such a man at a bargain price, so he immediately offered all he had: recognition of Constantine's real worth, through the grant of the title Augustus refused to him by Galerius the previous year, and marriage with his daughter Fausta, to whom Constantine had been betrothed fourteen years earlier, at the time of the creation of the Herculian dynasty by the elevation to the purple of Constantius Chlorus.

Maximian's proposals offered certain advantages, and Constantine did not hesitate long before accepting them. Marriage to Fausta would tie him firmly into the Herculian dynasty. An alliance with Maximian and Maxentius would mean that he could call on Italy, Spain and Africa for help if his old enemy Galerius, resentful of the mere fact that he had received Maximian at his court after failing to help Severus, should choose to strike north at him rather than take on the provenly formidable army of Italy. The assumption of the title Augustus would please those of his soldiers who had never understood why he had accepted his demotion by Galerius to Caesar and, as it was being granted to him by Maximian, the lustre of whose name was still not dulled in Gaul, it might help to overawe potential opponents of his rule. Moreover, it would be an effective snub to Galerius and his creature, the senior Caesar Maximin Daia.

The wedding of Constantine and Fausta was celebrated amid great military display at Augusta Treverorum on March 31, 307[10]. The panegyrist at the wedding, whose eulogy survives, did what must have been a most delicate task very creditably, avoiding all the pitfalls. He mentioned Constantine's divorce from his former wife Minervina, but not the existence of his son Crispus, now aged about six, and likely to be making his own alliances before the children of his father's second marriage were old enough to play any part in the political life of the empire except that of hostage or of partner in an enforced betrothal-of-convenience. He set Constantine's usurpation of power in an incredibly favourable light: 'The title of sovereignty [Augustus] has now accrued to thee, O Constantine, through thy father-in-law . . . When empire was left to thee by thy father, thou chosest rather to be content with that of Caesar, so that when one should appear wanting to add lustre to thy name, he might yet name thee Augustus.' He talked flatteringly about the genius and continuing strength of the old emperor, and the military prowess and administrative wisdom of the new. Tying together the welfare of the rebel armies in Italy and the future of the Herculian dynasty, he prayed, without actually mentioning Maxentius, 'May the world domination of Rome and the posterity of the emperors alike be immortal and eternal!' The future of the dynasty already seemed assured in Constantius' and Maxentius' children. In the course of the next fifteen years, Constantine and Fausta were to make the family's position look unassailable by the addition of five more children to the tally, three boys and two girls: Constantine, Constantius and Constans, Constantina and Helena. But by then Constantine would be poised to sweep Diocletian's artificial dynasties into oblivion.

That, however, was in the future. On his wedding day, Constantine became Augustus for the second time, under the auspices of Maximian[11]. This promotion was no more legal than the first; having once abdicated, even though only under protest, Maximian had no right to promote anyone to any position within the empire. And Constantine, having accepted the title and his new bride, was clearly expected to pay for the favours he had received with support for Maximian's plans. Everyone waited for him to send military aid to his new brother-in-law, Maxentius. However, when the news came that Galerius was in Dalmatia, on the point of invading Italy, Constantine declined to move. Whether the plan was that he should let Galerius weaken himself by attacking Maxentius, then fall on his rear, and seize control of the whole empire in the name of himself and Maximian, or whether in fact he callously abandoned his new in-laws to their expected fate at Galerius' hands, is a mystery. He had entangled himself in such a net of alliances that he could not emerge honourably from the situation, whichever side he supported, or even if – as in fact happened – he gave support to no one.

If Galerius had actually been as strong in that summer of the year 307 as had appeared at the beginning of his reign only two years earlier, he would no doubt have defeated Maxentius at Rome, and having brought Italy to heel, turned north to deal with his defaulting Caesar and fellow-consul. In fact, however, he had antagonized many of his people, not only by raising new taxes and persecuting Christians, but also by showing a typically military scorn for intellectuals by closing the schools at Nicomedia. Lactantius, himself once teacher of rhetoric there, was thrown out of work by Galerius' edict, and was remembering a time bitter in many memories when he wrote, 'Eloquence was condemned, advocates suppressed, jurists dismissed or put to death; literature was held to be a criminal occupation, and books were treated as enemies, destroyed, condemned.'[12]

When Galerius marched into Italy, Maxentius' continuing popularity, Maximian's easy defeat of Severus, the threat of taxation and oppression if the senior Augustus won the war, and a revival of patriotism for Rome fostered by agents of Maxentius and the Senate, all worked against his success; and by the time he had brought his army to the borders of the city prefecture, there were ominous signs of disaffection among his soldiers. He began to doubt his ability to retain their allegiance in the face of

Maxentius' propaganda against the violation of the sacred soil of Rome; and, before bringing them to battle, he turned back the way he had come, implementing a rigorous scorched-earth policy as he retreated. This failure of nerve left him puzzled about what to do next. He withdrew into Pannonia, regrouped his forces, and probably tried to consult Diocletian at Salona. Diocletian, however, continued to maintain total silence: he had retired, and it was all nothing to do with him . . . Meanwhile, in the North, Constantine waited. It was in fact all that anyone needed to do. Given time, Maximian and Maxentius were bound to destroy themselves.

They came close to doing so during their first winter at Rome together, that of 307–8. Maxentius had taken power partly, at least, to save Italy from taxation, but now after two invasions in two years, if he was to maintain authority, he had to raise extra money to pay and arm his troops and to feed Rome. Barred from taxing Italy, he imposed new taxes on the provinces of North Africa and raised the grain levy, which provided Romans with free rations at provincial expense, to unprecedented heights. The Africans naturally resented these fresh exactions, and in 308 they repudiated their offer of allegiance to him, declaring their provinces an autonomous principate of the empire ultimately subject to Galerius, and appointing a day-to-day Augustus of their own, the former Vicar of the Diocese of Africa, Domitius Alexander[13].

Spain also revolted at the idea of being penally taxed to enable Maxentius to buy his way out of his difficulties in Italy, and realizing that the Roman rebellion had been a mistake, withdrew support for it. Instead of claiming an independence which she could not maintain, however, she offered herself to Constantine, now the most legitimate of Herculians, holding his appointment from both Eastern and Western Augusti. He accepted the added burden of the Spanish diocese – no doubt with secret pleasure – and so extended his frontiers to those held by his father at the height of his power. It was less than two years since Constantius' death[14].

Meanwhile, at Rome itself, Maximian was trying hard to

supplant his son. Whether it was simply the old man's vanity, as has sometimes been suggested, which led him into extremes of antagonism towards Maxentius is very doubtful. His egotism probably did have some influence on the direction events took, but as an old hand at the power game he must have realized that Maxentius was set on a road which could lead only to destruction. Was Constantine deeply involved in his attempts to undermine support for Maxentius? The Herculian Caesar appeared to be merely sitting and waiting, but it may well be that he gave Maximian at least tacit encouragement. Maximian had been impressed by Constantine and would probably have been happier to see his son-in-law ruling Italy, rather than Maxentius, the son whom he had come to hate so much that he denounced him as a changeling, and no child of his by Eutropia of Syria. For Constantine not to have taken advantage of this situation would have been alien to his character. His understanding of his own ambition made him wary of friendship with any possible rival, and faith in himself as the only man fit to rule drove him to exploit the weaknesses even of his alleged allies.

Having defeated both Severus and Galerius, Maximian felt that he commanded enough support to put the case against his son openly before the Senate and the army of Italy. He argued that it was he himself who was the original Augustus Herculius, he who had won great victories, he who had defeated the Eastern emperors: it was he, and not his son, who was truly fit to rule. In the middle of one impassioned appeal to the soldiers lined up on the parade ground, he is said to have torn off Maxentius' purple cloak, declaring him to be no true emperor. If this tale is true, he is lucky to have survived: his son must have been very patient with him, or very uncertain of the soldiers' temper[15]. However, if Maxentius was willing to indulge his father, his friends were not. Maximian was made to realize that he had gone too far, and understanding at last that no one would draw a sword for him against Maxentius, he left Rome secretly. For a time, no one knew where he was, but he soon reappeared, at the court of his new hero Constantine at Augusta Treverorum. He could have taken refuge elsewhere, but he presumably thought that in joining Constantine he was openly allying himself with a fellow-conspirator, then and in the future. Whether or not Constantine shared this view is debatable. He was too clear-sighted to expect much from Maximian after his failure in Rome.

While this situation was developing at Rome, Galerius, camped with his army in the Danube provinces, wondered what to do next. It still seemed to him that there was only one man who could help him against Maximian, the latter's former superior Diocletian. It is clear that he had already decided to make another appeal to the retired Augustus soon after his retreat from Italy in 307, for at the end of that year he attempted to recall his 'father' Jovius' attention to his responsibilities towards the City by naming him as consul with himself for the year 308. Diocletian was still happy in retirement, and it took a good deal of correspondence to arrange a meeting with Galerius to discuss the future of the empire. He did finally allow his inertia to be overcome, and the two Jovian Augusti met at Carnuntem in northern Pannonia, in the late summer of 308. Maximian, now more bitter than ever against Maxentius, somehow inveigled for himself an invitation to their conference. The details of the discussions between the three emperors are not known, but their acrimony may easily be imagined. The outcome was the appointment of a new Caesar Augustus, a general named Licinius, to replace the dead Severus. Lactantius recorded: 'Diocles met his son-in-law, so that, in an unprecedented move, he might give the *imperium* to Licinius in place of Severus in his presence. Accordingly, this was done. So, at one moment there were six [Augusti].'[16] Because Diocletian, Maximian and Galerius were all present at Carnuntem, Eusebius said that Licinius was chosen 'by the common consent of all the emperors'[17]. The *History of the Caesars* adds a few details: 'Galerius, in council with Jovius, made Licinius, recognized as a Caesar because of their old friendship, an Augustus; and he was entrusted with the defence of Illyricum and Thrace.'[18] In fact, Licinius was expected not merely to defend Illyricum and Thrace, but energetically to attack the problem of Italy and Africa. Edicts were prepared, announcing his appointment, and proscribing Maxentius and any who continued to support him.

The date of the creation of the new Caesar Augustus was November 11, 308[19]. His appointment was, as Lactantius said, an unprecedented move, for his only link with the Jovian house was an old acquaintanceship with Galerius, with whom he had served in wars against the Danubian tribes and the Persians. No one admitted it, but at Carnuntem Diocletian was presiding over the first stages of the dismemberment of the dynastic system which he himself had so carefully designed to give stability to the empire.

Licinius was yet another Illyrian peasant whose military ability had brought him to the top. As Augustus, he claimed descent from the Emperor Philip the Arab, who reigned from 244 to 249, and assuming relationship with all the branches of the ruling families, called himself Gaius Flavius Valerius Licinianus. He was, in fact, like Severus, another of Galerius' old drinking companions – as Lactantius knew, but chose not to record, because in later times he became one of his heroes, a defender of the Christians: 'Galerius had Licinius always about him' was as much as he would permit himself to say. 'He was his old and intimate acquaintance and his earliest comrade-in-arms, whose advice he took on the management of all his affairs.'[20]

The struggle for power and influence in 308 must have been very intense indeed. A fascinating story must lie behind the sudden appointment of Licinius, without any formal period of probation as Caesar, but its details are lost. What was it that convinced Diocletian very much against his will that he must travel through the mountains from Salona to Carnuntem and once more apply his mind to the problems of the empire? What made Galerius accept Maximian as a member of the conference so soon after he had joined his son's rebellion, brought about Severus' death, and scared away the Senior Augustus' own army? And what kept Galerius out of Italy throughout 308? He is known to have been a man impatient for his own authority. The two unsuccessful Italian campaigns of 307 – before Maxentius had had time to become unpopular – would hardly have been enough in themselves to deter him from another invasion, at a time when Maxentius was already in difficulties. Of course, Diocletian may have made it a condition of his attending the conference that Maximian should also be there, and that no military action should be taken before the emperors met. Why, however, should the retired Augustus have made such conditions, or Galerius have accepted them? Surely only because the empire was in great danger from Maximian himself – or, rather, from Maximian and his new ally, Constantine.

It appears as though Maximian, having come to hate Maxentius and finally to have decided that in the long run he could not survive the opposition of the Eastern emperors, the instability of Italy, and the indifference of Constantine to his fate, had temporarily abandoned Italy together with his son, and made himself Constantine's ambassador at Carnuntem, representing the views of the ruler of the North and West to the Augusti. Having failed to regain real power for himself through Maxentius, he was perhaps aiming to do so through manipulation of his son-in-law. He attended the Carnuntem Conference in a dual role: as emperor-emeritus, with especial knowledge of the power structure and personalities of the West, and as champion of the only recognized ruler actually to have added to his stature as a result of recent events, the Herculian Caesar Constantine.

No doubt, once Galerius and Diocletian had taken the decision to appoint Licinius, they expected him immediately to set about destroying Maxentius' rebellion, but the army of the Danube was neither strong nor reliable enough to guarantee quick and certain victory – and the rulers of the East could not afford another rebuff in Italy. Licinius havered for a time. Meanwhile, over in the far east of the empire, the Caesar Maximin Daia felt that he had just cause for complaint. Diocletian's dynastic system had envisaged regular promotion from Caesar to Augustus: he himself was undeniably the senior Caesar, but now Licinius had been appointed Augustus ahead of him, without any formal training, and without his having been consulted. He put pressure on his patron. The Senior Augustus' position was too weak to permit resistance. He issued a decree naming both Maximin Daia and Constantine 'Sons of the Augusti'[21] – although this they already were, by virtue of their adoption into the Jovian and Herculian dynasties as Caesars. They both insisted that it was not enough, and early in 309, Galerius named each of them Augustus in his own right.

So at the beginning of 309, there were no Caesars, but eight Augusti: two officially retired, Diocletian and Maximian; four legitimately active, Galerius, Licinius, Maximin and Constantine; and two self-styled, Maxentius of Rome and Domitius Alexander of Africa. It speaks much for the efficiency of the administrative system created by Diocletian's reforms that the empire did not collapse into chaos. However, the strain of maintaining six armies and their staffs, and six imperial households (Diocletian was content with relatively little, and Maximian lived largely off Constantine's economy, in a new palace at Arles), hastened the decay of the monetary system. Alexander's and Maxentius' empires were particularly unstable; Maxentius' because, without Africa and Spain, Italy could not feed itself; Alexander's because the half-subdued peoples of the Atlas Mountains and the desert remained loyal only because of the permanent threat of massive intervention from overseas if they did rebel. In the East, Galerius and Maximin Daia were technically at peace, although continuing persecution of the Christians and the unending struggle between them and the various pagan groups perpetuated on the religious and philosophical plane the military unrest of earlier years. Both Constantine and Licinius had border troubles, but there was no serious unrest within their dominions, and they were both able to work at consolidating their hold on power.

From Constantine's point of view, indeed, the position early in 309 could hardly have looked more promising. His own troops recognized him as Augustus by virtue of his proven valour and his descent from Constantius. Provincial administrations in Britain, Gaul and Spain recognized him as Augustus by virtue of his nomination by Galerius and Diocletian. Maximian's surviving admirers knew him as old Herculius' son-in-law and chosen ally. He had come so far in a little over three years that it is hard to visualize him as the relatively unknown tribune who, in 305, had fled from Galerius' court at Nicomedia in fear for his very life. He was to advance much further yet.

CHAPTER FIVE

CAESAR IN GAUL

CONSTANTINE spent his first five years as an emperor in Gaul. Although he had been proclaimed in Britain, and Eusebius speaks of his visiting that diocese in about the year 310[1], there is no real evidence that he did so, or that he ever crossed the Pyrenees into Spain. Such of his time as was not taken up with intrigues concerned with the acquisition and retention of power, he devoted to the problems of Gaul.

He had inherited three major sources of trouble from his father Constantius: the Franks, the economy, and the need for reconstruction. So far as is known, he instituted no new policies, but in the intervals of peace, continued his father's work, achieving much that Constantius had lived too short a time to complete. The substance of his achievement is admirably summarized in Eusebius' *Life*:

> He showed much considerate clemency towards all those provinces which had been previously ruled by his father. When some barbarian tribes living on the banks of the Rhine and the shores of the Western Ocean dared to rebel, he brought them all back to their obedience, and led them from savagery to domesticity. He was satisfied merely to check the inroads of other tribes, driving from his dominions, like wild and dangerous animals, those he judged quite incapable of the settled course of civilized living[2].

The panegyric Eumenius declaimed before Constantius Chlorus in 299, praising him for his work in restoring Autun after the wars against the Franks and the *bagaudae*, finds a curious echo in his oration of 311, eulogizing Constantine for his endeavours to rebuild the same city thirteen years later[3]. In so unsettled a period, reconstruction was a labour for Sisyphus:

> If now, O Sacred Emperor, Flavia Aeduorum calls itself by an

> eternal name [that of the Flavians], it unanimously declares that it can do no less, because it was built and has come to its present state wholly through your munificence towards it, and it proclaims you its Restorer—or rather, I might more honestly say, its Founder—and gives thanks to you in this most mighty city [of Trier], where you have now begun work of the same kind....

Autun and Trier are the only two cities known from contemporary records to have been refounded by Constantine at this time, but no doubt similar work had to be undertaken in many parts of the country. At some time or another during the previous thirty years most areas of northern and eastern Gaul had been devastated by either rebels or invaders, and many had suffered from both. Those parts of the country not actually attacked had been neglected. Roads, towns, harbours, bridges, aqueducts, schools, military clothing factories, armouries and fortifications, all had to be planned and built. The difficulty was that money was still short. Constantine's main concern had to be the maintenance of his army in a state of instant readiness—and loudly as many must have grumbled at the expense of that policy, events showed that it was the correct one for the times. However, the cost of keeping so many soldiers, fortifying the Rhenish frontier, building palaces (which also functioned as administrative centres) at Augusta Treverorum and later at Arles, and of servicing essential legal and provincial institutions, was a constant drain on the damaged finances of the area. Constantine was a typical 'Illyrian' emperor, in that he was no more capable of thinking small than Galerius or Diocletian. The palace at Trier covered hundreds of acres and swallowed up hundreds of thousands of *aurei*. To satisfy the emperor's ego and demonstrate his greatness both to his own people and to his brother emperors, everything was planned on the grandest scale. The inevitable result was that little was done properly. 'Refounded' Autun was proud of its new buildings, but Eumenius admits that as late as 311, it had still not been possible to drain the inundated vineyards which had once been the city's chief source of income; and the main military road from the Saône Valley in central Gaul north-west to the Channel coast was so badly potholed that the couriers of the imperial post had difficulty in picking their way along it. Only Constantine's benevolence in remitting taxes, reducing the city's assessment from the equivalent of a poll-tax on 25,000 men to that of one on 18,000, had made it possible for the municipality to continue to function at all[4]. The picture is one of a countryside devastated by war and economic chaos. Yet Constantine was remembered in Gaul as a good emperor. The reasons are not far to seek. He cared whether the people were fed. His tax demands were reasonable. He forced no one into slave labour and he persecuted no one for his opinions alone. His people had nothing to fear from him, as long as they were loyal. In Italy, by this time, there was famine under Maxentius, and in the East, Galerius, Maximin Daia and Licinius all had to raise taxes and introduce unpopular new levies in order to keep themselves solvent. Life was not easy under Constantine, but at least there was a chance to earn some of his new *aurei* and save them under the hearthstone. He did not close the schools, as Galerius had done at Nicomedia, or fill the gaols and mines with persecuted Christians, as Maximin was doing, or earn personal notoriety for sexual excesses, such as Maxentius was winning for himself at least among the Christians. The taxes he raised for fresh campaigns against the Alemanni and Bructeri were unpopular, but the money was well spent, much of it being used to construct, equip and man a fleet and a line of forts on the Rhine, and build a bridge at Castra Divitensis, near the site of modern Cologne, over which his frontier guard could march straight into the heart of the Frankish homeland. No one could fail to see that the result was that at least some Gallic flocks and herds were kept safe which might otherwise have been driven off by rustlers, and some fields and homesteads preserved unburned.

The task of safeguarding the river frontier was in fact easier than it had been for generations, because the tribes living in what is now Germany were under pressure from the East and at war among themselves. No full-scale invasions of Gaul from across the river occurred for several successive years, while the Goths fought the Burgundians and the Alemanni, and these riparian tribes quarrelled with one another. Those who did cross the river were the dispossessed; already defeated once and driven from their lands, desperate and yet dispirited, they were a relatively easy prey for the disciplined, well-fed frontier legions. A century later, the pressure of the eastern tribes on the western was to lead to the uncontrollable Barbarian Invasions which heralded the so-called Dark Ages, but during Constantine's reign in Gaul the frontier was still an all-but-impenetrable barrier, with death or slavery waiting on the other side for those tribesmen who did succeed in piercing it. Constantine showed no mercy towards troublesome foreigners. The pattern of treatment he had set for prisoners after his first Alemannic Campaign in 306, with the execution of tribal leaders in the elaborate ritual of the circus, was followed inexorably in the years 307–11; but the magnificent amphitheatre which was one of the principal sights of restored Trier never again saw the beasts 'exhausted with slaughter', as they had been during its inaugural season.

Nevertheless, the rigidity of Constantine's policy towards captive Franks, and the undeniable cruelty with which they and condemned criminals were done to death in the presence, or with the approval, of the emperor, illuminates a side of his character which cannot be wholly excused by saying that he was a man of his time. The examples of his father and the golden Diocletian show that cruelty and the satisfaction of blood-lust were not essential characteristics of successful emperors either as individuals or as popular heroes and demigods. There is no evidence that the Gauls demanded bloody spectacles from Constantine (although, to be fair to him, there is equally nothing to show that they did not enjoy them when he provided them). He himself decided, at least in principle, on what the state's income should be disbursed – and he chose to spend one sizeable fraction of it on imperial display and another on circus performances. His family may have been 'Romans' for several generations, but there was a good deal of the barbarian in Constantine, as there was in most of the Pannonian friends, clients and favourites of Diocletian's immediate successors.

The difference of approach between Constantius and Constantine certainly marked a difference of temperament. The interesting question is, did it also mark one of religion?

In 312, at the end of these years in Gaul, Constantine was dramatically to make the Cross of the Christians his soldier's emblem (although, typically, changing its shape, to make it his own), and so turn a march on Maxentius which could have been simply and completely justified as a campaign to put down a rebellion into the first historical crusade. It has long been hotly debated whether he himself adopted the faith, as well as the badge, of the Christians at that time. He was not formally baptized until shortly before his death, but he had made himself master of the contemporary church long before submitting to Christian initiation. All that is known about his personal beliefs during his reign in Gaul is that, although he tolerated Christians and even favoured them, much as his father had done, his personal ethic, insofar as it can be distinguished from state policy, shows little relation to any standard recognizably Christian; but then as much could be said, for instance, of Lactantius' attitude to murder, or the general behaviour of Christian rulers in later times. His coins – one of the most potent of imperial propaganda weapons, and so commonly the best indication of the way an emperor's mind was working – show him in company with the old gods, especially Mars[5]. The three most testing challenges in the ethical field put to him in these years were the offer of marriage to Fausta, the opportunity of deifying Constantius Chlorus, and the question of the treatment of defeated enemies. By Christian standards he failed them all. He may already have been attracted by Christianity, by the personality of individual Christians and by the political advantages that an alliance with the Church could bring, but if so he certainly did not let his feelings on these points affect his behaviour. There will always be doubt as to whether Constantine adopted the cross in 312 merely for expediency's sake, or, at least partly, because he believed in Christ's power to help him overcome his enemies. In fact, he probably did believe in Christ's help – but it needed a vision to convince him. The question of how far he had moved along the Christian road before the vision remains unanswerable.

It would, however, be easier to guess at its answer if it were certain when he began calling Christians to court to work for him—when, for instance, Lactantius joined his entourage as tutor to Crispus.

Lactantius was one of that group of pagans – they appear to have been many – who, attracted either by the fervour of the Christians during the Great Persecution, or the spice of danger, or both, actually received baptism while the terror still raged in the East. The evidence suggest that he had already cast Constantine in the role of champion to the Christians, and moved to the West to be close to him, before the killing ceased in 311. Some manuscripts of his *Divine Institutes*, a study of Christian and biblical doctrines of the relationship between church and state written before *On the Deaths of the Persecutors*, contain two appeals to Constantine which may have been composed in Gaul before Galerius' death in that year[6]. The original edition of *On the Deaths of the Persecutors* was finished in 311, and it has often been pointed out that its mood exactly reflects Constantine's, during the march to Rome. Lactantius was an African by birth and for him Rome was still the capital of the civilized world. There is no proof that he was at Trier before 313, but the question remains, where was he in 311? May it not even have been he who inspired Constantine with the vision of a Rome where the merits of the old empire were blended with the virtues of a new Christian world? Or did Constantine, already imbued with that vision, invite the converted professor of pagan rhetoric to join his court because he knew that such a man could share it?

Another key figure in the situation whose movements in the crucial years 310–12 are unfortunately not known is Bishop Hosius of Cordoba. By 313, Hosius was already deep in the emperor's confidence, and had permanently deserted his see to act as his first fully-informed adviser on Christian affairs. However, it remains a mystery whether he was called to the court some time after the Spanish diocese revolted against Maxentius in 308, deliberately set out on his own initiative to attach himself to Constantine at that time, or first encountered the emperor at Rome after Maxentius' death at the battle of Milvian Bridge. It is tempting to speculate. As we have seen, there are hints of a Christian attempt to subvert the rule of the pagan emperors through Constantine as early as 305. May not the arrival of Hosius and Lactantius at his court from opposite ends of the empire some time before 311 have marked another stage in the development of Christian hopes? There is no need to postulate an actual plot at this stage. Constantine was moving nearer to the Christians in thought and outlook: it was natural that Christian individuals, persecuted elsewhere, should gravitate towards him.

However, there is no direct evidence to show what Constantine personally believed in the years 306–11. In his panegyric of 311, Eumenius spoke of 'our gods' as the source of the blessings of Constantine's rule, but the concept was a conventional one. During a visit to Autun, two years earlier, the emperor had consulted the oracle at Apollo's temple, and left magnificent offerings for the god[7]. This action may also have been conventional. An emperor was expected to pray publicly for the welfare of the state and pay homage to the gods. The choice of Apollo's shrine may, however, have had special significance. By this time, Apollo, for so long an independent god, was commonly recognized as one manifestation of *Sol Invictus*, Helios, the Unconquered Sun—just as the ancient Celtic sun-god of Gaul had long been identified with Apollo. Were Constantine's offerings, then, made to the generalized Helios, or to Apollo in particular? The pagan emperor Julian later claimed that his uncle had manifested a lasting devotion to Helios[8], and that claim seems to be borne out by inscriptions on Constantine's coins representing the sun god with the message 'in company with the undying sun'[9]. These coins are, however, all later than 310, when they replaced earlier designs celebrating the Herculian dynasty and the ancient gods. Was Constantine really turning from the polytheism of conventional paganism to the qualified monotheism of the worship of Helios as early as 308?

Can he really be said to have been a 'convert' to monotheism in that year? – or in 310, for that matter? This claim has sometimes been made, but his public 'conversion' in 310, as attested by the coins, can be accounted for as readily by political events as by adducing a personal change of heart. In that year, the Augustus Maximian, turning against Constantine as he had earlier turned against Maxentius, forced his son-in-law publicly to repudiate him and sever his connection with the Herculian house and its gods. His 'conversion' to Helios was a move in the political game – but was it merely just another move, or did he relinquish Jove, Hercules, Mars and the rest with something like a sigh of relief? It is quite reasonable to suppose, as many have done (basing their views largely on Julian's remark), that Constantine had always shared Constantius' monotheistic views, but if he had, until the upheavals of 310, he concealed them all but completely.

From our vantage-point in time, Maximian's attempt to seize power from Constantine in 310 looks inexplicably foolish and ill-conceived. Having been admitted in 308, with whatever degree of reluctance on Galerius' part, to the conference at Carnuntum, and seen his son-in-law raised to the rank of Augustus, he ought to have been content – and, indeed, he did lay aside the purple again and return peacefully to Gaul, seemingly once more ready to rest in retirement. At that stage, he may actually have intended to live out the remainder of his life in peace, but if so, he soon forgot his determination. Early in 310, he once more embroiled himself in a plot, his last, this time against Constantine himself.

There are two accounts of his last attempt to seize power. The earlier and more easily credible, related by Eumenius in the year it happened[10], suggests that his motive was simply ambition: just as, in 307–8, he had tried to undermine Maxentius' position at Rome, so now in 310 he tried to destroy Constantine. He may have been pushed to the desperate limit of rebellion by the death in Rome of his grandson Romulus, murdered during his first consulate, and by the childlessness of Fausta after three years of marriage: it must have seemed to him as though either

Crispus, who was not related to him, or his step-daughter Theodora's children would inherit his power, unless he could murder Constantine and marry Fausta to someone else. Probably also, Constantine's independence of mind did not please him, and there were too many Christians at court for his, Herculius', peace of mind.

According to Eumenius, he timed his attempt for a moment when Constantine was away in the north-east, leading a punitive raid against the Bructeri. He announced from Arles that the Augustus had been killed in a skirmish, and offering the army a donative so enormous that it emptied the treasury, called for a renewal of loyalty to himself as the divinely-appointed protector of the state.

When despatches announcing this change of regime reached Castra Divitensis on the Rhine, they stirred the legions to an anger more terrible even than Constantine's own. The troops insisted on abandoning operations against the Bructeri, and without even waiting for the commissariat to purchase supplies, set out on a swift march to the south. At Chalon-sur-Saône, they took to the rivers, free soldiers replacing slaves at the oars of the boats for speed's sake. Before Maximian could organize the defences of Arles, they were upon him. He fled from Arles to Marseilles. Constantine's army followed so close on his heels that the engineers had no time to prepare for the investment of the city. A first assault failed because the scaling-ladders were too short to reach the tops of the walls. Before a second attack could be mounted, the soldiers within the fortress opened the gates. Maximian was taken prisoner and 'his luck being the way it was, chose to make an end of himself', although Constantine had shown considerable restraint by neither torturing him nor threatening him with execution.

The other account of Maximian's last rising is altogether more romantic and closer to classical tales of dynastic and domestic intrigue. In its simplest form, as preserved by Jerome[11], it runs, 'During Constantine's third consulate, Herculius Maximianus, detected by his daughter Fausta while preparing a blow against her husband, fled to Marseilles and was killed'.

Lactantius tells a much more circumstantial tale on the same lines, beginning, like Eumenius, with the attempted usurpation while Constantine was at Castra Divitensis, and the army's forced marches through the length of Gaul, but continuing, after relating Maximian's flight to Marseilles:

> However, suddenly the gates were opened by somebody on his own side, and the soldiers admitted, and the rebel emperor – impious father, perfidious father-in-law – was dragged before the Emperor. He listened to the account of his wicked act, stripped him of his [purple] robe, and gave him his criminal's life. But he, instead of acting with the honour of an emperor and a father-in-law, chafing under his humiliation, fabricated fresh plots.

He begged Fausta to betray her husband to him. His plan was to stab Constantine while he slept. Fausta, however, decided that her loyalty was to her husband – in recent years there had been little in her father's attitude towards her brother Maxentius to commend filial piety to her – and disclosed the plot to Constantine. Instead of confronting his father-in-law with what he had learned, he let the scheme go ahead, merely substituting a palace eunuch for himself in bed on the night chosen by Maximian for the assassination. Maximian gained admission to the Sacred Bedchamber by telling the guards that he had just woken from a remarkable dream, which he must relate to Constantine immediately, and once there, stabbed the eunuch to death, while Constantine watched from behind a curtain. This time, Maximian could expect no mercy,

> and he was given the choice of his death. And so he whom the Romans had called the Supreme Emperor, who a little while before had celebrated his twentieth jubilee with vast splendour, was brought out and his proud neck broken, to end his detestable life with an ugly and ignominious death[12].

This account of Maximian's end is improbable but not impossible. However, given the ugly temper of Constantine's soldiers after the forced march on short rations from the Rhine to the Mediterranean, it is much more likely that, if Maximian did not commit suicide rather than risk capture, Constantine ordered his immediate execution, than that he would have forgiven his father-in-law and run the risk of the next plot against his life succeeding. Eumenius' account and that of Lactantius can be reconciled only by supposing that the official story, circulated immediately after the rising, deliberately suppressed the fact of Maximian's last act of treachery, perhaps for Fausta's sake; it seems more probable, however, that the incident of the eunuch's death was invented later to prove how evil a man Maximian had been and how worthy of the ignominious death divinely planned for him, according to Lactantius, as one of the persecutors of the Christians.

Maximian's death marked a turning-point in the development of Constantine's plans for himself and the empire. Before it, he may have nursed vague dreams of one day achieving absolute power over the whole Roman world; after it, he deliberately dissociated himself from the other emperors, abandoning the concept of himself as an emperor of the Herculian dynasty, and fostering the idea that he was divinely destined from birth to rule. The change made its first appearance in Eumenius' panegyric describing the events leading to Maximian's death. The orator expressly denied that Galerius or anyone else had given permission for Constantine to call himself emperor: 'it was no accidental agreement on the part of others, no sudden favour, that made you emperor; you merited the *imperium* because of your birth – by a divine gift.' The following year, Eumenius spoke openly of Claudius II, Gothicus, as Constantine's ancestor, and the first coins came into circulation showing Constantine on one side and Claudius' god, the Unconquered Sun, on the other. Although the break with the old gods was not yet complete, the break with their servants, the Jovians and Herculians, was already overt and irreversible.

Moreover, Maximian's death, and the repudiation of the Herculians, made war with Italy inevitable.

According to Lactantius, the first victim of this war was the late emperor Maximian's old comrade-in-arms, the Augustus Diocletian. He relates that after the failure of Maximian's attempt to seize Gaul and Vienne 'by Constantine's command, the statues of Maximianus Herculius were cast down and his portraits removed; but as the two old emperors were generally depicted together, the likenesses of both were removed at the same time. Thus Diocletian lived to see a disgrace such as no other emperor had ever seen, and . . . he resolved to die'[13]. He fell into a profound apathy at the collapse of all his plans for the future of the empire, and slowly starved to death. Or so Lactantius would have us believe – and, given Diocletian's history of mental instability, the story is credible enough. He may have survived until 313, but his part in the political life of the empire was finished.

Until the destruction of his father's statues and portraits, Maxentius had treated his brother-in-law with the respect due to a fellow-emperor, carefully avoiding disputes with him, and giving his acts the appearance of legality by coupling Constantine's name with his own in the preambles to his laws and inscriptions. Now, in an act of defiance, he not only deified Maximian, so that Herculius the Demigod joined Hercules the Hero in the pantheon, but declared Constantine a rebel and a murderer, ordering all the inscriptions and commemorations of him in Italy to be destroyed. His name was even cut out of the inscriptions on milestones. From this time on, Gaul and Italy were at war, although the actual outbreak of hostilities was delayed for nearly two years.

While Constantine had been fighting the Bructeri, and meeting the last challenge from his father-in-law, matters at Rome had gone from bad to worse. Romulus' murder in 309 was an act of protest against a regime daily becoming more intolerable. Even the Christians, whom Maxentius had at first courted, actually going so far as to restore to them some of the property confiscated under Severus, felt the weight of his anger, when they demonstrated against the severity of their newly-elected Bishop Marcellus.

Marcellus had probably suffered during the persecution. On attaining power over the Roman church, he began imposing penances of the utmost severity on Christians who had surrendered the Scriptures to the imperial authorities or offered incense to the gods, rather than endure torture. The Christians rioted in the streets against him, and Maxentius had to turn out the soldiers. When order had been restored, he exiled Marcellus. A new pope, Eusebius, was elected, but Marcellus' partisans denounced him as a usurper. Fresh disturbances occurred, and Maxentius promptly exiled Eusebius. There is nothing to show, however, that even after these provocations he was especially heavy-handed with the Christians. After Marcellus and Eusebius had both died in exile, the next pope, Melitiades, lived in peace at Rome. Yet Lactantius branded Maxentius a persecutor, and both he and Eusebius make much of his alleged terrorization of the City, relating how senators were murdered for their money, decent Roman matrons snatched from their homes for nights of debauchery, and children ripped open so that the omens in their entrails might be read. Worse than all this, in Eusebius' view, was the rumour, reaching the East in 311–12, that Maxentius had made a secret pact with Maximin Daia, the arch-persecutor[14]. The fact of the rumour alone was reason enough, in Christian eyes, for Maxentius to die the humiliating death of a persecutor.

After the murmurings of unrest at Rome had culminated in Romulus' assassination, it was clear that to survive, the administration would have to act quickly to relieve the famine ravaging the City and the South as a result of the loss of the African provinces and the destruction of the productive capacity of some of the best land in Italy by Galerius' retreating army in 307. Early in 311, Maxentius sent his Praetorian Prefect, Rufius Volusimus, to reconquer Africa with what contemporaries judged a ridiculously small army of only a few cohorts. He must have had secret information on conditions in the realm of the usurper Domitius Alexander, for the invading forces met with almost no opposition. Domitius' nominal recognition of Galerius as supreme emperor did not save him. He was captured and executed, and Africa made to pay a huge indemnity in corn and gold. This temporarily relieved the want of Italy, but trouble was laid up for the future by the army's fulfilment of Maxentius' orders that, in punishing the rebellion, it should methodically destroy 'the lands of Carthage and the more lovely parts of Africa'[15].

The African campaign made Maxentius appear secure, but with his superstitious and sexual excesses, he was rapidly digging not only his own grave, but also that of pagan Rome as the philosophical, intellectual and traditional capital of the empire. While his Praetorian Prefect was carrying out his orders in Africa, Galerius died, and Constantine, deciding – after much hesitation, it seems – that the time was ripe for the conquest of Italy, gave orders that his men should muster and be equipped for the march on Rome.

Having once determined to fight, Constantine set about ensuring that he must win. Eutropius maintains that it was now that he decided to make himself master of the whole Roman world: he provoked civil war with Maxentius deliberately, knowing that in the long run it would spread to the East, offering him opportunities for self-advancement everywhere[16]. A few years later, he himself was to tell the bishops in his *Oration to the Saints*, 'I believe our actions are noblest and best when, before attempting anything, we provide as far as possible for a secure result'[17]. In his own view, he was not the ardent, even foolhardy, champion of Christ his Christian admirers would have liked to have made of him. He planned his moves carefully, before acting with all the force at his command. He felt that he owed it to himself to win, and would risk his own life to do so, because the nature of warfare sometimes demanded it of a general, if he was to keep his men's loyalty and respect; but before committing himself to the field, he calculated the risks to a nicety, and 'provided as far as possible' for victory, by eliminating every foreseeable threat to his success.

In the confrontation with Maxentius, the main danger was from the East. He was not yet strong enough to risk war with Licinius, waiting in Illyria to take over the Italian diocese assigned to him by Galerius. War with Maxentius had, therefore, to be delayed until events in the East distracted his attention from Italy.

The Christian historians were convinced that their God

fought determinedly on Constantine's side throughout the Italian war. Although they seem not to have seen Galerius' death in May 311 as the most providential of preparatory miracles for Constantine's victory, they might well have done so. Galerius was the only man capable if not of permanently outmanoeuvring Constantine, certainly of opposing his self-aggrandisement with resolution and so delaying his accession to supreme power.

He died in great agony from cancer. As he was a persecutor until the last week of his life, neither Lactantius nor Eusebius spares the reader any nauseating detail of his terrible agony[18]. Already sick in 310, he spent that winter at his favourite city of Sirmium on the Save, in constant communication with his fellow-emperors in search of a formula to preserve peace. At the same time, his Sacred Chamberlain was in correspondence with the official Eastern capital, Nicomedia, where the Senior Augustus was expected, as soon as spring made the roads passable for a sick man, to make final preparations for the celebrations attendant on his twentieth jubilee. He was never to make the journey. In mid-April, he issued an edict of toleration in favour of the Christians, and a few days later 'his genitals being eaten away, he died'.

The Edict of Toleration was probably promulgated in the names of all the legitimate emperors, Galerius, Constantine, Maximin Daia and Licinius, although Daia's name does not appear in the version of it preserved by Eusebius in his *History*, presumably because his name and acts were later officially abolished. In it, the emperor affirms that the aim of all his legislation had always been that set before the empire by Diocletian 'to restore everything to the ancient laws and traditional discipline of the Romans', and especially to bring the Christians, who had abandoned the religion of their fathers, back to sound ideas. The Christians had, however, made their own rules and, deserting the ancient shrines, held 'different meetings in other places'. When the emperors had ordered them to return to 'ancestral customs', many had done so, but many others had 'persisted in their wrong-headedness, and we have observed that they neither give the gods the honour due to them, nor worship the god of the Christians. Wherefore . . . we feel we ought also to extend our indulgence towards them, permitting Christians to exist henceforward, and to re-establish their congregations, provided that they do nothing contrary to proper discipline. In a later letter, we shall explain to the magistrates the rules they should follow. In the light of this our indulgence, they must pray to their god for our health, for the state, and for themselves'[19].

This edict is a strange document, illogical to the point of absurdity unless it is supposed that in Galerius' last days he was willing to clutch at any straw, even the hope that his enemies the Christians might pray for him (or, perhaps, stop praying so effectively against him), and so his life still be saved. It is difficult to see why it was issued at all, unless it was Galerius' own idea, although it is remotely possible that it was a diplomatic concession to Constantine, granting him the lives of his favourites, the Christians, in exchange for some sort of undertaking that he would maintain the peace. There is, however, no other evidence that any such agreement was ever mooted, and whether Galerius signed the edict in the hope of a life-saving miracle or to preserve universal peace, he had left matters too late. Copies had barely been posted up in Nicomedia before a rumour reached the city that he was dead. Civil war in the West followed eighteen months later, when the inexorable Constantine was ready for it.

'This edict was promulgated at Nicomedia on the day before the kalends of May [April 30]', Lactantius records, 'and a few days later, having commended his wife and daugher to Licinius' care and given them into his hands, he was finished. And all this was known in Nicomedia that same month, when his *vicennalia* would have been due on the kalends of the coming March.'[20]

The edict was promulgated from Asia Minor to Britain, but not in the provinces ruled by Maximin Daia, where it became known only through letters exchanged between prefects and provincial governors. Even there, however, Christians were temporarily released from prison and the mines, and their worship permitted. At this juncture, Daia could not afford to make trouble for himself in Egypt and the East by ignoring an edict which, as one of Galerius' colleagues, he was technically assumed to have approved. He was avidly grabbing as much as he could of the rich quarter of the empire which Galerius had reserved for himself at Diocletian's abdication. As Lactantius put it:

> When [the death of Galerius] was announced and Maximin heard of it, having put things in order, he set off with all speed from the East to occupy the provinces [of Asia Minor and Thrace]; but Licinius realizing it, laid claim to everything as far as the Chalcedonian channel for himself, and entering Bithynia, to everyone's great joy abolished the census. Discord between the emperors brought them close to war. They held opposite shores in arms, but established peace and friendship on agreed terms and made a treaty,

by which Daia added Asiana and Pontica to his dominions, while Licinius held Moesia and Thrace[21].

With the armies of the Danube and Thrace added to his own, Licinius was now apparently much stronger than he had been. If he could have trusted Maximin Daia, he would no doubt have undertaken the 'liberation' of Italy forthwith. In fact, however, he could not trust him, and so, although the enlargement of his territory had brought more men and arms under his personal control, with Galerius no longer acting as a buffer between him and the Eastern Augustus, he was worse off than before, with an additional frontier to watch – a frontier along which danger was ever-present. The result was that when Constantine suggested an alliance between them, he welcomed the proposal. Their agreement was sealed by the betrothal to Licinius of Constantine's half-sister Constantia and, no doubt, a secret understanding that it should be Constantine who would actually undertake the conquest of Italy, while Licinius kept watch on Maxentius' ally, Maximin Daia. Lactantius asserts that it was news of this betrothal which frightened Maximin into secret negotiations with Maxentius: 'When Maximin heard that Constantine's sister was betrothed to Licinius, he feared that the two emperors, by creating a kinship between them, were making a league against him, so he secretly sent envoys to Rome, seeking a friendly alliance with Maxentius . . . and Maxentius . . . declared war on Constantine, allegedly to avenge the death of his father.'[22] There had, however, almost certainly been friendly contacts between Italy and the East long before Licinius' engagement to Constantia, and war between Gaul and Italy was Constantine's choice, not Maxentius'.

Whether it was the confirmation of his alliance with Maxentius, or Maximin's personal devils driving him on to destruction (as Lactantius might have claimed), which gave him the courage to act, within six months of the promulgation of the edict of toleration, and as soon as it was clear that Licinius was not contemplating an immediate invasion of Asia Minor, he recommenced the persecution. At the time of the promulgation of the edict, he had refused to circulate it, but had given verbal instructions for the easement of the restrictions on Christians. Sabinus, his Praetorian Prefect in the Orient, had written to provincial governors instructing them that it was the imperial command that, to save Christians from bringing themselves into danger over so small a question as that of offering sacrifice, 'if any Christian is found to be practising the religion of his own people, you must guard him from harm and danger, and not on that grounds alone hold anyone guilty of a punishable offence'[23].

Actually, there were grounds here for a sensible compromise in the general direction of syncretism. At the Christian Synod of Elvira in Spain a few years earlier (attended by Constantine's adviser, Hosius of Cordoba), it had been ruled that a Christian who became a magistrate, and on his appointment made the customary acts of adoration and sacrifice, should not be excommunicated simply on that account[24]; and at synods at Ancyra and Neo-Caesarea in 314 reasonable regulations were to be formulated to smooth over the difficulties of Christians who had weakened during the persecution[25]. Even so, fanatics on both sides drove their parties to extremes of action in the East and Egypt in 311–12. Compromise between Christianity and paganism was made impossible by men like Theocnetus of Antioch on the pagan side, who invented the cult of 'Zeus the Friend of Man' as a counter to the Christian god in his concern for individuals and who organized a private terror against Christians; and Bishop Meletius of Lycopolis on the Christian side, whose rigorism would not permit him even to be amiable towards his superior, Archbishop Peter of Alexandria, when they were in gaol together, because Peter showed understanding for those whose faith had wavered.

Maximin Daia appears to have been a genuine pagan fanatic. By the end of 311, his hand strengthened by popular petitions for the reinforcement of the established religion through the expulsion of Christians from the cities of Nicomedia, Antioch and Tyre, and the districts of Lycia and Pamphylia in southern Asia Minor, he initiated steps for the restoration of paganism by the reformation of its worship. His reform was intended to emphasize the dependency of the 'traditional' Roman empire on the gods, and with this end in view he established a pagan hierarchy paralleling the provincial administration of the state. In Lactantius' words 'he introduced a new style of government in matters of religion, and for each city created a high priest [the chief magistrate] chosen from among the persons of the highest distinction. The office of these men was to make daily sacrifices to all the gods, to prevent Christians from erecting churches or worshipping God either publicly or privately . . . and . . . compel Christians to sacrifice to idols and, on their refusing to do so, bring them before the civil magistrate. And as though this were not enough, in every province he established a superintendant priest [the provincial governor], a person of the highest eminence in the state, and he commanded that all these newly-instituted priests should appear in white garments, that being the most honourable distinction of dress . . . He forbade the slaying of God's servants, but commanded that they should be mutilated, and confessors for the faith had their ears and nostrils slit, their hands and feet cut off, and their eyes gouged out . . .'[26]

While Maximin Daia was thus demonstrating his zeal for paganism to his new friend Maxentius, and Licinius was consoling himself for being the man in the middle with the thought that Constantia's hand also brought him Constantine's friendship, Constantine himself was securing his northern and north-eastern flanks by a sweep through the Frankish settlements from his forts on the Rhine. He made his winter quarters for 311–12 at Colmar, and called for the muster there in the spring. When he was ready to march into Italy, his expeditionary force, according to Zosimus, totalled 90,000 infantry and 8,000 cavalry, drawn from Germany, Britain and the Celtic tribes of Gaul[27]. It has been estimated that this army represented somewhere between a quarter and a half of all the forces available to him. His caution in not draining every man from his frontiers suggests that he was not merely setting out on a glorious adventure, but intended to build a stable empire by enlarging his boundaries. He had made a careful calculation of Maxentius' strength, and set out from Colmar with just sufficient force to bring him down. However, he proved that he was staking his whole future on victory by taking command himself.

CHAPTER SIX

THE BATTLE OF MILVIAN BRIDGE

IF CONSTANTINE ever spoke at length about the causes and course of the Italian campaign, the record of what he said has unfortunately been lost; but there is an interesting reference to it in the *Oration* which, even if that work is not authentic, probably reflects the emperor's table-talk on the subject of Maxentius' bloody fall. It follows immediately on the account of Diocletian's abdication and the persecution of the Christians, alleging a causal connection between them:

> [During the persecution] so much blood was poured out, that if it had been shed in battle with barbarian enemies, there would have been enough of it to purchase perpetual peace. In the event, the Divine Providence finally took vengeance on these unhallowed deeds – but not without severe damage to the state. For the entire army of the empire I have just been talking about [Diocletian's], having become subject to the authority of a worthless person [Maxentius], who had violently usurped the supreme authority at Rome, . . . was destroyed in several successive battles. . .[1].

In these lines, there is the echo of the voice of a self-satisfied and censorious judge of men and events, anxious to give God his due, but concerned more especially to prove his own pre-occupation with the welfare of the state. When he reviewed his 98,000 as they marched and cantered out of Colmar, however, he was not yet committed to Christianity and might have been convicted of that cardinal crime of autocrats, identification of the welfare of the state with his own will for it. He was, he told several witnesses, tired, confused and anxious, but he had convinced himself that he was setting out on a war of liberation: in his own honest opinion, he was taking war to Italy in order to free Rome from the tyranny of Maxentius' rule, and it would have puzzled and angered him if anyone had suggested that what he was in fact doing was duplicating Maxentius' seizure of power, and had found him, rather than God or Diocletian, guilty of destroying the legions. He had no just claim to power in Italy: his territories were Gaul, Spain and Britain. There was little to distinguish his march on Rome from Maximin's invasion of Asia Minor the previous year, or Diocletian's revolution for the alleged purpose of restoring ancient customs, laws and discipline thirty years earlier. Although he called the war one of liberation, he was hard put to it to present convincingly to his own troops and to the Romans the thought that he came as a liberator, and not merely as another conqueror.

He seems to have found it difficult even to convince himself. Perplexity may seem an unlikely mood in which to set out to conquer the world, but he himself admitted to Eusebius that he was unsure of himself just before the experience – the famous Vision of the Cross – which spurred him on to victory at Milvian Bridge, on the road to Rome. For twenty years, he had been at the centre of affairs; for six years, he had been initiating them; in the last eighteen months or so, he had executed his father-in-law and repudiated the gods upon whom his authority allegedly rested. He said that he knew Maxentius to be a great magician with power over the pagan gods, and that, to counteract that power, he prayed long and often to the only deity left to him, the Supreme God whom his father had worshipped[2]. Psychologically, his state of mind was a classic one for conversion to a new ideology, and it is not surprising that he had psychic or spiritual experiences during the march, and gave several confusing accounts of them afterwards.

The fifth-century historian Socrates' account of Constantine's vision admirably reflects the emperor's condition before the decisive battle. His version of the story is the 'received' form, as it was current in the later Byzantine empire:

> The Emperor Constantine, being informed [of Maxentius' tyranny], set himself to free the Romans from their slavery under him, and began immediately to consider by what means he might overthrow the tyrant. Now, while his mind was full of this great objective, he debated within himself what god's help

> he should invoke in the conduct of the war. He had reached the conclusion that Diocletian's party had not profited at all from the pagan deities whom they had sought to propitiate, but that his own father Constantius, who had renounced the various religions of the Greeks, had passed through life far more prosperously than they. In this state of uncertainty, as he was marching at the head of his troops, a praeternatural vision transcending all description appeared to him. In fact, at about that time of the day when the sun, having passed the meridian, began to decline towards the West, he saw a pillar of light in the form of a cross on which was inscribed 'in this conquer'. The appearance of the sign struck him with amazement, and doubting his own eyes, he asked those around him if they could see what he did, and, as they unanimously declared that they could, the emperor's mind was strengthened by this divine and miraculous apparition. On the following night, while he slept, he saw Christ, who directed him to make a standard according to the pattern he had been shown, and to use it against his enemies as a guarantee of victory. Obedient to the divine command, he had a standard made in the form of a cross, which is preserved in the palace until this day . . .[3]

In another late version of the emperor's vision, Sozomen's, the explanation is said to have been given by angels:

> In the middle of his perplexity, he saw a vision, the sight of the cross shining in the heavens. He was amazed by this sight, but some holy angels who were standing nearby exclaimed: 'O Constantine! By this sign conquer!' And it is said that Christ himself also appeared to him, and showed him the symbol of the cross and commanded him to construct one like it . . . [so he] sent for some skilled workmen, and ordered them to make the standard the Romans call the *labarum*, converting it into the shape of the cross, and adorning it with gold and precious stones. . . . It is also asserted that no soldier who carried this standard ever fell from any dark calamity such as is wont to befall soldiers in war, or was wounded, or taken prisoner . . .[4]

So much for the later stories. In fact, the *labarum*[5], or battle-standard, of Constantine was not a cross; its nature was not explained by angels; and, in the earliest version of the story, he did not see it in broad daylight, but in a dream.

The earliest and most credible version of what happened is

Lactantius', written only a year or so after the events it describes. Lactantius says that during the night before the battle of Milvian Bridge,

> Constantine was directed in a dream to cause the heavenly sign to be marked on the shields of his soldiers, and so proceed to battle. He did as he had been commanded, and marked on their shields the letter X with a perpendicular line through it, turned over at the top, this being the monogram of Christ[6].

Christ himself appeared to the emperor – but only in the dream – and declared not 'In this conquer!' but '*Hoc signo victor eris*': 'By this sign you shall be the Victor'. The words were a promise rather than a command, and it is significant that in later years Constantine's favourite title was 'the Victor'. The god of the cross had kept his promise.

Lactantius was at Constantine's court within months of Christ's monogram being painted on the soldiers' shields in the dawn light before the battle, and may indeed have already been a member of the emperor's entourage at the time. He may previously have been unfamiliar with the symbol, but not necessarily so. It has been found in third-century Christian inscriptions from Asia Minor, and was actually used in pre-Christian contexts as the abbreviation of several Greek words beginning with the letters *chi-rho*, notably *chrestos*, 'useful' – the name, according to Suetonius (to whom 'Christos' obviously meant nothing), of the Jewish troublemaker whose activities in Rome led to the expulsion of the Jews under Claudius in A.D. 53. Another version of it, with the letter I running perpendicularly through an X, indicating Iesous Christos, forms part of an epitaph cut at Rome in 269. It is, therefore, possible that an X with a stroke through it was already a familiar emblem of Christ in 312; and that, by ordering his men to paint it on their shields before the battle for Rome, Constantine was not only giving them a badge to bind them together (personal loyalties forged in battle would do that more effectively), but also appealing to Roman Christians in Maxentius' forces to recognize who were their true friends, and to change sides.

Lactantius' story implies that the battle-standard with the

monogram on it was not used at Milvian Bridge. If Constantine's vision – or intuition – came to him on the night before the battle, there was certainly no time to do more than paint the shields before the fighting started. What little evidence exists suggests that in fact the *labarum* bearing the *chi-rho* symbol was not used before 317, when Crispus became Caesar and the monogram began to appear on coins; although, between 312 and 317, Constantine may well have worn it as his personal badge, on his helmet, as Eusebius' *Life* claims that he did from the time of the vision onwards[7].

However, when Eusebius wrote his first account of the expedition against Maxentius, in the last book of the earliest edition of his *Ecclesiastical History*, he apparently knew nothing of any vision, but had heard that it was Constantine's aim to liberate the Romans, and that he had invoked the name of Christ before the battle[8]. Twenty-four years later, when he came to compose his *Life of Constantine*, after he had enjoyed a long friendship with the emperor and studied the *labarum* then preserved at Constantinople, he told a very circumstantial story, midway between Lactantius' and Socrates', relating how, while still in the mountains of southern Gaul early in the campaign, the worried emperor had been further confused by a vision in the sky consisting of a cross surrounded by the words 'in this conquer!' The next night, it was explained to him in a dream that he was to make a battle-standard in the shape revealed to him. The following morning he related his dream to his staff, asking if anyone knew what the sign meant, and the Christians among them told him about Christ's cross; whereupon he promptly sent for workmen to make not the cross that his vision required, but the *chi-rho* monogram, which he afterwards wore in his helmet.

This version of the story is full of inconsistencies, the most damning of them the claim that Constantine did not know what the cross meant in 312, although in 303 (again according to the *Life*) he had watched the Great Persecution grow out of the allegation that it had been used as a magic sign to eradicate the omens from the livers of the sacred victims at Nicomedia. The

Life claims too much. Although it cannot be disproved that Constantine halted the march on Rome after his vision long enough for the construction of a gold-plated battle-standard with the *chi-rho* monogram set in a gold wreath, decked with precious stones, and with a portrait of himself hung beneath – for this was the *labarum* as Eusebius had seen it – the story seems highly suspect. The emperor told it to Eusebius on his word of honour – but only after the years had coloured what, even without the gold plating, had been a traumatic experience. Probably Socrates hit the truth when he said that the vision 'transcended all description'. Those who claim genuine mystical experiences usually also maintain that they are indescribable – before going on, precisely as Constantine appears to have done, to attempt the impossible. If the emperor did see anything visible to normal human eyes, it was the glittering halo, often apparently cut with a cross, produced by the sun high in the atmosphere, when it shines through a veil of ice crystals. It had no special meaning, but his troubled mind sought one, and 'explained' what he had seen by 'revealing' the monogram to him. He would have observed the halo-phenomenon in the Alps, but may not have had the revelatory dream until much later, perhaps not until the eve of the final battle, where Lactantius sets it.

To sum up, the evidence relating to Constantine's vision is conflicting, but it would be a mistake to assume that, because the descriptions of it are inconsistent, he saw nothing at all, and experienced nothing, before the battle for Milvian Bridge. In the nature of things, the debate about what precisely he saw and what form the *labarum* first took must be rather profitless. All that is certain is that, before the decisive battle, something changed him from doubt to certainty of victory. It may or may not have been sudden conversion to faith in Christ. We do not know how conscious Constantine was of leanings towards Christianity after the vision – or even if he was really aware of them at all. It is perfectly possible to argue that when he invoked Christ's name and made his banner his own, he himself felt not the slightest inclination to make Christianity his personal religion, but was merely using Christ and the Christians for his own ends. The pity is that Eusebius was so convinced that Constantine was throughout his life a kind of natural Christian, whose reactions at any time were instinctively orthodox, that he, the best placed of all men to learn the truth, never put to the emperor those searching questions which would have elicited as much of it as the emperor cared to recall. So, unfortunately, even Constantine's memory twenty years after the event of what his faith had been at the time is lost. When Eusebius asserts that Constantine called on the Supreme God and 'assuming the Supreme God as his patron and invoking Christ to be his preserver and helper, and setting the trophy of victory, the saving symbol, in front of his legions and *comitatus* . . . marched with his whole forces in an attempt to regain for the Romans the freedom which they had inherited from their forefathers . . .' his meaning appears quite straightforward, until it is remembered that the Supreme God and the Christian Father were not necessarily one and the same. The paragraph is propaganda for the Christians. It implies that the ancestral freedom of the Romans, stolen from them by Maxentius, gave liberty of conscience to all – and, especially, the freedom to be a Christian. This was simply not true. Throughout most of Rome's history before Constantine, Romans were bound to worship the gods of the state. Moreover, the propaganda here is not only Christian but also Constantinean: Eusebius is puffing up his hero in the very terms in which Constantine justified his attack on Rome, and his story is too loaded with special pleading to be trusted. Where it can be tested, it falls down on the question of Constantine's prior knowledge of Christianity, and on the course of the war itself.

Eusebius leaves his readers with the impression that, aided by the cross (or the *chi-rho* monogram), the whole army of Gaul marched from easy victory to easy victory, till it brought Maxentius to bay under the walls of Rome. From a panegyric describing the course of the campaign only a few weeks after it had reached its successful conclusion[9], and from the notices of it in Lactantius and the secular historians[10], however, it is clear that the outcome was by no means as certain from the beginning as Eusebius suggests. Maxentius was no man's fool; he really was 'the Unconquered Prince' and, since his last victory, he had been given more than a year's grace in which to plan his counters to Constantine's attack. His difficulty was that until the war actually began he could not be absolutely certain that he would not be simultaneously invaded by Constantine from Gaul and Licinius from Illyria. If he had known all along that his sole opponent would be Constantine, he could have arranged an ambush in the mountains which might have permanently ended Constantine's ambitions. His intelligence was, however, incomplete. He did his best to prepare for any eventuality, withdrawing troops from Africa, sending his Praetorian Prefect Ruricus Pompeianus – 'a most expert man in warfare and a pillar of the tyranny'[11] (and so, as a public enemy in Constantine's eyes, a man absolutely loyal to himself) – to fortify the cities of the north Italian plain, and remaining himself at the heart of the country, in Rome, with a massive reserve, in case the north was overwhelmed. Pompeianus showed his appreciation of the situation by his choice of the key-city of Verona as his headquarters. He strengthened its defences, and built or refortified an arc of strong-points further north, at the feet of all the Alpine passes, and on the eastern and western coasts. The forces at his disposal were considerably stronger than those commanded by Constantine, numbering 170,000 infantry and 8,000 horse. Some of his cavalry units were the heavily armed and armoured *clibinarii*, forerunners of the mediaeval knights. Their mail and tactics were borrowings from the Persians, and there is no evidence that they had previously fought in the West.

Constantine brought his army into Italy over Mont Cenis Pass. Whether or not he had already been strengthened by his vision as he marched on Susa, the first Italian city lying across his route, he was certainly already committed, as Eutropius realized, to an attempt to seize 'the principate of the whole world'[12].

Susa was taken by storm, but Constantine forbade his men to sack the city. He was fighting a war of liberation, not conquest. A massacre at Susa would have led to a hardening of resistance everywhere else. As it was, there was bitter fighting outside Turin, where the threat of the *clibinarii* was successfully countered by a special unit armed with iron-bound clubs, highly effective against both horses and men. The garrison commander had made the major tactical blunder of committing all the forces at his disposal to a battle outside the walls: when he tried to retreat within his fortifications, he found the citizens manning the gates against him. His men fought with their backs to the walls which should have protected them until their units ceased to exist. Then the city surrendered to Constantine. Again, he denied his men the right of plunder. The policy of restraint brought its reward: first Milan, then several other cities along Pompeianus' arc of defences, opened their gates to the conqueror. Constantine accepted their surrender, then rested and regrouped his forces at Milan before striking south-east towards Verona. At Brescia, he miscalculated the enemy's strength, and there was a desperate fight under the walls before the formations of the *clibinarii* were broken. It was either this battle, or that at Verona itself – an even more chancy affair – which left Lactantius, seeking to heighten the dramatic effect of the victory at Milvian Bridge, free to say without actually lying that 'Maxentius' forces outnumbered his enemy's . . . They fought, and the forces of Maxentius prevailed'. Actually, Constantine won both at Brescia and Verona, and in these battles the backbone of north Italian resistance was broken.

Verona was protected on three sides by the River Adige, and on the fourth, the western, by some of the strongest fortifications in Italy. Constantine advanced from the west, but realizing that an immediate frontal assault from that direction might well founder among the trenches dug outside the walls, decided to cross the Adige and encircle the city, mounting a classical siege. Pompeianus waited until his adversary had committed his army to the river crossing, then sent out a strong force to smash the invaders at the ford. He had underestimated the strength and determination of the enemy. His attack was thrown back with heavy casualties, and the ford lost. That night, before his lines of communication could be cut, he himself slipped out of the city to collect reinforcements. Their approach was detected, and an untidy running fight developed, with fresh elements joining the battle piecemeal throughout the hours of darkness. At some time during the night, Pompeianus was killed, and in the morning the garrison surrendered. Constantine pushed on to Aquileia, then to Modena. The fighting grew no easier although the defending general had been killed. The stubbornness of the resistance gives the lie to the suggestion that all Maxentius' people were groaning under his tyranny, longing for freedom. By the middle of October, however, the road to Rome lay open.

So far, Maxentius had not personally taken part in the war – except, the Christians said, by making ever more bloody sacrifices to sway the will of the gods in his favour. Eusebius charges him with cowardice: 'And whereas Maxentius, trusting more in his magic arts, than in the affection of his people, dared not even venture outside the City gates . . . the emperor, confiding in the help of God, advanced . . . And he was already very close to Rome itself when, to save him having to fight all the Romans for the tyrant's sake, God drew the tyrant, as it were by secret cords, a long way outside the gates . . .'[13] This is scarcely fair to Maxentius, who had merely stayed in his capital, at the centre of his lines of communication, trusting his Praetorian Prefect and sub-commanders to hold his outer defences for him. Now that the decisive battle was at hand, and the Prefect dead, he chose his moment to throw his final reserves into the struggle, commanding them himself.

The first clash of the final battle occurred at Saxa Rubra, 'Red Rocks', on the Via Flaminia, some eight miles north-east of Rome. A limit was set to the battlefield on Constantine's left by the ox-bows of the Tiber and on his right by broken, rising ground lying between his flank and the Via Cassia, running south from Viterbo to meet the Via Flaminia at the Milvian Bridge. Between the old stone bridge and the city itself, two miles to the south, Maxentius had built a complicated system of trenches and forts to supplement the protection offered by the walls. It was a grave error to advance beyond them, and put the river at his back; but he had clearly planned a tactical retreat, damaging Constantine's forces as much as possible while drawing them on to these defensive strong-points, for next to the stone bridge he had constructed a strong bridge of boats, so made that it could be broken in the middle to prevent its use by an enemy after his own men had withdrawn over it. It was guarded by barricades and a tower, so that a sudden advance could be held while engineers separated its parts.

It is said that Maxentius consulted the Sibylline Books before committing himself to battle on October 28, the sixth anniversary of his accession, and accounted by him his lucky day. To demonstrate his own continuing confidence and to keep up the morale of the people, he had ordered that the usual festivities should be observed during the anniversary week. However, at the races on the 26th, he was jeered by some elements in the crowd, and on leaving the circus, asked that the prophecies might be consulted to confirm him in his conviction of victory. The sentence against October 28 was as ambiguous as the oracle from Delphi which had sent King Croesus to his doom against the Persians centuries earlier: 'On this day, the enemy of Rome shall perish,' but Maxentius declared that it was an omen of good fortune. Constantine was the enemy of Rome[14].

Thus, when the battle was joined, both commanders were assured of victory by their protecting gods, and at least in as much as they were both acutely aware of the fact, the chroniclers were right to see the battle in retrospect as one of the decisive clashes between Christianity and paganism.

The battle started according to Maxentius' plan. His advance guard found Constantine's van at the Red Rocks, and after a brief engagement, broke off and withdrew. But once again, Maxentius' intelligence officers failed him. He apparently did not know that Constantine commanded not only the Via Flaminia, but also the Via Cassia. Before an orderly, fighting retreat could be made to the bridges, his enemy had turned his left flank and his rear was threatened by a clash on what becomes here the north bank of the river. The brunt of the encounter fell on the Praetorian Guard. They acquitted themselves well, offering stubborn resistance, while all around them other

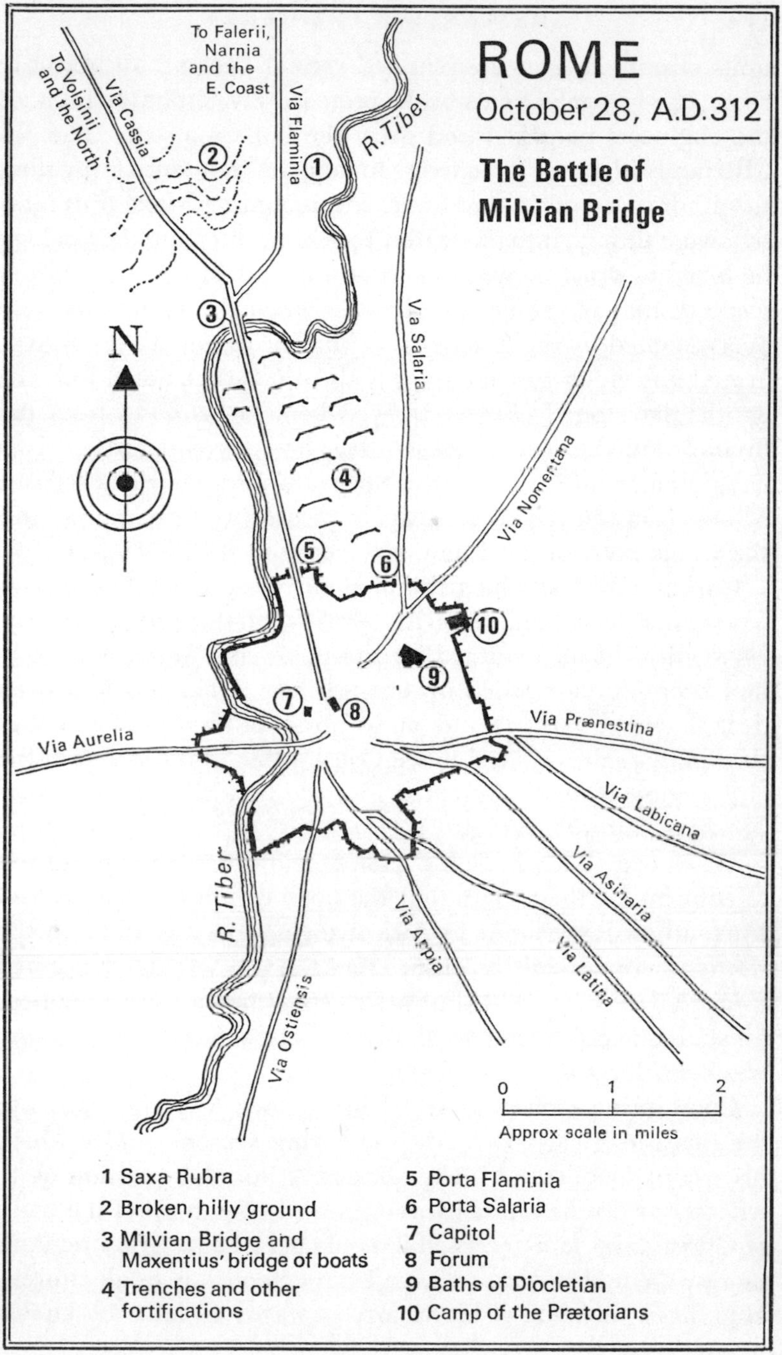
ROME
October 28, A.D.312
The Battle of Milvian Bridge
To Falerii, Narnia and the E. Coast
To Volsinii and the North
Via Cassia
Via Flaminia
R. Tiber
Via Salaria
Via Nomentana
Via Aurelia
Via Prænestina
Via Labicana
Via Asinaria
Via Latina
Via Appia
Via Ostiensis
R. Tiber
N
0
1
2
Approx scale in miles
1 Saxa Rubra
2 Broken, hilly ground
3 Milvian Bridge and Maxentius' bridge of boats
4 Trenches and other fortifications
5 Porta Flaminia
6 Porta Salaria
7 Capitol
8 Forum
9 Baths of Diocletian
10 Camp of the Prætorians

units crumbled, and the planned retreat became a disorderly rout. The bridge of boats broke prematurely, probably because the engineers panicked and drew the bolts too soon. The old Milvian Bridge was too narrow to take the thousands struggling to withdraw across it, and hundreds, including Maxentius himself, were thrown into the water. Eusebius, pursuing the analogy he loved to draw between Constantine and Moses, likened the scene to that in the book of Exodus when the Egyptians were overwhelmed by the Red Sea, 'so Maxentius and all the heavy-armed and light-armed troops with him "went down into the depths like stone" (*Exodus* 15, 5) when, in his flight from the divinely-aided forces of Constantine, he essayed to cross a river lying on his route . . . and after the example of His great servant Moses, Constantine entered the imperial city in triumph, and the whole body of the senate received him with joy . . .'[15]

Constantine made his triumphal entry on the anniversary of Maxentius' accession. A grisly trophy in the procession was Maxentius' head, mounted on the point of a lance. His body had been found, washed up on the river bank, and had been decapitated to provide undeniable proof of his death. Whether the senate really rejoiced to see Constantine in the streets of the city or not, it hurriedly voted him the honorific title *Augustus Maximus*, 'Supreme Augustus'[16].

When everybody in Rome had been afforded an opportunity to confirm for themselves that the head on display was indeed Maxentius', it was sent to Africa, together with orders to the *vicarius* there designed to ensure that the war was not continued from that diocese. All Maxentius' enactments were annulled, his statues overthrown and his inscriptions defaced. The tyranny was over. Or had it just begun?

Constantine himself ascribed his victory over Maxentius to the quasi-magical powers of 'the saving symbol' under which his troops fought at Milvian Bridge[17], but the question as to whether or not he himself was even now convinced of the truth of Christianity and accepted it as his personal religion remains unanswered. However, unless all the evidence is totally unreliable, from the time of his victory onwards he let it be known that he regarded the faith of the Christians as that of the Free Romans. His victory at Milvian Bridge made him sovereign from Hadrian's Wall to the Atlas Mountains, and from the Atlantic to the Rhine and the Adriatic, and, by his alliance with Licinius, gave him a considerable amount of influence from Illyria to the Bosphorus. It was, therefore, a matter of wide significance that, in Eusebius' words, 'he made the saving symbol known to everybody, expressly causing it to be cut in indelible characters that the saving symbol was the safeguard of the Roman government and the whole empire . . . and immediately ordered a long spear in the form of a cross to be placed in the hand of the statue representing himself erected in the busiest part of Rome, and the following inscription to be carved on it in the Latin language, "By virtue of this saving sign, which is the true test of valour, I have preserved and liberated your City from the yoke of tyranny. I have also set at liberty the Roman senate and people, and restored them to their ancient distinction and splendour." '[18]

As much ink has been used in argument about the actual appearance of the statue referred to as in discussion over the unknowable in connection with Constantine's vision. Since the Age of Reason, scholars have tried to 'prove' either that the statue never existed or that, if it did, either it showed Constantine with the accoutrements of Apollo, or Eusebius mistranslated the inscription. However, even if the statue was a figment of Eusebius' or another, more fertile, imagination, there can be no doubt that, during the months from October 312 to January 313, Constantine, now the sole Western Emperor, promoted Christianity as vehemently as possible without actually laying himself open to a charge of persecuting pagans. Bishop Hosius was already there, acting as his ecclesiastical intelligence officer, supplying him with information about the state of the church in Spain and Africa, where conflict between the *traditores* and the confessors was made more bitter by political and racial differences[19]. At Rome itself, Pope Marcellus, taking advantage of Maxentius' liberal attitude towards Christians during the early part of his reign, had raised the number of titular churches to twenty-five: they were now not only permitted to exist, but enriched by donations from Constantine's private purse and, recognized as corporations under the law, had their property – consisting mainly of cemeteries – returned to them[20]. The cancellation of all the acts and edicts made under Maxentius had restored the persecuting legislation of Maximian and Galerius: Constantine cancelled it in a series of letters to vicars and provincial governors ordering not merely that Christians should be permitted freedom of worship, but that 'the Catholic [that is, universal] Church of the Christians' should be subsidized from state funds – just as Maximian Daia was subsidizing his new pagan church in the East[21]. Pope Marcellus and Eusebius both having died in exile, a new pope, Melitiades, had been elected. When Constantine left Rome, in January 313, he presented Melitiades with the palace on the Lateran Hill which the Empress Fausta had used as her personal residence throughout the winter. It remained the palace of the popes for more than a thousand years, and next door to it was built the first of the Constantinean basilicas of Rome, St. John Lateran, the City's cathedral[22].

Constantine's three months in Rome were not, however, devoted solely, or even largely, to promoting Christianity. Maxentius' mismanagement and the devastation of civil war made the need to restore the administration, with the primary aim of feeding the people, the most pressing of all the tasks facing the regime. Eusebius mentions it as one of Constantine's acts of charity, along with his benefactions to the churches, but it was rather an act of good government, and must have gone a long way towards reconciling the people to their new ruler[23]. It was thus rather a realistic than an altruistic act of benevolence, as was also the confirmation in office of as many of Maxentius' administrators as would loyally serve the new government. Such officials as the aristocratic Senator Aradius Rufinus, who, until October 28 had been Maxentius' governor of Rome, were rapidly restored to their posts; it was actually less than a month before, on November 22, Rufinus received new letters of appointment from Constantine[24]. There was no purge after the battle of Milvian Bridge, except of the Praetorian Guard. Severus' legislation concerning it was confirmed and enforced, and so the Guard ceased to exist, after three hundred years. It had been severely mauled on October 28, the commanders who might have rebelled rather than obey orders to disarm their men were dead or demoralized, and there were no disturbances at its passing[25].

Whether or not such senators as Rufinus really approved of Constantine's assumption of power in Italy, there was nothing effective that they could do to end it. The senators acquiesced readily in his plans for the government of Italy, appeared at the Victory Games with which he celebrated his triumph, accepted what jobs he offered them, and raised in his honour the triumphal arch which is still one of the wonders of Rome. Completed before his second visit to the City as emperor in July 315, to celebrate the tenth anniversary of his accession to power, and constructed partly of stone originally cut and dressed for trophies and memorials of the Emperor Trajan, the arch bears a series of panels depicting units in Constantine's army, trophies of his conquests, sacrifices of thanksgiving to the pagan gods, and an inscription which, in neither decidedly Christian nor indubitably pagan terms, dedicates the memorial

TO THE EMPEROR CAESAR FLAVIUS CONSTANTINE WHO BEING INSTINCT WITH DIVINITY AND BY THE GREATNESS OF HIS SPIRIT WITH HIS FORCES AVENGED THE COMMONWEALTH IN A JUST WAR ON BOTH THE TYRANT AND ALL HIS PARTY[26].

It would be difficult to find a phrase less explicit than that used on the arch to describe what inspired the emperor or how it affected him. The words are *instinctu divinitatis*, 'being instinct with, imbued with, inspired by, full of, godness, the divine, whatever-god-is'. If Constantine and the bishops who by then were his constant companions chose to read this inscription in a Christian sense, they were free to do so. The senators who ordered it, read it as they pleased. If it made no one happy, it offended no one. The Christian Scriptures were full of references to men being filled with the Spirit of God, while the idea of being 'instinct' with or by the gods or the goddesses, or by evil spirits, was, although not a familiar one, certainly not unknown in paganism. The senators chose the inscription, but Constantine must have approved it before it was made public. Both they and he were walking warily, they being careful not to give open offence to his notoriously touchy Christian friends, and he not yet willing definitively to opt for the church and against the temples. In the nineteenth century it was fashionable to maintain in some circles that Constantine merely used Christianity as an instrument of his policy of self-aggrandisement; early in this present century, a reaction set in against that theory, and it was argued that from 312 onwards he was committed to Christ, although for political reasons he remain unbaptized. It is now perhaps possible to take a view midway between these extremes, and admit that even a simple soldier can be more complicated than either of them suggests. Constantine did need the Christians, just as the Christians needed him. He also needed – certainly before the battle of Milvian Bridge, and probably also during later crises – the moral strength that awareness of being personally 'instinct with the divine' gives to the naturally religious mind. It obviously pleased him, satisfied something in him, to believe that he was specially singled out by the Supreme God to fulfil great tasks, that he had – as the panegyrist of 311 put it – 'some secret communication with that divine mind which, delegating the care of the rest of us to the lesser gods, deigns to reveal itself solely to you'. On the available evidence, he was committed to furthering Christianity as an organized religion from 312 onwards, but felt himself above the ministrations of archbishops and bishops. He called himself 'the bishop of those outside' the church and later 'the equal of the apostles', and this he indeed was in so far as he was willing to oversee everyone's morals, provide for the church's welfare and actually perform as a kind of lay missionary, encouraging people (such as Helena) to join the church, while refusing to submit to its discipline himself. Had he been 'converted' in 312, as a fanatic is converted to a system or organization, he would not have delayed baptism. He would have accepted it as soon as possible, and forthwith begun to force conversion on unwilling pagans.

He was, however, not a fanatic, except for peace and unity within the empire under his benevolent autocracy. He was impulsive sometimes and bad-tempered often, but he did not find it easy to adopt courses of action from which there could be no sure retreat – of which accepting baptism would have been one. He was ready to commit others to the care of Christ and the Christians, even his beloved son Crispus, but in 312 he was not yet ready to commit himself.

CHAPTER SEVEN

TWO TO RULE THE WORLD

ALTHOUGH a triangle appears so stable, and in mechanics a triangle of forces often is, a triangular division of political power rarely subsists for long. The division of forces and the tensions between Constantine, Licinius and Maximin Daia after the death of Maxentius was so blatantly unstable that even the most apolitical observer of the times must have realized that war was inevitable, and might come at any moment.

Licinius had done nothing whatsoever to help the army of Gaul in the Italian Campaign. Although it had probably been agreed beforehand that he should not interfere beyond keeping a watchful eye on Maximin Daia, his inactivity was held against him in the West. The panegyrist eulogizing Constantine in 313 emphasized and re-emphasized the fact that his emperor alone had freed Italy, doing so with a minute army and at great personal risk to himself[1]. His manner was much more pointed than it would have been if official policy had not aimed at the denigration of Licinius, probably to prepare public opinion for a blunt refusal to hand Italy over to its legitimate ruler. A panegyrist was not a licensed fool. He could not afford to offend his patron by voicing political judgements at variance with received opinion. Yet in the months following the Battle of Milvian Bridge, all was officially well between the victor and his dilatory ally. They still needed one another. Maximin Daia was stronger than ever, and the enemy of them both. Although it was Licinius who was in immediate danger from the East (an invasion of Constantine's new provinces in Tripolitania from Libya was unlikely to be a rapidly profitable adventure), it was Constantine who had killed Maximin's ally and was encouraging his declared enemies, the Christians. By the time the news of Constantine's arrival in Rome had reached Sirmium and

Nicomedia, winter was closing down over the Alps and the mountains of Asia Minor and Thrace, and storms had ended the Mediterranean sailing season. No one was in immediate danger from invasion, but the winter was only a respite, and they all knew it.

Constantine used these months of grace to consolidate his position in Italy and Africa, organize food supplies, make a tentative peace with the *honestiores* of the senatorial aristocracy, and refit his battered assault units. Licinius passed them at Sirmium with his court. With a declared enemy to the East and an uncertain ally to the West, he must have been a very unhappy man. As far as he knew, the promise to marry him to Constantia still stood, but he can have been certain of nothing except that trouble lay just over all his horizons, and that only continual vigilance would ensure his surviving the coming spring. It was probably a great relief to him to receive an invitation to share the consulate with Constantine in 313, and celebrate the marriage at Milan in February, before the opening of the campaign season. Even these gestures must have left him with some mixed feelings, however, for if he had been bolder, or better endowed by Galerius with arms and trained men, he himself might have controlled the Senate and Milan might have been his own capital for the previous two years. He can scarcely have hoped that Constantine would present him with Italy, although the Gallican army had 'liberated' it in the names of the legitimate emperors. The old agreed divisions of the empire had effectively been swept away with the disappearance, first of all the Caesars by Galerius' mass promotion of them, and then of so many Augusti, both false and true. The most that he could hope for was acceptance by Constantine of the frontiers as then constituted, leaving him free to push back Maximin Daia, and enlarge his own territories at the expense of the Eastern emperor.

In the event, this is precisely what happened. Constantine was temporarily satisfied to have added Rome and Africa to his holding. As Zosimus summed up the events of the winter of 312–13: 'After [Milvian Bridge], Constantine did justice on a few of those who had been useful to Maxentius, rubbed out the Praetorian soldiers, and emptied the prisons of those in them; then, having thus arranged things at Rome to his liking, he set out for the Celtic lands and Gaul. And having sent for Licinius, he married him at Milan to his sister Constantia, who had been promised to him earlier. And when all this had been done, Constantine returned to the country of the Celts[2].'

Maximin Daia recognized the threat represented by an accommodation between Licinius and Constantine, and he seems quickly to have realized also that if he continued to persecute Christians the war, when it came, could easily be represented as a struggle 'to restore ancient liberties'. After the news of Constantine's successful invasion of Italy reached him, he showed much less zeal in persecution. To make quite sure that he understood his danger, Constantine, recently voted Augustus Maximus by the Senate, wrote to him, warning him to ease the pressure on the church[3]. However, for him simply to have ended his war against the Christians would have resulted in an intolerable loss of face. His ambiguity at the time of the publication elsewhere of Galerius' Edict of Toleration, and the welcome he had given to municipal and provincial appeals for the expulsion of Christians from their homes, had given a new lease of life to paganism in his dioceses. Artificial though his pagan church was, it was enjoying temporary success. A powerful weapon in its armoury was a scurrilous pamphlet, in that genre of fictional works popular among early Christians now known as the Apocryphal Acts, entitled *The Acts of Pilate*, in which Christ and the Apostles were shown in the worst possible light, although its style was close enough to that of standard Christian literature to provide seemingly authentic *testimonia* (proof texts) for unscrupulous pagan controversialists. This book had an influence far beyond its obvious significance. Christians prided themselves on being the possessors of a divinely-inspired Sacred Text; many of them owed their literacy to Christianity; written texts were their guarantee of the authority of their teaching. But the canon of the New Testament was not yet completely fixed. A good parody of the authentic texts was a very

Coin-portraits of (*l. to r. top*) Diocletian (284-305) and Constantius Chlorus (293-306); and of (*l. to r. bottom*) Galerius (293-311) and Licinius (310-324)

Photos: British Museum

A stylised, but probably not unlifelike, bust said to represent the pagan reactionary Maximin Daia (305-313)

Photo: Cairo Museum

real threat. Something of how seriously Christian controversialists felt compelled to take the *Acts of Pilate* can be glimpsed in Book One of Eusebius' *Ecclesiastical History* where, discussing the chronology of Christ's ministry, the author is careful to point out that the writer of 'the *Acts* recently published denigrating our Saviour' was in error about even so elementary a point as the date of Pilate's procuratorship in Palestine[4]. To Christians, a text composed in their own style, dealing with the lives of their sacred heroes, and blaspheming all their most sacred beliefs, was the cruellest of attacks. At the beginning of the persecution, they had been willing to die rather than hand over the genuine scriptures to the magistrates: now the children in the schools were being taught to read from this evil book (as they saw it) the *Acts* of Christ's executioner. Even its choice of hero was important, underlining as it did the fact that Christ had died a rebel against the state. With such ideas being relentlessly hammered into the minds of the pagan population, it is hardly surprising that the Christians obtained small relief from Maximin Daia even after Constantine had written to him, reminding him of the existence of Galerius' Edict. His response was hypocritical. It took the form of a rescript of Sabinus, his Praetorian Prefect, warning him of the dangers of extremes in persecution: 'It is rather by acts of grace and exhortations that you should increase the care for the gods in our provinces. If anyone voluntarily chooses to worship the gods who ought to be acknowledged, it behoves us to welcome him, but if some wish to follow their own religion, let them do what it is legal for them to do . . . But let no one trouble our provinces with violence . . .'[5] This attempt to push responsibility on to Sabinus was unconvincing, at a time when Christians dispossessed of their homes were dying from hunger in the streets, and the client king of Armenia was so incensed at the invasion of his country by pagan Roman missionaries in pursuit of Christian refugees that he was planning a breach of his treaty with Rome and a retaliatory attack on the empire[6].

Eusebius suggests that the rescript to Sabinus followed the delivery at Nicomedia of not merely a single letter from

Constantine, but a bundle of despatches prepared jointly by Constantine and Licinius, including a report of Maxentius' fall, 'an account of the miracles God had wrought on their behalf', and 'a most perfect and thoroughly detailed law on behalf of the Christians' which they had jointly drawn up, 'with one will and intention'[7].

Constantine had already made dispositions in favour of 'the Catholic Church of the Christians' for those parts of the empire under his direct rule. It looks as though at Milan he brought pressure on Licinius to extend toleration as far as the Bosphorus, and join him in trying to frighten Maximin Daia into co-operating with them in this new policy. Success would mean not only peace for the Christians, but also that Maximin Daia, Constantine's oldest rival, the man who had been named Caesar instead of him in 305, had acknowledged him as the Supreme Augustus, whose will was law throughout the empire.

This bundle of despatches can only have been prepared in January and February 313, when Constantine and Licinius met at Milan with their staffs to finalize the details of the alliance between them and seal it by Licinius' marriage to Constantia. This being so, the 'perfect and thoroughly detailed law on behalf of the Christians' was that famous Edict of Milan which has caused more controversy among scholars than any other piece of Constantinean legislation.

At various times it has been denied that such an Edict was ever promulgated, that Constantine had any part in its preparation, that it had any connection with Milan, and even that any special legislation was necessary to end persecution and give peace to the church[8].

In fact, as Galerius' legislation was still the law of the empire, it should have been unnecessary to write a new decree in favour of the Christians; but there can be little doubt that a law of some kind 'on behalf of the Christians' did issue from the meeting at Milan. Both Lactantius and Eusebius claim to reproduce its text, the one in his *Deaths of the Persecutors*[9], the other in his *Ecclesiastical History*[10]; both believed it absolutely fundamental to the freedom of the church, and there is no record that any of their contemporaries, however bitter about the triumph won by Christianity in gaining imperial favour, ever accused either of them of forging the text he reproduced. The text of the edict copied by Lactantius in Latin differs slightly from the Greek translation made by Eusebius, but the variants are so slight as to be immaterial to any but a specialist in this controversy. Lactantius' version of the main paragraph of the text, as he claims it was promulgated by Licinius at Nicomedia after the fall of Maximin Daia on June 13, 313, runs:

> When I, Constantine Augustus, and I, Licinius Augustus, met under happy auspices at Milan, and went over in discussion everything pertaining to public welfare and security, we judged that the one thing above all others which we saw would be of benefit to most people was that relating to the regulation of the worship of the Divine: that we should give to Christians and to everyone else the right freely to follow whatever rule of faith [*religionem*] they chose, so that, whatever divinity [is] enthroned in heaven may be well-disposed and propitious towards us and all those under our authority.

The main differences between this text and that reproduced by Eusebius is that Eusebius substitutes the phrases 'to all' for Lactantius' 'to most people', and 'whatever divine or heavenly thing exists' for Lactantius' 'whatever divinity is enthroned in heaven'. He omits the tautological phrase 'and propitious' but adds the instructions which accompanied the Edict itself when it was transmitted to a local administrator – instructions mainly designed to ensure that property confiscated from the Christians during the persecution was promptly and fully restored to them.

The main difficulty in identifying this law with that 'perfect and thoroughly detailed law on behalf of the Christians' mentioned by Eusebius as among the bundle of despatches sent to Maximin Daia from Milan is that it is manifestly not a law to the advantage solely of the Christians, detailed enough to make them totally secure. Although it singles them out for special mention – largely, in all probability, because they were the chief sufferers under current conditions – it also sets other formerly proscribed sects, such as the Manichees, free to teach, worship and make converts. It is an Edict of general religious toleration, with additional concessions to the Christians, rather than a specific and exclusive charter of Christian freedom. It reflects official recognition of the bankruptcy of the state cults and seems to admit confusion and concern about the real identity of the godhead. It mentions Christians, but not Christ. Acknowledging that the state needs divine help, like the inscription on the Arch of Constantine, it is scrupulously, all but superstitiously, careful to avoid offending the *divinitas* dwelling in heaven by naming It and perhaps naming It wrongly. If Eusebius' 'perfect law' was the Edict of Milan as we know it, the text must have been accompanied by an extensive collection of imperial letters showing how it was to be applied 'on behalf of the Christians' alone. No such collection is known. This is, however, the only law promulgated jointly by the emperors which could have been described in Eusebius' terms. There was no meeting between them and their staffs except at Milan when the draft of so fundamental a piece of legislation could have been thoroughly discussed – as, surely, this joint edict must have been. Although not a persecutor, Licinius had no special love for Christians, or any other religious group, and must have needed convincing that they deserved a degree of cosseting beyond the laconic 'Christians may exist' offered them by his old friend Galerius almost with his last breath, in April 311. As it is, there is nothing to show that he promulgated any edict of toleration before the war with Maximin Daia which followed the conference at Milan as soon as the roads became passable to armies in the spring of 313; and it is known that as soon as he discovered how confused Christian affairs were in the East, he washed his hands of them, although he probably never became the arch-persecutor Eusebius later called him. In the light of subsequent events, however, the view that Licinius alone produced the 'Edict of Milan', without prompting from Constantine, is manifestly untenable.

It seems reasonable to suppose that what actually happened was this: after the victory at Milvian Bridge under the protection of the monogram of Christ, Constantine repaid his debt to the Christian God by favouring his devotees in Italy and Africa, enriching his churches and honouring his ministers, throughout the months of his stay in Rome. During that period, he was in correspondence with Licinius about the forthcoming marriage and the terms, both declared and undeclared, of the marriage contract. Constantine, still repaying his debt to God, made toleration a condition of the alliance, possibly even sending to Sirmium a draft of the edict, which he may have already promulgated in his own provinces. (The theory that a law promulgated by any Augustus was automatically effective throughout the empire had already proved no more than that in practice: only when a law had been posted by a local Augustus could it be held to bind his provinces.) These preliminary exchanges led to the agreement of a final text in Milan in January–February 313, and this was possibly promulgated by Licinius at Sirmium in March or April, and certainly published in Nicomedia in June.

If Constantine had not previously promulgated an earlier draft valid in his dioceses from Rome, he may actually have issued the Edict itself in February from Milan, as its popular name suggests, for Milan had been Maximian's capital and was still officially the chief city of the Italian diocese, despite the attention recently accorded to Rome.

The subsidiary enactments necessary to make the law effective in each of the provinces of the West according to its needs were already going out to local governors and commanders. Two of them, addressed by Constantine to Anulinus[11], his Proconsul in Africa, have been preserved; one orders the restoration of Christian property sequestered during the persecution, on the grounds that 'we are not merely not hesitant, but rather are anxious, to restore to others what is morally theirs', the other extends to ministers of 'the Catholic Church of the Christians' the immunities, including immunity from taxation and conscription, already enjoyed by pagan priests.

The 'many other matters' which the Edict of Milan says were discussed by Licinius and Constantine probably also included the question of the future government of Italy. Certainly, within a few months of that historic meeting, Constantine had agreed to the appointment of a Caesar there. He was one Bassianus, a distant relative of Licinius, but married to Constantine's half-sister Anastasia. His brother, Senecio, was still working for Licinius, and seems to have been his trusted agent. Within months, the brothers were intriguing against Constantine at Rome. According to the anonymous chronicler quoted by Valesius, Constantine himself suggested that Bassianus should be promoted, and used his half-brother – Anastasia's and Constantia's brother – Julius Constantius as his go-between in the negotiations: 'Constantine sent [Julius] Constantius to Licinius, urging that Bassianus, who was married to his other sister Anastasia, should be made Caesar. And Bassianus, embroiled in Licinius' plots through Senecio his brother, who was loyal to Licinius, took up arms against Constantine, but these moves becoming known, he was defeated and overthrown by Constantine's command. But when punishment was demanded for Senecio, the instigator of these plots, Licinius refused, and their friendship was broken.'[12]

However, in February 313, Licinius' plots against Constantine still lay hidden in the future. Before the talks at Milan had reached their formal conclusion, news reached Licinius that taking advantage of his absence from his dominions, Maximin Daia had broken the truce made between them in a boat in the middle of the Bosphorus only a little over a year earlier, and, defying the winter, had crossed the straits into Europe with an army at his back, to take the ancient fortress and market town standing at their Black Sea entrance, the little city of Byzantium.

This was the kind of direct challenge that Licinius' temperament and training best fitted him to meet. Leaving Milan immediately, he took the road to the East with a force consisting of little more than his *comitatus*, and drove himself and his men so hard that Maximin had time only to advance about seventy miles along the coast road, from Byzantium to Tzirallum, the first posting station west from Heraclea-ad-Europa, before the disconcerting news reached him that the next posting station, Drizipara, only eighteen miles away, was already occupied by Licinius. It was still only the last week in April.

Licinius reached Drizipara with a minuscule force of perhaps

30,000 men, infantry and cavalry. Maximin had used a larger army at the brief investment of Heraclea, and the whole army of Asia was within a few days' call. Licinius called for a truce, and a peace conference, but Maximin, certain of an easy victory, refused to meet him except in battle. The unequal armies clashed in the Serene Fields, midway between the posting stations, on April 30[13]. Immediately before the battle, Licinius announced – whether truthfully, or so as not to be outdone by Constantine, we cannot tell – that he had received a revelation in a dream: an angel had appeared to him, and taught him a prayer to the Supreme God which his soldiers were to chant in their advance as a paeon to the defeat of their polytheistic enemy:

Supreme God – we beseech thee!
Holy God – we entreat thee!
Committing all justice to thee!
Committing ourselves to thee! [*or* our safety *or* salvation to Thee]
Committing our command [*imperium*] to Thee!
Through thee we live!
Through thee our lives are victorious and well-omened [*felices*]!
Supreme, holy God, hear our prayers!
We stretch out our arms to thee!
Hear [us] Supreme and holy God![14]

If the soldiers actually shouted more on the battlefield itself than the chorus line of this litany to the Supreme God, '*Summe, Sancte Deus!*', they must have had angelic help, or breathlessness would surely have defeated them. But that line may well have been their battle-cry, if it had occurred to Licinius that the propaganda which had worked for Constantine before the battle of Milvian Bridge might also work for him on the Serene Fields. His men may have taken extra fire from the belief that they were fighting for the Supreme God, their emperor's friend, against the godlings, and that the-one-who-actually-is-enthroned-in-heaven was helping them. Licinius was an unlikely subject for a divine revelation, but he may have remembered the prayer during the night, as it seems to have been a well-known one. Eusebius' *Life* puts it on the lips of Constantine[15].

With or without special divine help, Licinius was a good

general. Within hours, his 30,000 had destroyed Maximin's army, 'and he,' Lactantius gloats, 'threw off the imperial dress so ill-becoming him, and hid himself with unmanly timidity in the crowd about him, seeking safety in flight, lurking about the fields and villages thereafter in the dress of a slave, hoping thus to be effectively concealed. But he had not escaped the mighty, all-seeing eye of God . . .'

While in the Taurus Mountains, trying to collect an army with which to reconquer his lost empire, Maximin fell sick, and died at Tarsus, in a manner unpleasant enough to be fitting, in Lactantius' view, for an arch-persecutor: 'his whole body was consumed . . . and nothing remained but dry bones . . . his eyes protruded and fell out . . . until at length, surviving even these sufferings, he too implored the pardon of the god of the Christians, and confessed his impious warfare against god . . . and . . . by laws and ordinances explicitly acknowledged his error in worshipping those he had formerly called gods . . .'[16]

His death – perhaps from cholera – ended what might otherwise have proved a long and bitter civil war, leaving Licinius triumphant from Illyria to the Euphrates. At Nicomedia, on June 13, he paid his debt to 'whatever divinity is enthroned in heaven' by promulgating the agreed edict of toleration, the 'Edict of Milan'. In the ninth book of Eusebius' *History*, written about that time, he is represented as a divinely-inspired hero, second only in glory to Constantine himself.

When Licinius entered Nicomedia in triumph, Constantine was once more in the North, demonstrating to the Franks by a tour of the Rhenish forts and with punitive raids into their lands that they should not attempt to take over parts of Gaul just because he appeared to be busy somewhere else, and might have forgotten them[17].

The previous October, when he had defeated Maxentius, he had been certain enough of his own popularity and superiority to leave in peace all those who did not actively continue to oppose his will. Licinius sensed that he could not afford such leniency in the East. He executed many of Maximin Daia's chief ministers, including his finance minister, Peucetius, his

Augustal Prefect of Egypt, Culcianus, and Theocnetus, whose pagan church at Antioch had inspired Daia's religious reforms. He also proscribed all Daia's relations, and so outlawed the families of the late emperors Galerius, Severus and Diocletian. The proscription was ruthlessly executed. Ultimately, even Galerius' wife Valeria and mother-in-law Prisca, Diocletian's widow, whom Galerius had entrusted to Licinius himself as a sacred charge only days before his death, were seized in their home at Thessalonika and beheaded[18]. The bloodbath went on until there was no one in the East to be held up as a figurehead to rally opposition. The Jovian imperial family had ceased to exist. The effect of this purge was that the only persons left in the empire with any justifiable claim to imperial power who were not members of Constantine's family were Licinius himself, and his infant son by his Syrian concubine Mamertina, Licinianus. If he had children by his new wife, Constantia, they too would be Constantine's kin.

He seems to have realized the danger of this situation himself – and the opportunities it offered, for if Constantine were to die, he could claim to be head of the family. In the late summer of 313, while Constantine was still on the Rhine, he initiated the intrigue with the Caesar Bassianus, designed to eliminate Constantine and leave him as Augustus Maximus, with his cousin as Caesar at Rome – for as long as Bassianus would be permitted to survive. The plot was detected and Bassianus summarily executed, but when Constantine demanded that Licinius should surrender the go-between Senecio to him, Licinius not only refused to deliver his cousin to certain death, but early in the following summer brought his *comitatus* menacingly into western Pannonia 'and their friendship was broken'[19].

Only fifteen months before, they had agreed to share the empire between them at Milan. Now they were on the brink of war. Licinius pushed them over it. At Aemona, the Italian frontier post (now Ljubljana), he declared war by throwing down Constantine's portraits and statues. 'The war thus begun,' the anonymous chronicler in Valesius says, 'suited them both. They both led armies to Cibulae. Licinius had 35,000 infantry and cavalry; Constantine led 20,000.' This manoeuvre actually involved Licinius in a retreat, but left him in a strong defensive position, on dry ground in the middle of the Hiucla Marshes filling the valley of the Save near Cibalae. Constantine, however, nullified his opponent's advantage by mounting an attack under cover of darkness. The battle fought before dawn on the morning of October 8 must have been a very cold, uncomfortable affair. At the end of it, Licinius had 'lost at least 20,000 infantrymen by the sword, and he fled, night helping him to Sirmium, with the greater part of his cavalry. And picking up his wife [Constantia], son [Licinius Licinianus] and treasure there, he pressed on into Dacia, where he proclaimed his General Officer Commanding the Frontier, Valens, as Caesar . . .'

The breaking of Constantine's statues at Aemona was Licinius' declaration of war, but it is probable that Constantine deliberately provoked him into making this defiant gesture by pin-pricks additional to his initial demand for the surrender of Senecio. Eutropius – no friend of Constantine's memory, but a reluctant admirer of his ability, and well-placed as secretary to the Emperor Arcadius to study the surviving documents – had no doubt as to who was the real aggressor: 'Constantine, a mighty man and one who made a point of bringing about whatever he planned to do, once he had decided to rule the whole world, occasioned a war with Licinius, although bound to him by a treaty of friendship and affinity, [his] sister being Licinius' bride . . .'[20] It was a dynastic war in the old tradition. The two armies represented no more than each emperor's bodyguard of Protectors, Lancers and Shieldsmen, and neither apparently took steps to involve the general population in the quarrel. Constantine pursued his fleeing rival all the way to Thrace, where at last, rejoining the main body of his forces at Hadrianopolis (now Edirne, where modern Greece, Turkey and Bulgaria meet), Licinius prepared to make a stand, declaring Constantine deposed, and naming the *dux limitis*, Caius Aurelius Valens, Caesar and Augustus in his place. Coins were struck inscribed with the portrait and titles of the new Emperor Caius Aurelius Valerius Valens Augustus and in praise of Jupiter, the

Preserver of the Emperors. In this crisis, the revelation of the Supreme God was forgotten[21].

Constantine advanced to Philippopolis in eastern Thrace, and there received legates from Licinius. It appears that this embassy was instructed to keep Constantine talking until the armies of Asiana and Pontica could be ferried over to Europe; but, before either commander-in-chief was ready to take full advantage of his military strength and tactical skill, the forces under their command stumbled into battle on the Plains of Mardia, in the wide valley of the River Hebrus (Maritza), flowing the fifty miles or so between their headquarters. The result was that they dissipated one another's power without either of them decisively gaining the upper hand, and at the end of the day Licinius had little difficulty in slipping away from the battlefield, heading north, towards Beroea. The next morning, Constantine – perhaps believing that he was in pursuit of a defeated enemy, but more probably aiming to cut the lines of communication of a man whom he knew to be still dangerous – pushed on eastwards through Hadrianopolis to Byzantium. Once the citadel and harbourworks there were in his hands, he was the master of every main road and port in the European empire, and Asia apparently lay open before him. But there was still a cohesive army in his rear, poised ready to strike either west or south. When Licinius sent a new embassy to him, led by one Mestrianus, he first received it with honour, but then made Mestrianus a hostage until the first of his demands was met, by the deposition of Valens and the public recognition of the legitimacy of his own rule as Augustus Maximus.

In a generous demonstration of good will, Licinius not only removed his former frontier commander from imperial office, but also executed him, so establishing an atmosphere in which two sensible generals could talk to one another without fear of interruption from a fool. They soon reached a compromise. Licinius ceded Upper Moesia, the Pannonias, Macedonia and the Greek peninsula to Constantine, and in exchange was confirmed in his possession of the toehold in Europe represented by Thrace, together with all Asia, the County of the East, Egypt, the Libyas, Constantine's half-sister Constantia and Constantine's friendship. Constantine withdrew his soldiers from the Bosphorus and, finding Galerius' old palace at Sirmium a convenient place from which to rule the West, took up residence there[22]. So by the end of the year, when preparations were already well in train for the celebration of his tenth jubilee at Rome in July 315, he had made himself absolute master of the Empire in Europe, with the sole exception of the diocese of Thrace, and of all North Africa as far east as the Province of Tripolitania; and was ruling these vast possessions from the city which had been the seat of his father's first administration, as Governor of the Pannonias, back in the days when Diocletian had murdered Numerian, just thirty years earlier, and he himself had been a child.

On the day when, in the summer of 315, Roman plaudits for his first visit since his victory over Maxentius marked the beginning of a triumphal month of celebrations, his ambitions and his European empire both seemed to be at peace. There was, however, a newer and subtler conflict brewing, a struggle for dominance between the all-powerful emperor and the once-sovereign senate, between the new men, many of them Christians, whom the emperor was making, and the old aristocrats, usually still pagan at Rome, whom he threatened by his promotions to destroy.

To flatter the emperor with the title Augustus Maximus or with a fanciful inscription on a decorative arch was one thing. To co-operate with him while he dismantled one's world around one was quite another. Constantine showed himself indifferent to the feelings of Rome's pagans from the beginning of this visit. Although he did not actually forbid pagan sacrifices, or surrender the title Pontifex Maximus (Supreme Pontiff), and the control it gave him over appointments within the colleges of pagan priests, he refused to make the customary offerings of thanksgiving for past benefits and petition for future blessings which were a traditional part of the emperor's duties. Instead, Eusebius says, he 'ordered general celebrations, and offered prayers of thanksgiving to God the King of All, as sacrifices without flame and smoke. And he derived much pleasure from doing so'[23].

In pagan eyes, sacrifices consisting only of words offered nothing but insult to the gods. Constantine may have enjoyed his celebrations and bloodless sacrifices, but to the aristocratic senators, they appeared to be an attempt to curry favour with the mob, by giving them games to entertain them and sharing their predilections in worship – for most Christians were still poor and underprivileged. They concluded that Constantine was an atheist – that is, a Christian – himself, and sensed that he mistrusted and disliked them. They expected him to turn on them at any moment, as Licinius had already turned on the aristocrats of the East, robbing and murdering them while passing measures to ingratiate himself with the peasantry and urban poor. They were studious in their avoidance, not only in 315 on the Arch of Constantine, but for many years to come, of the admission that the emperor's vision had been of Christ, his monogram, his cross or his person. To the Roman mint master, Constantine was the *liberator orbis*, 'the Liberator of the World', and 'the Companion of the Unconquered sun'. To orators and officials, he was the specially-favoured of the gods, 'instinct with divinity', the blessed recipient of a special revelation of the divinity – but who that divinity was none in Rome but the Christians would admit, although they, of course, were delighted to proclaim it. Not every aristocratic pagan at Rome condemned Constantine and worked against him. Many took office under him loyally. All, however, regretted his links with the Christians and, as the years passed, their regrets hardened into bitterness and finally into outspoken opposition. On August 20, 315, he appointed one of the most honoured of pagan administrators, the aged Vettius Rufinus, to be his governor of Rome[24]. Rufinus was an *augur*, a high priest of the sun cult, and a priest of the temple of Mars on the Palatine Hill, but his and similar appointments, although accepted by the senators, won Constantine no confidence from them. In the end, he had to take extraordinary steps to weaken the old aristocracy, by creating a new class of aristocrats, the Admirables, *clarissimi*, from respectable provincial families, and importing them into the city to outvote the senatorial *honestiores*; and then, to counteract the violence with which individual members of the former ruling class tried to bolster its failing powers and work off their own sense of personal failure and inadequacy, by issuing edicts removing the power of jurisdiction over Honourables from local courts presided over by their sympathetic friends and relations, to others where the law was administered by strangers.

'Anyone of the class of Honourables,' one of these laws, dated before 321, and preserved in the Theodosian Code, rules, bluntly defining the commonest of offences, 'who abducts a virgin or encroaches upon the estates of others, or is detected in any other guilt or crime, instead of being subjected to the public laws of the Province in which the offence was committed, shall either have his name brought to our notice, or be tried by another jurisdiction . . .'[25]

Such measures appear to have met with small success, and Rome remained a problem until the founding of Constantinople and its success as 'the New Rome' with a senate of its own (which although subservient to the emperor nevertheless commanded respect in some quarters, and clouded the issue generally) started to drain away both the respect and the resources of the old Rome on the Tiber.

However, the beginning of war with the senate was not permitted to destroy either the splendour of Constantine's decennial celebrations, or his delight in them. Eusebius said that he greatly enjoyed them, and that was probably true, for he loved to cut a fine figure, and was always willing to work for popular acclaim, putting himself and everyone else to a great deal of trouble for the sake of making a favourable impression. Enjoy a Roman holiday though he might, however, he was not really comfortable in the City, and never allowed himself to be distracted for long from the business of governing the empire. By the autumn of 315, he was once more in Gaul, where he spent nearly a year, overseeing the work of strengthening the frontier fortifications and rebuilding the cities which had been continuous since the beginning of his reign. In 316, he moved the court south-eastwards, into the Danube region and the provinces of his frontier with Licinius. He wintered at Sirmium, and it was from there the following year that he named his teen-age son by Minervina, Flavius Valerius Crispus, and his infant son by Fausta, Flavius Valerius Constantinus II, as Caesars of the West; while simultaneously at Nicomedia his fellow-Augustus Licinius named his son Licinianus Caesar in the East[26]. By this move, following as it did the deaths of Herculius and his son at Constantine's hands and the deaths of all traceable Jovians at Licinius', Diocletian's dynasties-of-merit ceased to exist, and the normal principle of inheritance by heredity was restored.

Two men now ruled the world, and they were determined that their sons should rule it after them. There is evidence that Licinius had planned this end for Diocletian's experiment as early as 314, at the time of his peace treaty with Constantine. He had coins struck that year, showing the three boys as Caesars together. Why Constantine did not accept their promotion at that time is not known. Possibly, he then had no real intention of sharing the *imperium* with Licinius and his family, even for a few years. By 317, however, Crispus was growing up, and provision had to be made for his future. To have named him alone as Caesar would have been a direct challenge to Licinius, who would doubtless have answered by clothing Licinianus in the purple, and probably also with gravely provocative frontier incidents. Constantine had just removed the image of Mars from his coins and was using the currency to popularize the slogan that his was a reign of 'Blessed Tranquillity'[27]. He was not ready for another war – yet.

CHAPTER EIGHT

WHAT IS A CATHOLIC CHRISTIAN?

IN THE year when Crispus was made Caesar, his father Constantine, although careful not to provoke trouble with Licinius, actually found himself with two battles on his hands: one the continuing war of attrition on the economic front, the other, almost as long drawn out, in the field of power and authority. The measures he took during this period of military inactivity to defend and strengthen the currency were ultimately crowned with a remarkable degree of success. The other conflict, in the field of power, was the only war he fought in which his victory was equivocal. Faced in Proconsular Africa and Numidia with what amounted to an ideological revolt against his vision of a unitary empire secure in the 'Blessed Peace of the Augustus' (as some of his coins put it), he ultimately lost his temper, and loosed his armies against dissident and independent Christians there. Although his soldiers were generally victorious, he lost the struggle for the minds of the people. A century later, Catholic Christians like Augustine of Hippo were still expending a great deal of energy trying to end what has become known as the Donatist Controversy[1].

On one level, that at which it is usually presented in histories of Christianity, this conflict sprang directly from the Great Persecution, and, like the riots at Rome which drove Maxentius to exile Pope Marcellus, revolved around the post-Persecution status of those who had surrendered the Scriptures, or otherwise betrayed the church, at the imperial command. On another, perhaps more profound, it was an expression of revulsion against the monolithic state being constructed by Constantine and run for him by his friends, so many of whom called themselves Catholic Christians; and thus, paradoxically, it may properly be compared with the revolt against

Constantinean ideas and methods of the pagan senatorial class at Rome.

The original leaders of the Donatist party were scions or protegees of the rich in Africa and Numidia, who were naturally anxious to preserve what they considered the true African tradition against the upstart Constantine. In the first half of the fourth century, Africa was one of the most 'Roman' of the provinces, and its citizens were proud of the fact. Later, control of their movement was to pass into other hands, as the pagan masses of the countryside and mountains were converted, and Donatism, the religious expression of the African spirit, took on the political hue of African nationalism, but in the beginning it was a revolt not against Rome, but for the preservation of Rome against the emperor himself.

The attitudes revealed in these very Roman Africans by the first stirrings of the controversy were, not surprisingly considering their aristocratic background, a neat reversal of those disclosed by the troubles following the election of Pope Marcellus at Rome, where the Christians were often the dispossessed, and frequently not native-born. At Rome there was no permanent church building within the walls until Constantine endowed St John Lateran: at Carthage, the capital of Proconsular Africa, the Donatists owned three magnificent basilicas in the centre of the city before the year 320. At Rome, it was the hard line on *traditores* taken by Marcellus which sparked off riots. At Carthage, where discipline was traditionally harsh, it was the election of a soft-liner, Caecilian, that led to trouble.

Carthage had a long record of aristocratic independence in ecclesiastical thinking, and of aristocratic steadfastness under persecution. Both these traditional attitudes had found expression in the life of her great martyr bishop Cyprian. During the Decian Persecution (A.D. 250–1), he had dealt summarily with the *lapsi*, those who had betrayed the faith by offering incense to the gods, granting them reconciliation with the church only at the moment of death and on condition that they were rebaptized. And he had ended his life as a consenting victim to imperial displeasure, by voluntarily surrendering himself to the headsman's axe. Cyprian thought of himself as a Catholic Christian, a true representative of the universal church, and his doctrines as Catholic doctrines. His teachings, however, were not universally accepted. In fact, it was more generally held that lapsing from the church did not invalidate baptism; that the sacrament, once administered, should not be repeated. Those holding this view also called themselves Catholics. The question as to which view was truly Catholic was still a live one at the time of Constantine.

The last of the apostates under Decius had hardly disappeared from the African scene before the Great Persecution reaped a new harvest of martyrs there and sowed a new crop of apostates, the *traditores*. Many died for their faith in Africa before the abdication of Diocletian and Maximian, but many more prudently handed over their copies of the scriptures to be burned. While the persecution raged, it was not safe for the bishops to meet in synod and choose successors for those of their number who had died, either naturally or violently, during the months of terror; but when, on the appointment of Severus as Caesar with title in Italy and Africa, it became clear that the worst was over, local synods met at several places in Africa and Numidia to appoint bishops and re-establish discipline. One of these gatherings assembled at Cirta in Numidia, under the presidency of Numidia's senior bishop, Secundus of Tigisi, a venerable priest, widely honoured as a 'confessor' who had suffered for the faith in prison. Unfortunately, although a brave man, he was not otherwise an admirable one. He turned the synod into a witch-finding commission, devoted to ferreting out traitors to the faith, turning his pack of fanatical followers on to the trail of the beloved Bishop Mensurius of Carthage. Mensurius, although not technically a *traditor*, had shown a very human love of life during the persecution, saving himself and the treasures of his congregation at Carthage by substituting secular books for the sacred texts when imperial officers called on him to surrender the scriptures, and going into hiding, taking the scriptures with him – a pusillanimous trick, in Secundus' opinion, one proving that he was unfit to rule. Secundus himself, so he boasted, had met the imperial commissioners' demands for the scriptures with the flat refusal, 'I am a Christian. I am a bishop. I am not a *traditor*.' As Mensurius had not formally apostatized, the Synod at Cirta could not demand his deposition, but a noisy war of words followed its censorious debate, in the course of which Mensurius, leaning on a ruling already well over a century old, warned his congregations against honouring Secundus, on the grounds that to invite martyrdom, as Secundus claimed to have done, was not meritorious, but foolhardy. For good measure, he also spoke slightingly of confessors in general, maintaining that many of them were criminals who had hoped to win their way back to favour by one act of courage, and that others had grown fat in prison, accepting the gifts offered to them by the charity of simple-minded Christians, whether they were in need or not. The acrimonious dispute between Carthage and Cirta was not an edifying one, but neither Mensurius nor Secundus could hurt one another very seriously at this stage[2].

The situation changed, however, when Secundus, or one of his clique, identified a deacon of Mensurius' church named Felix as the author of an anonymous pamphlet grossly libelling Maxentius of Rome. Felix was betrayed to the authorities, but when an attempt was made to arrest him, Mensurius concealed him and refused to divulge his whereabouts. Maxentius summoned the bishop to Rome, and he stood trial, but was acquitted for lack of evidence, although several of his fellow-Christians, members of Secundus' faction, appeared as witnesses against him. He was freed, and began a triumphal journey back to Africa, but did not live to complete it. Falling sick on the way, he died at just about the time of Maxentius' defeat at Milvian Bridge.

The election following his death was inevitably a crucial one. At Carthage, it was generally held that the man most fitted to succeed him was his archdeacon, Caecilian, who had always supported his liberal views, and within days of the announcement of his death, the local clergy had in fact held an election and secured Caecilian's consecration by bishops from three neighbouring towns, the minimum number required by Christian tradition. The three consecrating bishops were Felix of Aptunga, Faustus of Thuburo and Novellus of Tyzica[3]. Their action in enthroning Caecilian was hasty, but not irregular, except in so far that since the persecution it had been customary to hold general synods—like that called by Secundus at Cirta in 305—before making important appointments, so that there could be no argument about them afterwards. As news of Mensurius' death spread, confessor-bishops who shared Secundus' rigorist views hurried to Carthage to participate in the synod to elect his successor. When, on arrival, they discovered Caecilian already in power, trouble was inevitable.

Secundus himself reached Carthage to find himself the natural head of a faction of sixty-nine bishops sworn to secure Caecilian's deposition. He knew that there was no hope of proving that Caecilian had been irregularly elected by the Cathaginian clergy, or that he was personally unfit to rule, so he made enquiries into the lives of the three bishops who had consecrated him, hoping to find some irregularity there. He thought he had found the lever he needed to unseat Caecilian when someone denounced Felix of Aptunga to him as a *traditor*, and therefore, as an apostate, incapable of consecrating a true bishop.

The question of whether an unworthy minister could administer a valid sacrament was a matter of long-standing debate in Africa. To most Christians, the sacraments were divine gifts, unaffected by the worthiness or unworthiness of those bestowing them, but rigorists of Secundus' stamp were convinced that an unworthy minister could not convey a valid sacrament. In Secundus' view, if Felix of Aptunga was a *traditor*, his participation in Caecilian's consecration was enough to invalidate the ceremony, Caecilian was no true bishop, and the see of Carthage was still vacant. It meant nothing to him that it could be proved, and later was, that Felix had been away from Aptunga when his deacons had surrendered the scriptures there. He was out for blood, not justice. Caecilian offered to be reconsecrated at his hands, but he brushed the proposal aside. Nothing would satisfy him but Caecilian's deposition and replacement by a more worthy man—one who belonged to his faction and shared his views.

It is at this stage in the controversy—the stage it had reached when Constantine's administrators arrived in Africa—that its political elements are first apparent. Caecilian was one of the new men. Constantine's religious adviser, Hosius of Cordoba, recognized him immediately as just the kind of person the empire needed, secured for him an immediate subsidy of 3,000 *folles*, and drew up, probably with his help, a list of approved clerics who alone were to be allowed to share in the imperial bounty. At Hosius' instigation, as well as writing to his Proconsul Anulinus, ordering the restoration of Christian property in Africa sequestered during the persecution and granting immunities exclusively to 'the clerics . . . of the church of which Caecilian is president'[4], Constantine wrote to Caecilian personally, informing him of the subsidy, explaining that it was for the support of his partisans in 'the Africas, the Numidias and the Mauretanias' and commanding him to pay out the money 'in accordance with the list already sent to you by Hosius'[5]. Throughout, he treated Caecilian exactly as though he were an honorary servant of the administration. Later, he was to be accused of turning the empire into a police state; in 312, his intelligence service was obviously already excellent. The decision as to which of the factions in Africa the empire ought to support was probably Hosius', whose views on rebaptism and the sacraments in general Caecilian shared. If any bishop in Africa was likely to accept a quasi-official position under the New Flavians, that man was Caecilian, to whom the emperor must have seemed omniscient as well as incredibly benevolent when he revealed that he already knew about the difficulties that 'a crowd of turbulent persons' were making for him, and had 'personally commanded Anulinus the Proconsul and Patricius the *Vicarius*' to hold themselves ready to protect him from his enemies.

To Constantine's agents it must have been significant that one of the most vociferous of these enemies was a rich widow with aristocratic connections whom Caecilian had rebuked for superstition verging on idolatry on learning that she had sent her private chaplain to Syria to beg or buy the relic of a martyr and that she ostentatiously kissed it before receiving Holy Communion. This lady, whose name was Lucilla, paid the expenses of the Numidian bishops during their months in Africa. It has been suggested that she did so out of personal spite against Caecilian, but it is more likely that her actions were inspired by dislike and distrust not merely of him personally, but rather of the school of thought which he represented – a school with wide support in Italy, Gaul and Spain but alien to Africa. Lucilla belonged to the old aristocracy of landed and monied gentry. Caecilian's acceptance of Constantine's subsidy confirmed people of her class in their distrust of him. In their view, he had sold himself to the new government and its church. She was almost certainly not the only one of their number to match Constantine's generosity to Caecilian's party with substantial gifts to Secundus' men.

When Secundus called for Caecilian's replacement by a more worthy man, Lucilla put forward her own candidate, a priest named Majorinus. He was duly elected by her grateful pensioners (later Catholic claims that she bribed the bishops to vote for him were only an unpleasant way of saying that they recognized their debt to her and her friends) and a synodal letter announcing his appointment was sent to every church in Africa.

Clearly, the real argument was no longer between the 'confessors' and the 'traditors', although these labels were still used to hold the parties together. The split was between the old world and the new.

However, although Caecilian's enemies were Constantine's – as the emperor's letter showed that he realized – Secundus and his puppet Majorinus had undeniable rights as citizens under the law, and on April 15, 313, they set in motion the machinery which allowed any citizen to exercise his legal privileges, presenting to Anulinus two documents stating their case against Caecilian, the first a public 'Appeal to Constantine', the second a private (and now lost) Statement of the 'Charge of the Catholic Church concerning the Crimes of Caecilian'.

The 'Appeal to Constantine' read:

> Most Excellent Emperor Constantine –
> Whereas there are disputes between us and other bishops of Africa, we pray you – since you are of a just stock, in as much as your father did not prosecute the persecutions with the other emperors, and Gaul is free from this crime – we pray you that Your Piety may command that judges be given us from Gaul.[6]

The signatures on this document were Lucianus, Dignus, Nasutius, Capitonius, Fidentius 'and other bishops'. Secundus' name did not appear, as Tigisi was not in Africa.

Anulinus forwarded this 'Appeal' together with the 'Charge' to Constantine, with a covering despatch which seems to suggest that even if Majorinus' party had right on their side, they would not receive justice: he at least had prejudged the case, but intended to do his duty, even though it apparently involved taking seriously the contentions of a gang of trouble-makers. He had, he wrote, just completed the necessary arrangements for the protection of Caecilian and the granting of immunities to his clergy in accordance with Constantine's instructions, when 'a few days later, some people arrived, bringing a mob with them', and offered him the enclosed sealed packet and open letter, to be forwarded to the emperor. He had accepted them, but declined to take any further action on his own initiative, telling the emperor, 'Caecilian continues to hold his present office.'[7] As far as Anulinus could see, there was nothing in what the petitioners had to say which would have justified his suspending Caecilian. He would continue to treat him as the loyal servant recent imperial favours had indicated him to be, until other instructions arrived in Africa.

By the time that this letter and its enclosures had reached Constantine in Gaul, and he had acted on it, Majorinus was dead. On his death, a synod was immediately called in Africa to elect his successor. When it met, the claims of Caecilian to be the true bishop of Carthage were once more pressed on the bishops, but Secundus of Tigisi was still in the city, and he and his Numidians persuaded the assembly to endorse their choice, a priest named Donatus from Casae Nigrae, and, according to all reports, a fitting representative of a haughty aristocracy, a man who 'believed himself superior to all other men', one 'out to conquer all Africa'.

No sort of accusation against a recently-appointed official made by persons of good standing could be simply ignored. Whatever Constantine thought of the points made in the sealed 'Charge of the Catholic Church concerning the crimes of Caecilian', he felt bound to act on them. He accepted the suggestion made in the 'Appeal' that Gallic bishops should be appointed to hear the case, naming three to form a board of assessors under the presidency of another Christian leader to whom he had recently given signal honours, Militiades of Rome. The choice of Militiades showed how well Constantine and his advisers understood the difficulties of the Christians following the persecution. Having lived at Rome during the terror, and seen for himself the riots following the appointments of Popes Marcellus and Eusebius, he was less ignorant of the baleful effects of persecution on the psychology of its survivors than the Gauls might have been. Constantine wrote to Militiades, warning him to expect the arrival in Rome of Bishops Reticus of Autun, Maternus of Cologne and Marinus of Arles, who would sit with him 'and Mark' (otherwise unknown), in the case of Caecilian of Carthage. The African authorities, the emperor said, had already been instructed to send Caecilian to Rome, together with ten of his supporters, and ten of his accusers. Militiades would study the documents in the case, copies of which were appended, and then 'Your Reverence will decide how the above-mentioned case may be most fully examined and justly resolved, since Your Diligence must be aware that from my great respect for the legal Catholic Church, I wish you to leave no possible division or discord anywhere'[8].

As Militiades could easily discover (even if the documents did not reveal the fact to him) that Constantine, although aware that Caecilian had enemies, had nonetheless exclusively subsidized his 'Catholic Church', these instructions could hardly have been much more explicit without actually spelling out for him the judgement he was expected to reach. He duly reached it, although not without first having put on a show of independence. Taking advantage of the freedom of procedure granted to him by his letter of commission, he enlarged the committee of five into a local synod, by inviting fifteen Italian bishops to join the Gauls, Mark and himself in their deliberations.

The commission heard the evidence on October 2–4, 313, at Fausta's former palace of the Lateran, Donatus appearing in place of the dead Majorinus as chief plaintiff[9]. When the hearing was over, Militiades wrote to his master that, Caecilian's orthodoxy not being in question, 'no accusation having been made against him by those who came with Donatus' in respect of it, and the accusations that had been made having proved groundless, he should be retained in office. The Synod of Rome condemned Donatus, on his own admission that he had rebaptized those members of Caecilian's church who had wanted to join his congregation, but did not condemn the other members of his party, even those who were in fact ruling schismatically, claiming sees already occupied by members of Caecilian's church. It merely ordered that where there were now two bishops (except at Carthage), the one first consecrated should continue to rule; if he died before the second appointee, the second should then reign; after they were both dead, a fresh election should be held. Nothing should be done tending to perpetuate the divisions among Christians. Constantine wanted peace, even at the expense of theological exactitude, and this remained his attitude to quarrels among Christians throughout his reign. At this first synod held under imperial auspices, Militiades tried to obtain it for him, but failed. His judgement, although apparently equitable, meant that Donatus would have to resign any claim to the see of Carthage, at least during Caecilian's lifetime. This he was unwilling to do. He led his party in an appeal from the synodal verdict to Constantine himself—exactly as he might have done if the case had been heard in an ordinary provincial court. The grounds of the appeal was that injustice had been done because the Gauls had been drowned in a sea of Italians and 'not all the case had been heard: the bishops shut themselves away somewhere, and passed the judgement that suited them'[10]. As soon as the Donatists had discovered that they were not to be heard by a purely Gallic court, they had realized they would receive not justice but condemnation. However, their new appeal was granted a hearing, Constantine demonstrating how important the matter was to him by indicating that he would consider it himself, although the president of the new court would be Bishop Marinus of Arles, sitting in his own see city.

Eusebius has preserved the imperial summons to one of the chosen assessors at this Council of Arles, Chrestus, the Bishop of Syracuse. In it, after briefly outlining the course of events so far —and, incidentally, representing the Donatists as disaffected people who were persisting in keeping the affair alive although it had been 'thoroughly examined and finally settled', so that Chrestus knew before even he left Syracuse whose side the emperor was on—it continued:

> therefore, in as much as we have commanded numerous bishops from many parts to assemble at Arles before August 1, we have decided to write to you also. Be so good, therefore, as to obtain an official carriage from my Corrector in Sicily, the Illustrious Latronian . . . and present yourself by the appointed day at the place aforesaid . . .[11]

Chrestus was permitted to take with him two presbyters and three servants at public expense. Constantine wanted the support of the bishops; he knew that they were mostly poor men, not yet very sophisticated or spoiled by being made much of, so he put on a display for them. He was to do the same again at Nicaea, in 325. On neither occasion were his efforts wasted.

While his letters were on their way to bishops like Chrestus, the emperor also wrote to Aelius Paulinus, his new Vicar in Africa, asking him for a report on the case of Felix of Aptunga and his activities during the persecution. Paulinus passed the question on to the Proconsul of Africa, and thanks to the efficiency of the public records office, although there had been four violent changes of regime in the province during the intervening years, one of the two men who had acted as magistrates at Aptunga during the year 303, and had demanded the surrender of the Christian scriptures there, a man named Aelfius Caecilianus, was traced and, on August 19, brought to the Proconsul's court[12]. Not surprisingly, the documents relating to the seizure of the scriptures at Aptunga had disappeared, but Aelfius Caecilianus had little difficulty in remembering the details of what was probably the most important event of his year of office. He maintained that he and his fellow-magistrate had burned the scriptures, the episcopal throne, 'the letters', and the doors of the church at Aptunga, in accordance with the imperial edict, but that Felix had played no part in their destruction. The scriptures had been peacefully surrendered to him, but not by the bishop. 'We sent to the house of this same bishop Felix,' he said, 'but the town officials reported that he was away.'

So far, the enquiry in Africa was producing precisely the kind of evidence required to support the hearing at Arles, opened just nineteen days earlier under Bishop Marinus and in the presence of Constantine himself, Caecilian and Donatus, and their leading supporters. The arguments at Arles were bitter, but the conclusion reached there was what everyone must have expected. Donatus was condemned again. Unlike the members of the Roman synod, however, the bishops did not leave matters there. They went on to approve a set of disciplinary canons designed to unify the practice of the church throughout Constantine's empire. From the fact that these canons were closely modelled on the series elaborated at the Spanish Synod of Elvira in about the year 300, which had been attended by Hosius, but were noticeably less severe and puritanical, it would appear that an attempt was being made to establish norms of Christian discipline undistorted by persecution: at Arles, the standards of unpersecuted Spain were modified for general use in the cool atmosphere of unpersecuted Gaul, to guide the church into normal life in an empire ruled by Blessed Tranquillity. So, for instance, the first canon of Arles dealt not with contemporary controversy, but with the ancient question of the date of Easter. The bishops could not, however, totally ignore the problems stemming from persecution. They defined *traditores* as 'those who had handed over the scriptures, or the Dominical vessels, or the names of their brethren' to the imperial officers, and condemned them to be 'cut out from the clergy'. Going right back to the questions raised by the first purge of the army under Galerius in 298, they denied that Christians had the right of conscientious objection to military service in peace-time (they could envisage circumstances in which a man might be forgiven for throwing away his arms in war). More significantly in the context of the argument with Donatus, they rejected the decision of a Synod of Carthage held under Cyprian more than sixty years earlier, that the lapsed were to be rebaptized when they were readmitted to the church[13]. In the Western theology of Constantine's new men, untried by persecution, there was only one church, to which baptism admitted a convert eternally: all dissensions were quarrels within the church, just as all wars within the frontiers of the monolithic empire were civil wars. The Donatists could not agree. Like Cyprian before him, Donatus had rebaptized lapsed persons and heretics applying to join his 'Church of the Martyrs'. To him and his supporters, it seemed that their opponents were selling out to the world—an impression which can only have been confirmed by the synod's ruling that a Christian given public office should not be excommunicated merely because, when he accepted it, he made the pagan sacrifices traditionally required of those holding it (a ruling which, in effect, emptied the sacrifices of all meaning and hastened their decay, while opening the top posts in the state to Constantine's new men).

After Donatus' condemnation at Arles, the trouble ought to have been at an end, but he was not beaten yet. At Carthage, his counsel at the Proconsul's enquiry, one Maximus, suddenly produced new evidence which re-opened the whole question of Felix's role at Aptunga in 303. It took the form of a letter, which a scribe named Ingentius would swear to having written to Felix at Aelfius Caecilianus' dictation, quoting Felix as having said at the time of the inquisition at Aptunga, 'Take away the key and the scrolls on the throne, and the books on the stone ...' —which, of course, made Felix a *traditor* of the worst kind, one who had helped the magistrates, without apparently even having first been threatened with torture.

This part of the letter, quoting Felix, was a forgery, but because other parts of it were genuine, it took six months to obtain the facts. The enquiry re-opened at Carthage on February 15, 315, before the new Proconsul, Aelianus. The scribe Ingentius had been found, and was submitted to close questioning. The story he told showed Felix in a very bad light, but was too unlikely not to be true. According to him, he had a grudge against Felix for denouncing a friend of his, now masquerading as a rigorist member of Donatus' party, as a *traditor* during the persecution, so when an opportunity had arisen of doing Felix an injury, he had taken it. Felix was not the complete innocent that Caecilian's party claimed. He had sold some precious copies of the scriptures entrusted to his care by a third party, who now wanted them back, and to save himself from denunciation as a thief had written to the former magistrate Aelfius Caecilianus, asking him to certify that these books had been destroyed with the others at Aptunga in 303. Aelfius had been horrified by this suggestion, and had dictated a letter to Ingentius for transmission to Felix reminding him of what exactly had happened during the persecution. To revenge his friend, Ingentius had added to this letter the lines making Felix appear the worst of *traditores*.

Surrender of the scriptures was the only charge against Felix. As he had not been denounced for theft by the owner of the missing books, the Proconsul cleared him of suspicion, committed Ingentius to prison as a material witness, and wrote to Constantine, telling him the facts as he had established them. Shortly afterwards, his term of office ended, and it was to his successor, Probianus, that Constantine addressed an order commanding that the wretched scribe should be sent to his court, so that the whole question could be thrashed out once more, to silence those 'who are continually appealing, day after day'[14]. Actually, it was Donatus, the only man condemned outright at both Rome and Arles, who had appealed again to the emperor. Constantine informed the bishops of this new elaboration of the plot in a letter which seems to mark a development in his personal religion, and might be regarded as his own commentary on the panegyrist's assertion that he had received a personal revelation making him specially fit to rule. In this letter, after remarking generally on the mercy of 'our God', who lets no one wander long in 'darkness' and will not permit the 'evil desires' of the few to prevail for long, he continues:

> I draw this same conclusion from my own case. For at the outset, there was much in me that seemed lacking in righteousness, and I did not believe that there was any power above who could see into the secret recesses of my heart, and the thoughts nurtured there . . . But God Almighty, enthroned in heaven, has granted me what I did not deserve: blessings innumerable . . .

He then goes on to tell the bishops that, acting 'like a pagan' (adopting the bishops' own usage, he is already thinking of a worshipper of the gods of the state as his enemy), Donatus has just avoided their proceedings at Arles of juridical significance by appealing from them to himself, as from a lower court to a higher: there is nothing that he can do but send them home, and attend to the matter personally, when he can find the time, after the Vicarius in Africa has sent him details of all the latest evidence[15].

One of the most interesting points about this letter is that Constantine's words imply that before 'our God' made himself known to him, he had been an atheist, or at best a follower of those philosophers who thought the Supreme God too remote from the world to be interested in human morality. He does not admit that just before the vision which was one of the most imperative of those blessings to force faith on him, he was seeking for a personal god in whom to believe, although later in life he made much of his uneasiness just before the Italian campaign. Writing to the bishops, he is more concerned to present himself as a former sinner, converted by undeserved benefactions, than as a wretched seeker who ultimately found what he sought. There is an unpleasant flavour of hypocrisy here.

Donatus' direct appeal to the emperor, although no doubt very annoying, could not legally be ignored, but its hearing could be delayed during Constantine's pleasure. In fact, Donatus, together with his supporters, was kept in prison until the celebration of Constantine's *decennalia* at Rome in July 315.

Then he was released, but refused permission to leave the City until Caecilian had presented himself once more at court for what must, under the law, be the final review of the evidence. Constantine told him that if, face to face with Caecilian, he could prove just one point against him, the court would accept that any charges he liked to make were true. The emperor's temper was wearing dangerously thin. It snapped when, on the day fixed for the hearing, Caecilian did not appear. The case was held over until October, at Milan, when at last all the witnesses were brought together. Constantine now made it quite clear that he had no more time for Carthaginian affairs, by ordering that both Caecilian and Donatus should be interned at Brescia, while two of his loyal bishop-bureaucrats, Eunomius and Olympius, went to Africa, solved the problems of the church there, and oversaw a fresh election to provide an acceptable substitute for both pretenders to the see[10].

From the Christian point of view, this solution to the problem was wholly unacceptable. Everyone knew—although Constantine's episcopal courtiers were obviously willing to overlook the fact—that a true bishop held office for life, or until his teaching could be proved unorthodox. Bishops might serve the state, but they were not mere civil servants, to be reproved and replaced if their service appeared unsatisfactory. Militiades' synod had been at pains to point out that Caecilian's orthodoxy was not in question: if he were the true bishop of Carthage, he could not be deposed. For similar reasons, the Donatists could accept no one but Donatus as the bishop of that see. Eunomius' and Olympius' mission was doomed before it began. The people of Lucilla's class, who were backing Donatus against Constantine's lackeys, would certainly not accept a solution imposed by envoys from the court, even if they were indubitably bishops. The poor, who had been encouraged by Constantine's support for 'their' bishop Caecilian, could not understand why he was not allowed to return to them. There were riots at Carthage, before Eunomius and Olympius had finished their work there. In their report, the two bishops recommended a return to Constantine's earlier policy of unqualified support for Caecilian: 'The sentence formerly handed down by the twenty-nine bishops [of Militiades' synod, presumably, although only twenty are known to have attended it] cannot be overturned.'[17]

Meanwhile, however, Donatus had escaped from what was manifestly a somewhat lax internment at Brescia, and Caecilian had been released to make his way back to Africa. Constantine's anger rarely lasted long. If one could survive its first outburst, one could rely on his losing interest in one's fate as soon as another matter caught his attention.

With Caecilian and Donatus both free, by February 316 only four Donatist bishops and one priest remained under guard, being dragged as material witnesses from prison to prison in the wake of the peripatetic court. On the 26th of that month, they too were released, perhaps under a birthday amnesty, and an order was signed at Trier commanding their conveyance back to Africa at public expense. Constantine had a new idea for the final solution of the problems of Africa. He wrote to Domitius Celsus, his current Vicarius there, informing him that he planned an official visit to the diocese, personally 'to make plain . . . what kind of worship is to be offered to the divinity'[18]. His irritation at the unreliability of his chosen ministers and the obstinacy of controversialists was driving him ever closer to the opinion that he was intended to rule the church himself: 'I shall unhesitatingly,' he wrote, 'cause those I judge hostile to the divine law . . . to pay the penalty.' He demanded a report on the riots sparked off by Eunomius and Olympius and ordered that no further measures should be taken against the Donatists until he had studied conditions in Africa for himself. In fact, in 316 he went no further south than Milan, and did not visit Africa in that or any other year, although later he built two basilicas for the church at Cirta, graciously accepting the compliment when, in gratitude for these and other gifts, the city changed its name to Constantine.

That autumn, he once more reviewed the whole body of evidence in the case against Caecilian, and came back to the viewpoint from which he had started and to which his two-man episcopalcommission had been driven by the violence of Donatist

The triumph of Constantine at the Battle of Milvian Bridge, by Piero della Francesca. The first 'crusade' as reconstructed by the imagination of a renascence romantic

Coin-portraits of (*l. to r. top*) Constantine (306-337) and Helena (Augusta, *c.* 327-330); and of (*l. to r. bottom*) Fausta (Augusta, 307-326) and the Caesar Crispus (317-326)

Photos: British Museum

opposition to imposed solutions: Caecilian was his man, and no crime having been proven against him, he deserved continued support. For a short time, angered by Caecilian's ineptitude, distracted by political events, and perhaps anxious not totally to alienate powerful families in Africa during the period of his confrontation with Licinius, he had vacillated; but it is difficult to see how his deliberations could have reached any other final conclusion without shaking to its foundations the confidence of his true allies among the Christians, the moderates, such as Hosius, to whom the opportunities offered to the church for expansion and influence through association with imperial policies seemed valuable enough to outweigh the disadvantage of having ecclesiastical affairs continually under imperial scrutiny. In a letter addressed to Eumelius, the Vicar of Africa in 316, dated November 10, he once again set out the details of the case before expressing his final judgement, against which there could be no appeal in law:

> It seems clear to me that Caecilian is a wholly innocent man, who observes all the duties of his religion and serves it fittingly. It is quite clear to me that no one has been able to demonstrate any fault in his behaviour, despite the accusations brought against him in his absence by the lying hypocrisy of his adversaries[19].

This verdict left Donatus condemned as a troublemaker; Constantine threatened him, but he was not arrested. It also voided of effect the compromise over who should occupy the various sees of Africa and Numidia propounded by Militiades' court in 313. Donatus' faction having been condemned, Donatist congregations had no standing as corporations under the law, and the fine churches build by the munificence of their aristocratic benefactors to replace those destroyed during the persecution or to serve their rapidly growing congregations in newly converted areas were reckoned to belong to dissident criminals. No general persecution of the Donatists began at this time, but on March 12, 317, the army moved in to occupy the three Donatist basilicas at Carthage itself[20]. This development, which proved disastrous in the long run for the cause of Blessed

Tranquillity in Africa, was probably instigated by members of Caecilian's party, to whom the existence of Donatist churches in their leader's own city must have been a continual affront. The Donatist leaders had somehow received prior warning of the army's movements, and the three churches were vigorously defended by their congregations. It was only at the cost of a massacre of men, women and children that the buildings were taken and handed over to Caecilian's Catholic Church. When the noise of that day's fighting died away, an uneasy peace settled over Africa. It lasted for three years, punctuated only by angry murmurings which found their loudest voice in a flood of pamphlets and libellous accusations, denunciations and threats. Edicts dated March 29, 319[21] and December 4, 320[22] proposed draconian punishments for their authors, but without effect. Perhaps because the Donatist cause was tinged with nationalism, or perhaps because its adherents, being fanatics for their faith, were better preachers than Caecilian's clergy, they made more converts from among the pagan masses than their opponents, so that both the number and the size of their congregations continually increased. What the Catholic (but still unbaptised) emperor thought of this development is not recorded. Apart from his edicts against the pamphleteers, he seems to have made no statement, official or unofficial, relating to the Donatists from 316 to 320, when a document which can only have been a daring forgery came to light, offering 'proof' that not only Donatus, but Secundus of Tigisi and several other leading Donatists had themselves been *traditores*, and that one of their earliest supporters, Bishop Purpurius of Limiata – who had once declared that he would like to smash Caecilian's skull – was a self-confessed murderer.

This document, purporting to be the minutes of an episcopal synod held at Cirta in 304 or 305 under the presidency of Secundus of Tigisi, was offered in evidence at the trial before Zenophilus, the Consular of Numidia, on December 13, 320, of Silvanus, the Donatist Bishop of Cirta, one of the consecrators of Donatus' predecessor Majorinus, and so one of the 'elders' among the schismatics[23]. Silvanus had quarrelled with a deacon named Nundinarius, and in a moment of spite Nundinarius had accused him of having been a *traditor* in the days of the persecution, and of theft and sodomy. In those days, the bishop had been only an insignificant subdeacon. The Consular Zenophilus was perhaps not greatly interested in whether Silvanus had been a *traditor* or not, but the accusation of theft was a grave one. All the charges were probably trumped-up, and there may have been collusion between the Consular and the Catholics, who were certainly dismayed by Donatist successes and were planning counter-moves, as is proved by the consequences of Silvanus' trial, if not by the fact of the trial itself. Zenophilus found the bishop guilty on all counts, and exiled him. This sentence, and the forged minutes of the Synod of Cirta, are said to have done much to discredit the Donatist cause among the Africans. But they did more than that. They proved to Constantine's satisfaction that he had been right all along to back the Catholics against them. To him, these latest revelations were a clear demonstration that the founders of the sect were liars and hypocrites, just as he had said in his judgement in favour of Caecilian. It was time that he used against them the powers of coercion granted to him by God. In an edict and letters which have not been preserved, he ordered all Donatist bishops into exile, and the confiscation of their churches and other property.

This action was bitter proof to the Donatists and their backers that they for their part had been right constantly to withstand the imperial will. All emperors were by nature persecutors – this one, who claimed to be a Christian, no less than the rest. They denounced a last appeal for unity, issued in 321, and prepared to resist the order sequestering their churches, attributing it to their arch-enemy, the courtier-bishop Hosius, who had first singled out Caecilian as the fitting recipient of imperial favour, and so begun the process of the enslavement of the African church and the attenuation of its faith. As imperial troops moved from place to place, arresting Donatist bishops and expelling them from their churches, African Christians suffered and died, as their predecessors had suffered and died in every persecution from the beginning of the African church, absolutely convinced of the rightness of their cause. They had always claimed that their church was 'the Church of the Martyrs', priding themselves on their loyalty to leaders who had faced death rather than surrender anything to an arbitrary government. Now the piecemeal annihilation of their congregations achieved nothing but the hardening of their resistance. Donatists killed in the struggle for the possession of their churches became Christian martyrs and National heroes. After the massacres of spring 321, the Donatist church became the chief rallying-point of all resistance in Africa. There can be little doubt that Constantine ordered this military action in a fit of anger such as he had often displayed in the past, and was to show with increasing frequency over the next few years. Within three months, he had regretted his order, and accepted with relief an appeal from the Donatists for clemency, immediately taking steps to mitigate the evil effects of his displeasure, by signing an order rescinding the edict and permitting the exiled to return to their homes.

The Donatists showed no gratitude, but promptly claimed that they had won a victory. This naturally offended the Catholics, and soon Constantine had to bend himself to the task of smoothing their feathers, reminding them in a letter that it was for God to judge who was right and who wrong, and telling them that, if the Donatists ill-used them, they must endure it patiently, for he himself could do nothing more for them[24].

He has often been criticized for ineptitude in handling the Donatist affair, but it is difficult to see how he could more effectively have met the threat to the unity of his empire represented by their movement, without totally disowning and betraying Caecilian's loyal Catholics. Painfully impaled on the horns of a dilemma as he was, it is not surprising that his views about the role he ought to play in African affairs changed from year to year. One moment he saw himself as, in his own words, 'God's servant', his Praetorian Prefect on earth, empowered to judge causes and execute his own sentences. The next, he was a helpless worm, going in fear of being divinely crushed.

It was the divinely-inspired Prophet of God who, writing to the Vicarius of Africa to command the attendance of Caecilian and his opponents at the Synod of Arles, two years after annihilating the enemy of truth at Milvian Bridge declared, 'I think it is quite contrary to the law of God that we should take no account of such disputes and dissensions,' and the somewhat superstitious worm who could continue that sentence, 'for if we did, the Supreme God might be moved to anger, not only against humanity, but also against me personally', before remembering once more his role as God's regent and ending, 'to whose care he has by his heavenly will committed the government of all terrestrial affairs'.

But was it the regent or the worm who in 322 piously told the Catholics that suffering would be good for them? It sounds like the weary suggestion of a man thoroughly bored with the whole question at issue. By that time, he was deeply involved in other, apparently more pressing matters, but his failure to pursue the Donatist question to the end cost his successors dear.

The controversy in Africa was damaging to the unity of the empire and the persecution there ought to have proved disastrous for Constantine's reputation. However, although the monolithic unity of the empire that he was then still building was threatened by this crack in the fabric of the church, it was powerfully reinforced by Constantine's unconscious answer to the question lying at the heart of the controversy: What is a Catholic Christian?

The Christian answer was that a Catholic was one whose doctrines and practice were those of the whole church throughout its history, one who was in communion with bishops throughout the Christian world. Constantine's practical answer, never defined in words, but revealed time and again in his attitude to Bishop Caecilian, was that a Catholic Christian was one loyal to his emperor's concept of the universal empire. By it, without perhaps knowing that he had done so, he had elaborated the theory of caesaro-papism, and imposed it on the church. Centuries later, Western Christianity was to break free of it by asserting the universal sovereignty of the pope, but for the meantime, Constantine had defined the Catholic Church as the church supported by the state, and had made the 'catholic' (that is 'universal') bishops into superior civil servants. Later emperors were to claim that episcopal power derived from God through the throne. It has sometimes been said that Constantine worked this revolution cynically, claiming to be a Christian so that he could use the flattered bishops to forward his own ambition. His own piety, was, however, not cynical, but a very genuine and potent compound of superstition, fear of the wrath of God and the fanaticism of the 'twice-born' convert. If he made use of the bishops, it was because his own vocation, by which he believed God had committed to him 'the government of all terrestrial affairs', demanded of him that he should make efficient use of all the resources of the state. There can be no doubt that he thought he was honouring the bishops, not abusing them, when in 318 he signed an edict making them civil magistrates and permitting the transfer of cases to their courts, as superior to those already existing[25]. By that time, his policies were proving, if anything, too successful, and the church was recognized as a high road to promotion in the empire. Even the Jews were worried by the number of converts from their ranks, and their uneasiness translated itself into occasional acts of violence against any of their people who became Christians – or so it would appear from an edict signed in 319, threatening any Jew who 'stoned a convert to God' with death by burning[26]. The privileges given to Christian priests and the favours showered upon them led to a rush of applications for ordination of such frightening dimensions that action had to be taken lest the civil administration and the corps of officers should be left understaffed and the number of taxpayers drop below a level dangerous to the economy. In 320, an edict was promulgated forbidding the admission to the ranks of the clergy of anyone qualified for curial service in his city, unless imperial sanction for his ordination had first been obtained[27]. If wholly effective, this law should have both ensured that the majority of those ordained were poor men who, if ambitious, would eagerly adapt themselves to the imperial system for the sake of self-advancement, and facilitated imperial screening of candidates from the upper classes, so making it possible to prevent the kind of situation which had produced Donatism in Africa from arising again. However, it was not wholly effective, and it came too late. A situation somewhat similar to that in Proconsular Africa had already arisen in Egypt and was waiting, like a time-bomb, to explode under Constantine when he came to power there. Fortunately for his peace of mind, although he sometimes grew bored with individual bishops, he seems actually to have enjoyed theological debate. He was to be involved in many hundreds of hours of it in the years of life remaining to him.

CHAPTER NINE

THE VICTOR

THE year 317, when Licinius named his son Licinianus Caesar in the East, while Constantine made Caesars of Crispus and Constantinus in the West, was the high water mark in the flow of relations between them[1]. Their friendship had never run very deep. Two years earlier, they had shared the consulship for the last time – for each of them, it was his fourth term of office – and although for the next two years they bowed to tradition by each accepting the office with the other's Caesar, the tide had already turned.

For the years 315 to 319, the table of consuls reads:

315: Constantine Augustus IV; Licinius Augustus IV

316: Sabinus and Rufinus

317: Gallicanus and Septimus Bassus

318: Licinius Augustus V; Flavius Julius Crispus Caesar I

319: Constantine Augustus V; Licinianus Caesar I

but in 320, as the first public indication of troubles to come, the names announced were:

Constantine Augustus VI; Constantinus Caesar I

and in 321: Crispus Caesar II; Constantinus Caesar II.

By Galerius' appointment, and under the terms of the old Jovian-Herculian dynastic law, unilaterally abrogated by Constantine, Licinius was the Senior Augustus. By the vote of the Senate, however, taken under duress in 312 at the peremptory demand (however mildly expressed) of a conquering general, Constantine was the Augustus Maximus. While the two emperors agreed to share the world between them, in the period after they had composed their differences in 314, it was, perhaps, only of legalistic significance which of them claimed seniority. Once tensions had reappeared, however, the naming of Constantine for the sixth time in 320, out of turn, must have been a matter of concern to Licinius, and the naming of Crispus and Constantinus for the second time in January 321 was an open slight to Licinianus, and a direct challenge to himself – as he showed he realized by refusing to permit publication of their names in his dioceses, so that the year had no official name there. In 322, when the Senate, with Constantine's approval, named as consuls two of its own aristocratic pagan members, Petronius Probianus (who was to be Constantine's City Prefect from 329 to 331) and his cousin Anicius Julianus (City Prefect from 326 to 329), Licinius nominated himself consul for the sixth time and Licinianus consul for the second, without reference to the senators. The following year, 323, Constantine again approved the names of two Romans, Aelius Severus and Vettius Rufinus, and Licinius again ignored them. The consuls for 324 were Crispus and Constantine II, both for the third time. By the end of the year, they were universally recognized, for the empire of Licinius was no more.

The gradual worsening of relations between East and West was reflected elsewhere than in the table of consuls. As early as 314–5, Constantine had moved the seat of his administration from the old Herculian capitals of Trier and Milan to Sirmium in Western Pannonia. By 317–8, he had transferred it still further eastwards, to Serdica, the modern Sofia in Bulgaria, where in a short time his architects had completed a grandiose enlargement of Galerius' palace, so that for size and majesty it rivalled the great palace of Diocletian at Spalato. Soon he was saying, by his actions if not actually in the words attributed to him by an unknown author, 'Serdica is my Rome'[2]. His prolonged residence there was both an insult to the old Rome and a challenge to Licinius. The choice of Sirmium as a permanent capital could have been justified on several counts: it was well served by roads, and was equally convenient for the administration of the Rhine and the Danube, Italy and Africa. Serdica, on the other hand, was undeniably inconvenient for controlling the only active trouble-spots of the time, Africa and the Rhine Frontier, but manifestly well-placed for surveillance of Licinius' European provinces – districts which had been ruled by Galerius when he had made the city one of his chosen residences. For Constantine to settle there was an overtly provocative move.

Both Eusebius' *History* and the *Life of Constantine* claim that it was the hardening of Licinius' attitude towards the Christians which made Constantine his enemy[3]. Licinius, they claim, was struck with the self-same madness which had affected Maximin Daia before him, and as a madman, possessed by devils, he had to be destroyed by God's champion, the New Moses, Constantine. In this view, Licinius brought destruction on himself. In fact, however, it was Constantine who provoked war. He had decided to unite the empire under himself by eliminating the Eastern Augustus, and Licinius' growing dislike for the Christians was simply one of the justifications for war found by Constantine's propaganda machine: it is impossible to free Constantine wholly of the burden of blame, as the *Life of Constantine* tried to do, with the claim that Licinius was an intolerably unreliable neighbour, 'pretending friendship one moment, claiming the protection of solemn treaties the next, then suddenly violating every agreement, only to beg forgiveness again through envoys, before finally breaking his word shamefully, declaring open war . . .'

There was, however, a difference between the two emperors' attitudes towards the church. Even while Constantine was growing bored to the point of irritable persecution with the Donatist-Catholic conflict in Africa, he continued to promote the welfare of those Christians in his empire willing to fall in with his plans for the church. The acid test was, however, loyalty to himself rather than religious orthodoxy. He did not persecute loyal pagans. He did persecute rebellious Christians. His only measures against paganism in the decade 312–322 were a law of 318, forbidding the making of magic to charm away the life or chastity of a neighbour[4], and laws of 319 and 320, repeating the substance of former edicts against private divination, on the age-old judicial assumption that what is secret is suspect[5]. In fact, the law of 318 expressly permitted spell-making to cure sickness and the law of 320 emphasized that only private divination was prohibited: 'Go to the public altars! . . . We do not forbid the performance in daylight of ceremonies hitherto practised;' while a related law of the same year confirmed the traditional role of soothsayers in elucidating the omen if 'any part of our palace or some other public building has been struck by lightning', and permitted private persons also to consult them if similarly afflicted from the skies. The edicts condoning, while seeking to control, pagan and magical practice were, however, a minuscule corpus compared with the significant body of legislation apparently influenced by Christian sentiment. Following the edicts of toleration, as early as 316, Constantine forbade the branding of convicts on the face 'which is formed in the image of heavenly beauty'[6]. In 318, he gave the bishops their role as magistrates[7]. The following year, he forbade masters to kill their slaves for any offence[8]. In 320, he abrogated the law, going back to Augustus, prohibiting celibacy and laying disabilities on childless couples[9], and approved a law designed to protect prisoners against brutality[10]. Except for the edicts of toleration, and that regarding the bishops, none of these laws can actually be shown to have Christian inspiration, but the presumption must be that they had. The same is true of the most famous edicts in this group, the two relating to Sunday observance, dated March 7 and July 3, 321, both of which scrupulously avoid mentioning Christ:

> All magistrates, city-dwellers and artisans are to rest on the venerable day of the sun (*venerabilis dies solis*) But country-dwellers may without hindrance apply themselves to agriculture . . .[11]

and

> Just as we thought that the day celebrated by the veneration of the sun should not be devoted to the swearing and counter-swearing of litigants, and their ceaseless brawling, so it is a pleasing and joyful thing to fulfil specially urgent petitions on this day. Therefore, let all be permitted to perform manumission and emancipation [of slaves] on this day, and let nothing pertaining to this be prohibited[12].

The question of whether or not these laws are Christian has been exhaustively debated. They would be equally pleasing to

Christians like Hosius and worshippers of the sun like Aradius Rufinus, without giving any particular offence to more traditional pagans. Hosius and his friends may well have been pressing at this time for more definite pro-Christian statements from the emperor. Despite the generous start marked by the Edict of Milan and the executive instructions associated with it, and imperial patronage of the Synod of Arles, Constantine was still unwilling either to be baptized himself or forcibly to christianize the empire. Although he was openly scornful about the value of pagan worship – the law of 319 against private divination sneers at continuing pagans, characterizing them as 'you who believe that it will benefit you' to worship the gods – he still feared the power of pagan magic.

Meanwhile, on the other side of the Thracian frontier, Licinius was having difficulties with his Christian subjects. Like Constantine's troubles in Africa, his also grew out of the Great Persecution, and ultimately drove him to become a persecutor. Unlike Constantine, however, he was basically uninterested in the problem of religion, and had not bound any party among the Christians to himself by special favours, although Eusebius, the Bishop of Nicomedia, had a place at his court, and tried to influence him as the bishops of the West influenced Constantine. Two schisms in the church in Egypt, those of Meletius and Arius,* seem to have convinced him that the Christians were a danger to his empire. At the beginning of his reign in the East, he allowed them complete freedom of worship and association, under the terms of the policy agreed at Milan; but free synods, such as were held at Ancyra in 314 and Neo-Caesarea a little later, soon became focuses of unrest, and about the year 320 he promulgated a law, which has not survived, prohibiting them, much to the consternation of the Christians, to whom they had become essential as the occasions for the election of new bishops to replace those who had died or been deposed for heresy. According to Eusebius, in whose works alone Licinius' drift towards persecution is reported in any detail, his next anti-Christian move was the expulsion of bishops and priests from his

* See Chapters Ten and Thirteen.

service; but he probably dismissed only known troublemakers, for Eusebius of Nicomedia continued to work in and about the palace, under the protection of the Empress Constantia, and even held a synod at Licinius' capital, to determine the policy to be adopted towards Arius' teaching by the churches of Asia Minor and the County of the East. His next step was to publish a second edict, ostensibily aimed at suppressing immorality at Christian meetings, but really (if it ever existed) intended to disrupt them altogether. 'Being himself of a nature hopelessly debased by sensuality,' the *Life of Constantine* records, 'he . . . denied that the virtues of chastity and continence exist among men. Accordingly, he passed a second law, ordering that men and women should not attend houses of prayer together, and forbidding women to attend the sacred schools of virtue, or receive instruction from the bishops, directing that women should be appointed to instruct those of their sex'[13]. Next, 'he ordered that the usual congregations of the people should be held outside the gates, in the open country'. By this time, Constantine was arming, and there was little time for persecution to become more intense, although some bishops were arrested and tortured, before Licinius' empire was swept away.

It may well be that those arrested by Licinius' orders were suspected of Constantinean sympathies and defeatism, or even of treasonable correspondence with the enemy. In a roundabout way, the *History* admits as much, reporting that churches were demolished and bishops arrested 'because he would not believe that prayers were offered for him . . . but convinced himself that we did everything and made our petitions to God only for the emperor whom God loved'[14]. If any bishop made it clear before or during the war that he believed that God cherished only Constantine, he deserved to be arrested. Licinius is known to have been afraid of Constantine's Christian magic. His laws against Christian assemblies are comparable to Constantine's against private consultation of the auspices. Both were inspired by superstitious fear.

Eusebius claims, then, that the war between Constantine and Licinius marked another stage in the confrontation between

Christianity and paganism. The *Life* describes Constantine as marching to battle behind his personal standard, the *labarum* with its religious motifs, and with priests as well as soldiers on his staff[15]. The battle-cry chosen for the Western armies was '*Deus summus Salvator!*', 'God, the Supreme Saviour'. God's champion used the *labarum* against Licinius, as he had used the monogram of Christ alone against Maxentius, because he had convinced himself that he had been promised victory if he did use it. It had become his totem, the invincible sign of his own unbreakable power. His faith in it was absolute. He knew by experience that its magic worked powerfully for him. To identify himself with it completely, he had his own portrait, and probably those of his Caesars, mounted on it, immediately below the *chi-rho* symbol itself. Just how superstitiously he regarded it is clear from the stories he told about its miraculous protectiveness at the Battle of Chrysopolis, on September 18, 323: how the soldier delegated to carry it lost his nerve, and thrusting his precious burden into the arms of the fifty-strong Labarum Guards around him, made off at a run, only to die within seconds with an enemy javelin in his belly, while, although the new standard-bearer

> was attacked with a continual rain of javelins, he remained unhurt, the staff of the standard itself taking all the weapon-points. It was a really remarkable sight: all the enemies' darts struck and remained within the thickness of the spear-shaft, so that the standard-bearer was saved from death.

Behind the scholar's words lies the old soldier's tale, related under oath, but nonetheless not spoiled in the telling: 'Not a man who did this job was ever wounded[16].'

Licinius, on the other hand, is said to have dedicated himself on the outbreak of war at a grove sacred to the gods, and received promises of victory from a specially recruited corps of 'Egyptian diviners and soothsayers, with sorcerers and wizards, and the priests and prophets of those he imagined to be gods'.

The speech which, in the manner of ancient historians, the author of the *Life* attributed to him on this occasion is interesting for the glimpse it gives of the pagan view (although seen, as it were, through Christian eyes) of the advance of Christianity:

> Friends and fellow soldiers! These [the statues in the grove] are the gods of our fatherland, and we venerate them with a form of worship handed down to us from our remotest ancestors. But he who leads the army now confronting us has shown himself false to the religion of his fathers, and, taking as his own the views of the atheists, has adopted some strange and hitherto unheard-of god, with whose despicable standard he now disgraces his army, and trusting in whose aid he has taken arms, not so much against us, as against the gods whom he has betrayed. However, the business on which we are about to embark will show which of us is wrong . . .[17]

But, was the war between Constantine and Licinius simply, or even chiefly, a war of religion? It seems unlikely. Although Constantine was convinced that he fought with the help of the Christians' God, there is no conclusive proof that he ever fought any war for religion's sake, except the brief but disastrous campaign against the Donatist Christians of Africa and Numidia. He belonged to the ancient world. Like all the kings of antiquity, he fought in his god's name, and carried his worship to all the lands he conquered. It was, however, not religion which inspired him to conquer, as religion inspired the successors of Mahomet to conquer. What drove him on to seize the whole empire was his belief in himself, his unique ability and consequent right and duty to rule.

The circumstances in which the war began suggest deliberate provocation on his part, forcing a declaration from his opponent, so that a war of aggression could be represented as an act of self-defence. To see the pattern unfolding, it is necessary to go back to the year 317, when Crispus was made Caesar. After the celebrations connected with that event were over, Constantine sent his son to Gaul, in nominal command of the Rhine frontier[18]. It was already being said that no good would come of the honours that he and Licinius had given to their sons, because the year was overshadowed by an eclipse of the sun, observed from Upper Egypt on December 31, 316, and so was inauspicious for the making of kings[19]. However, the first four years of Crispus' principipate were without untoward incident, and in fact, campaigning against the Franks in the winter of 320, he did well enough for the panegyrist Nazarius to be able credibly to acclaim him a hero in his father's image, a worthy Caesar 'filling his adolescent years with triumphant glories. For now already the Most Noble Caesar enjoys the respect of his father and all his brethren, and presents himself before us as deserving the admiration of all. In this last cruel winter, with its fierce frost, he marched with incredible speed over vast distances deep in snow' to win a signal victory. 'Is not thy breast filled with a sweet joy, O Supreme Constantine, melting to see thy son after so long a time – and to see him a conqueror?'[20]

Constantine recalled Crispus from the frontier to celebrate his fifth jubilee at Serdica on March 1, 321. Like his father and grandfather before him, he contracted an early liaison with a woman later judged unworthy of him. She was his grandmother's namesake; nothing is known about her except her name, Helena, and the fact that, in September or October 322, she bore him a child[21]. By then, he had been for some time back on the frontier, commanding the Rhine army in yet another campaign against the perennially restless Alemanni, but there appears to have been no hard fighting that year: like his father in 313, he was showing the Franks that the emperors were not so preoccupied as to have forgotten them. Already Constantine was deepening and enlarging the harbour at Thessalonika, in preparation to receive the fleet which was to sail from there to force the Hellespont in the final confrontation with Licinius.

A century earlier, the Roman fleet had consisted of ten squadrons worthy of comparison for efficiency and tenacity with the best units of the imperial army[22]. These ten squadrons had now shrunk to one major unit, the British fleet, guarding the northwest coasts of Europe from piratical attacks, and a number of small flotillas, each operating from, and protecting the approaches to, a single port. Constantine had succeeded in blockading the Tyrrhenian seaports during the war against Maxentius only by using every available boat, whether or not it had been designed for war. Now his agents scoured every harbour in the

West for bottoms capable of transporting troops and supplies, while Licinius' officers commandeered ships throughout the East. By chartering, seizing and building ships wherever he could, Constantine had assembled some 200 thirty-oared warships and 2,000 transports by the summer of 323, while Licinius' Duke of the Fleet, Abantus, commanded 350 of the larger and more dangerous triremes[23].

Meanwhile, an occasion of war had been found – so opportunely that Constantine has sometimes been accused of having prearranged it. In the autumn of 322, the barbarian King Rausimond of the Sarmatians led his tribe across the Danube into Dacia and Moesia, where they destroyed villages and farms, and took many prisoners for ransom or sale into slavery. Constantine marched north to intercept them. After a series of sharp engagements on Roman soil, the tribesmen were thrown back over the Danube, Rausimond was killed, and his men harried until they surrendered their prisoners and sued for peace. Constantine brought his troops back into the empire, and himself returned to Thessalonika, where he was building a palace as well as overseeing the new harbour-works. That apparently was that[24]. Crispus may have been recalled for this campaign (which would suggest that it was premeditated), for after it coins of both Augustus and his Caesar were struck with the inscription 'Sarmatia Subjugated', and Crispus, his military apprenticeship completed, was named Duke of the Fleet.

Constantine's critics through the ages have argued that this brief Sarmatian campaign was a cleverly disguised, pre-planned provocation, which went wrong when King Rausimond was killed. Pursuit of the Sarmatians had taken Constantine into Licinius' European provinces: the theory is that Constantine had promised the king rich pickings for leading him there. Constantine himself claimed that the incursion was accidental, and, even if it had not been, was justifiable, as it led to the rescue of citizens from barbarians. Licinius, already touchy on the subject of Constantine's intentions, rejected his explanations, maintaining that it had been a probing attack, a reconnaissance in strength, preparatory to a full-scale invasion. A few weeks later, he brought the bulk of his army to Hadrianopolis, his most westerly city, and waited there, to see what the Western emperor would do next.

In the course of the following months, Constantine massed an army of 120,000 infantry and 10,000 cavalry on the frontiers of Thrace, while his mint-masters struck propagandist coins, reminding all who used them of his illustrious and victorious forebears: Claudius II, Conqueror of the Goths; Constantius, Conqueror of the Franks and Britons; and Maximian Herculius, conqueror everywhere until Constantine had killed him[25]. Crispus sailed the war-fleet south from Thessalonika to rendezvous with the transports at the Piraeus. The army of the West crossed the Thracian frontier in the last week of June.

Licinius let the Westerners cross the Plains of Mardia unopposed. He had 150,000 infantry and 15,000 cavalry waiting for them in a strong defensive position commanding a steep hill-face, just outside Hadrianopolis. The armies met on July 3; it was a long, savage struggle, but Constantine's leadership, his men's better discipline, and the magical power of the *labarum* gradually wore the enemy down, although 34,000 of Licinius' soldiers were dead, and thousands more had deserted, before he ordered a general retreat. Despite Licinius' determination not to yield, he may actually have helped to defeat himself, for, according to the *Life of Constantine*, he was as superstitiously afraid of the *labarum* as Constantine was convinced of its quasi-magical powers of support, and he betrayed his fear to his men, in as much as 'he had warned his soldiers never to direct their attack at this standard, or even incautiously to look at it, for he believed it possessed a terrible power, and was specially hostile towards himself'[26]. A general convinced that his enemy has a secret weapon of 'terrible power', is lucky if he has time to order a retreat before his men panic. Although Licinius lost the Battle of Hadrianopolis, he proved his generalship that day, if only by his success in disengaging and organizing a fighting retreat. It is said that the battle was so hard-fought that to win it Constantine had to expose himself to extreme danger at a moment of crisis, coming close enough to the enemy to receive a spear-thrust in the thigh. Physically, it was not a disabling wound. He managed to remain in command, and fight on. Its propaganda value, however, must have been very high, if only because every sun-hero in mythology was wounded in the thigh at some time in his career, usually just before his greatest victory, and Constantine was still being proclaimed by his coins 'the Companion of the Unconquered Sun', although the issue made in 324 proved to be the last of the series. Licinius fell back from Hadrianopolis to Byzantium, and both sides prepared for a siege. While he could hold the city, Licinius was safe. Essential supplies would reach his forces across the narrow channel of the Bosphorus, separating Europe from the granaries of Asia. From the citadel guarding the precious harbour, he proclaimed his defiance to the world, declaring Constantine deposed, and announcing that he had appointed the head of his civil service, the Master of the Offices Marcus Martianus (or Martinianus), as Augustus in his place[27].

He had tried the same tactic ten years earlier, promoting Valens before the Battle of Mardia. It had availed him nothing then, and brought him little more reward now. No one in the West took up arms to fight for the Emperor Martianus. The only real effect of his promotion was to give added emphasis to the declaration of Constantine's deposition, and so make a negotiated settlement that much more unlikely. With Valens' fate to warn him, it is surprising that Martianus accepted his moment of spurious glory, if Licinius gave him any choice in the matter. Once he had accepted it, knowing Constantine's ruthlessness towards any who opposed his rule, he must have known that he was fighting for nothing less than his life. By making him his fellow-emperor, Licinius had created for himself a subordinate commander whom he knew he could trust. Having proclaimed him, he sent him to Lampsakos, on the southern shore of the Hellespont, to muster the army of Asia there, and reinforce Abantus' fleet, lest Crispus should force a landing in Asia, to cut the lines of communication between Byzantium and Asia.

While Constantine sat outside Byzantium, waiting for Crispus

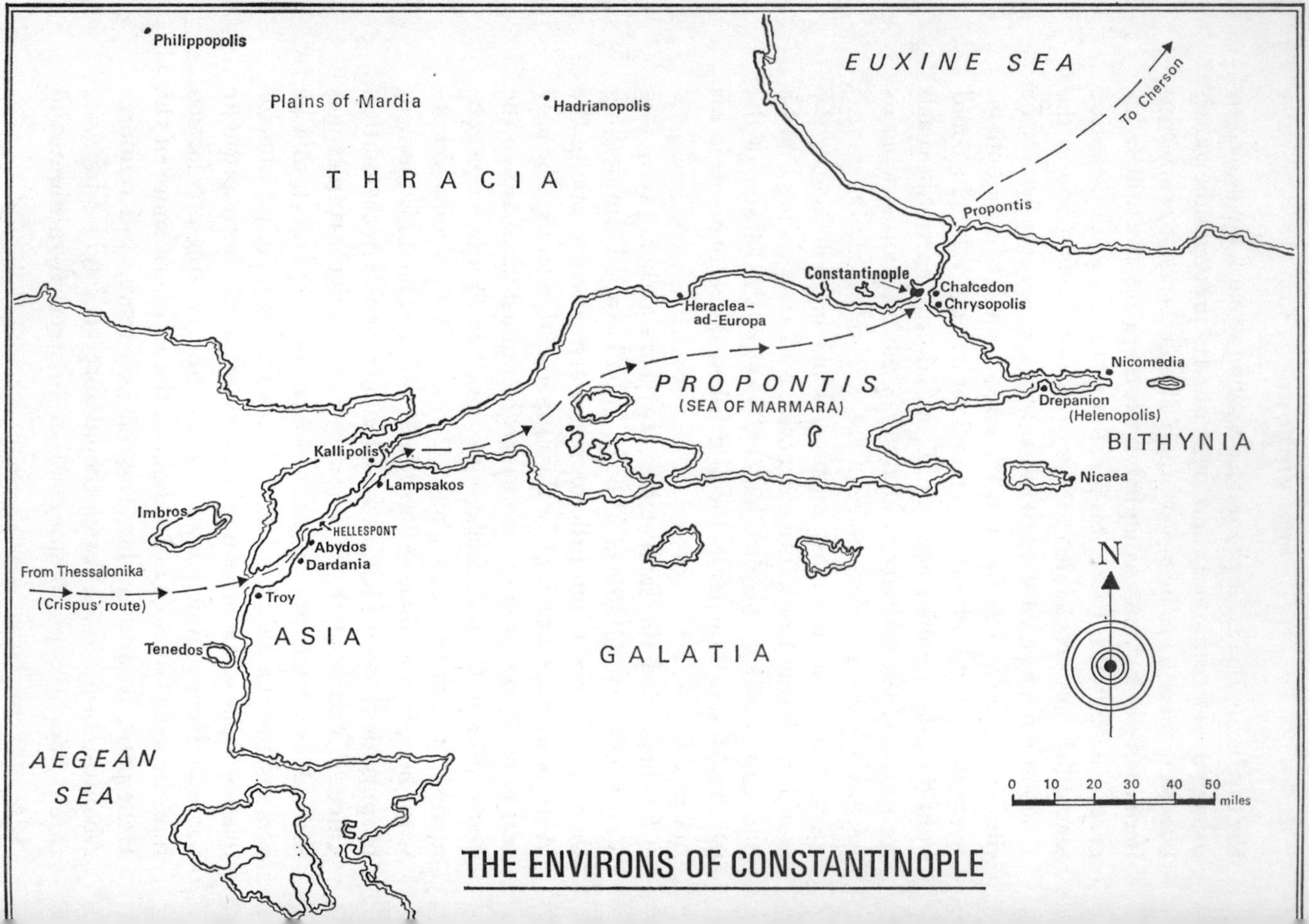

THE ENVIRONS OF CONSTANTINOPLE

to play his part in the war, he had ample opportunity to realize the natural strength of the city, which was approachable by land only on a narrow front over open ground, and to think about the implications of the fact that the Goths, whose homeland was north of the Black Sea, were on the move again, after thirty relatively quiescent years.

The previous year, Rausimond's people, the Sarmatians, had either crossed voluntarily into the empire, to escape Gothic pressure, or had actually been forced across the Danube by raiders from the East. Now news reached Constantine that Gothic auxiliaries were joining Martianus' Army of Asia. The situation was interesting, if not yet alarming.

Moreover, the Persian kingdom, powerful as ever, still lay east of the Euphrates. The loss of the Mesopotamian provinces still rankled there, and Galerius' forty years' peace had little more than ten years to run.

The European half of the empire needed a strong eastern outpost, to guarantee the County of the East from ever being overrun. It is doubtful whether, while besieging Licinius at Byzantium, Constantine actually considered that the city should be the new capital of the whole empire, but it was now that he decided to enlarge and strengthen it, to ensure that once he had united the empire, it could never be cut in half by an invasion reaching the Bosphorus.

With 350 war triremes lying in the Sea of Propontis, between Lampsakos on the Asian shore and Kallipolis (Gallipoli) on the European, Abantus should have been able totally to deny the narrows of the Hellespont to Crispus' thirty-oared ships and wallowing transports. Naval strategists studying this campaign have, indeed, maintained that his superiority in strength was so marked that, if he had had any training in war at sea, he would have sailed out to intercept and destroy the Western fleet in the open waters between Mytilene and Lemnos. However, he had as little experience as Crispus in managing a fleet, and probably believed that he could use his ships as though they were army units on land, massing them to close to the enemy 'the pass' represented by the straights. When Crispus' fleet appeared,

Abantus committed too many ships to battle for any of them to be able to manoeuvre freely. He held up the Westerners for two days off Gallipoli, but his losses were heavy, and when during the second night a storm swept over his constricted anchorages, piling up ships on the shore, his fleet ceased to exist. A hundred and thirty of his vessels were lost, and 5,000 sailors drowned. Next day, the surviving ships surrendered, and Crispus sailed on in triumph towards Byzantium, from where 'Licinius, despairing of hope from the sea, fled with his treasure to Chalcedon', as the unnamed chronicler quoted by Valesius put it; 'thus Constantine took Byzantium, and celebrated Crispus' naval victory in a suitable manner'[28].

So all Europe came to acknowledge Constantine as its sole ruler.

From Chalcedon, dangerously close across the Bosphorus from Byzantium now that Constantine commanded all the sea transport he could want, Licinius withdrew south-westwards to Chrysopolis, half-way to his capital of Nicomedia; and, all danger that Crispus would force a landing at the Hellespont being passed, ordered Martianus up from Lampsakos to reinforce his twice-depleted army. Meanwhile, Constantine celebrated Victory Games for Crispus, then ferried his men across the straights to the Chalcedon shore. It was the first time that he had set foot on Asian soil since his dramatic flight from Galerius, eighteen years earlier. By the middle of September, he was camped outside Chrysopolis. Within the walls, Licinius had restored his army to within 20,000 of the total with which he had begun the war, but only by the expedient of hiring the help of the Goths under their King Aliquaca – fierce, but unreliable allies, ready to fight in the hope of plunder, but not to stand and die in a Roman cause.

The battle for Chrysopolis started not when the general staff decided, but when Constantine's intuition told him that the moment for the charge had come. Eusebius relates that, by this stage in his life, the emperor had so firmly convinced himself that he was divinely inspired in every action he undertook to defend and expand his empire that he had ordered a special tent to be made, where he could say his prayers and wait for the heavenly word of command to come to him.

> He pitched the tabernacle of the cross at a distance from the camp, and there passed his time in a pure and holy way, offering prayers to God, so following the example of the prophet of old [Moses], of whom the oracles testify that he pitched the tabernacle outside the camp. He was attended only by a few whose faith and pious devotion he held in high regard. He always acted in this way when he was meditating on a battle with an enemy. For he acted only after deliberation, so as to be more sure of a safe outcome, and he longed to be guided by divine advice in all circumstances. And, praying thus continually to God, he was always soon visited by some token of his presence. And then, as if thrust into it by a divine push, he would suddenly rush out of the tabernacle, and give orders to his army to move at once, with drawn swords. When this happened, they would immediately begin the attack, fighting so fiercely as to win victory with incredible speed[29].

The question as to whether or not Constantine actually was inspired on these occasions is one for faith, not history. He himself certainly believed that he was, and managed to convey his conviction to his soldiers, and despair to the enemy. He must have been a superb showman to bring it off. The line between being awe-inspiring and looking ridiculous is very narrow.

Chrysopolis was another fierce and bloody engagement. When Licinius finally fell back on Nicomedia, he had lost 25,000 dead, and thousands had panicked and fled. Nevertheless, he was still capable of making a last stand in defence of his capital. He had money and a coherent army, in spite of the fact that his rearguard 'seeing Constantine's legions coming through Liburna, threw away their arms and surrendered to him'. However, the Empress Constantia was at Nicomedia, and, it seems, in the course of a single night, persuaded him that further resistance was futile 'and the next day, she came to her brother's camp, and implored and begged him to grant her husband's life'. Whether or not her friend, and Constantine's natural ally in the city, Eusebius of Nicomedia, joined her either in convincing Licinius that he should ask Constantine's clemency, or in her embassy to her brother, is not known. Neither is impossible. At any rate, Constantine granted his favourite sister's petition, and that same day, victor and vanquished dined together, before Licinius went off to internment at Thessalonika, with the promise of an estate to support him in a suitable style[30]. Martianus was also granted an amnesty, and was despatched to comfortable exile in Cappadocia, but the former government was proclaimed tyrannical and all Licinius' personal property was confiscated. Constantia and the Caesar Licinianus remained at Nicomedia, where they lived as pensioners of Constantine's household.

All Licinius' acts were annulled on May 16, and on the following November 8, Constantine clothed his second son, Constantius, in the purple cloak of a Caesar. At about the same time, on Constantine's orders, Licinius and Martianus were both murdered. But in which year did these events occur?

Strange as it may seem, the fact is that the year in which Constantine made himself sole master of the whole Roman world is by no means certain. All that is incontrovertible is that he took Nicomedia and the East some time after he had killed King Rausimond in 322 and before the end of the year of the third consulship of Crispus and Constantine II, 324.

Jerome's Chronicle laconically records that in the Year from Abraham 2339, Constantine's seventeenth, which ran from July 322 to July 323, 'Constantius the son of Constantine was made Caesar; Licinius was put to death secretly at Thessalonika, in defiance of civilized custom when oaths have been sworn (*contra ius sacramenti*)'[31]. This correlation between Constantius' promotion and Licinius' death may be correct, but the date 322–3 is unacceptable, because it would mean that Licinius' empire was destroyed in the year of the Sarmatian war – which in its turn would require that Rausimond's people were routed and all Constantine's preparations made for a second war before the end of June, when he advanced on Hadrianopolis: an incredible set of propositions in itself, even if its falseness were not confirmed by the fact that Constantine's consuls for the year 323, Severus and Rufinus, were not recognized in the East. If the war did not end before the autumn of 323 (which is the assumption here), it is possible that Severus' and Rufinus' names remained generally unfamiliar there, but that could not have happened if Constantine had actually been ruling in Nicomedia when their year of office began on January 1.

The war, then, was fought either in 323 or 324. The year 324 has been generally favoured by historians, and is supported by Idatius' Chronicle in a notice almost identical with Jerome's, but dated in the year of the consulate of Crispus Caesar III and Constantine Caesar III. It is, however, difficult to believe either that all the events from the Battle of Hadrianopolis on July 3 to the promotion of Constantius and the death of Licinius occurred in the same year, or that Licinius' murder and the promotion of Constantius were delayed until 325. It is even less credible that two years separated Constantine's provocative invasion of Thrace in pursuit of King Rausimond and the outbreak of hostilities with Licinius. It would seem more likely that the Sarmatian Campaign of 322 was followed by the overthrow of Licinius in 323, and his murder in 324.

Another problem is raised by the dating of the law in the Theodosian Code requiring the annulment of all Licinius' acts: 'All the constitutions and laws of Licinius now being set aside, the observance of all our former laws and customs is strictly enjoined'[32]. The date of its promulgation is given as May 16 'In the Year of Flavius Julius Crispus III and Constantine Caesar III' – again, 324. The most natural time for the abrogation of Licinius' edicts was immediately after Constantine's triumphal entry into Nicomedia. (He had destroyed Maxentius' portraits and annulled his acts immediately after his entry into Rome in October 312.) Constantine's forces, however, occupied Nicomedia at the end of September. How, then, can the date 'May 16' be accounted for? It may, of course, simply be wrong, but if it is not, either Licinius' acts were declared void as a move in the war of propaganda, six weeks before the actual fighting started in Thrace (and the year was after all 324), or Licinius was not declared a tyrant and his edicts cancelled until it became expedient to murder him, more than seven months after the fall of

Nicomedia. So long a delay in the cancellation of Licinius' edicts in general need not have been fatal to the claim that by the war Constantine was bringing liberty to the Christians of the East, if, immediately the fighting ended, special orders were issued to provincial governors and magistrates in the 'liberated' areas suspending recent anti-Christian executive orders and re-establishing the Edict of Milan as the fundamental law on the status of Christianity. The Edict was Licinius' law as much as it was Constantine's. Something of this kind appears in fact to have happened. The *Life of Constantine* remarks that, after the fall of Nicomedia, 'the Emperor's edicts, permeated with his humane spirit, were published among us [the Easterners] also, as they had been previously among the people of the other half of the empire'[33], and lists the blessings they brought as the return of exiles to their homes, the restoration of Christian property, the reinstatement of soldiers dishonourably discharged, and the naming of the church itself as the heir to those martyrs who had died leaving no immediate kin. This was the basic pro-Christian legislation, very similar to that which Licinius himself had promulgated at Nicomedia immediately after his defeat of Maximin Daia. Once this adjustment had been made in favour of the Christians, Constantine may well have let other Licinian edicts run until he had convinced himself that it was necessary to end the life and blot out the memory of the brother-in-law with whom he had dined on the day of his surrender.

So while readily admitting that other solutions to these and related chronological problems are possible, a tentative reconstruction of the order of events is:

322 (the consulate of Probianus and Julianus): defeat of the Sarmatians; gathering of the fleets; the propaganda war

323 (Severus and Rufinus): July 3, Battle of Hadrianopolis
- July-September, Siege of Byzantium; principate of Martianus; Crispus' victory off Kallipolis
- September 18, Battle of Chrysopolis
- September 19-21, surrender of Licinius; Constantine's triumphal entry into Nicomedia
- Winter, legal adjustments in favour of the Christians in Asia Minor, Egypt and the County of the East.

324 (Crispus III and Constantine Caesar III): Winter-Spring, gradual spread of the news of Constantine's victory to all the provinces (under favourable conditions, Alexandria was three weeks from Nicomedia, and Rome six).

at unknown dates: murder of Licinius and Martianus

May 16, annulment of all Licinius' acts

November 8, promotion of Constantius

According to the fifth-century Christian historian Socrates, Licinius brought death on himself by conspiring with trans-Danubian barbarians, his mercenaries in the recent war, to rescue him and restore him to power. When his plot was discovered, the army threatened mutiny if he were not executed, and Constantine unwillingly acceded to its demands, although he gave the execution an additional sheen of legality by first referring the matter to the Roman senate. A still later tradition maintains that Licinius actually escaped to his former allies, the Goths, but was killed by them[34].

These stories should probably be regarded as whitewash, applied to brighten Constantine's memory. Eusebius carefully avoids giving any details of Licinius' and Martianus' deaths – which would imply that there was something shameful about them. They were not spectacular deaths, richly deserved, of the kind by which, according to him and Lactantius, Providence generally paid off persecutors, but were, rather, expedient murders. In fact, there is no contemporary evidence that Licinius planned to subvert Constantine's government, and what probably happened is that Constantine, remembering the treachery of Maximian and the Bassianus-Senecio affair at Rome, gradually convinced himself over a period of seven or eight months that he had allowed his affection for Constantia to cloud his judgement in dealing with her husband. There may have been pressures on him of which no trace now remains – from the Christian confessors, perhaps, who, as the history of the Donatist controversy shows, could be very vindictive. In the end, he ordered the murders 'secretly, in defiance of civilized custom when oaths have been sworn', before any plots could be evolved. He may have asked the Senate to approve his secret orders: he had used it as a cover before, notably when it 'voluntarily' voted him Augustus Maximus.

Asked why Licinius had to die, Constantine would doubtless have answered simply that his death was necessary for the peace of the world. There was no room in the empire for anyone who might ever be tempted to challenge his own divinely-approved power. He may even have regretted the executions, as that later inspired tyrannicide, the Lord-Protector Cromwell, is said to have agonized over the 'cruel necessity' of the murder of King Charles I of England. However, if he did, he gave no sign of it. He now called himself 'the Supreme Emperor, Constantine the Champion': Victor Constantinus Augustus Maximus. The God under whose protection he had placed his fortunes at Milvian Bridge had given the government of the whole Roman world into his hands. It was his plain soldierly duty not to let it slip from misplaced clemency or lack of vigilance, let alone for love of his sister.

CHAPTER TEN

THE ARIAN CONTROVERSY: NICAEA

ONCE Constantine had united the Roman world and made himself its sole master, his primary ambition was to cement it firmly together in tranquil subservience to his own will. 'My own desire is,' he prayed in a letter circulated throughout the empire to announce the universal enforcement of his enactments in favour of the Christians, 'for the welfare of the whole world and the advantage of all humanity, that Thy people should enjoy a life of peace and untroubled concord'[1]. It was a very public prayer, rather a statement of policy than an act of devotion, yet it was probably quite genuine. Throughout the rest of his life, he showed himself ready to go to almost any lengths to avoid discord and civil war.

He was, for instance, entirely willing to murder for the sake of peace, as the cold-blooded elimination of Licinius and Martianus clearly demonstrated, and his determination to preserve it drove him both to start rebuilding Byzantium as Constantinople and to reconstruct the military and civil administration of the whole empire. Pursuit of it made him set energetically about the task of bringing uniformity to the faith and practice of the hitherto semi-autonomous churches of the East, while converting them into departments of his empire-wide Catholic Church; and at the same time replacing independent pagan aristocrats as administrators wherever possible by Catholic Christians more willingly subservient to himself, as the sole source of patronage for themselves and their church.

The *Life of Constantine* says that, after the defeat of Licinius, he openly championed the Christian God, 'maintaining that He and not himself was the Author of all his past victories. He caused the following declaration, written in both Greek and Latin, to be circulated throughout every imperial province . . . "Constantine the Victor, Supreme Augustus, to the people of the Province of [Palestine]: It has long been obvious to everyone . . . [that blessings are reserved for Christians, while persecution of them leads to nothing but misery] . . . Many a time, armies have been slaughtered, or put to flight . . . and . . . there has followed a scarcity of the necessities of life, and a crowd of consequent miseries, and the authors of these impieties have either met disastrous deaths of extreme suffering, or dragged out shameful existences . . . What relief has the Deity then devised? . . . I myself am the instrument he chose . . . With the aid of divine power, beginning at the remote Ocean of the Britains, where in accordance with the law of nature the sun sinks beneath the horizon, I banished and utterly abolished every form of evil then prevailing, in the hope that the human race, enlightened through me, might be recalled to a proper observance of God's holy laws . . .[2]" '

All memory of the fact that his accession was an act of usurpation had been suppressed, together with that of his agnostic doubt before the Italian campaign concerning what god to pray to. In his view, his career of aggressive conquest had been from the outset a pilgrimage and a mission; now he had fulfilled his every ambition by the 'utter abolition' of 'every form of evil', and by establishing the reign of God through that Divine Instrument, himself, Constantine the Victor.

The letter continued with the announcement of the measures already noted lifting disabilities from the Christians of the East: the recall of exiles, the restoration of sequestered property and the reinstatement in the forces of Christian soldiers cashiered when they had refused to offer sacrifice at Licinius' command.

The Victor followed this encyclical letter with a personal note addressed to Constantia's friend, Bishop Eusebius of Nicomedia, offering special subsidies for the restoration and enlargement of churches, such as he had already given to the bishops of Italy and Africa: 'We empower you, and others through you, to demand what you need for this work from both our provincial governors and the Praetorian Prefect'[3]. This generous offer to buy Eusebius for the Constantinean Catholic Church was followed in its turn by a second encyclical letter, containing a long, rambling attack on paganism, but finishing with the ruling that, despite the manifest shortcoming of the old religion, it would continue to be tolerated. It was in this letter that the Victor made his policy-statement in prayer: 'I beseech Thee, most mighty God, to be merciful towards Thine eastern nations . . . My own desire is . . . that Thy people may enjoy a life of peace and untroubled concord. Let those, therefore, who still delight in error be assured of the same degree of peace and tranquillity as those who already believe . . .' At this point, the letter became not so much a prayer to God as a stern warning to Christians, an order to leave continuing pagans in peace. It ended with a reminder to Christians that it would be wrong to try and force conversion on anyone: 'it is one thing voluntarily to take up the fight for eternal life; it is quite another to compel others to do so from fear of punishment.'

If, however, he was firmly against the coercion of unwilling pagans into joining the church, he was not averse to strong measures intended to compel existing Christians to conform to the norms of his Catholic Church. Only by the narrowest of margins did he avoid repeating in Egypt in 324–5 the mistakes for which his name was already reviled in Donatist Africa and Numidia, when he allowed himself to become involved in the confusion arising from the schisms of Meletius and Arius, the former of which was directly, the latter indirectly, the result of the Great Persecution.

When Constantine inherited Egypt and its problems, the Meletian Schism was already more than twenty years old[4]. In the year 300, a priest named Peter had been elected to rule the huge Patriarchate of Alexandria. A little under three years after he had accepted this charge, the Great Persecution had broken over his church. He was arrested and imprisoned under the terms of Diocletian's second persecuting edict, that ordering the detention of the senior clergy. In the same prison was one of his bishops, Meletius of Lycopolis, a provincial city in Upper Egypt, an insignificant place in comparison with cosmopolitan Alexandria.

Theologically, Peter was a generous man who, although not condoning the apostacy of those who had complied with the imperial edicts, understood their dilemma, and argued that the church ought to forgive them, readmitting them to communion with their fellow-Christians when the persecution ended. He was, however, also an autocrat by nature, and took it badly when Meletius disagreed with him. Like the Numidian Secundus of Tigisi, Meletius thought that the lapsed and the *traditores* had cut themselves off for ever from the church and should be told so bluntly. There was obviously a clash of temperaments, as well as of doctrine, between the two men. Soon they were refusing even to share the same prison yard, and Peter had a blanket hung down the middle of their communal cell, inviting anyone who would not accept his authoritative ruling to leave his half of the prison. Few did so apart from Meletius – but those few naturally felt superior to the mass of Christian prisoners, believing themselves misunderstood, ill-treated and right.

Real trouble seemed inevitable when persecution eased, the bishops were released, and it became possible, between Easter and Pentecost 306, to hold a synod to determine a common Egyptian policy towards the lapsed. The rules it adopted were similar to those later approved at the Synod of Arles: a penance of forty days' fasting for those who had given way only after flogging or torture, a year's penance for those who had surrendered after being merely imprisoned, three years for those who had bowed to threats alone or had forced their slaves to sacrifice, reversion to the lay state for clergy who had lapsed, but complete pardonfor temporary apostates who had later repented and confessed their Christianity to the imperial authorities, and for those whom fear had driven to forge certificates or persuade pagan neighbours to impersonate them before the imperial commissioners[5].

The leniency of these canons disgusted Meletius. He decided that they proved that Peter was not worthy to rule Alexandria, and began to act as though he himself were the archbishop, ordaining priests to work not only in the see of Lycopolis, but throughout the patriarchate.

The renewal of persecution in Egypt under Maximin Daia sent Peter into hiding and afforded Meletius a heaven-sent opportunity, as it seemed to him, to subvert the clergy of the city of Alexandria to his views. Full of zeal, he went to the city to preach against Peter, making no attempt to conceal himself – he would have considered that the act of a coward – and was inevitably arrested for a second time. While in prison in Peter's own see-city, he declared Peter deposed and consecrated a bishop to replace him. Peter provisionally excommunicated him and his adherents, until the restoration of normal conditions made it possible to hold a synod to regularize the whole situation. This sentence brought several of his supporters to their senses. Among them was Arius, then a pious layman from Libya, a strangely magnetic personality, whose faith in his own insight was later to change the pattern of church history for centuries to come.

Also in prison at the same time as Meletius were Eusebius Pamphilus, a friend of Arius', who was later to become the bishop of Caesarea and author of the *Ecclesiastical History*, and a priest named Alexander, a loyal follower of Peter the Archbishop, later himself to be consecrated archbishop of Alexandria. Eusebius and Alexander appear to have been gaoled only briefly, but Meletius' sufferings were severe. The magistrates sentenced him to slave labour in the mines at Phaeno in Southern Palestine. What he endured there only strengthened his convictions regarding the lapsed. While working as a slave, he ordained more priests and consecrated at least one bishop, so deliberately founding a 'Church of the Martyrs' to confront the compromised Catholic Church. Released under Galerius' Edict of April 311, he returned to Lycopolis determined to fight to the end against the soft line taken by his archbishop. His cause received a severe set-back when Peter was suddenly seized and summarily beheaded in December 311, thus himself becoming a martyr in the most spectacular manner; but nevertheless his Church of the Martyrs continued to grow. He denounced Peter's successor, Achillas, as another compromiser, and continued his opposition into the reign of Alexander when, a month or so later, on Achillas' sudden death, he succeeded to the patriarchate.

So Alexander of Alexandria found himself faced with a rival church organization in Egypt, little less formidable than that threatening the 'Catholic' Caecilian at about the same time in Proconsular Africa; and throughout Licinius' reign in the East had to combat not only increasing hostility from the authorities, but also a continually growing dissident church. He was, however, more fortunate than Caecilian. Traditional rivalry between the Delta and the Desert gave some political colouring to Meletius' movement, bringing suspicion on everyone, and naturally the pagans made capital out of it. But the Alexandrian archbishop was spared the embarrassment of overwhelming imperial patronage, so that the church of the Meletian schismatics never had the national and 'Roman' appeal which made Donatism so strong in Africa.

There was, however, further trouble for him in the person of Arius[6]. As one of the first defectors from the Church of the Martyrs, he had been welcomed by Peter, who had made him a deacon, but when Peter had excommunicated his former leader, he had objected so violently that the archbishop had felt compelled to close the doors of the church to him also. He had, however, later expressed repentance, and, recognizing his magnetism and energy, Achillas had ordained him priest, while Archbishop Alexander in his turn had given him the cure of the church at Baucalis, in the suburbs of Alexandria, where his skill as a preacher brought him many disciples among the clergy and especially, it is said, among the women. He was tall and dramatically thin. He dressed very simply and the asceticism of his way of life showed in the lines of his face. Like Eusebius of Nicomedia and Eusebius Pamphilus, he had sat at the feet of one of the most brilliant if enigmatic of Syrian Christian teachers, Lucian of Antioch, who, before his execution at Nicomedia on January 7, 312, had inspired a whole generation in Asia Minor and Palestine not only with his own views on Christianity but also with intense loyalty to himself and one another. Arius called this circle of friends the Collucianists, 'those who were with Lucian' and trusted them to stand by him in any circumstances[7]. They rarely failed him. Their loyalty would nearly disrupt the empire.

Lucian had based his teaching on the doctrines of the masters of his own native Antioch, where the approach to Christianity was subtly different from that made by the theologians of Alexandria. At Antioch, emphasis was laid on the uniqueness of God the Father, on the humanity of Christ and the practical aspects of the Christian life as shaped by the Scriptures. At Alexandria, teachers dwelt on the mystical union between the eternal Christ and the Divine Father, the pre-existence of the Word of God and the harmony of heaven. Antiochene teaching tended to stress the difference between the Father and the Son, and to grant the Father precedence; Alexandrian to point to what they had in common, and insist that they shared it eternally. From Lucian, Arius had learned not so much a special doctrine, as a particular way of looking at God. It led him to the conclusions that the Divine Father was, as it were, the senior partner in the Godhead, that the Son was eternally subordinate to him, and that – granted the correctness of the Father–Son analogy, which was affirmed by Scripture, and therefore divinely guaranteed – although there is no time in eternity 'there was [? a time, a state] when he, the Son, was not'.

To strict Alexandrian theologians, this doctrine was shocking, because they believed that God was unchanging: if Christ was ever the Son of God, the Second Person of the Godhead, he was so from all eternity; but many ordinary Christians found Arius' arguments convincing, partly no doubt because they were propounded by a man who looked and spoke like everyone's dream of an ancient prophet returned to earth. By about the year 320, Arius had collected around himself at Baucalis a mixed but influential following of priests and fashionable lay people. Epiphanius describes him as the spiritual master of a school consisting of one bishop (a Collucianist, Secundus of Ptolemais), seven priests, twelve deacons and about 700 dedicated virgins[8]. He had been promoted to second priest in the diocese under the Archpriest Colluthus, and his teaching had attracted the attention of Archbishop Alexander himself.

It was probably Colluthus who denounced him as a heretic. Alexander could not ignore the charge, but refused to move precipitately. He called first for one public debate, then for another. At the second, Arius committed himself to extreme subordination and claimed that his doctrines were those of the bishops of Nicomedia, Caesarea, Lydda, Tyre, Berytus and Anazarbia – all Collucianists, old friends of his, prominent men in the church not of Egypt but of the County of the East and Asia Minor. He defended himself so ably that although Alexander personally found his views unacceptable, he did not suspend him from all clerical duties, but merely forbade him to teach until a synod of bishops had ruled on the validity of his opinions.

Before such a synod could be assembled, however, Colluthus, jealous perhaps of Arius' success and sickened by Alexander's timid handling of him, came to the conclusion that the Catholic Church in Alexandria was dead, and that it was his own vocation to resurrect it. He started to call himself Bishop Colluthus, and to ordain priests on his own account. To outsiders, it looked as though the church in Egypt was crumbling away. The pagans took fresh heart.

When Alexander's synod met, it comprised just over a hundred bishops from Libya, Tripolitania and Egypt. Only Arius' fellow-Libyans and Collucianists, Secundus of Ptolemais and Theonis of Marmarica, refused to vote for his condemnation. They were both declared deposed and excommunicate, together with Arius himself, six other priests and six deacons. Shortly afterwards, a local synod met at Mareotis in the Delta and condemned two more priests and four deacons. Arius wrote to one old comrade, now Bishop Eusebius of Nicomedia, seeking his support, and left Egypt for a council of war with another, now Bishop Eusebius of Caesarea. He was still convinced that he was right. In his letter to Nicomedia, he wrote of himself as 'the man persecuted unjustly by Patriarch Alexander . . . because we said "the Son has a beginning: God is without a beginning".'

Eusebius of Nicomedia wrote back encouragingly, with the declaration, 'Your views are right.' Eusebius of Caesarea addressed letters attacking Alexander to all known Collucianists in

Egypt, calling them to arms. Within months, Eusebius of Nicomedia had agreed to receive Arius and his own namesake from Caesarea at the capital, and hold a synod there to pass judgement on Alexander of Alexandria, who not unnaturally complained that he was acting as though the whole future of the church depended on him alone. The Nicomedian synod, packed with theologians of the Antiochene School, many of them former disciples of Lucian the Martyr, found little to complain of in Arius' teaching, and wrote to Alexander, urging him to reinstate those he had excommunicated and expelled. Alexander refused, complaining of intolerable interference in the affairs of his archdiocese in letters he sent to sixty-nine archbishops and bishops, including Silvester of Rome.

These letters show that Alexander was cut out by nature to be one of Constantine's Catholic bishops, working as a dedicated bureaucrat for the peace and unity of the church within the framework of the Constantinean empire. 'There is,' he wrote, 'only one body of the Catholic Church, and the precept of Holy Scripture is that the bond of unanimity and peace must be preserved.' The pity was that when Constantine took over the East, he had little opportunity of observing Alexander's qualities. He was prematurely brought into too close contact with the two bishops Eusebius. One of them was his sister's favourite. The other had recently finished the first nine books of his *Ecclesiastical History* with a glowing eulogy of Constantine and Licinius, but now that the political climate had changed was already talking about writing a tenth, describing how Licinius became possessed of the devil, and God's Champion, Constantine, had destroyed him. In this situation, Constantine was not free to decide who would be most useful to him. During 324, he did in fact use Alexander's bishops as his delegates at talks with the continuing Donatists of Africa and Numidia, hoping no doubt that as fellow North Africans they would all understand one another, but the stories he heard about schisms against Alexander soon convinced him that as an ally 'Egypt is a broken reed'.

By this time, the question of Arius' orthodoxy had split the

Eastern church from end to end. Arius himself had revealed a genius for propaganda. He made up slogans that were chalked on walls and chanted in the hippodromes. He wrote songs with catchy words and melodies, for sailors, merchants, travellers and schoolchildren, all teaching his doctrines. He claimed that the best Christian tradition backed his opinions, and his claims were widely believed. He wrote a book, the *Thalia*, 'Happy Thoughts', expounding his teaching in that mystical, high-flown style which his half-educated contemporaries found so appealing. Its opening sentences stated his position: 'According to the faith of the elect of God, those who understand God, budding saints, orthodox men, possessing the Holy Spirit of God – what follows is what I learned from those granted the privilege of Wisdom, distinguished men, taught by God, skilful in every way. It is in their footsteps that I walk, walking with them – I, of whom they are saying so much, who have suffered for the glory of God, who have received from God such learning and wisdom as I possess.' Those who accepted his claims were willing to back their faith in him with action against his critics. Arianism was fast becoming a mass-movement, offering as real a threat to the peace as any politically-inspired movement today.

After the synod of Nicomedia, Eusebius of Caesarea had called a Syrian synod, which had predictably found Arius' teaching orthodox and purported to authorise him to resume his duties at Baucalis. Armed with the resolutions of both synods, he tried to reinstate himself at Alexandria, but Alexander refused to receive him, and there was rioting in the streets. Meanwhile, Bishop Asterius of Cappodocia was neglecting his duties to preach Arius' views throughout the County of the East. His support was not as welcome to the Collucianists as it might have been, because he had been accused of lapsing during the persecution, but as everyone knew that Arius had been an admirer of Meletius, the founder of the Church of the Martyrs, had himself been imprisoned for the faith, and was a devotee of Lucian the Martyr, Asterius' enthusiasm was not instantly fatal to his cause. The whole situation was, however, very confusing to the ordinary Christian, without special theological training. It is not surprising that Constantine, coming on the scene at its most complex point, failed to understand it.

What worried him during 324 was the threat to the peace in his new territories. As soon as he realized the danger, he sent Hosius to Egypt, empowering him to do whatever was necessary to restore unity to the church. Hosius' position, although never officially defined, was effectively that of Special Vicarius in Ecclesiastical Affairs. There was no precedent for his function in the Eastern church, and his only authority, ecclesiastically speaking, was that voluntarily surrendered to him by Alexander. It is a measure of the respect currently afforded to Constantine by the Christians that no one seems to have challenged Hosius' right to intervene in Egypt. (It was certainly not fear of the emperor which led to his universal acceptance: bishops like Alexander, who had spent long months in prison for defying imperial edicts, would not have acquiesced in his mission from fear.)

Despite Hosius' and later reports, Constantine probably never understood the details of the quarrel over Arius' teaching. Time and again in the years that followed, he sought a compromise where compromise was in fact impossible. Perhaps as time passed, he did begin to glimpse something of the truth, but the letter which he sent by Hosius impartially to Alexander and Arius in 324 displayed an almost twentieth-century impatience with theology, and a longing only for the restoration of Blessed Tranquillity:

> Constantine the Victor, Supreme Augustus, to Alexander and Arius:
> [A short while ago] finding that the whole of Africa was imbued with a spirit of madness, through the influence of those who, with reckless frivolity, had presumed to rend the religion of the people into sects, being anxious to check this disorder, I could find no other remedy equal to the occasion but to send some of yourselves to try and restore natural harmony among the disputants, after I had removed that common enemy of mankind [Licinius], who had by his lawlessness prohibited your holy synods . . .
> . . . but now, how deep a wound has not my ears only but my heart received from the report that divisions exist among your

selves more grievous even than those still persisting in that country! . . . Yet, having enquired carefully into the origin and foundation of these differences, I find their cause to be of a truly insignificant nature, one quite unworthy of such bitter contention . . . You, Alexander, asked your priests what they thought about a certain passage in the law [Proverbs 8, 22], or, rather, about one insignificant detail of it, and you, Arius, imprudently voiced an opinion which ought never to have been conceived or, once it was conceived, ought to have been silently buried . . . So now let each of you, displaying equal forbearance, accept the equitable advice of your fellow-servant. What is that advice? Primarily, not to propose such questions, or to reply to them if they are proposed . . .

Restore my quiet days and untroubled nights to me, so that that joy of undimmed light, delight in a tranquil life, may once again be mine . . .

I was hurrying to see you and had already accomplished [in imagination only] the greater part of the journey, when the news of this business made me change my mind, so that I should not be compelled to see with my eyes what I could scarcely bear to hear about. . . .

Hosius' mission to Egypt was not a total failure. He called a synod and thoroughly explored the problems. Colluthus' schism was dealt with summarily. He had little to complain about now that Arius was being taken seriously, and readily accepted a ruling that he was to cease pretending to be a bishop. He even urged one of the priests whom he claimed to have ordained and who had appeared before the synod, a man named Ichyras from a village in the Delta, to desist from claiming the privilege of celebrating the Holy Eucharist. Hosius was, however, to hear of Ichyras again.

The problem of Arius proved much more intractable. There can be little doubt that the synod examined him, or at least some of his episcopal supporters, but unfortunately its records on this examination have not survived. However, it is known that when Hosius returned to Nicomedia to make his report, he was followed there by both Arius and Alexander, neither of whom was satisfied with whatever judgement he had given. Arius travelled by land, and may have broken his journey for consultations on strategy with Collucianists in Syria and Asia Minor. Alexander took a ship, reached Nicomedia first, and so temporarily won Constantine's ear – or perhaps, even more importantly, that of Hosius, in whom, no doubt, he recognized not only the real power behind the throne in ecclesiastical matters, but also a man of his own stamp; their co-operation was to have a decisive influence on the history of the whole church.

By the end of 324, Constantine was surrounded by Christians, all clamouring for his attention. At the palace were Hosius and Alexander, the one his private adviser, the other undeniably head of the 'catholic' church in the civil diocese of Egypt; Eusebius of Nicomedia, the bishop of the palace, Arius, and probably also Eusebius of Caesarea, who, according to one possibly apocryphal account had just been excommunicated by a synod at Antioch, all three certain that their cause would succeed because it had the support of Constantia, and perhaps also of the Dowager Empress Helena, for she was certainly in Nicomedia only a few months later, and was soon to become the greatest patroness the church in Palestine ever had, and a lively advocate of the cult of Lucian the Martyr.

We shall probably never know whose idea it was that a council of the church, bigger and more authoritative even than the Synod of Arles, might succeed where Hosius had failed. Philostorgus, a Christian historian, suggests that the plan originated with Alexander; Eusebius, with Constantine himself[10]. It was probably first mooted in conversation between Alexander and Hosius, and presented to Constantine in such a way that he could make it his own if it appealed to him. He accepted it unhesitatingly.

The site first chosen for the council was Ancyra in the civil diocese of Asiana, but when the imperial summons went out, the meeting place had been changed to Nicaea, close to Chalcedon, and thus to Byzantium, where 'Constantine's City' was already being marked out beside the Bosphorus: 'Although it was previously arranged that the synod of bishops would be held in Galatia, at Ancyra', Constantine wrote, 'for several reasons it has now been decided that it should gather at Nicaea in Bithynia – because bishops are coming from Italy and other parts of Europe, because the climate is more pleasant, and so that I may be close at hand, to watch and take part . . .[11]'

Despite the emperor's confidence that bishops from all over Europe would attend his Council of Nicaea, when the moment came in May 325 for him to open its proceedings, only a handful of delegates were present from non-Greek-speaking churches west of Macedonia: Hosius of Cordoba, Caecilian of Carthage, Marcus of Calabria, two Roman priests representing Pope Silvester, a bishop from Gaul and another from Illyria, in a total attendance of, according to Eusebius of Caesarea, about 250.

Other chroniclers made the total attendance larger: Eustathius of Antioch, who was present, counted 270 bishops; Athenasius, Alexander's deacon, 300; Constantine's civil servants, just over 300; St Hilary, writing about the year 360, 318. This last figure was, however, a mystical and not a realistic number, chosen to equate the total of bishops of Nicaea with that of the servants of Abraham when he rescued his brother Lot from the five kings. Yet such is the attraction of a significant number that for centuries Hilary's count was preferred to that of any of those who had actually attended the council.

Constantine welcomed the unsophisticated bishops, many of whom had recently been released from imperial prisons, at the palace of Nicaea with a show of splendour which, thirteen years later, still lived with dream-like clarity in Eusebius' memory[12]:

> The council met for the final solution of the points at issue at a central room of the palace, which seemed bigger than any of the rest. On each side of this room, there were rows of seats, to be occupied by those summoned to attend in order of precedence. When the whole assembly was seated with fitting dignity, a general silence prevailed in expectation of the emperor's arrival. First of all, three of his immediate family entered in order of rank, then others heralded his own approach – not the soldiers or guards who usually attended him, but only friends in the faith. And then, all rising at a signal indicating the emperor's entrance, at last he himself proceeded through the midst of the assembly, like some heavenly Angel of God, clothed in a garment which glittered as though radiant with light, reflecting the glow of a purple robe, and adorned with the brilliant splendour of gold and precious stones. . . . When he had advanced to the

> front of the seats, he remained standing at first, but when a low chair of wrought gold had been placed for him, he waited until the bishops had signalled him to sit down and then did so, and after him the whole assembly did the same. Then the bishop who occupied the chief place on the right hand side of the assembly [Sozomen says that it was Eusebius of Nicomedia; Theodoret, Eustathius of Antioch] rose and, addressing the emperor, delivered a concise speech couched as a thanksgiving to Almighty God on his behalf. When he had resumed his seat, silence ensued, and all regarded the Emperor with fixed attention, at which he looked serenely round the assembly with a happy glance, and having collected his thoughts, said the following words –

The whole scene was beautifully stage-managed. Constantine wanted results from this conference, and needed them quickly. He was also determined to establish his domination over the bishops. His advisers knew, even if he did not, that he was unlikely to achieve these ends by his intellect, so his splendid physical presence and love of display, together with the charm he could exert when circumstances warranted it, were employed instead.

The speech with which he opened the council was not that of an Angel-messenger, but very much in his own rambling and involved style. It reveals him as still superstitious, still proud of his part in overthrowing the persecutors, still convinced that he was God's chosen agent, equal in his own sphere with the bishops in theirs, and still interested above all else in seeing them attain peace and unity:

> My friends: it has long been my supreme desire to see you come together, and now it is fulfilled. I publicly give thanks to the King of the Universe who, capping all his other blessings, has granted me this supreme blessing of seeing you all gathered together here in a single spirit of concord. May no malevolent enemy disturb our present peace! At this moment, when by the grace of God the Saviour, the tyrants who had risen up against God have vanished away, may no perverse devil expose the divine law to blasphemy! For my own part, I hold any sedition within the Church of God as equally formidable as any war or battle, and much more difficult to bring to an end, and am more opposed to it than to anything else. . . . Delay not, then, dear

friends! Delay not, O ministers and faithful servants of him who is our common Lord and Saviour! Begin now to cast aside the causes of that disunity which has existed among you, and eliminate the confusion of controversy by embracing the principles of peace! For by so doing, you will with one stroke be acting in the manner most pleasing to the Supreme God, and confer an extraordinary favour on me, your fellow servant.

He spoke in Latin and an interpreter translated his words into Greek, but when, as soon as the general debate began, acrimony emerged, he delighted the bishops by using what Greek he had in an attempt to impress on them that peace must be their supreme object, showing himself, Eusebius says, 'in a truly attractive and amiable light, persuading some, convincing others by his arguments, praising those who spoke well, and urging unity of sentiment on all'. He was, however, probably happiest with those whose language and pattern of thought was Latin, Marcus, the Roman priests, Caecilian and Hosius; and the Hosius-Alexander combination gradually won him away from his former attachment to the Collucianists and Arians as he came to see in Alexander the Egyptian who would be most useful to him in building up the catholic empire of his dreams.

When the word *homoousios*, consubstantial, 'of one substance', was first heard at Nicaea, or who used it to define the relationship between the Divine Father and his Son as that of two persons sharing one essential nature, that of co-equal and co-eternal divinity, is another insoluble mystery[13]. Once the word had been introduced, and Constantine had assured himself that its Latin form would be acceptable throughout his own catholic church of the West, and would satisfy Alexander and his fiery deacon Athenasius, he put himself enthusiastically to the task of making it the key to lock the whole church together into one universal department of state, working with the unanimity and efficiency of those other two great departments of the catholic empire, the civil offices and the army.

For twenty-five years, charm and authority had been carrying him from success to success, but as he himself had said, schism within the church was 'equally formidable as war . . . and more difficult to bring to an end'. Those bound together by common admiration for Lucian were among the ablest of Christian logicians and historians. In Arius, they had a leader as fanatically convinced as the emperor himself that he was always right, and with a manner equally convincing. Although he was condemned early in the proceedings, following a debate where excerpts from his 'Happy Thoughts' were read to prove that he did not really believe that Christ was God, imposing the word *homoousios* on the bishops was a long, slow business. The difficulty was that although the Latin form 'consubstantial' had long been used in the Western church, in the East *homoousios* was a suspect word. Archbishop Dionysius, who had ruled in Alexandria during the persecution under Decius and Valerian, had condemned it, and it was widely known only as one of the key-words in the teaching of Paul of Samosata, a former patriarch of Antioch, declared deposed by a synod in his own city in 268 for his scandalous life, and for teaching that hymns in praise of Christ as God were 'too modern and written by men too progressive' to be used in church. Christ, he had said, had been only a man on whom the Word of God had rested, and the Word could not be separated from the Father, but was 'consubstantial' with him. Theologians of the Antiochene School had long feared that Egyptian mysticism would finally commit Egypt to a theology like Paul's, and Alexander of Alexandria's acceptance of the word *homoousios* seemed to justify their fears. Gradually, however, they were worn down. When Constantine put himself out to attain something, he was hard to resist.

Despite his efforts, however, the desired result was not obtained by argument alone, and he had to resort to threats. As Philostorgus tells the story:

> Arius' partisans being unwilling to adhere to the faith of the council, the emperor declared that those who refused to accept the general ruling of the bishops, whether they were priests or deacons, or other members of the clergy, would be exiled. Philomenos was charged with the execution of this order: he was what the Romans call the *magister* [*officiorum*, head of the civil service]. So he presented Arius and those with him with the agreed formulary, and gave them the choice of signing it . . . or being exiled. . . . They chose exile[14].

Even among those who did sign, many probably still had doubts. In later years, the story circulated that several, including Eusebius of Caesarea, inserted an *iota* into the middle of the word *homoousios* in the copies of the formulary Philomenos presented to them for signature, so that it read *homoiousios*, 'of like substance'. They may well have wished that they dared to do so. Socrates preserves a letter written to the Christians of Caesarea by their bishop which shows how uneasy the imperial creed left him. It was he who had initiated the idea that all the bishops should subscribe to a common statement of faith, proffering that used at baptisms in his own church as a model. Now he had to tell his people that it had been declared unacceptable, because its clauses on the nature of Christ were too ill-defined: 'Our most pious emperor was the first to admit that they were probably correct . . . exhorting all present to give them their assent, and subscribe to them as they stood . . . with the insertion of the single word *homoousios*, an expression which the emperor himself explained did not relate to corporeal parts or properties. . . . However, our conception of such things can only be in divine and mysterious terms – such was the philosophical view of the subject taken by our most wise and pious ruler[15].'

In other words, Eusebius had compromised, on the understanding that he and his congregations need not take the offensive word literally, unless they chose. No doubt others signed on the same conditions.

Bishops Secundus and Theonas, Arius himself, and a handful of priests and deacons would not sign, and went off to exile in Illyricum. The rest of the council, probably among sighs of relief from Constantine and those like him who were happier arguing in Latin than in Greek, turned to the consideration of other problems: the date of Easter, the Meletian Schism and the formulation of disciplinary canons which, whether the bishops realized it or not, were designed to have the effect of cementing the church into the fabric of the unitary empire.

Constantine may not have taken part personally in these later debates. Discussion of the schism of Meletius must, however, have awakened in his mind unpleasant echoes of the Donatist

Affair. Just as Donatus had made charges against Caecilian, so Meletius had laid information against Alexander – and, just as at Arles, so now, Constantine submitted the case to the judgement of the council. Although the bishops found the charges baseless, their discussions revealed that there was a great deal of sympathy for Meletius, and they refused either to depose him or to order the priests he had made to revert to lay status. They ordered him to cease consecrating new bishops in competition with Alexander's, and proposed the integration of the Church of the Martyrs into the Catholic Church by repetition of the ordinations he had already made and by giving the right of succession in Catholic sees to Meletian bishops, provided that they submitted to the Catholic archbishop of Alexandria. Similar proposals had been made at Arles with regard to the Donatists (except that re-ordination, foreign to Gallic and Italian tradition, had not been proposed there). They had proved ineffectual, partly for political reasons. Now they were to prove ineffectual again. The differences between the Delta and Upper Egypt were too marked to be eradicated by a decision taken at far-off Nicaea.

The conciliar rulings in the Meletian Affair might have been seen as a victory for those personally or doctrinally antagonistic to Alexander of Alexandria, but the balance was restored in the vote on the perennial question of the date of Easter. At Antioch and in the East generally, the church had always calculated that date from the Jewish New Year's Day as announced by the rabbis. At Alexandria, Rome and in the West generally, a specifically Christian system prevailed, by which Easter was held to fall on the Sunday after the full moon following the Spring Equinox, itself artificially fixed as falling on March 21. As the Jewish calendar was lunar, and took no account of the equinox, but consisted of sometimes twelve and sometimes thirteen months, Easter was seldom celebrated simultaneously at Antioch and Alexandria, and their feasts might be as much as a month apart. The question seems unimportant today, but at the time of the Council of Nicaea it had been causing bitter strife for over two hundred years. The Council itself heard some violent debates before the Syrians finally capitulated, agreeing for unity's sake to adopt the Alexandrian and Western system.

The final task of Constantine's universal council was to fix rules to ameliorate the lot of those who had lapsed under persecution and prevent future scandals like the Meletian schism or the Collucianists' interference in the affairs of the Alexandrian church. Leaning heavily on the work of the synods of Ancyra and Caesarea, Arles and ultimately Elvira, the council passed twenty canons, all reflecting in some way Constantine's desire that the past should be forgotten as soon as possible and a peaceful church integrated into a tranquil empire. The first drafts of most of them were probably produced under Hosius' guidance in the imperial *scrinia*. Many were concerned with what classes of person might and might not be ordained, and are of little interest today. Six, however, were of special significance to those to whom it was important to fit the church into the empire, and bring the vagaries of those who believed themselves inspired under control.

Canon four ruled that new bishops ought to be consecrated by all the bishops then living in their province, failing which no consecration should be accounted valid unless three bishops had played a part in it, all had given written assent to it, and it had been confirmed by the metropolitan archbishop.

Canon five made the point that persons who had been excommunicated in one diocese ought not to be received in communion elsewhere (as Arius had recently been), but that the cases of excommunicate bishops ought to be reviewed twice a year, in spring and autumn, by synods of bishops from their own provinces.

Canon six granted special precedence to Rome, Antioch and Alexandria, so that their bishops were legally recognized as having peculiar juridical powers, equivalent to those of the Praetorian Prefects in the civil sphere. Under canon seven, Jerusalem was granted a unique status, its bishop becoming an honorary patriarch, as it were, with precedence after the ruler of Antioch, but no extraordinary judicial functions or authority.

Canons fifteen and sixteen forbade bishops, priests and

deacons to leave the sees to which they had been consecrated or ordained in order to work elsewhere – and were dead letters from the first as far as such imperial administrators as Hosius were concerned, but helped to prevent schismatics from spreading rival church organizations by making it possible to deport them back to their own dioceses[16].

An old tradition says that the Council of Nicaea began on May 25 and ended on June 19, but that the bishops remained in Pontica as members of the imperial entourage until late July, as Constantine's guests at the celebration of his twentieth jubilee. Recent precedents would have taken him to Rome for the festivities, but he was far too busy in 325 with his new city and the task of impressing the bishops to go there that year. 'Public festivals were celebrated by the people of the provinces generally,' Eusebius related, 'but the emperor himself invited and feasted with those of God's ministers whom he had just reconciled, and thus offered as it were through them a suitable sacrifice to God. Not one of the bishops was missing from the imperial banquet, the arrangements for which were splendid beyond description. Detachments of the bodyguard with drawn swords surrounded the entrance to the palace and the men of God proceeded through their ranks without fear into the inmost of the imperial apartments, where some shared a table with the emperor, while others reclined on couches set at either side. One might have thought it a foreshadowing of Christ's kingdom, and a dream rather than a reality . . .[17]'

The bishops, so recently persecuted, may have wondered if they were dreaming, but Constantine knew that he was not. His gesture of feasting the bishops, like that of kissing the empty eye-sockets of Bishop Paphnutius, blinded under Licinius, may have been entirely uncalculating when he first thought of it, but his propagandists made certain that it was not overlooked afterwards.

Meanwhile, the report of the council's proceedings was circulating in Egypt, the Pentapolis, Libya and probably elsewhere, in a synodal letter, issued on the authority of the bishops. Constantine, however, had no intention of leaving matters there. He had guided the council, if he had not inspired it: by summoning and attending it, he had transformed it from a synod of bishops, significant only to Christians, into a Sacred Imperial Council, whose rulings were law everywhere. Now he despatched letters in various directions to announce its conclusions as imperial sentences and so give them executive effect. He wrote to the churches of the East, informing them officially of the decision made regarding the date of Easter, and to the bishops in Alexander's archdiocese, telling them that 'the three hundred and more bishops who have been meeting at Nicaea have declared that there is only one faith, the same everywhere, which alone is conformable to the truths of the divine law, and that the egregious Arius appears to have been the victim of the power of the devil', but that now all the 'dissensions, schisms, disturbances and fatal poisons of discord have, by the Will of God, been overcome by the refulgence of the truth'[18].

It was not true. There was half a century of life still in Meletius' Church of the Martyrs, two centuries in the Easter Controversy, and more than three in the Arian conflict. Hardly had the council broken up, before Eusebius of Nicomedia, Maris of Chalcedon and Theognis of Nicaea wrote to the emperor repudiating their signatures to its creed. 'We committed an impious act, O Prince,' Eusebius declared, 'by subscribing to a blasphemy from fear of you.'

Nevertheless, Nicaea had achieved a great deal, not least by confirming Constantine in his conviction that he could work with the Christian bishops and that his vision of a universal church in a catholic empire was capable of realization. In the coming years, he time and again demonstrated his authority over the church by such acts of government as ordering recalcitrant bishops into exile and authorizing the election of replacements for them, as though they had been no more than unsatisfactory officials. Although opposition to the creed of Nicaea continued, there was very little outcry against Constantine's arrogation to himself of power in the church, and none on reasoned doctrinal grounds, where it would have been most difficult to refute.

In a moment of crusading zeal, he promulgated on October 1, 325, a law against 'the cruel spectacles' of gladiatorial contests[19]. Towards the end of the year, he addressed another to the vicarius of the City Prefect forbidding the magistrates to compel Christians to offer any sacrifices other than those of prayer at the Feast of the Imperial Vows[20]. Apparently, he was at last ready to start dismembering the old world whose allegedly lost liberties he had undertaken the war against Maxentius thirteen years earlier to preserve and restore. His obvious bias towards the Christians during this vicennial year frightened the pagans and was to lead to a disastrous clash with them at Rome a few months later. He had stopped calling himself 'the Companion of the Unconquered Sun', and had persuaded his mother Helena to join the church. Yet even now he was not ready to make a definitive break with paganism, and he successfully resisted any temptation he may have felt towards being baptised himself.

CHAPTER ELEVEN

A FAMILY TRAGEDY

CONSTANTINE went to Rome in 326, for a second celebration of his twentieth jubilee. He intended the festivities to be a magnificent expression of both his power and the continuing importance of the City. The fact that he had chosen to keep the anniversary itself at Nicaea was, however, an insult that the aristocratic Roman Senate could not forgive.

Although Byzantium was later to become New Rome, nothing indicates that Constantine had yet decided that it should replace old Rome as the capital of his empire. Optatianus Porphyrius, his court poet, had, it is true, called it 'another Rome' in verses composed to mark the jubilee[1], but the reference was clearly intended only to flatter Constantine for his flair as a city planner, and cannot be shown to reflect either imperial policy or the common talk of the court. Nevertheless, the aristocracy of old Rome was doubtless disturbed by reports of the intense energy which he was putting into the reconstruction of the city on the Bosphorus, and pagans generally were made uneasy by the fact that he had preferred to celebrate his twenty years of power with the Christian leaders at Nicaea, rather than with the high priests and nobility of the empire at Rome. The announcement that the celebrations at the capital would be all the more glorious because they would also mark the tenth anniversary of the promotion to the purple of everybody's favourite prince Crispus and his younger step-brother Constantine II was hardly enough to compensate Rome for the snub. Indeed, as Crispus had been exposed for so long to the influence of a Christian tutor, he may well not have been as popular in the City as he was elsewhere. Too much had happened for the Romans easily to accept any Christianized imperial favourite as a particular friend of theirs. During the past four years, as well as witnessing the destruction of Licinius' pagan empire and the postponement of the *vicennalia* for the Christians' sake, they had also watched grow up within the walls of their own city the first Christian church building to threaten its monolithic paganism, the Lateran *basilica constantiniana* with its baptistery, the magnificent *fons constantini*; and, worse still perhaps for their morale, they had seen the appointment to the city on January 4, 325, of its first Christian governor, Acilius Severus, an old associate of Crispus' teacher Lactantius. Nevertheless, Rome prepared to welcome its emperor, and on January 1, 326, duly voted him the consulship he demanded – his seventh – associating with him his new Caesar, Constantius. On the surface, all was peaceful, but in fact the Blessed Tranquillity of the Augustus lying over the empire late in 325 was only the calm before the storm.

Constantine and his family spent the autumn of 325 in Nicomedia, but by February 326, they were at Serdica and by March, in Sirmium. From there, the emperor had travelled by April 1 to his father-in-law Maximian's old palace at Aquileia, where many years earlier there had reputedly hung a family portrait of the Herculians, showing Fausta as a child, handing a helmet to an equally immature Constantine. If that portrait still hung there, it looked down on a family split by dissension and distrust. March should have been the months of Crispus' decennalial feast, but by then, he was dead, executed by his father's order, allegedly for treason.

When Constantine had begun his progress from Nicomedia to Rome, among the royal party had been his mother Helena, the Augusta Fausta, Licinianus, the son of the murdered Augustus Licinius, probably the ex-empress Constantia, and the Caesar Crispus. Since his mother's return to public life, Constantine had been calling her 'that most noble lady' (*nobilissima femina*) and, probably at his Christian *vicennalia*, had proclaimed her Augusta in her own right, granting her permission to wear the diadem, so putting her in a position of equal honour with Fausta. Both women must have been acutely aware that his handling of the situation had been inept, and Helena was soon to give proof that she had not forgotten that Fausta was a Herculian, whose family name she had had cause to hate since Theodora had taken her husband Constantius Chlorus from her thirty years earlier.

Nor were the two empresses the only members of the party leaving Nicomedia with grudges and fears to nurse. Licinianus had seen his father murdered and his chance of empire snatched from him. His own position was still uncertain, and he cannot have enjoyed the thought that if luck had not turned against him, he would have been preparing to celebrate his own tenth jubilee simultaneously with Constantine's sons.

As for Crispus, he may well have been labouring under the burden of the greatest sense of injustice of them all. After his brilliant victory off Kallipolis, he must have expected some greater reward than a banquet and games at Byzantium and a set of rather indifferent verses from Optatianus. It would have been a fitting gesture if Constantine had named him as his fellow-Augustus, but far from honouring him, his father seems deliberately to have focused the attention of the empire solely on the legitimate neo-Flavians. The command of Gaul had been taken from him and given to the barely adolescent Constantine II; it was not he but Constantius who was named consul for 326; and the approved design of the coins issued to mark his jubilee coupled his famous name with the untried boy-Caesar's, giving him no special distinction, but merely marking 'the tenth year of our Caesars' and 'of our Lords the Caesars'.

An explosion was not, of course, inevitable, but with an imperial family so cruelly divided, travelling towards an uneasy City, it is not surprising that several occurred. Constantine, well characterized by Victor as 'a man rather given to mocking than honey-tongued'[2], had spent 325 putting himself out to be specially smooth and easy with the bishops, however much they had annoyed him. He was fatigued by thirty years of public life, and concerned about the future. When – probably through a common informer, seeking a reward under the terms of an edict dating from the crisis-year 324[3] when his control of the East had still hung in the balance – the rumour of a threat to his authority from Crispus reached him, 'he put to death', Eutropius records, 'that exceptional man his son, his sister's [adopted] son, and soon afterwards his wife, and later, numbers of his friends'[4].

Crispus was not undeserving of the description 'exceptional'. In his nine years as Caesar, he had won victories on the Frankish and Gothic frontiers, at sea with the fleet, and in the hearts of the people. It was this last triumph which his father grudged him. Constantine was not willing, at this stage in his life, to share his popularity with anyone. The edict of 324, like several of Constantine's laws, was a peculiar mixture of ferocity and piety. Promising to informers of whatever 'status, rank or position' a fair hearing of any treason charge against 'any of my officers, senior officials, retinue or family' and rewards in the form of honours and estates if such charges proved well-founded 'so that the Supreme God may continue to be merciful towards me and preserve me for the happiness and well-being of the State', it reflected a new concern on Constantine's part for his own safety and apparently marked his transition from youthful and daring adventurer to suspicious ageing tyrant.

What precisely Crispus' crime was has never been clearly established, and is probably now unascertainable. Contemporary accounts pass over in silence the reasons for the executions marring this year of Roman jubilee. Those later chroniclers content to report only established facts are almost equally reticent. Only the historical gossips claim to inside knowledge of the affair. So, under the date 'from Abraham 2341' (A.D. 325–6), the sober Jerome records only that 'Crispus, Constantine's son, and the younger Licinius, son of Constantia and Licinius, were most cruelly put to death in the ninth year of their reign', while Eutropius notes simply, 'being forced to it by necessity, he executed that exceptional man', and Victor, 'of his children, he who was born the eldest was judicially executed by his father for an undisclosed reason'[5].

If these were all the records, they would be enough to satisfy anyone that Crispus had been executed for treason. The phrase 'being forced to it by necessity' is another way of saying 'for reasons of State' and hints at the same clash between the generations, carefully concealed afterwards by a regretfully triumphant father, as 'judicially executed . . . for an undisclosed reason'. From these notices alone, the natural conclusion would be that Crispus, sickened by Licinius' murder 'after oaths had been sworn', and reading a warning in his own failure to receive promotion, plotted with Licinianus and perhaps also with his stepmother Fausta, the daughter of the executed Herculius, to overthrow Constantine's government between March and July 326, before the splendour of his own jubilee could be eclipsed by the glories of his father's. The plot was, however, discovered, and the conspirators were legally executed as and when their guilt could be proved: Crispus and Licinianus together, then Fausta, and afterwards 'many friends', in waves of terror, spreading outwards like ripples on a pond. The pattern is similar to that of events in Nazi Germany following the failure of the July Plot against Hitler.

If this had been unequivocally the pattern of events, Constantine's revenge would be unpleasant to contemplate, but politically justifiable. Unfortunately for his reputation, however, there is another group of references to the events of this year which put him and his mother in a much more unfavourable light.

In his *Histories*, Victor is content to admit that as far as he knew the reason for Crispus' execution had never been disclosed, but the *Epitome*[6] reports the rumour 'they say that it was by the prompting of Fausta that he ordered his son Crispus to be killed', so plunging everyone back immediately into that world of boudoir intrigue in which Fausta appears to have flourished. Eutropius' 'being forced to it by necessity' now assumes a more sinister hue. Philostorgus hints that the charges made were untrue, but does not list them: 'It is said that Constantine killed his own son Crispus because of slanders made against him by his stepmother'[7].

Zosimus, however, the enemy of the neo-Flavians, says bluntly, 'Crispus, having demanded honours [and been refused them] . . . was suspected of having cohabited in adultery with his step-mother Fausta, and was executed'[8].

Sidonius Apollinaris rounds out the story of Crispus' quasi-incestuous adultery with his father's wife by recording that in his day it was said that Constantine was warned of what was afoot not by Fausta herself, but by his favourite Ablavius, whom he later made Praetorian Prefect and Consul, and 'by lines such as these which were put up on the gates of the Palatine Palace, "Who misses now the golden years of Saturn? They are come again, gem-studded – but Neronian!" '[9] The mythical 'golden days of Saturn', reflected annually in the revels of the Saturnalia, held in December at Rome, were notorious for their sexual license, and Nero had been popularly, if not judicially, convicted of incest with his mother Agripinilla, the daughter of the hero Germanicus Caesar. The pinning of these verses to the gates of Fausta's former palace made their meaning only too obvious.

According to Zosimus, who speaks of the celebrations as already having started when the arrests were made, Crispus was seized at Rome during the summer, but if, as Jerome says, he was executed with Licinianus 'in the ninth year of their reign', the order must have been issued from Serdica or Sirmium before March 1. The two Caesars were executed secretly at Pola, in Istria, near modern Trieste ('most cruelly' Jerome says; 'with cold poison' according to Apollinaris), so leaving Fausta's children, the grandchildren of Herculius, as the only obvious claimants to the empire. If Fausta did make false charges to Constantine against Crispus, it was clearly to obtain this end that she cast herself in the role of Wicked Step-mother.

Apollinaris' version of this family tragedy, however, accounts for Fausta's own execution by the implied assertion that Crispus' attempts to seduce her were successful. Saturnine days had come again, although with a Neronian cast, and Constantine executed both his favourite son and his legal wife on the evidence of favourites and anonymous denunciations*. If this account is true, Licinianus was either simply unlucky, the jealousy of the

* Actually, Apollonaris' account suggests that Ablavius wrote the verses attached to the Lateran Palace gate. It is difficult to see why he should have done so, unless it was to arouse the populace. As Constantine's favourite, he had only to whisper a word in his master's ear to bring about Crispus' downfall.

tyrant dragging him into the net of suspicion, or perhaps convicted of having acted as a go-between. Apollinaris' story is, however, contradicted by another, which has gained wider credence. This brings Helena's name into the affair. According to this version, Fausta, having secured Crispus' arrest and execution by her denunciation of his, possibly unsuccessful, attempt to commit incest with her, was herself denounced by Helena for having done her grandson 'a great injury', whether by slandering him or in some other way, the *Epitome*, which records it, does not make clear:

> They say that it was by the prompting of Fausta that he ordered his son to be killed. And afterwards he had his wife Fausta herself killed by being immersed in a scalding bath, when his mother Helena accused her of having done her grandson a great injury.

Jerome dates her execution in the year from Abraham 2344, a few months after Crispus' death. Philostorgus has an even more titillating version of the story, in which Helena's name does not appear, but to which it has often been attached: 'And sinning again [after bringing about Crispus' death unjustly by slander], by committing adultery with a circus hand, she was ordered to be suffocated in the hot room of the bath, Constantine meanwhile giving the justice of the sword to the young man. . . .'

If the story did in fact become as complicated as this, with Crispus, Helena, Licinianus, Fausta, Ablavius and a stableboy all involved, it is not surprising that Constantine afterwards ordered the execution of 'many friends'. He had his full measure of that suspiciousness common to most autocrats. Even if the intervention of Helena is discounted as the invention of anti-Christians and anti-Constantineans, the story remains a very unpleasant one. It is rendered even more unsavoury by the suspicion, frequently reiterated, that two edicts on sexual immorality posted in April 326 refer to Crispus and his step-mother. The one, dated from Aquileia on the first of the month, lays down savage penalties for abductors of virgins, and for the girls themselves, whether consenting or not, providing also for the execution of slaves acting as pandars in such cases by the stopping of their mouths with molten lead, and the exiling of parents acquiescing in the offence[10]. The other, promulgated at Nicomedia on April 25, and so probably issued in Italy or Pannonia sometime in March, removed adultery from the list of crimes punishable on the evidence of a common informer, making it a private crime, as it were, punishable only if the information was laid by a husband or other close relative of the guilty woman[11].

In fact, neither of these edicts has an obvious and direct connection with the case of Crispus and Fausta as it is recorded in the chronicles and histories. The edict of April 1 would seem, with additional refinements of cruelty in the punishments envisaged, to widen the scope of the edict sent to the City Prefect alone some time before 321, reserving cases of abduction by members of the class of *honestiores* to the imperial court. The severity of the revised edict suggests that it was in fact provoked by an actual case, the details of which nauseated Constantine; but to argue that the case in mind was Crispus' is to accuse the Caesar of a new crime in the total absence of evidence against him. It is, of course, possible that he carried off a virgin as well as trying to seduce Fausta, but there is no proof that he did, even in the tenuous form of an anonymous denunciation.

The edict on adultery dated April 26 can only be linked with Fausta's case by supposing that it was not the Most Noble Empress Helena who denounced her, but only anonymous verse-writers and similar witnesses, or that although Constantine accepted Helena's evidence, he was afterwards ashamed of having done so, and wanted to make it illegal for mothers-in-law to denounce daughters-in-law for the future. If this were so, however, we should expect to find some evidence that he turned against his mother when remorse struck him, but there is nothing to suggest that he did so. His mother remained in favour until her death from natural causes in the year 330, and was then buried at Rome in a porphyry coffin apparently, from its military decoration, originally intended for Constantine himself. She had a palace at Rome, all the money she wanted for founding churches and other purposes, and her every whim was indulged. A year after Fausta's death, Drepanum in Bithynia was entirely rebuilt at her request, because the body of her favourite saint, Arius' master Lucian of Antioch, was buried there; at the same time, Constantine renamed the city Helenopolis, perhaps because she had been born there, but more probably as a graceful mark of respect. On this evidence, if Helena had indeed betrayed Fausta, because she in her turn had falsely denounced Helena's grandson Crispus, Constantine was not disgusted with her action, but delighted by it.

Yet another edict of 326 which has sometimes been said to relate to the Crispus-murder, one dated June 4 prohibiting married men from keeping concubines[12], would seem even less likely to have any direct connection with the family entanglements of that year. Like the law of April 4, forbidding tutors to commit fornication with their pupils[13], it would seem rather to belong to that large body of Constantine's legislation bearing the impress of his puritanism. If, as we have already suggested, Constantine was a sexual puritan, with little time to spare from the lust for power for the pursuit of Venus, all the 'sexual' legislation of this year may well fit into this category, its only link with Crispus and Fausta being that their lapse or lapses perhaps drove the emperor actually to issue it at this time, and propose punishments for breaches of the law more savage than he would otherwise have made them. If these laws had been directly inspired by events within the imperial family, they would have mentioned that family. Nothing in Constantine's character would have restrained him from legally forbidding sexual congress with ladies of the imperial household if that is what he had wanted to forbid.

The news that the executions had been carried out might have been expected to relax the tensions threatening to tear Constantine apart, and allow him to sink thankfully into the celebrations, but it appears not to have done so. Having faced a challenge, real or imaginary, from within his family, he himself suddenly threw out a challenge to his pagan detractors in the army and the city, by an open display of contempt for their religion, thus deliberately staking his credibility as a leader on the chance that their loyalty to himself was stronger than their fidelity towards the gods.

On what should have been Crispus' jubilee day, March 1, he

had entered the camp at Aquileia to shouts from 'the prefects and tribunes, and most eminent men' of 'O Augustus Constantine! May the gods preserve you for our sakes! Your safety is our salvation!'[14] The last thing he could afford to do in this turbulent year was to risk undermining such loyalty in his still-pagan guards by openly repudiating their gods. Yet after he had entered Rome in July, that is precisely what he did. As Zosimus tells the story:

> When the festival of the ancestors came round, when the custom was to go up from the camp to the Capitol and there fulfil the tradition ceremonies, Constantine was to have taken part in the festival with the soldiers. But the Egyptian [Magician: a contemptuous epithet for Hosius] told him of an oracle to the effect that to go up to the Capitol Hill would be a shameful thing, so he stayed away from the holy rites of the temples, thus demonstrating hatred of the Senate and people[15].

His refusal to take part in the ceremonies of the feast seems to have been a sudden decision on his part. It is said that the parade was already drawn up, waiting for its imperial Commander in Chief, when he announced with an oath that he would not march in it. Like many sudden decisions, this one had disastrous results. It earned Constantine the curses of the Senate and people, and threatened to split the army into Christian and non-Christian factions. If the emperor had been willing to go the whole way with the Christians, the situation might have been different, but he was still refusing to be baptised. Zosimus was not the only pagan who blamed Hosius' influence for Constantine's ill-mannered display at this feast, but his story that after it the emperor was baptised, to free himself from the guilt of the murder of Crispus, must be rejected in the light of Eusebius' testimony that he himself baptised him some ten years later. The loyalty of the soldiers withstood this assault, but it was a foolhardy risk for even an absolute ruler to take.

The claim that Hosius was behind the incident might not be true, and in fact the whole story may have been invented for propaganda purposes by pagans aiming to blacken Constantine's memory. There can, however, be no doubt that he showed reckless disregard for pagan susceptibilities at Rome that year, and took no care to hide his preference for Christian company. During the months of his stay, he endowed at least one and possibly two new basilicas, St Peter's at Nero's Circus in the Vatican, an area formerly sacred to Apollo, and the Church of the Holy Apostles (now St Sebastian's) on the Appian Way. The basilica of St-Paul-without-the-walls may also have been founded at this time, at the traditional site of St Paul's martyrdom, on the Ostian Way.

According to mediaeval tradition, the emperor himself marked out the foundations of St Peter's with his own hands, just as he personally drove the plough outlining the walls of Constantinople, and carried the first twelve baskets of earth from the site, one in honour of each of the Apostles[16]. If there is any truth at all behind this story, it must have seemed to the pagans an insult almost as great as his refusal to take part in the Capitoline ceremonies. Both Peter's and Paul's basilicas were endowed with estates, mainly from Licinius' former holdings in Egypt, although St Peter's was also granted land from the imperial estates around Antioch, in commemoration of the apostle's rule there, and St Paul's received some income from Tarsus, Paul's native city. The amount of the original endowments is uncertain – as is also their date – but by the end of the reign St Peter's was receiving 3,170 *solidi* a year, and St Paul's, 4,070; while both churches also rejoiced in the possession of priceless treasures given to them by Constantine and his mother (although her main gifts were made to the church built a few years later at her palace in Rome, Holy Cross in Jerusalem, the *basilica sessoriana*).

It must be held somewhat to the discredit of Constantine's Christian advisers and the Roman patriarch that they appear to have been so dazzled by his friendship and munificence – and, perhaps, so afraid of his losing patience with them – that none of them did anything to stop the judicial murders which went on throughout that summer. They acquiesced, publicly at least, in the poisoning of Licinianus, just as they had in the beheading of Licinius. There is not the slightest hint anywhere that Lactantius' friend Acilius Severus, or Bishop Hosius, or anyone else, objected even to the murder of Crispus, although until his death he was manifestly being groomed for a future as a Christian emperor. Constantine's behaviour that year was as Neronian (although in a different sense) as that ascribed to his son by the anonymous verses preserved by Apollinaris. It was a scandalous example of Christian rule, and may well have given the death-blow to the last hope of converting pagan Rome and making it the capital of the Christian empire.

There is an interesting footnote to the story of Fausta's disappearance from public life in 326, one which – if it were credible – would explain why no outcry followed her alleged murder by suffocation and scalding. According to a tale picked up from an unknown source centuries later by the Orator Monodius she was not killed in 326–7, but merely immured in the women's quarter of the palace, where she survived to emerge in mourning at the funeral of her son Constantine II in 340. It was probably the privacy of her execution, coupled with a natural desire on the part of the Christians to clear their hero's name of cruelty and murder charges, which gave birth to this tale. There was never an official account of Fausta's death, and by the end of the century, John Chrysostom seems to have believed that she had died in the amphitheatre 'from exposure to wild beasts'[17]. Yet another tradition maintained that she committed suicide after Constantine learned of her adultery with the circus hand. She may have done so, from fear of his anger, but it is more probable that this story, too, was circulated in the hope of relieving his name of the burden of the guilt of having killed her.

There is, however, nothing to suggest that during his lifetime Constantine ever reproached himself for her death, or any other executions carried out at his order. After his own death, her sons put her portrait on some of their coins, but at the time of her murder, her name and Crispus' were chipped out of inscriptions everywhere, and the citizens were expected to forget them both.

But Crispus' victories had fired the imaginations of many in the empire, and he was not forgotten. On the contrary, over the years a body of legend grew up around his name until, during the period of the Turkish occupation of Greece, over a thousand years later, he was still remembered as *the* Caesar, the hero-prince, the Christian Theseus, as it were, founder of the modern Greek nation. The story of his execution was too well established for it to be forgotten or explained away, so no attempt was made to deny it, but it was said that hardly had the order been carried out before his father was overcome by remorse. Leaning perhaps on Zosimus' story that it was at this time that, in order to be freed from blood-guilt, Constantine was baptised 'for the remission of sins', legend related that the emperor did penance for the canonical period of forty days, and ordered a golden statue of Crispus to be exhibited in a prominent place, with the inscription: 'To my son, whom I unjustly murdered.' But no reliable witness ever claimed to have seen it.

CHAPTER TWELVE

CONSTANTINOPLE

CONSTANTINE is best remembered for his championing of Christianity, and his decision to rebuild Byzantium as Constantinople, making it the new capital of the Roman world. It would be difficult to decide which of these policies had the greater effect on the evolution of Europe during the thousand years following his death. They were, in fact, so closely linked that they ought not to be separated. In the last resort, it was because Constantine made himself champion of the Christians that he was forced to build a New Rome. If he had chosen to persecute them, Serdica or Nicomedia would have served him well as an administrative centre, and it would have been unnecessary for him to make Constantinople anything more than a strong military base and trading post, serving to link Asia and Europe, while guarding the Bosphorus against the Goths and Persians.

There is some evidence that this was the future he planned for the city, when he first began to rebuild it, after unifying the empire by defeating Licinius. Throughout the mediaeval period and into modern times, legend had it that when he drew up plans for a new metropolis, his first choice of site was not Byzantium, but the plain of Troy, at the western end of the narrows of the Hellespont. If his intention was deliberately to found a new Rome and restart the history of the world, setting it to run on Christian lines, Troy was the ideal place for the venture. Throughout the Greek-speaking world, the siege of Troy by the Achaeans under Agamemnon had for centuries been held to mark the true beginning of civilized history, and Homer's accounts of it and its consequences had long been used not only as standards of eloquence but also as primary textbooks in almost every subject taught at the schools. Moreover, Roman legend had it that the Eternal City had been founded by Aenaeas, the son of Priam, who, escaping with divine help from the sack of Troy, had carried the mysterious *palladium*, in which Troy's luck was embodied, into Italy, where it had ultimately passed into the safe keeping of the Vestal Virgins. So to any educated citizen of the empire, Troy was the beginning of everything that was best in the world, and for Constantine to have founded his new capital on the site of the old city would have been an act of profound symbolic significance.

In the event, however, he did not do so. He may actually have started a city development at the site of ancient Sigeum, on the plain below Troy, but there is no reliable evidence that he ever planned to make it his Second Rome. He himself said in one of his laws that he was divinely inspired to give that honour to Byzantium[1]. The story of the rebuilding of Troy first appears in late histories of his life. There is an interesting version of it in Sozomen's *History*, where writing of Byzantium, he records that

> [Constantine] made great improvements at this last city, making it the equal of Rome in power and administrative function. After he had organized the empire as he wanted it, and had settled foreign affairs by wars and treaties, he decided to found a city to be called after himself, equal in renown to Rome. With this intention, he went to the plain lying below Troy near to the Hellespont, close to the Tomb of Ajax, where, they say, the Achaeans had their ships beached and tents standing during the siege of Troy, and there he marked out the groundplan of a large and beautiful city, and built its gates on a rise in the ground, where they are still visible to anyone sailing that way. However, when he had reached this point, God appeared to him by night and commanded him to seek another site. So led by God's hand, he came to Byzantium in Thrace, beyond Chalcedon in Bithynia, and was ordered to build his city there, making it worthy of the name of Constantine. So in obedience to divine commands, he enlarged the city of Byzantium, surrounding it with high walls. He also built wonderful palaces in all its southern districts. Then, realizing that its former population was not large enough for so important a city, he peopled it with noblemen and their households, summoning them from the elder Rome and the other provinces. To cover the cost of his building projects, of decorating the city, supplying its inhabitants with food, and providing it with all the necessities of life, he introduced new taxation. He beautified it sumptuously with a hippodrome, fountains, porticoes, and other buildings. . . . He built a new

Council House (which they call, a Senate), and ordained that it should be granted the same honours and celebrate the same holidays as those traditional among the other Romans[2].

Later legend further embellished this pious tale. According to one Byzantine account, when Constantine, led from Troy by the divine hand, hesitated at Chalcedon, uncertain whether or not God intended him to cross the Bosphorus into Thrace, the eagles of the mountains flew down to pick up the architects' instruments, builders' tools and building materials, and carry them to the acropolis of Byzantium[3]. According to another, well known in the West centuries later, not only did God personally order the conversion of Byzantium into Constantinople, but the city herself also appeared to the emperor in a dream. In its final form, as told by William of Malmesbury, this version ran:

> As Constantine was sleeping, he imagined that there stood before him an old woman, one whose forehead was furrowed by age, but that presently she was transformed into a beautiful girl, so charming his eye by the elegance of her youthful graces that he could not refrain from kissing her. His mother Helena, who was present, then said, 'She shall be yours for ever, and shall not die until the end of time.' When he awoke, the emperor implored heaven by fasting and almsgiving for the explanation of this dream. And lo and behold, within a week, having fallen again into a deep sleep, he thought he saw Pope Silvester, who had died some little time earlier, complacently regarding his convert and saying, 'You have shown your customary prudence in seeking a divine explanation of this enigma: it is certainly beyond the comprehension of man. The old woman you saw is this city [Byzantium], worn down by age, her time-eaten walls, threatened by approaching ruin, needing a restorer. But you, having renewed its walls and affluence, shall make it famous with your own name, and the descendents of emperors shall reign here for ever'[4].

A little earlier, Adhelm of Canterbury had told the same story in his *In Praise of Virginity*, but perhaps out of deference to the nature of his subject had not permitted the emperor to kiss the girl. In his version, Constantine clothed Byzantium with his own purple cloak, and putting his gold and bejewelled diadem on her head, made her queen of the world.

The city gates which Sozomen described as standing in his days on the site of Sigeum may have been built there by Constantine, but it is very unlikely that he ever intended the city beyond them to be his capital or that he was led from there by the hand of God to begin the reconstruction of Byzantium. Work on Constantinople was in fact begun immediately after Constantine had become 'the Victor', 'to mark his victory' as the *Origins of Constantinople* and the unnamed author quoted by Valesius both record[5]. If he ever did toy with the idea of building a capital at Troy, it was after, and not before, he had begun to rebuild and beautify Byzantium, where reconstruction work had already commenced before the quarrel with the pagans in 326. It was this quarrel which, as Zosimus knew, drove him to the decision to make the rebuilt city his New Rome – or, as he put it, to carry the *palladium* (whether physically or metaphorically) from Rome to the new city, so making it heir to the destiny of world leadership which the old Rome had inherited from Troy[6]. Even after he had determined to make Constantinople his New Rome, he was hesitant about broadcasting that decision to the world. When the time came, in 330, to dedicate the city as Constantinople, the official reason for rebuilding Byzantium was still being given as the commemoration of his – and the unmentionable Crispus' – victory over Licinius. Certainly, the original aim – before 326 – was the same as that behind most grandiose building schemes at this time: primarily, that is, for the aggrandisement of the name of Constantine the Victor, and this aim probably remained paramount for some time after the final quarrel with Rome's pagan leadership. So much is clear from the design of the first coins issued to mark the dedication, a bronze issue with on one side a female head, the embodiment of the city, with the word CONSTANTINOPOLIS around it, and on the other a reminder of the victory of Kallipolis, in the form of a ship at sea, with Victory (or perhaps *Tyche*, the destiny and luck of the city) bearing a wreath at the prow, and the inscription 'the Victory of the Augustus'. These coins were actually minted at Rome, simultaneously with another issue showing on the reverse Romulus and Remus and the stars of the *Dioscuroi*, the Twins, and on the obverse a female head and the inscription URBS ROMA[7].

How soon after the fiasco of the Roman *vicennalia* the idea of making Constantinople first rival then surpass the old Rome took root in Constantine's mind, he never revealed. The thought may have germinated while he was still at the old capital in 326, but it would have been in keeping with his character to throw himself into an agony of doubt about it, then resolve his difficulties by claiming a divine revelation, so putting the burden of the decision on to God. A vision in 312 had given him victory over Maxentius, and brought the Romans 'freedom' to live in the peace of Constantine. By 326, it was clear that they had decisively rejected that freedom, so after a period of indecision, Constantine experienced a vision of God telling him that the moment had come to replace Rome with a new, more compliant, capital city. Even after he had convinced himself that God wanted him to build a new Rome, his attitude towards the decision to do so remained ambiguous. He spared no effort to solve the practical problems involved, but gave Constantinople institutions which, although often superficially paralleling those of old Rome, were in fact only potentially a challenge to them. So, for instance, although the new senate was expected to rival and soon outshine the old, he was too wily to permit it immediately to reveal the full scope of its threat to the aristocracy which had snubbed him. He invited the old senatorial families to transplant themselves to the shores of the Bosphorus, offering them estates in Bithynia and Pontus to support them, remitting all taxation to the few who accepted, and building them palaces on the Bucoleon waterfront which were replicas of their old homes at Rome. When, however, it became clear that the majority were not willing to move, he accepted this fresh snub, and instead of compelling them to obey him, created a new order of noblemen and, as a chronicler put it, 'made a new senate there of the second rank; they were called *clari*'[8] – whereas the nobles he had created at Rome to ouvote the old class of *honestiores* after the defeat of Maxentius had been given the more resounding title *clarissimi*. At first, this new senate at 'Byzantine Rome' was thus openly admitted to be inferior, but how long would it be so in fact, if he and his successors used and honoured it, while generally ignoring the senators of old Rome?

Many of the new *clari* were Christians, only too anxious to see pagan Rome eclipsed. It may, indeed, have been the Christians who first planted the thought in the emperor's mind that a new capital would solve many old problems. The poet Optatianus, who first called Constantinople *altera Roma*, 'another Rome', was a Christian. The vision of a new Rome, capable of giving a new lease of life to the empire, may not, however, have been wholly unwelcome even beyond Christian circles, for there was a widespread fear that the old Rome, the Head of the World, was about to be cut off, and would carry the provinces with it into ruin.

Superstitious fear about the imminent destruction of Rome was fostered by gloomy forecasts of a black future for the whole empire, made by a number of self-appointed prophets whose prognostications found wide credence at this time. One of the most interesting of them, from our present point of view, was Crispus' tutor Lactantius, who, during the period while he was unemployed after Galerius had closed the schools of rhetoric and philosophy at Nicomedia, had written a treatise entitled *The Divine Institutes*, a large part of which was devoted to proving that the world had been made to last six thousand years, and that its time was about to run out. 'The fall and ruin of the world will soon occur,' he declared, but added that it would not come about 'while the City of Rome continues to stand. But when the Head of the World has been cut off, and has become a rough track, as the Sibyls foretell, who can doubt that the end of man's history and the orb of the world itself will have come? That city, and she alone, upholds all. . .'[9] Lactantius was an African by birth and at the time he wrote the *Institutes* had only recently been converted to Christianity. The semi-mystical acceptance of Roman world-leadership reflected in these sentences was a typical pagan and Afro-Roman attitude, not necessarily shared elsewhere in the empire. Optimistic Eastern Christians may well have argued that the fulfilment of the punning Sibylline oracle that 'Roma' would one day become a *rhume*, a path for pack animals, would not have the dire results predicted for it if a new Christian city was ready to slip into the role of Head of the World as soon as the old capital collapsed. Lactantius and his fellow pessimists were, however, ready with another prophecy to kill all such hopes: 'The sword shall run through the world, mowing done everything, laying everything low, like a harvest. And – my mind recoils from relating it, but I must tell it, for it is on the point of happening – the cause of this desolation and confusion will be this, that the Name of Rome, by which the world is now ruled, will be taken from the world, and government will return to Asia, and the East will rule once more, and the West serve'[10]. The prophesied result of any attempt to remove the capital to the East was, then, instant destruction.

Constantine was manifestly superstitious. Lactantius had shared his ideas with him over many years. The emperor shared a good deal of the ex-rhetor's respect for Rome, although he did not like the city. His internal conflict over the decision to transfer power to Constantinople may well, therefore, have been very intense, although it was not strictly speaking the 'Asian' city of the prophecy, and this – as well as fear of a pagan reaction – may account for the diffidence and ambiguity with which he made the future role of the city known to the world. As the Easter Chronicle expresses it, Constantine chose and dedicated Byzantium as his capital 'because the hegemony of Rome was ending'[11]. To the superstitious mind, Byzantium was a safer choice than either Troy or Chalcedon, because it was not technically in Asia, although an Eastern city; and its foundation-oracle, allegedly given to the Megarans by Apollo at Delphi in the seventh century before Christ, seemed to imply that the city would be twice-founded, and that its second foundation, made under the auspices of a fish, would have a more glorious outcome than the first. The fish was a Greek symbol of the saving Christ. Byzantium's foundation-oracle thus appeared to cancel out the oracles against moving the centre of government from Rome: might not Constantine hope that the foundation of a New Rome on a lucky site in the name of the saving

Christ would turn away the evil fortune hanging over the world?

There can, naturally, be no proof that any of these prophecies were in the forefront of Constantine's mind when he went to Byzantium after his Roman *vicennalia*, but at the very least they coloured the thinking of some of his contemporaries and so had some effect, however minimal, on his own outlook. He was still superstitious enough to consult augurs and astrologers before choosing the day for the solemn ritual of marking out the line of the new walls with the point of his spear.

The actual date of this new *consecratio* remains uncertain, but it was in the autumn of either 326 or 328, on both of which occasions Constantine is known to have been in Byzantium. According to one account, the date was November 4, 328, 'in the first year of the 276th Olympiad, when the sun was in the constellation of the Bowman and at an hour dominated by the Crab'[12]. Early Christian chroniclers of the city's foundation are all adamant that it was planned as a Christian centre from the first. So Sozomen says, for instance, that 'as this city became the capital of the empire during a period of religious advance, it was not contaminated with altars, Greek temples or sacrifices, and although Julian later authorized the introduction of idolatry for a short period, it soon afterwards became extinct'[13]. (Ironically, Julian the Apostate was the first emperor actually to be born in Constantinople, in the year 331, while his father Julius Constantius 'the Patrician', Constantine's half-brother, who had married Basilina, the daughter of a wealthy senator, was a member of Constantine's staff there.) Yet two pagans, Sopater the Neoplatonist and the High Priest Praetextus, played very prominent roles in the consecration ceremonies, and two temples are known to have been built in the city before Constantine's death, one at the Hippodrome, to the Heavenly Twins, the other to the *Tyche* of the city, although probably no sacrificial cult was permitted at either of them, any more than at the temples to the genius of Constantine and the *Gens Flavia* which he permitted to be founded at about this time at Hispellum in Umbria[14]. What little evidence exists, suggests that Sozomen and his fellow Christian historians present a distorted picture of Constantine's thinking about Constantinople in 328. Although the Christians already claimed him as their own, Sopater's influence over him was strong, and the ceremonies of the *consecratio* were largely pagan, in marked contrast to those of the dedication only two years later. He seems to have dug into the foundations all the varieties of luck he knew. For a time, he entertained the idea of calling the city not Constantinople but 'Anthusa', 'flourishing', the Greek form of 'Flora', the secret name used by the pagan mystagogues for Rome – perhaps to ensure that, whatever disasters struck Italy, the 'name of Rome' should not disappear from the world. It may well have been 'Anthusa' and not 'Constantine' that he had in mind when, in a law of as late a date as 330, he said, 'At the divine command, we have bestowed upon this city an eternal name'[15]. Tradition has it that when, following the precedent set by Romulus at old Rome, he personally marked out the line of the walls, he enclosed within them an area so great that a member of his entourage protested, only to be put in his place with a sublime 'I shall go on until He who is walking ahead of me stops'[16]. Who was this 'he', walking ahead of the spearpoint? The Christians unhesitatingly claimed that he was Christ, but Constantine never said so, and it is remarkable that although he used the *chi-rho* symbol and the cross, he almost never spoke of Christ as his God, even when addressing bishops. Despite the active part he played in Christian affairs, he was still at heart an agent of the Supreme God, one aspect of whose nature was revealed in Christianity, rather than a monotheist, dedicated to Christ. The 'he' who walked before him right across the peninsula from the Golden Horn to Propontis probably had no personal name, though he was known by a host of them, being made up of the best attributes of such divine beings as Apollo, Christ, the *Tyche* of the city and the Genius of Constantine himself.

Constantine's continuing ambiguity in religious thinking found expression in the statue of himself which he set up in the heart of the new city. It stood at the top of what was said to be the tallest column in the world, a hundred feet of red porphyry, brought from Heliopolis, the Sun-City in Egypt, and erected in the new forum on a twenty-foot high base of white marble. Under this slab, he was alleged to have secretly buried the original Trojan palladium, as a *telesma*, a foundation-offering to bring good fortune through the years ahead. The body of the statue was an Apollo by Phidias; its head was a portrait of Constantine himself. It carried a sceptre in its right hand and an orb in its left. Equivocally, the orb bore a cross – equivocally, because the cross could be interpreted as a symbol either of the sun-god or of Christ. Inside the orb, however, was placed a fragment of the True Cross, recently discovered by the Empress Helena at Jerusalem. Around the statue's head was a metal crown or halo made to represent the sun's rays, and the inscription on the base spoke of the emperor shining like the sun[17]. Who was being honoured in this confection – Christ, Apollo or Constantine? It looks very much as though Constantine was claiming that he summed up all religion in himself, and that he was well on the way to megalomania – a conclusion which finds support in the murder of Crispus and Fausta, the challenge to Rome's pagans in 326, and the scale of Constantinople itself.

The original walls of Greek Byzantium had been about a mile long. They ran in a loop southwards from the south shore of the inlet known as the Golden Horn, to take in higher land where the acropolis was built, then back north-eastwards to the western shore of the Bosphorus. Under Septimus Severus and Caracalla, at the end of the second Christian century, they had been moved westwards some thousand yards along the Golden Horn, to bring within the fortified area the suburbs which had grown up on the plain to the west and south of the acropolis. Constantine's plan moved the northern boundary another mile inland along the Golden Horn, then struck due westwards for almost three quarters of a mile, before curving gently west and south to the shores of Propontis, so including within the city some four miles of the southern shore of the peninsula on which it stood, together with four new harbours[18]. The result was that the new city had at least five times the area of the old. It would have been a hopeless

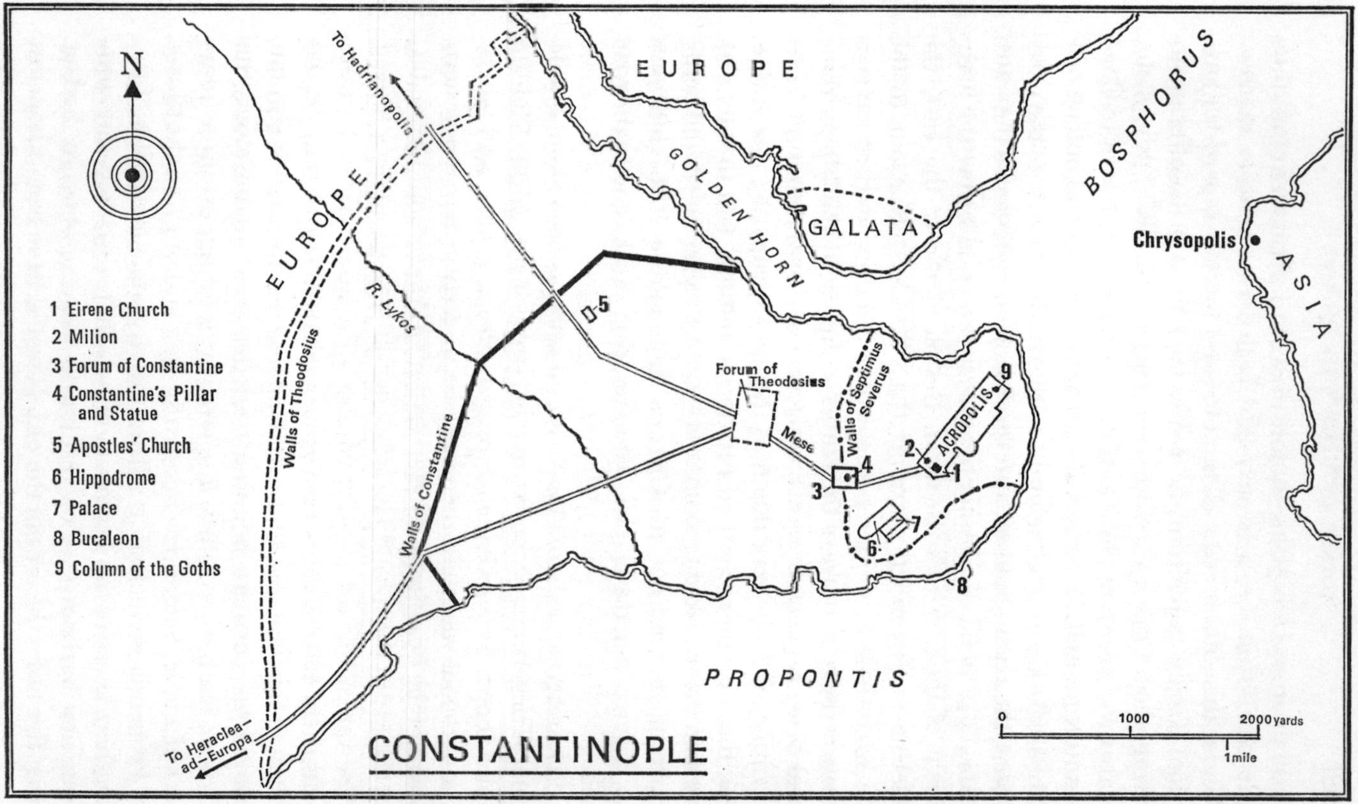
N
EUROPE
GOLDEN HORN
GALATA
BOSPHORUS
Chrysopolis
ASIA
To Hadrianopolis
EUROPE
R. Lykos
Walls of Theodosius
Walls of Constantine
Forum of Theodosius
Mese
Walls of Septimus Severus
ACROPOLIS
PROPONTIS
To Heraclea-ad-Europa
0
1000
2000 yards
1 mile
1 Eirene Church
2 Milion
3 Forum of Constantine
4 Constantine's Pillar and Statue
5 Apostles' Church
6 Hippodrome
7 Palace
8 Bucaleon
9 Column of the Goths
CONSTANTINOPLE

task to attempt to fill the whole area with permanent buildings within the two- (or at most four-) year period between the consecration and the dedication envisaged by the emperor's plans. He expected the city to be ready for formal dedication at the beginning of the celebrations marking the twenty-fifth anniversary of his accession, in the early summer of 330. Instead, efforts were concentrated on certain areas, notably the main harbour, the line of the walls, the plain to the south and west of the acropolis, the acropolis itself, and the Bucoleon Harbour to the south of it. The main development was on the plain below the acropolis, in the triangle between the old walls to the east, the Severan walls to the west, and the Bucoleon Harbour to the south. It was here that the tangle of buildings and courtyards constituting the Great Palace grew up, with the hippodrome forming its north-western boundary, and beyond that the heart of the 'public' part of the city, the oval Forum of Constantine, with the statue of the Founder in the middle. Just to the north of the palace complex, within the area of Byzantium's old walls, was placed a *milion*, a First Milestone, marking the beginning of all the roads in the empire – it actually lay at the end of the road from Hadrianopolis, which within the city became the main thoroughfare, the *mese*. The erection of the *milion* here made the claim that this spot was now the centre of the world. Like the new Senate built on the Forum, the *milion* was planned as a conscious challenge to its counterpart at Rome: without a word being said or written on the subject, Anthusa was taking over from Flora, the new Rome from the old. On the acropolis itself, the site of the temple of Aphrodite became that of the city's principal church, dedicated not to a martyr but to *Hagia Eirene*, Holy Peace, the Holy Peace of God and the Blessed Tranquillity of the Augustus. Such limited archaeological exploration of the site as has been possible suggests that a pagan shrine to peace may have stood within or near the area sacred to Aphrodite before the reconstruction. If this was so, was the new dedication an exercise in propaganda or in syncretism? It could be read either way: by Christians, as a sign that their new world was swallowing the old, by committed pagans as a direct challenge, by waverers as a sign that things were not going to be so different after all.

In addition to the walls, the Great Palace, the Eirene Church, the hippodrome, and the forum with its law courts and senate house, the only other structure within the city known to have been sufficiently near completion to be formally inaugurated in 330 was the enlarged baths, known since the time of Severus as the Baths of Zeuxippus, in honour either of Zeus Master-of-Horses or of one of the two men (the other was Byzas) honoured as the city's original founder. Like the hippodrome, this was intended as a popular foundation, and no expense was spared in reminding all using it of the munificence of its restorer. Its walls were covered with marble and more than sixty bronze statues, brought from all over the empire, stood in niches around its pools. Unfortunately, neither the baths nor any other of Constantine's buildings in his own city survives in anything like its original form. Not only have time and conquest destroyed them, but also the haste in which they were erected made it necessary to begin restoration work on them within a few years of their completion. Although Constantine wrote to provincial governors ordering them first to send their best architects to Constantinople, and then to set up schools of architecture and building science to provide a steady flow of skilled men to work at the city, too much was currently being demanded of the resources of the empire for all that was being produced to be of the best quality[19].

Constantinople was not the only major building project under way at this time. In the West, new basilicas were under construction at vast expense at Rome (notably Holy Cross in Jerusalem) and other cities, and in North Africa the whole of Cirte in Numidia was being rebuilt as Constantine; while in Asia Minor Drepanum was becoming Helenopolis, and at many places churches were being built or enlarged with the help of imperial funds, especially at the Christian Holy Places in Syria and Palestine, where the work was undertaken at the instigation or in imitation of the zeal of the Empress Helena.

Eusebius says that Constantine had by his influence made his mother in her last years 'so devout a worshipper of God – although she had not previously been one – that she seemed to have been instructed from her earliest days by the Saviour of Mankind himself . . . and had granted her [together with the title Augusta] . . . authority over the imperial treasury, to use and disburse its funds entirely at her own will and discretion'[20]. In 327, she used this freedom to make a pilgrimage through Syria to Jerusalem where she was shown by Bishop Macarius the alleged site of the Crucifixion, recently excavated there. The culminating moment of her visit came with her discovery of the True Cross in a cistern. Her benefactions to the Christians of Palestine included the endowment of the basilicas of the Holy Nativity at Bethlehem and the Ascension on the Mount of Olives. At the same time, Bishop Macarius was using funds provided by Constantine and a large number of skilled labourers to build a rotunda over the Holy Sepulchre, with an accompanying basilica, paved courts and colonnades, living quarters and offices; while Eutropia of Syria, Maximian's widow, another imperial pilgrim to the Holy Land, had written to her daughter's murderer asking whether he knew that the tombs of the patriarchs at Mamre near Hebron were now the site of a pagan grove and shrine, and demanding that a suitable church should be built there also. Constantine passed on her request as an order to Bishop Macarius, and earmarked additional funds for this development[21]. Meanwhile, important church building projects were also in progress at Antioch and Tyre in Northern Syria. . . . The list went on and on. The result was that, plead though Constantine would, there was simply not enough skilled labour in the empire to make Constantinople durable as well as impressive.

The greatest loss of all has perhaps been the Eirene Church. It was destroyed not by decay, but by hooligans in the course of the Nike Riots, during the reign of Justinian, and completely rebuilt, so that even its original ground-plan cannot be determined. Probably Holy Peace, like most other Constantinean churches, was a simple basilica, based on a plain rectangle, divided into a nave and two narrower aisles by rows of columns, and having an apse at one end with a raised floor-level, approached by steps, the platform so produced being used for the bishop's throne, as in secular buildings of a similar kind it was often used for the magistrate's curial chair. It may, however, like the first St Peter's at the Vatican, have been enlarged in width by additional side aisles, or like the basilica at Antioch have been beautified with additional apses; and the steep-pitched timbers of its roof may well have been concealed by a sumptuous coffered ceiling, rich with gold, such as Constantine offered to have installed for Bishop Macarius at the Holy Sepulchre in Jerusalem. As Constantine had a hand in its building, it was certainly rich, certainly splendid, and almost certainly in barbaric bad taste. At this point in his life, still flushed with triumph at finding himself master of the world despite the pain that mastery had brought him, he was in the grip of a passion for perpetuating his name in buildings, and would have welcomed any grandiose scheme for expressing his power and authority in stone and timber, plaster and bronze. Regrettably, but predictably, he had developed a liking for designs allowing for masses of gilding.

It was planned from the outset that the New Rome should be a treasure-house of all that was considered best from the ancient world, and Constantine's agents travelled widely to collect from every province whatever was biggest, most precious, most sacred, whatever would best adorn the new capital and bring most honour to its founder. The porphyry column was the biggest in the world; the statue placed on it had been cast by the world's best sculptor. The world-famous statues of the Muses were brought from Mount Helicon in Greece to decorate the new Senate; Zeus was requisitioned from Dodona, Pallas from Lindos, Apollo from Delphi. Among the many precious trophies assembled to ornament the *spina* of the hippodrome was the serpent column from Delphi, the memorial set up at the temple of Pythian Apollo in the fifth century before Christ to commemorate the unity of the Greeks which had brought them victory over the Persians under Xerxes at the Battle of Plataea. So many works of art in so many contrasting styles were brought together in the forum and other public places that the total effect must have been overwhelming.

This collection may be seen merely as a heaping-up of treasures, the loot of an empire stacked up to celebrate the victory of a megalomaniac, fascist-like autocrat. The systematic stripping of pagan shrines and the melting-down of their gold, silver and bronze treasures to decorate Constantinople, which became common practice after 330, supports this view. Both Christians and pagans of the time, however, saw in it a propagandistic and political significance going beyond the mere aggrandisement of Constantine. Socrates, for instance, argued that in founding Constantinople 'not only did [the emperor] improve the situation of the Christians in the ways I have shown, but he also damaged the superstition of the pagans, for he brought their images into the common light of day to adorn the city of Constantinople, and set up the tripods from Delphi publicly [that is, not on a sacred site] in the hippodrome. . . . And at this period, Christianity grew faster than at any other'[22]. From the pagan stand-point, it looked as though the emperor was deliberately setting out to destroy the old world which Diocletian had striven so energetically to preserve, and shortly before the day set for the dedication ceremony a pagan philosopher named Canonaris earned himself summary execution with a public address to Constantine on the theme 'Do not think yourself above our ancestors, simply because you have brought our ancestors down to nothing!' Constantine is said to have reasoned with him before killing him, but he was of the stuff of martyrs, and the emperor found it as frustrating to talk to him as pagan magistrates had found it to discuss theology and imperial policy with Christians set on dying for their faith[23].

To the Christian, then, the exhibition of the temple treasures in the streets and public buildings of Constantinople was an exposure of the hollowness of pagan superstition, while to the pagan it was a ridiculing of the true gods and true Roman values before the mocking eyes of an atheist crowd. But what did it signify to Constantine himself? He probably saw it primarily as public proof of his victory, but it was also a public expression of his own confused thinking – the confusion of mind which could build both a church to peace and a temple to the Dioscuroi, and lead him to divide his time between such diverse men as Hosius and Eusebius on the one hand and Sopater and Praetextus on the other. . . . Unless, of course, his dreams really were megalomaniacal, and during the months while the city was taking shape he was obsessed with a vision of uniting all religions and all opinions in himself, the alter-Christus, alter-Apollo, the embodiment of the Good Fortune and Blessed Peace of the empire, the spirit of the Supreme God in imperial form. This is not impossible. A little later, he talked as though he believed himself to be Christ come again.

He may have been a little unbalanced at this time on the question of religion, but when it came to that of the practical organization of the life and laws of his New Rome, he quickly demonstrated that he had lost none of his old flair for administration. To support the new Senate of *clari*, and carry on the day-to-day work of the city, he offered extraordinary privileges to any commoners who would come and settle between his forum and the new walls. He gave the city the ancient *Ius Italicum*, a body of laws enshrining the privileges of freedom from taxation and conscription hitherto enjoyed only by the citizens of old Rome, but put its daily government into the hands not of an all-powerful City Prefect but of an imperial proconsul. Once again, there was deliberate ambiguity here: the grant of the *Ius Italicum* proclaimed Constantinople's equality with Rome, while the appointment of a mere proconsul as its chief administrator seemed to deny it. In other ways, however, the challenge of the new city to the old was demonstrated without any ambiguity. Landowners at Constantinople paid neither the new capitation-tax nor the old land-tax. Like the Romans, the common citizens of the fourteen districts spread over the seven hills (numbers exactly paralleling the topography of Rome) received free rations of corn, wine and oil, at first as a special bounty, but after 332 as a right under the law. Their supplies were a levy, chiefly on Egypt, but were paid for when necessary by taxes not on themselves but on the inhabitants of less privileged cities. The new imperial taxes necessitated both by the unimaginable cost of building the city and by the obligation to provide for its people was a new burden on an empire already grossly overtaxed – a burden which the individual could avoid only by moving to the city itself. Unfortunately but foreseeably, it was, generally speaking, only the rootless, the work-shy and those with an eye to the main chance who felt themselves free enough from home ties in the provinces to accept the emperor's invitation to move voluntarily to the shores of the Bosphorus. So Eunapius writes indignantly:

> He collected at Byzantium a population from the cities subject to him, so that a great corps of drunkards could applaud him in the theatre one minute and throw up their wine the next. He was quite satisfied with the applause of those who had lost control of their faculties, and was happy to hear his name shouted, even though only by men who knew it merely because it was impressed on them every day[24].

Constantine's name was certainly thrust continually on the new population. Constantinople was his city from seawalls to landwalls, and none was allowed to forget it. It is impossible accurately to estimate how many millions he spent on construction work during the years between the consecration and the dedication. A century ago, Burkhardt put the total expenditure on the city during Constantine's lifetime at sixty million gold francs – a guess likely to be as close to the truth as any[25]. Much of this money must have been spent in the first few months, to bring the city to the point where, although obviously unfinished, it could be regarded as capable of an independent existence, and so fit to be dedicated. When that stage was reached, it was still not, as Socrates claimed, 'equal to imperial Rome' either in magnificence or authority, but 'it was established by law that it should be called New Rome' and this name was publicised in 330, 'being carved on a pillar of stone set up publicly in the *stratageion*, the law courts'[26].

By the time dedication-day came, the rest of the empire was feeling the burden of the city's cost. Jerome came close to the truth when he noted laconically against this year in his *Chronicle*, 'Constantinople dedicated; almost every other city stripped naked'[27].

The choice of the day for the dedication was made as carefully as that for the consecration had been. The astrologers agreed on May 11 as the most auspicious date close to Constantine's accession-day in July. By now, however, Sopater's influence was waning, and the Christians felt strong enough to demand a bigger part in the ritual. On dedication-day, therefore, as well as the customary processions and dedicatory games, there was a ceremonial mass, and prayers were offered by both Christian and pagan priests. It is, however, clear from the histories that the person granted the highest honours at the ceremony was Constantine himself.

For forty days, he was praised at every turn, and at one ceremony in the hippodrome he was all but worshipped. On this occasion, with the benches crowded and Constantine in the magnificent imperial box on the south-eastern straight, a procession of soldiers in long white tunics marched around the course with candles in their hands, as a guard of honour to a vast statue of the emperor. As the statue passed, those who had room to do so knelt in their places and all shouted their acclaim. After the circuit of the track had been made, the statue was carried back to the forum in a sacred procession led by a Christian priest chanting a part-pagan, part-Christian litany with the response 'Lord have mercy', *Kyrie eleison*.[28] But which Lord was it, the devout asked themselves, whose mercy was being implored? It is not surprising that within a few years a cult of Constantine had developed at the porphyry column. Candles were burned there, and prayers offered to the sacred emperor. The ceremony in the hippodrome set the precedent for a Founder's Day parade held annually at Constantinople through many succeeding reigns, in which the living emperor and his family did pious homage from the imperial box to a statue of Constantine bearing in its outstretched right hand the figure of the city's *Tyche*. After that, no one could be surprised at any claim he made for himself, not even when he designated as the site for his tomb a spot in the middle of the cruciform Church of the Holy Apostles (work on which was begun after 330), so that he might lie till the end of time with six apostles on the left hand and six on his right.

CHAPTER THIRTEEN

THE ARIAN CONTROVERSY: THREATS TO THE PEACE

SOPATER the Neoplatonist did not long survive the dedication of Constantinople. The circumstances of his fall from favour and subsequent execution are obscure, but it is known that Ablavius, by then holding the post of Praetorian Prefect, played some part, and was rewarded for it and other services by a consulship in 331[1]. Although Constantine's dream was still of an empire united under himself in which all might find a place, Sopater's execution really marked the end of the hope that the pagans would, some day, somehow learn to live with him and he with them – a hope which, as the pagan role in the consecration and dedication of Constantinople proved, had managed to survive the buffeting it had received at the Roman *vicennalia*.

For Constantine's dream of unity to find fulfilment, those with conflicting opinions on religious and other matters had to learn to live with one another. Pagans could generally co-exist with pagans, but not with Christians. The Christians hated and feared the pagans, and fought among themselves. The exiling of Arius and his most obdurate supporters during the Council of Nicaea no more ended the controversy centering on his name than the war against the Donatists in Africa and Numidia in 321 had ended the conflict between them and the compromised 'catholic' Church of Caecilian and his successors. Moreover, the Meletian Church of the Martyrs survived in Egypt despite Meletius' own surrender to expediency. The temporary recrudescence of paganism and pagan influence at the imperial court during the years of Constantinople's rise from the foundations of Byzantium is partly explicable by a temporary loss of confidence on Constantine's part in his own ability to make the 'Catholic' Church play that role in the state which he had designed for it. Although such men as Hosius of Cordoba were always prepared to fall in with, or even to initiate, plans to bind the church closer to the state, while the co-operation of others could often be bought for cash and privilege, few of the Christian leaders were willing to consider surrendering their doctrinal principles for the sake even of life and freedom, let alone of peace and unity. The result was that throughout the last decade of Constantine's life the monolithic solidarity of the empire was constantly threatened by religious strife.

Alexander of Alexandria, a man fitted by nature to be a pillar of Constantine's catholic church, but prevented by circumstances from always filling that role, lived only three years after the Council of Nicaea. In 328, he was succeeded as Archbishop of Alexandria by the most eloquent of Arius' opponents, his chaplain Athenasius[2]. The new Alexandrian patriarch was to prove one of the most uncompromising of all Christian leaders, a thorn in the flesh not only of Constantine but also of several of his successors. His unyielding attitude ultimately forced Constantine into his enemies' camp, but even before his election Alexandrian intransigence on the subject of Christ's nature had driven the exasperated emperor to accede to the constantly reiterated appeals of the Asian bishops and lift the order restricting Arius and his companions 'to a remote place'. Meanwhile, important events in Asia Minor and Syria had shown that, although temporarily bested at Nicaea, the disciples of Lucian the Martyr had not abandoned the struggle to impose their master's view of Christ on Constantine's church, and so on the whole body of Christians.

The two bishops Eusebius, of Nicomedia and Caesarea, were key figures in the manoeuvrings of the three years 325–8; they were so important that the party they led has often been called the Eusebians. Their aim was two-fold: to regain Constantine's confidence, and to secure the election of disciples of Lucian to the principle sees of the East, especially to Antioch and – once Constantine had decided to create a new capital – to Constantinople.

In their campaign to win Constantine, they had geographical

advantages over Alexander, Athenasius and their followers. Alexander's allies were in North Africa and the West. While Constantine spent most of his time in Asia Minor and Thrace, it was difficult for the Egyptians to organize swift counters to Eusebian moves against them. The Eusebians, moreover, had powerful support in the two women who alone seem to have exercised lasting influence over Constantine, the Empresses Helena and Constantia, both of whom had conceived intense devotion to Lucian the Martyr. Through the emperor's mother and sister, and by their own willingness to co-operate in imperial plans for the future of the church, as long as these did not involve repudiation of Lucian's theology, they gradually succeeded to a large extent in weaning Constantine away from both the day-to-day guidance of Hosius in doctrinal matters and adherence to the policy that the creed of Nicaea, with its catchword *homoousios*, was forever immutable.

Immediately after the Council of Nicaea, however, their cause went through a period of difficulty. The more autocratic and all-powerful Constantine grew, the more determined he became to force unity on the church. He demonstrated just how strongly he felt on the subject in an edict promulgated on September 1, 326, designed to compel a variety of heretics to submit to his catholic bishops. Its violent tone seems to reflect his own mental disturbance following his Roman *vicennalia* and his murder of Crispus and Fausta:

> Understand now by this present statute, Novatians, Valentinians, Marcionites, Paulinians, you who are called Cataphrygians . . . with what a tissue of lies and vanities, with what destructive and venomous errors, your doctrines are inextricably interwoven! . . . We give you warning. . . . Let none of you presume, from this time forward, to meet in congregations. To prevent this, we command that you be deprived of all the houses in which you have been accustomed to meet . . . and that these should be handed over immediately to the catholic church[3].

He further commanded the collection and destruction of all heretical books, and seemed on the point of drifting into persecution. Weeks later, he authorized the circulation of a supplementary constitution exempting the Novatians from the general condemnation of the sects, because they were not so much heretics as extremely puritanical ascetics; but uniformity with catholicism was rigidly enforced on other Christian groups, much to the satisfaction of the leaders of the official church, as is apparent from Eusebius' comment on the ban and its effects:

> So the members of the whole body were united and made to cohere in one harmonious whole, and the one catholic church, at unity with itself, shone with an unblemished radiance, while no heretical or schismatical group continued to exist anywhere. And our heaven-protected emperor . . . could attribute solely to himself . . . the credit for having accomplished this mighty work[4].

While Constantine was in this savagely repressive mood, only fanatics dared to draw attention to themselves, and nothing more was heard of the Arian conflict for some time. Then the emperor learned that a handful of priests in Egypt were still opposing their archbishop. He summarily ordered their deportation, not to a remote place, but to Nicomedia, presumably so that his Western chaplains could subject them to a process of thought-reform and spiritual re-education. At the former capital, they quickly made the acquaintance of the Collucianists, and it was soon reported to Constantine that Eusebius of Nicomedia and Theognis of Nicaea were plotting to do away with the creed of the Council. His response to this information was swift and uncompromising. He issued an order deposing both bishops and empowering synods to convene and elect successors to them. Their fellow-bishops objected to this arbitrary condemnation, but their revolt was not strong enough to withstand Constantine's determination. He wrote to the Nicomedians, reminding them of the creed signed at Nicaea and denouncing Eusebius as a traitor to the church who had, he alleged, cooperated with Licinius in organizing the persecution before 324, and was now plotting with certain Egyptian dissidents to disturb the peace of Alexandria. This letter was so strongly worded that both local synods meekly submitted to his orders, the one electing Amphion to rule at Nicomedia, the other Chrestus to preside at Nicaea. Loudly protesting their innocence, Eusebius and Theognis went into exile[5].

The corrupt and partisan character, and frequently late date, of the surviving sources make it difficult to be certain of the precise order of events during the next few years. What is clear is that, having reduced the East to a state of quiescence by frightening the bishops, Constantine set vigorously about the task of exploiting the situation to his own advantage. He wrote time and again to Arius, trying to convince him that the creed of Nicaea was not unacceptable to anyone professing Christianity, but Arius was not easily persuaded to say, as the Nicene bishops had, that Christ exists eternally and is eternally of one substance with the Father. As he understood it, this was the doctrine of Lucian's arch-enemies, the Sabellian heretics, who had 'confounded the substance' by claiming that the Father and the Divine Word were one and indivisible in every respect. Constantine first invited, then ordered, him to come to court:

> Constantine the Victor, Supreme Augustus, to Arius.
> It is a long time now since Your Gravity received an invitation to come to my court, so that you might enjoy my presence. I have been very surprised that you did not come immediately. So take a public carriage now, and hurry to my court, so that, having experienced my benevolence and solicitude, you may return to your native city.
> May God keep you, beloved[6].

Realizing the danger of ignoring so direct an instruction, Arius drew up a statement of faith in collaboration with one of his fellow-exiles named Euzoius and, armed with it and a petition to the emperor, went to Asia Minor. His new creed, although carefully avoiding the word *homoousios*, could be interpreted as orthodox by Nicene standards and his petition was skilfully calculated to appeal to the pious side of the imperial nature:

> We pray thy religion, God-beloved Emperor, because we are clergy and because our faith and thoughts are those of the church and holy scriptures, that thou wouldst reunite us by the exercise of thy peace-loving and devout piety to our mother the

> church, so that there may be an end to these interminable debates and that we and thy church being at one may all pray as it behoves us to do for the peace of thy kingdom, and for thy family[7].

Constantine appears at this time to have been planning to reconvene the Council of Nicaea, for he also wrote, on at least two occasions, to Alexander of Alexandria, trying to persuade him to reconsider the question of Arius' excommunication. Alexander did not want Arius back in his patriarchate, but could hardly say so openly, so he prevaricated. Constantine wrote to him again:

> Arius – Arius himself – came to me, to the Augustus. He was supported by the recommendations of a large number of people. He swore that what he believed about our catholic faith was what was decided and ratified by the Synod of Nicaea – by you yourself, that is, I myself, your fellow servant, being present and myself concurring in the decision. . . . So I am sending to you, not simply suggesting, but imploring that you will take these men back. . . . Let me hear what I desire and yearn to hear, that there is peace and concord among you all[8].

Alexander, however, was not accommodating. He kept postponing a decision until at last he died. The scheme to revive the Council of Nicaea also met with little response: if any meetings were held, they resembled more those of a local synod than of the general debates of Nicaea. Then, on May 21, 328, the Alexandrians demonstrated that they were as opposed as ever to Antiochene theories, and as indifferent as ever to imperial dreams of universal tranquillity, by accepting the nomination of Athenasius to rule their church.

The election was not wholly undisputed, although in a synodal letter written seven years later Athenasius himself claimed that it was accorded 'an enthusiastic welcome'. Philostorgus relates that the consecration was performed in a dark corner of the Cathedral of St Dionysius at Alexandria, by only two Egyptian bishops, and that Athenasius was censured by the Alexandrian synod for consenting to such irregular proceedings. The Councils of Arles and Nicaea had required consecrations to be performed by at least three bishops, and preferably in public. The story of Athenasius' secret consecration is probably apocryphal, but moderates at Alexandria may well have hesitated to endorse the candidature of so well-known a firebrand.

Meanwhile Constantine, having accepted Arius' and Euzoius' petition as providing at least a basis for discussion, could hardly reject a petition for reinstatement made by Bishops Eusebius and Theognis. Apart from the intruded bishops, Amphion and Chrestus, few seem to have objected to their restoration, and Eusebius of Nicomedia resumed his service to Constantine as though nothing had happened to mar their happy relationship. For a while, the whole church seemed at peace, but the Eusebian party was still convinced that Arius' opponents were wrong, so when Eustathius of Antioch, one of the few substantial theologians of the Alexandrian school holding an important appointment in the County of the East, put himself in an untenable position, they attacked him so determinedly as to drive him from his see, and thus captured for one of their party the first of their objectives, the chief city of the East and their own spiritual home, the birthplace of their hero Lucian.

Eustathius had been elected to Antioch at the end of the year 324, and, before taking leave of his people to attend the Council of Nicaea, had held in his cathedral that synod at which Eusebius of Caesarea is said to have been condemned for the first time for refusing to accept its excommunication of Arius. This synod also passed canons laying down reasonable penalties for witchcraft, superstitious practices and sexual offences. At Nicaea, Eustathius was stubbornly antagonistic towards Arius, led the bishops in their condemnation of his 'Happy Thoughts', and persuaded them that the creed presented by Eusebius of Caesarea was too vague to be meaningful. In the months following the council, he set himself the task of demonstrating that the whole speculative method of Origen, an Egyptian theologian who had died a century earlier but was still widely revered as an exegete and as founding father of the Antiochene school of thought, was wrong in every respect, and so clashed again with Eusebius of Caesarea, whose own allegorical speculations were based on Origen's method. In his studies, he identified the Word of God and the divine Father so closely and made so clear a distinction between the eternal Word and the human Christ that the Antiochenes accused him of adoptionism and Sabellianism. He was a skilful enough theologian to meet these charges, but he could not shrug off those next brought against him, of insulting the Empress Helena and fathering an illegitimate son.

Neither of these accusations can be shown to have been justified. Only a madman would have insulted the emperor's mother during these years of her glory, and the baby's mother later said that his father had been not Eustathius the Bishop of Antioch, but Eustathius the Coppersmith there. However, they were believed at the time, and a synod convened at Antioch to consider what action should be taken, while rioting mobs roared through the streets. 'The people, even the magistrates themselves,' Eusebius says, 'were roused to such a pitch that the argument would have been settled with swords if the watchful Providence of God, as well as fear of the emperor's displeasure, had not restrained the fury of the mob'[9]. The synod declared Eustathius deposed, and both the bishops and a group of prominent citizens wrote to Constantine telling him that they wanted to break the rule against moving bishops from see to see established at Nicaea by electing Eusebius of Caesarea as their patriarch. Constantine sent a general to impose martial law on the city, and wrote to its citizens: '. . . reading your memorandum, it is obvious to me, from its glowing praise of Eusebius, the bishop of Caesarea – whom I myself have known well for a long time, and esteemed for his learning and tolerance – that you feel a strong attachment to him, and would like to make him your own. . . . But why do we covet those things which would destroy our reputations? . . . [The translation of Eusebius to Antioch could only lead to fresh controversy, so] take fitting care to elect [another] man to supply your needs, carefully avoiding quarrels and tumults, for such dissentions are always wrong. . .'[10].

Despite this letter (or perhaps before it arrived), the synod did offer the appointment to Eusebius. He prudently declined it, and Constantine wrote to him, 'Your Prudence has done very well indeed to refuse to rule the Church at Antioch, and to prefer to continue at that church oversight of which was first made yours by the divine will. I have written on this matter to the people of Antioch, and also to your fellow-labourers in the ministry, who had themselves consulted me about it. On reading my letters, Your Holiness will readily perceive that, as Justice made what they wanted impossible, I was divinely directed in what I wrote to them. Your Prudence ought to attend their assembly, so that the Church in Antioch is left in no doubt about this decision. . .'[11].

His letter to the synod has an important place in ecclesiastical history, for in it he set the precedent for imperial and later royal direction of episcopal elections: 'I have studied the letters written by Your Prudences, and thoroughly approve of the wise decision taken by your fellow-bishop Eusebius. Moreover, having informed myself about the circumstances of the case, partly from your letters and partly from those of our Illustrious Counts Acacius and Strategeius, and so probed the matter sufficiently deeply, I have written to the people of Antioch suggesting a course of action simultaneously pleasing to God and beneficial to the church. . . . My information is that Euphronius the Presbyter, a citizen of Caesarea-in-Cappadocia, and George of Arethusa, also a presbyter, one appointed to that position by Alexander of Alexandria, are men of tried faith . . .'

Both Euphronius and George were notorious adherents to Arius. Constantine's selection of their names, and his high praise of Eusebius, make it clear that he had already moved a long way from his position immediately after the Council of Nicaea. The insults offered to his mother, constant propaganda by her and Constantia on behalf of the Collucianists, and the sheer usefulness to him of the Bishops Eusebius, had worn away his resistance.

Obedient to the imperial will, half the synod at Antioch duly voted for Euphronius to be their archbishop. The other half, however, complained bitterly of imperial interference in ecclesiastical affairs, and refused to recognize the election as valid. Eustathius and his friends retired from the city, but neither Constantine's reiterated arguments nor his threats succeeded in persuading everyone that the deposition and new election were justified. For the next eighty years, there were two churches at Antioch, each claiming to be catholic, and each electing a new bishop whenever its leader died. The first such election took place very soon in the 'official' church. Euphronius survived his election only one year, to be succeeded by a certain Flacillus, who also soon died; naturally, the Eustathians claimed that God was showing his displeasure, and relations between the factions deteriorated.

Meanwhile, another leading anti-Arian, Marcellus, the Bishop of Ancyra, had put himself in the wrong with an attack on the doctrines of an ex-rhetor, ex-apostate named Asterius, an ambitious and apparently unscrupulous man, whose lapsing during the Great Persecution had made it forever impossible for him to realize his dream of being consecrated bishop. Asterius was an Arian – the subordinationism taught by Arius held a special appeal for those, like him, well educated in paganism – and in attacking him, Marcellus went further towards Sabellian 'confounding the persons' than even Eustathius had done. The affair caused so much controversy that Constantine ordered a synod to meet at Constantinople to apportion blame. This assembly was not a general council, in the sense that Nicaea had been, but it was attended by many bishops from Asia Minor and Thrace. Marcellus' arguments were ably countered by Narcissus of Neronias and the two Bishops Eusebius. Constantia, primed by the Collucianists, took up the case personally with her brother, and as a result of the proceedings, not only was Marcellus deposed and exiled, but within a few months many other anti-Arians also, including Bishop Paul of Constantinople[12]. So the Eusebians gained both their objectives: Constantine's confidence, and some power in Antioch and the new capital.

The chronology of this period is very obscure. Some accounts, for instance, place the Synod of Constantinople after one held at Tyre in 335. However, it must have been at about this time that Constantine, still in pursuit of his policy of unity and tranquillity, published a prayer for use on Sundays throughout the army. Coming from the pen of a man so deeply involved in Christian affairs that he was prepared to argue with the best living theologians, it is remarkable only for its bland inoffensiveness:

O Sole God –
Thee we acknowledge
Thee we honour as our king
Thine aid we implore!
By thy favour, victory has been ours.
Through thee, we have been made stronger than our enemies.
We give thanks to Thee for Thy past benefactions
And put our trust in Thy future blessings.
With one mouth, we pray to Thee
Beseeching Thee long to preserve for us
Safe and triumphant
Our Emperor Constantine and his Pious Sons[13].

While the emperor continued to worry about unity and peace, and the alliance led by the Bishops Eusebius slowly strengthened its grip on the court and the church in Asia Minor and the County of the East, Athenasius, the man who was ultimately to outmanoeuvre that alliance, was floundering ever more deeply into trouble at Alexandria. Meletius, the original leader of the Church of the Martyrs, had died at Lycopolis, but his church, now headed by Bishop John Arkaph, was as bitter as ever in its opposition to the officially-recognized patriarchate of Alexandria. Athenasius later claimed that his first clash with Arkaph's supporters was provoked by Eusebius of Nicomedia, whom he had annoyed shortly after his election by renewing his predecessor's ban on Arius. At Eusebius' instigation, Constantine had written to him:

> You know that what I want is to be assured that admission to the church will be open to all who ask for it. If I learn that you forbid admission to the church to anyone who wants to form a connection with it, I shall immediately have you deposed and exiled[14],

but despite this warning, he had still felt unable to sanction Arius' return to communion. Eusebius had therefore set out to harry him into submission or resignation and as part of his campaign had incited John Arkaph to send four of his suffragans to Constantine to accuse him of the serious crime of having imposed on Egypt a tax of his own devising to provide striped linen cloth for church use. Whether Eusebius was actually involved or not, the charge was certainly made by four Meletians named Ision, Eudaemon, Callinicus and (the description is Athenasius') 'that fool Hieracammon who, ashamed of his own name, calls himself Eulogius'. Fortunately for Athenasius, two of his own priests happened to be at Nicomedia, and were able to speak for him, denying the accusation. When no evidence to support the Meletian case reached Constantine from Egyptian officialdom, he concluded that Athenasius was being slandered, and would no doubt have dismissed the affair from his mind if the Meletians had not immediately produced two new accusations more difficult to counter, those of bribery and sacrilege.

The bribery charge could not be ignored, as it involved a high official named Philomenos. Athenasius' enemies said that he had paid this man a large sum in gold to persuade him to intrigue against the emperor, but so little was subsequently heard of this accusation that it may be assumed that it was made simply to ensure that Athenasius would be brought before a magistrate, so that the sacrilege charge would receive an airing.

This accusation was to haunt the courts of ecclesiastical affairs for the rest of Constantine's life. As the Meletians told it, the story was that while Athenasius had been making a visitation of the Mareotis district of his archdiocese, he had sent a priest named Macarius to bring before him for questioning Ichyras, the village curate whom Meletius himself had urged to stop pretending to be a priest at the Council of Nicaea. Macarius had broken into the village church during mass, overturned the altar and smashed the wine cup which Ichyras used as a chalice. In law, Athenasius was responsible for everything his agents did, therefore, Athenasius was guilty of sacrilege.

Athenasius' version of this affair, as it made its suspiciously piecemeal emergence over a number of years, was that Father Ichyras was not a true priest, but one of those laymen whom Archdeacon Colluthus had pretended to ordain after his quarrel with Archbishop Alexander during the Great Persecution; that he had later claimed to be a Meletian; that his 'church' had in fact been a house belonging to an orphan named Ision; and that

The Arch of Constantine (erected 315) by night

Photo: the Author

A detail of the Arch: the siege of Susa in 312, the first major battle in the campaign to wrest control of Italy and Sicily from Maxentius

Photo: Mansell Collection

The interior of Constantine's Basilica of St. Peter, from a seventeenth-century fresco. Although in the course of the centuries additions had been made to the structure, the essential form of the Basilica had been clearly preserved.

Photo: Mansell Collection

he had not been saying mass there when Macarius had called, but lying ill in bed at his own home. Macarius had not insisted on seeing him, but had asked his son to warn him to stop masquerading as a priest, and had then quietly left the house, having broken nothing. Under great pressure at a later date, Athenasius admitted that there had been some trouble at Ision's house, during which Father Ichyras' chalice may have suffered some harm: it had apparently been standing with a number of identical cups on a kitchen table which had unfortunately been overturned during an altercation.

One thing is clear: both sides were lying. That the Meletians may have been lying more stoutly than Athenasius is suggested by the fact that when the archbishop presented himself before Constantine to answer the charges against him, he came armed with a document, signed by Ichyras and witnessed by fourteen ecclesiastics, in which Ichyras admitted that he had not made his accusations spontaneously; they had been forced from him by the threat of violence. The difficulty about accepting this document at its face value is that Athenasius himself had probably also used force to obtain it – at least, Ichyras was later to claim that he had[15].

However, as Constantine's current favourite, Ablavius, a profound admirer of Athenasius, was at the palace when the case was heard, there was no danger that the archbishop would be convicted, whoever was lying. In fact, Constantine heard the evidence, then immediately released him, in time for him to return to Alexandria to keep the Easter of 332 with his people. He carried with him an imperial letter to the Alexandrians warning them to avoid any disturbance of the peace, and telling them 'for my own part, I have received your Bishop Athenasius with a large measure of humanity, and treated him as a man of God. Now you must understand that it is not my business to pass judgement of this question of sacrilege'[16]. The political charges having been dismissed, only the religious question remained, and with friends on both sides, Constantine was uncharacteristically hesitant to make a ruling. He wanted peace and unity. A broken chalice belonging to a man who probably was not a genuine priest seemed a small thing to stand in the way of his attaining them. Athenasius' return to Egypt was, however, the signal for a riot.

Meanwhile, Arius was still trying to reach his parish at Baucalis, and the Athenasian party was still determined to prevent him. By the end of 332, when the emperor had again asked that Arius should be re admitted to communion, and the man whom he had 'received with a large measure of humanity' had again refused his request, unrest was so widespread that Constantine felt compelled to send a special commission of two officials from the department of the Master of the Offices, Syncletius and Gaudentius, to Egypt with orders to deliver letters to Arius (whom it seems was in the country, although banned from Baucalis) and the Athenasians, and enforce peace on the basis of their contents. The letter to Arius was a reply to one which he had written claiming that all Libya and most of Egypt was behind him, and it ordered him to go to court and discuss the position with 'the man of God', Constantine himself[17].

Arius' boast of general support had both angered and worried the emperor. His letter to the Athenasians was in essence an edict of persecution against Arius' party, whom it identified with the Porphyreans, the most virulent of the Christians' pagan enemies. It ordered the seizure and burning of Arian books, and made death at the stake the mandatory punishment for those caught twice with Arian texts in their possession. The years were beginning to tell on Constantine, and his character was deteriorating. His diatribe against the Arians was far less rational than even the edict promulgated by Diocletian against the Manichees in 296. Most disturbing, however, was the ease with which favourites could sway his opinions, so that imperial policies changed month by month. In 332, it was Athenasius who was briefly in favour, despite his refusal to admit Arius to communion, and the Bishops Eusebius who were in eclipse. Later, he was to fall from grace and they were to rise again, but until Constantine's mood changed he would see Athenasius as the only man in Egypt honestly trying to serve his obsessive ends of unity and peace, and Athenasius would be able to do no wrong.

Bishop John Arkaph set himself to change Constantine's opinion about Athenasius by producing new charges against him. Whether or not the Eusebians were forewarned of the plot is not known, but once it was under way they certainly co-operated wholeheartedly in it.

In 334, the Meletian Bishop Arsenius of Hypsela suddenly disappeared from public life and John Arkaph accused Athenasius of having procured his murder, producing as evidence a human hand, crudely chopped from a corpse, claiming that it was all that was left of his colleague after Athenasius' servants under Bishop Plusianus had finished an interrogation of him. Athenasius denied that his men had ever killed anyone. John Arkaph countered by filling in the background to the murder: Arsenius had been tied to a pillar in his own house and flogged till he died; then the house had been set on fire and the corpse chopped up and buried. He was not the only Meletian victim of Athenasius' barbarity. Others would give evidence of their own ill-treatment. Everyone should remember the story of Father Ichyras and his chalice, and the violence offered to them. . . . As the case against Athenasius grew more circumstantial, riots occurred at Alexandria and other Egyptian cities.

By the time a report of Arsenius' disappearance reached Constantine, over a year had passed since he had seen Athenasius, and the memory of the man who had so impressed him was fading, while the Eusebians had daily been making the most of their opportunities to demonstrate their usefulness to their ageing master. They had represented Athenasius as a dangerous and violent man; Arsenius' murder seemed to prove them justified. They pressed Constantine for a full enquiry, so that the whole matter could be thrashed out and forgotten before the joyful celebrations to mark his thirtieth jubilee in July 335. He curtly refused to re-open the trivial case of the broken cup, but agreed that there should be an enquiry into the fate of the vanished bishop. He appointed his half-brother Delmatius, for whom he had revived the honorific title 'the Censor'[18], to hear the case at Antioch, from where, as Count of the East, he administered the affairs of Asia.

The trial before the Censor collapsed in farce when Athenasius proved that Arsenius was still alive and unmaimed. In later years, the popular version of what happened was preserved by Theodoret[19]:

> Aresenius was a bishop of the Meletian sect. The men of his party put him in hiding and told him to remain there as long as possible, then they cut off the right hand of a corpse, embalmed it, put it in a wooden box, and carried it about everywhere, declaring that it was Arsenius' hand, and that he had been murdered by Athenasius. But the Eye which sees all things did not permit Arsenius to remain hidden for long. First he was seen alive in Egypt, then in the Thebaid. Later, the Divine Providence led him to Tyre, where the infamous hand was produced before the synod. Athenasius' friends tracked him down, and took him to an inn, where they compelled him to lie hidden . . .

When the charges against Athenasius and his aides were made before the Censor, and the hand was produced as evidence, Athenasius brought Arsenius, alive and well, into the court, and asked sarcastically, 'Is this really the right Arsenius? Is this the man I murdered? Is this the man these people mutilated? – after his murder? – by cutting off his right hand?'

The truth made an even better story. What actually seems to have happened is that after Arsenius' disappearance, one of Athenasius' agents traced him to a monastery in Upper Egypt, but before he could be apprehended, the monks smuggled him out on a river-boat. When his escape was discovered, two of the monks were seized and taken to Alexandria, where a confession was extorted from them in the presence of the military governor. They managed to send a warning to John Arkaph, but by the time it reached him, Delmatius had already been ordered to hear the case and it was too late to withdraw the charge. Before the trial opened, Athenasius had traced Arsenius to Tyre and had him identified before Paul, the local bishop. Whether he also later produced him before the Censor's court, suddenly confronting his accusers with him, is uncertain but inherently unlikely. What is clear is that John Arkaph wrote to Constantine, admitting that he had been deceived by his own followers and had maligned Athenasius. Constantine was delighted with his frankness and, inviting him to court, set himself to make a full reconciliation between him and the archbishop. He was temporarily successful. Athenasius himself recorded that in 334 he and the Meletian leader seemed to have reached an understanding[20].

However, the troubles of the Egyptian church were not at an end. Arius' petition for reinstatement had still not been granted, and despite Constantine's ban on his books, they were still widely popular. Constantine, for his part, was still longing for universal peace. He had decided that the thirtieth anniversary of his accession should be the greatest Christian festival that the world had yet seen. He planned to convoke a huge council at Jerusalem, to culminate in the dedication of the world's most magnificent church, the basilica of the Holy Sepulchre. All the bishops of the world would meet in concord, to the everlasting glory of their Pious Protector. . . . Such was the dream. But if peace was not universal, how could that dream be realized? Athenasius was the stumbling-block. . . . When Constantine reached this conclusion, early in 334, his admiration for the Alexandrian archbishop turned to bitterness and anger, and he ordered Eusebius to convene a synod at Caesarea 'for the cleansing of the Holy Christian People'[21]. Athenasius declined to attend, on the grounds that no one should be made to face a court composed entirely of his enemies. Constantine accepted the validity of this objection, and the proposed synod was cancelled at the last moment. However, when a year later the situation had still not improved and the Eusebians again called for a synod, he welcomed the suggestion and uncritically approved the list of delegates they submitted, summoning them to meet his own representatives at Tyre before proceeding to Jerusalem for the celebrations:

> Delay not, then, but hasten with redoubled zeal to bring these disputes to an end. . . . You will find no evidence of lack of pious zeal on my part. I have done everything your letter suggested. I have sent to those bishops whose presence you requested, so that they will attend your deliberations. I have sent Dionysius, a Consular, both to remind those bishops ordered to attend the

> council with you of their duty and to be present himself to oversee the proceedings, with the special task of maintaining good order. This time, if anyone should attempt to defy my order and refuse to attend – although I think that unlikely – someone will be despatched immediately to banish him by imperial edict and teach him that it is unseemly to resist imperial decrees issued in defence of the truth. For the rest, it is up to your Holinesses to . . . find a fitting remedy . . . to free the church from blasphemy and lighten my cares[22].

The Synod of Tyre was apparently difficult to arrange, and bickering among the Christians cast a shadow over the whole of what should have been the triumphal year of 335. It was already July, the month of the accession itself, before the synod – or, rather, the trial of Athenasius before the Military Count Flavius Dionysius – actually began.

In spite of the fact that forty-eight of his bishops were prepared to sail with Athenasius and speak for him at Tyre, he hesitated to expose himself to the uncertain justice of the Count's court. A contemporary letter relates how he had his luggage put on board ship at Alexandria and taken off again, refusing for some time to start the journey, despite repeated summonses and appeals[23]. When he did reach Tyre, he found the court packed with his enemies and complained so to the Count, but Dionysius had orders to settle the business as quickly as possible and, brushing Athenasius' objections aside, pressed on to examine the first charge, the case of Father Ichyras' chalice.

Ichyras had by now repudiated his retraction of his first story, and contributed many new and telling details, maintaining among other things that he had been wrongfully detained and brought before the Augustal Prefect Hyginus on a charge of having thrown stones at a statue of the emperor, and as a result had been made to serve an undeserved term in goal. Other Meletians then came forward with tales of similar injustices, and Arsenius' original disappearance after his house had been set on fire was said to have aroused justifiable suspicion because Athenasius' men were known to be ruthless and brutal. Arsenius claimed that he had gone into hiding because he had been afraid. Every possible slander was levelled at the archbishop.

Even the story that he had been uncanonically elected and consecrated was revived.

In his rebuttals, Athenasius revealed that he was himself no angel of truth and justice. He answered calumny with calumny, lie with lie, and when the situation began to look really perilous, tried to smuggle Macarius out of Tyre before he could be asked any more awkward questions – and then protested that Macarius could not give evidence freely, because he had been handcuffed to prevent further attempts at his escape. Finally, Count Dionysius ruled that a special commission should go to Egypt and the Thebaid to collect additional evidence: Athenasius objected that all the evidence had already been collected. We are left wondering what more he had to hide. His objections were overruled, and when the six members of the Commission of Enquiry were named, not one of them was his supporter, or even neutral towards him. Protests showered on the Count, not only from the Athenasians, but also from others, notably the meticulously honest Alexander of Thessalonika, but he contented himself with warning the commissioners not to bring dishonour on to the court by too obvious a display of bias.

The Commission's behaviour in Egypt shocked even imperial officials there, and they felt compelled in September 335 to make an official complaint. The commissioners refused to listen to anyone whom they suspected might have a word to say in Athenasius' favour and not even pro-Athenasian riots made them wonder if there was anything that could be said. When news of their methods filtered through to Athenasius, he appealed for his case to be transferred to the imperial court. According to Sozomen, his life was in danger at Tyre, so Count Dionysius allowed the appeal, and helped him to leave the city secretly. Other accounts, however, suggest that while the special commission was still at work in Egypt, the rest of the synod moved on to Jerusalem for the dedication of the Holy Sepulchre, Athenasius accompanying his judges, and that it was from there he slipped away, going ultimately to Constantinople. Sozomen's story is probably the true one, because a sentence of deposition seems to have been recorded against Athenasius at Tyre in his absence; the commission had reported that it found him guilty on all counts relating to Father Ichyras' chalice, and Count Dionysius ruled that he had disobeyed an imperial command by failing to present himself at Caesarea in 334 and had shown disrespect to this present court at Tyre. Remembering at the last moment that it was a holy synod and not a witch-hunt, the court then issued a synodal letter, announcing Athenasius' sentence to the world and decreeing the reinstatement of those Meletians whom he had slandered and harmed[24].

Spurred on by a letter of encouragement from Constantine the bishops left Tyre in time to reach Jerusalem and consecrate the new basilica, amid scenes of great magnificence, on the anniversary of the Augusta Helena's discovery of the True Cross: September 17 according to some accounts, but the 14th in the calendar of the Western church. Constantine had entrusted the task of organizing the celebrations to the *Notarius* Marianus who, according to Eusebius, did all that could have been expected of him:

> The director and chief of these officers received the synod with the customary hospitality, and entertained them with feasts and banquets on a most splendid scale. He also distributed lavish supplies of cash and clothing among the naked and the needy. . . . Moreover, he decorated and beautified the church itself[25].

The ceremonies of dedication included the celebration of the Eucharist according to many different rites, sermons and expositions of the Scriptures by some of the best Antiochene theologians and, of course, 'prayers for the universal peace of the church of God, for the emperor and author of these blessings, and his pious sons'.

Athenasius, legally deposed and condemned, secretly entered Constantinople with a handful of faithful followers on October 30. A few enquiries soon told him that Constantine was in no mood to grant him an audience in the usual way, so he took extraordinary steps to gain a hearing. Describing their meeting in a letter to the members of the Council of Tyre, Constantine said that it took place as he was approaching the city from a palace in the country. Athenasius suddenly appeared in the path of his horse, weeping and lamenting. He was so changed that the emperor did not recognize him 'until, when I asked, some of my servants told me who he was, and what injustice you had done him. He and those with him looked so troubled and depressed that I felt an ineffable pity for him, when I realized that this was Athenasius, the holy sight of whom had once been enough to draw the very Gentiles to worship the God of All'.

'I did not know,' he continued – according to one of the several differing versions of this letter which have been preserved – 'what sentences your court had passed in the midst of tumult and disturbance; but the truth seems to have been crushed under noise and discord; and among all your quarrels you gave no thought to what would be pleasing to God . . . So come here with all speed, and be assured that I shall strive with all my heart to ensure that everything is made firm and stable, and that the enemies who multiply blasphemies under pretence of defending His Holy Name are scattered, destroyed and completely annihilated'[26].

Only six members of the council actually travelled to Constantinople and presented themselves at court. Among them were the two bishops Eusebius. They arrived with such suspicious promptitude that they must have left Jerusalem immediately after the dedication ceremonies, and certainly before Constantine's letter could have arrived there, to try and ensure that Athenasius had no opportunity of presenting his case unopposed. According to the synodal letter circulated after the Council of Rome in 340 (a council composed entirely of Athenasius' friends and supporters), the six were careful to say nothing of Father Ichyras' chalice or his stone-throwing, but brought a new accusation against Athenasius. He had, they said, threatened that if things went badly for him, he would bring the port-workers of Alexandria out on strike, the grain-ships would not sail, and Constantinople would starve[27].

Mere rumour of such a threat to his beloved New Rome was enough to throw Constantine into a blind rage. Ignoring Athenasius' plea that he was only a simple bishop and not influential enough among the quayside labourers to induce them to commit what could be represented as an act of rebellion for his sake (which was probably a lie: events had shown and were to show again that the bishops of that century commanded fanatical devotion), Constantine ordered him into exile, and on November 7, only eight days after his appearance had touched the emperor with ineffable pity, he left Constantinople on the first stage of a sad journey to Augusta Treverorum. It was the first of five periods of exile, and was to last until after Constantine's death.

Convinced now that Athenasius had been the enemy of truth from the outset, Constantine devoted himself wholeheartedly to the support of the Eusebian party, and they joyfully set to work to restore Arius to his parish. In the name of the Synod of Tyre, which had now become the Council of Jerusalem, they wrote to the Church of Alexandria: 'We are sure that it will give you great joy to receive back the members of your own body: great will be your joy, great your consolation: they are your intestines, your brothers, your fathers: you will recognize them and take them back.'[28]

When, however, Arius actually tried to return to his parishioners, there was renewed rioting at Alexandria, led by the monks of the desert under the famous Anthony who, in this crisis, left his cave to fight for his archbishop and the Alexandrian faith. Anthony wrote several times to Constantine, asking for Athenasius' recall. Constantine replied with a general letter to the people and clergy of Alexandria and a personal one to Anthony himself. In the general letter, he described himself in terms so remote from the facts that it is difficult to believe that he could so deceive himself, as a man who never went back on his decisions, and not the sort to recall a troublemaker regularly condemned by an ecclesiastical court. Therefore, he claimed, riots could achieve nothing, and the people would do well to return calmly to their daily routine. In the letter to Anthony, he maintained that although a handful of secular judges might make a mistake, so large a group of wise bishops as had assembled at Tyre would not have condemned an innocent man[29].

These imperial sops did not calm the Alexandrians. It appears that Arius made a final attempt to return to Baucalis, and once more the mobs filled the streets. Certainly Constantine began to wonder if he had made a mistake after all, and summoned him to court, for a final examination as to his orthodoxy and an enquiry into his part in the disturbances. What happened at Constantinople was vividly described by Athenasius in a letter to his friend and ally, Bishop Serapion of Thmuis:

> I was not at Constantinople when he died, but Macarius the presbyter was there, and I heard the circumstances from him. The Emperor Constantine was induced by Eusebius and his party to send for Arius, and on his arrival the Emperor asked him whether he upheld the faith of the catholic church. Arius swore that he was orthodox, and Constantine dismissed him, saying, 'If your faith is orthodox, your oath is justified, but if your faith is blasphemous, and yet you have sworn, may God judge you from heaven!' When he left the Emperor, the Eusebian party, with their usual impetuosity, wanted to take him straight to church, but Alexander of blessed memory, the Bishop of Constantinople, refused his permission, alleging that one who had invented a heresy ought not to be admitted to communion. Then the Eusebians started to threaten. 'Just as a short time ago we succeeded in prevailing on the Emperor to decide in favour of Arius despite you, so tomorrow Arius will join us in Holy Communion at this church, whether you forbid it or not.' All this took place on a Saturday. . . . [Bishop Alexander prayed with Macarius all that evening, while] Arius, made bold by the protection of his faction, engaged in light-hearted and foolish conversation, until he was suddenly compelled by a call of nature to retire, and immediately, as it is written 'falling headlong, he burst asunder in the midst' and gave up the ghost, so being deprived both of communion and of life[30].

Arius' ignominious death in a lavatory, although it convinced the superstitious that he had perjured himself before Constantine, neither ended the controversy nor persuaded the Emperor that he ought to reconsider the injustice done to Athenasius. Constantine himself now had less than two years to live, and during that time he allowed himself to be ruled in ecclesiastical affairs totally by the Bishops Eusebius. Such had been the violence of the Alexandrian reaction to Athenasius' exile that the

Eusebians made no attempt to impose a nominee of their own on the see, but the Arian party survived there nonetheless, forming a small dissident church around a certain Pistis, one of the original Arian party excommunicated before the Council of Nicaea. Athenasius' triumphant return to his see, six months after Constantine's death – he actually re-entered his cathedral on November 23, 337 – stirred Pistis' faction into renewed life. It made contact with the Eusebians and soon elected a schismatic bishop of its own to oppose Athenasius. The Eusebians rejected the man it had chosen, and themselves consecrated Gregory of Cappadocia to rule Egypt. Athenasius' loyal congregations reacted to his double insult by barricading themselves into their churches and defying the army to install Gregory's clergy. It is as well, perhaps, that Constantine did not live to see this final breach of the Blessed Tranquillity imposed by the God-beloved Emperor.

CHAPTER FOURTEEN

AN ARBITRARY GENIUS

In a perfectly ordered world, no crowds of naked and hungry citizens of Jerusalem would have rejoiced in September 335 to be fed and clothed in the emperor's name by his *Notarius* Marianus. Their existence is proof that after thirty years of power, Constantine had not solved all the problems confronting his administration. Jerusalem was a bustling, expanding city. If large numbers there were in need of imperial charity, what must conditions have been like in less prosperous parts of the empire? Recent excavations at a fortress at Portishead in England, abandoned by the army early in Constantine's reign and afterwards occupied by squatters, suggest that they must have been appalling. Yet he is remembered, and rightly remembered, as an administrative genius. Although after thirty years of power he had not ended world poverty, he had brought more order and prosperity to the world than it had seen for many generations.

It would be difficult to overestimate the importance of his personal role in the administrative revolution characterizing these years. His own character, personality and methods had so profound an influence on his world that some historians have claimed that with his accession ancient and classical history came to an end and the middle ages began. So, for instance, the *Cambridge Mediaeval History* opens with an account of his reign. The line between one era and another ought not, perhaps, to be so firmly drawn, but by his founding of Constantinople and his reforms, Constantine certainly initiated the transformation of the Roman into the Byzantine empire, with all that change implied for the future of Europe and the Near East. Within his empire, his personal influence was so all-pervasive that any attempt to assess his achievement must begin with an estimate of his true character.

He was not altogether an admirable man, and his personality seems to have deteriorated as he grew older. Eutropius says that he started with every advantage, but that

> after a little, want of use of his good qualities changed him from his former spirit of gentleness. . . . A man who at first had the imperial spirit of the best princes, at the last he was comparable to the most mediocre. His innumerable advantages both of mind and body are undeniable. Greedy for military glory, he was lucky in war, and did not, it must be admitted, hold it beneath him to work for success. In his last years, he put mighty efforts into making peace with the Goths, and his memory is preserved with gratitude among those barbarous peoples. He was liberal towards civil arts and studies and gave the impression of loving justice, pursuing it with all honour and gentleness. Although he behaved dubiously towards some of his friends, he was uncommonly good to the rest, letting pass no occasion of making them richer or raising them higher. He made many laws, some good and equitable, the majority superfluous, but none oppressive[1].

Although harsh in some respects, this judgement is generally fair. Victor agrees that he was 'more greedy for praise than it is possible to tell'[2] and this weakness had the unfortunate result that in his later years his readiness to listen to favourites often overrode his love of justice, while a growing impatience with small minds masked his readiness to make plans and await an opportune moment before acting. He had a high opinion of himself, and liked to hear it echoed by those around him. It must have been difficult sometimes to endure his pride in the conviction that he had been chosen by God to rule the world. The Christian bishops, for instance, cannot have been happy to hear him tell them that he himself was a bishop, although he had not yet been baptised: 'at a banquet he gave for the bishops, he declared,' Eusebius says, 'that he too was a bishop. He added these words – I heard him with my own ears – "but you, of those who are in the church, while I, of those who are outside, having been made so by God himself" '[3]. Absolute power corrupted him. He loved display, fancy uniforms and fancy titles. He enjoyed pleasing his friends, and sometimes overlooked the larger issues in order to do so. He was probably somewhat effeminate, but there is no evidence to show that, as some writers have claimed, in his later years he became aggressively homosexual.

Although many people flattered him, professing to find him admirable in every respect, he was not really likeable, though he could be agreeable and was always efficient. Eutropius does him less than justice in suggesting that he was willing to work for glory only in war and that most of the laws he made were superfluous. He was willing to plan for success and put himself out to achieve it not only as a military commander but also as an administrator. His genius for the exercise of power revealed itself both in an ability to propose unexpected yet valid solutions to the multitudinous problems of the empire and in a readiness to spend himself on detail in order to achieve his aims. Moreover, despite his shortcomings in the field of human relationships, he obviously aroused great loyalty in a huge corps of officers and officials, most of whom cannot have known him personally, or at best can only have met him once or twice. It was the loyalty inspired by his leadership which gave him power in the first instance, and loyalty to him personally which kept him in power for three decades without a serious rebellion. No emperor had ruled longer except Augustus, the first of them all. His vigilance played a part in his survival, but he could not have lived so long had his servants wished him dead. The admiration they felt for him, especially those of them whose work lay far from the palace, must have been based as much on his industry and success as on his good looks.

The amount of work that he undertook personally was incredible. The effort he put, for instance, into reconciling the Christian factions at Alexandria in 324–5 might well have been considered enough in itself for a professional arbitrator, but so great were the demands of the newly unified empire that he cannot have afforded to give it more than a small fraction of his time. There is little wonder that his temper suffered. Officials from all departments expected him to be on daily call and from the volume and range of his surviving decrees and letters, all bearing the impress of his personal style, it is clear that he rarely disappointed them. Not surprisingly, he had to institute a new department in the civil service, the *scrinium dispositionem*, with the primary task of arranging his appointments and ensuring that he kept them. He had, of course, an army of clerks to advise him generally and carry the burden of routine work, but the personal note, and especially the reflections of transitory mood, in so many of the documents bearing his name makes it obvious that little went out under his seal which he had not seen, and suggest that a great deal was modified at his dictation if not by his own hand. Perhaps if he had felt able to delegate more, he would have lived longer and displayed less ill-tempered impatience. It is questionable, however, if his reign would then have been more memorable than in fact it was. The true and lasting achievements of his thirty-two years of power were those which bore his personal stamp most clearly: the brilliant leadership which brought him continual victories, the general stability won by his unceasing insistence on the value of peace, the integration of the Christians into the state, the foundation of Constantinople, the stabilisation of the currency, the re-organization of the army and the reduction of its political influence (at least while he lived), and the rationalization of the civil service – all these developments resulted from his application of his own powers to the problems of the day.

His most spectacular and lasting achievements were undoubtedly the creation of the 'catholic' church and the foundation of the new imperial capital. Simply because they were so significant, for good or evil, it is easy to do him less than justice by overlooking the range of his financial, military and administrative reforms. Yet they were of very real importance, not only in his own times, but for centuries to come. The dedication with which he strove to complete the work begun under Diocletian in stabilizing the currency was alone enough to win him a permanent place in the history of Europe.

It is usual nowadays to maintain that a sound economy is the indispensable foundation for a stable state. Constantine would have denied that. Soundness in religion and a firm hand on the reins would have seemed to him much more essential than the mere collection and disbursement of funds. Nevertheless, he understood the importance of a stable monetary system, and as soon as he controlled the resources of the north-west, set himself to provide the basis for one, by introducing a gold coin, the *solidus*, which was to be the standard for Byzantine and European currencies for more than a thousand years.

Shortly after 284, Diocletian had introduced an *aureus* weighing one sixtieth of a Roman pound, and in 290, another weighing one seventieth of a pound, but neither issue was minted in sufficient numbers to overcome the pressure on individuals and institutions, during a period of inflation and monetary uncertainty, to treat all gold as bullion, to be hoarded rather than spent. The result was that as fast as they were minted, they disappeared into temple treasuries and private hiding-places. Constantine, better provided with bullion – especially late in his reign, after he had persuaded himself that it would not be dangerous to strip the temples of their wealth – did not make the fundamental mistake of monetizing too little gold. His *solidus*, the first examples of which were struck at Trier in 309 with the inscription 'Victories everywhere', was intended to be a real coin, and was minted in sufficient quantities to remain in circulation[4].

From the first, it was minted at seventy-two to the pound – the weight, apparently deliberately chosen for its propaganda value, of the oldest silver *denarius* (the Roman 'penny'), about 4.55 grams. It was given a fixed value in relation to the silver *milliarensis*, weighing one ninety-sixth of a pound, one *solidus* equalling twenty-four *milliarenses*. The copper *nummi* continued, however, to be a problem. So many types of differing weights and nominal values were in circulation that all attempts to fix the value of the smallest coins, or of the *solidus* in terms of the nominal *denarius*, still used by bankers and international merchants in making their accounts, foundered before they were well launched; although in the 320s frequent recourse was had to the desperate measure of demonetizing old issues when new ones were made. All the measures taken before 330 had already proved unworkable by the time Constantinople was dedicated, and the copper issue struck to commemorate that event was considerably lighter than the first issues made after the defeat of Maxentius, although intended to have the same value. Yet constant fluctuations in the value of small change, even if they frustrated tax reform and made frequent special levies and unpopular taxation in kind inevitable, did not destroy the value of the gold and silver currency. Over the reign as a whole, however, inflation appeared catastrophic in terms of nominal *denarii* or real *nummi*. In 324, the *solidus* was already reckoned not in hundreds but in thousands of *denarii*, and by 337, when Constantine died, it stood at over three-quarters of a million on the Alexandrian exchange. The rise in prices was not so frightening in terms of gold or silver, although, naturally, abnormal circumstances, like the local famine which in 331–2 nearly sank Constantinople before it was well launched, led to localized and uneven price rises. Nonetheless, despite such adverse facts as that before the reign ended it had become uneconomic to collect any taxes in copper, and the complaint frequently made that high levies in gold, the number and range of special exemptions from all taxation (like that granted to the Christian clergy), and the unhealthy incidence of corruption, combined together to make it impossible for an honest man to make a living by working, the reality of the revolution begun by the introduction of the *solidus* cannot be denied. Gross inequalities had always been a feature of the Roman economic system and were to continue to mar the face of the Byzantine empire. Sumptuary laws introduced from time to time by early emperors had always failed in the long run because the economy depended on conspicuous and apparently wasteful consumption by the rich. The richest man in the state was the emperor; he was forced to pour out money on building projects, banquets, donations and charitable causes not only to prove that he was a sufficiently magnificent and god-like figure to deserve to rule, but also to keep the economy fluid and provide work for those whose trades were so skilled that without imperial or aristocratic patronage they would have found no one who could afford to keep them in work. No doubt Constantine's levies and his expenses were at times unjustifiably high, so that he was open to accusations of both avarice and luxury, but the army of men employed in building cities like Trier, Constantinople, Constantine, Constantia in Cyprus and Helenopolis, and basilicas like Holy Sepulchre, Holy Cross in Jerusalem and the Holy Apostles, as well as in keeping the imperial household clothed and fed, the armies supplied, and the administration moving, might have joined the naked and the starving if by taxation and expenditure the emperor had not constantly redistributed the wealth of the empire. The system was no doubt a bad one, but it would have needed a revolution unimaginable in Constantine's day to change it to one fundamentally more equitable or efficient in operation.

The one systematic change in the direction of equity which was attempted, the reform of the tax laws begun under Diocletian, unfortunately collapsed under the pressure of inflation[5]. The theory behind Diocletian's reform had been that everything in the empire had a value and could be reckoned to produce a profit comparable in money terms to the nominal value set on the individual human being by the poll-tax (*capitatio*). Obviously, the fertility of the soil varied from place to place, and the profitability of agriculture from crop to crop, many factors being involved in the final computation; but when all the factors were taken into account, it was possible to equate the taxable value of, for instance, an area of cornland in Gaul with an area of vineyard in Cyprus, or of a flax-field in Egypt. The area of cornland, or vineyard, or flax-field which would yield a profit taxable at the level of the head-tax on a single individual was arbitrarily defined as one *iugum* (so that the 'yoke' ceased to be a fixed area of land, and became a rate of tax) and, when all the calculations had been made, it became possible to assess cities at equitable tax levels throughout the empire. The survey of resources entailed took many years to complete, but when it was finished, Constantine became the first emperor actually to know what he was worth. The special levies about which so many complaints were made were based on an accurate knowledge of the wealth of the province called upon to supply them, and petitions for temporary reductions of taxes received more equitable consideration.

As no accurate and complete record has survived of the stages through which Diocletian's reforms had already passed at the time of his abdication, or of how far Constantius Chlorus may have modified Diocletian's provisions before his death fifteen months later, it is impossible to determine where precisely Constantine began his work of reform in the army and civil service. His achievements in the field of military affairs are somewhat more clearly charted than those in the civil sphere.

When Diocletian abdicated in 305, the army was bigger, better equipped and more trustworthy than it had been for many years[6]. Its supplies were guaranteed through a system of well-sited, officially-maintained armaments and clothing factories, and although many of its new recruits were barbarians, incapable of the well-disciplined manoeuvres of the legions of old, its morale was apparently very high. (The defections of Severus' and Galerius' men to Maxentius may be accounted for as much by the shortcomings of the men who rose to the top in Diocletian's artificial dynasties as by reference to a failure of discipline for which the men could be blamed. As the success of Constantine's own usurpation demonstrated, barbarians were loyal to men rather than to concepts. Division of the empire invited them to make invidious comparisons between commanders.) It has been estimated that at the beginning of Diocletian's reign, there were thirty-four legions, each consisting of the traditional number of 5,500 infantrymen with cavalry and auxiliary support. Twelve of the legions were on the Danube frontier or in garrison towns of the Danube provinces. In the twenty years of his rule, he raised an additional thirty-four legions, which with their auxiliary forces, gave him a total of some 350,000 men under arms. Of his sixty-eight legions, he used forty-six as front-line troops, and sixteen as divisional reserves. Thus he had a final reserve, uncommitted to any specific task and ready for use as a mobile force anywhere in the empire, of only six legions with their auxiliary cavalry – less than 40,000 regular troops in all, leaving foreign auxiliaries out of the account, to act as the bodyguard to four emperors. The danger was obvious. If any part of the frontiers came under a major assault, its garrison could be meaningfully reinforced only by stripping a neighbouring sector first of its tactical reserve, then of its first-line troops. Similarly, to collect together an army capable of striking hard at an enemy beyond any particular sector of the frontier involved seriously weakening the defences of neighbouring fronts. A defensive system built on the pattern of large units more or less permanently posted to a particular province of the empire had been Roman practice from the outset. It had worked well in the early years, but less efficiently as time passed. In the course of his service with Diocletian and his own father, Constantine realized that the army was now so barbarianized that the system could no longer be said to work at all. Though dressed in Roman uniforms, the legions lacked true loyalty to the idea of Rome. Worse still, they lacked true Roman discipline, and could not be trusted to stand and die for an emperor they had never met. He saw that many of the problems would resolve themselves if the bulk of the army was brought into more immediate contact with its supreme commander, himself. Semi-barbarian troops fought best in fast-moving actions under inspiring leadership. It had been demonstrated time and again that the new type of soldier was happiest as a member of a small unit, under a commander he knew well. Constantine decided therefore to treat the whole army as though it were composed of subject allies, and as a first step in that direction, cut the size of the infantry legion from 5,500 to 1,000 men. The legions of the old army had been general-purpose units, liable either for frontier duty or to be redeployed as part of the imperial field army, as the needs of the hour dictated. Many barbarians, however, did not make good all-round soldiers, so he decreed that there should in future be in effect two armies: a frontier guard and garrison force (*limitanei* and *castriciani*) and a mobile field army of infantry legions and cavalry vexillations (*comitatenses*). By reorganizing the available manpower, settling the least adaptable troops on the frontiers, and stripping their units of their cavalry wings to form new elements in the field army, he succeeded in building up a strategic reserve, immediately available for service under the emperor, consisting of some 260 small but powerful units. The creation of this new army meant that the frontiers were more lightly guarded than for centuries (although some two-thirds of the armed forces were still on frontier duties); but, as the constant incursions of the Franks and Goths in Diocletian's reign had shown, the old deployment could not keep out a determined enemy, and the task of the frontier force could only be to delay an invader until a sufficient army was brought up to destroy him. For this task, a small force could be as effective as a much larger unit, as long as the men felt that they were fighting for something tangible. They were therefore granted the right to cultivate imperial lands close to their well-protected and -equipped forts, and became almost settlers on the frontiers, owing military duties to the emperor when required. For counter-attack and pursuit (as well as for putting down rebellion within the empire), the new small legions and cavalry vexillations were much more practical than the old reserve garrisons.

The new army required a new command structure. After the Battle of Milvian Bridge, Constantine took their military duties from the Praetorian Prefects and gave it to two new officers of field rank, a Master of Infantry and a Master of Cavalry (*magister peditum praesentalis* and *magister equitum praesentalis*). This reform also had the valuable effect of making the very necessary distinction between the military and civil administrations. Both military Masters had permanent places at the Consistory, but the Master of Infantry was always reckoned the more senior, and thus the first soldier in the empire after the emperor himself. When, in 335, Constantine divided the empire to give commands to his sons and nephews, a Master of the Horse was appointed as senior general under each of them, but overall command of the armies remained in the hands of his own Master of Infantry.

The division of the old ponderous legions into many smaller formations led to the institution of new ranks in the chain of command, and references to military dukes (*duces*, leaders) and counts (*comites*, 'comrades of the *Augustus*') are increasingly frequent from Constantine's later years. Promotion to the higher ranks of the army was usually through service in the imperial bodyguard, a centurion from a field unit becoming first a protector, then a tribune, before being appointed either *dux* or *comes* in command of an area. Masters were commonly appointed only from the ranks of the Counts, most of whom seem to have had special claim to be reckoned as 'comrades', having performed some usually meritorious service for the emperor, or been judged by Constantine himself to deserve his favour. Appointment as a military duke usually meant that a man was barred from further promotion.

Constantine's critics claimed that he put an intolerable burden on the empire by doubling or even quadrupling the number of men under arms. The actual figures which survive are from a much later period, but it would seem that his reconstruction of the army quadrupled only the number of units and made soldiers a more common sight in many cities by dispersing units more generally throughout the empire. His army was more efficient than Diocletian's, but probably not much more expensive to maintain, except in so far as continuing inflation made everything more costly and an increase in the number of units postulated more unit commanders being paid.

The structure and quality of the society which the armies guarded did not alter fundamentally during Constantine's reign, although superficial changes were many. Apart from official records, few documents survive to throw light on the attitudes and way of life of the poorer and middle classes. Something of the qualities, good and bad, of both administrators and administered does, however, emerge from such records as this courtroom exchange between the Most Distinguished Consular Zenophilus and a somewhat shifty, probably frightened schoolmaster named Victor, during the examination of Nundinarius the Deacon's charges against Bishop Silvanus on December 13, 320:

Zenophilus: What is your name?
Witness: Victor.
Zenophilus: What is your occupation?
Witness: I am a Professor of Latin Literature, a Latin grammarian.
Zenophilus: What is your background?

Witness: My father was a decurion of Constantinia, my grandfather a soldier who served in the bodyguard, but by blood we are originally of Moorish descent.

Zenophilus: Remembering your honour and dignity, outline simply the causes of the quarrel among the Christians.

Witness: Although I am of the Christian community, I do not know the origins of the quarrel, but I was at Carthage when Secundus the Bishop came there one day with a Carthaginian, and they said that it had come to light – I do not know how – that Bishop Caecilian had not been consecrated properly, and they had put someone else up in opposition to him. This quarrel started at Carthage at that time, but I cannot tell you in detail how the argument began. We always had one church in our city before this, and if there ever had been a quarrel, we knew nothing about it.

Zenophilus: But if his innocence was obvious, why was this man suspended? . . . Remember: others besides you are quite positive that Silvanus is a *traditor*. Admit the truth.

Witness: I know nothing about it.

Zenophilus (to Nundinarius, the plaintiff): Victor denies knowing that Silvanus was a *traditor*.

Nundinarius: He did know it. It was he who handed over the books.

Witness: I ran before *that* storm. May I drop dead if I'm lying! When persecution broke so unexpectedly over us, we fled to Mount Bellona. I lived with the Deacon Martus and the Presbyter Victus, and when they came to this Martus, searching for all the books, he denied that he had any. Then Victus gave them the names of all the Readers. They came to my house when I was not there. Someone came from the magistrates, and my books were taken away. When I came back, I found my books had been taken.

Nundinarius: According to the reports, you have already admitted that you did hand over the books. Why deny it when they can be produced?

Zenophilus: Just admit it. If you will not, you may have to be interrogated under torture.

Nundinarius: Have the reports read.

Zenophilus: Read them!

(The records were read, proving Nundinarius right)

Zenophilus: Now – admit it.

Witness: I was not there.

(Letters were then read, showing that Victor and Silvanus were both *traditores*)

Zenophilus: The records and letters prove that Silvanus was a *traditor*.
(*to Victor*) Just confess that you knew that he had surrendered something.

Witness: He did surrender something, but not in my presence.

Zenophilus: Well, then, who allowed Silvanus into the ministry?

Witness: The persecution began under Bishop Paul, and Silvanus was a subdeacon then.

Nundinarius (*interrupting*) And what happened when he was made a bishop? Did not the people say: Let it be someone else! O God, hear us?

Zenophilus (*to Victor*) Did the people say: Silvanus is a *traditor*?

Witness: I myself was unhappy to see him made a bishop.

Zenophilus: Because you knew he was a *traditor*? Just admit it.

Witness: He was a *traditor*.[7] . . .

Examining magistrates like Zenophilus have been breaking down reluctant witnesses like Victor since judicial enquiries first began. One of the mainstays of the empire was the respect felt by men like Victor the Grammarian for its institutions and the self-respect they drew from their awareness of their own place in it. It was important to Victor, to Zenophilus and – they both instinctively felt – to Constantine himself, that Victor's father had been a decurion, liable to serve as a magistrate if elected, and that his grandfather had been in the imperial bodyguard. By the drastic expedients of war and political murder, Constantine reduced the number of imperial courts to one, his own, and restored to the empire its original monolithic structure, but he did nothing to destroy the belief of such men as Victor in their place in it. He did not change the essential structure of society, but rather strengthened the old structure by binding it together in loyalty to a single head. Such measures as the creation of new orders of knights at Rome and Constantinople, and the invention of new titles, such as *comes* and *patricius* (Julius Constantius became 'the Patrician', but there were others), did not involve a large enough number of families immediately to deform the social pattern. He was, it is true, continually although not always openly at war with the old aristocracy – a struggle which emerged most frequently into the light on the religious issue – but although he took steps to reduce its independence and freedom of action, he did not introduce legislation designed to strip its members of their landholdings and accumulated wealth. The aristocracy complained that he raised barbarians and nobodies to positions of power and authority, and he did in fact make it his policy to employ anyone who would be useful to him – but Victor, a Christian by conviction, and a Moor by blood, would have seen that rather as a sign for hope than a cause for complaint. His favourites joined the aristocracy, as far as that group permitted them to do so. His half-brother Julius Constantius' first wife was Galla, a sister of the Senator Rufinus, one of the Anicii. His half-sister Eutropia married a rich senator named Nepotianus. Although he did raise men like Ablavius, the Praetorian Prefect in Attendance for an unprecedented period of twelve consecutive years, to dizzy heights of power, it was not merely because he liked them and wanted to set them up against the ancient nobility, but because they were efficient and valuable. His bias was rather against possessions and connections likely to interfere with efficient service of himself and his administration, than against wealth and noble birth as such. He was always ready to use those aristocrats – like Anicius Julianus, his governor of Rome from 326–9 – whom he believed trustworthy and loyal to himself. It was because he knew that he could not trust most aristocrats that the overall effect of his rule on their class was to depress it.

Thus the trend already discernible in the reign of Diocletian, away from Rome and unfavourable to those previously recognized as important people in their own districts, was continued and reinforced by the operation of Constantine's character and personal predilections on the course of affairs. Under Diocletian, the number of the provinces had been increased and the actual power of provincial governors and magistrates proportionally reduced. This gradual reduction in the importance of the province was accelerated under Constantine, partly because he could not fully trust the class from which governors and magistrates were traditionally drawn; partly because he did not really share 'Jovian' devotion to ancestral practices and institutions; but largely because the creation of a strong central administration, effectively directed by an emperor with a good grasp of the realities of life and carried on by a professional civil service geared to provide him with a constant flow of essential information from every quarter, made many aspects of the old provincial administrations irrelevant. Even the senate of Constantinople, which he had deliberately created to play an essential role in the government, remained largely an ornamental body while he lived to control the empire.

The structure of the civil service through which he ruled was so complicated that it demands a special study, and innumerable books and papers have been devoted to analyzing it[8]. Essentially, however, it depended on efficient co-operation between the four praetorian prefectures and the central government on the one hand and the handful of officials who made up the Sacred Council, the Consistory, on the other. The Consistory varied in size and composition as the needs of the moment dictated, but its permanent members in the early days appear to have been the Praetorian Prefect in Attendance (Ablavius for many years), the Master of the Offices, the Master of the Soldiers, the Great Chamberlain, the two chief financial officers of the empire, the controller of the huge private purse (*magister res privatae*) and the general finance minister (*rationalis rei summae*), the chief legal officer (*quaestor sacri palatii*) and the *primicerius* 'of the tribunes and notaries', whose office it was to oversee promotions and appointments, and ensure that the decisions of the Consistory were carried out by the proper departments.

In general, duties and tasks in the civil sphere fell into the province of one of the masters of the *scrinia* subject to the Master of the Offices. As the administration grew in complexity, the responsibility of this last officer also grew – so also, therefore, did his importance, together with that of the *primicerius* and the *quaestor*, who took precedence before him and were responsible for his efficiency to the most senior of all civil officers, the Praetorian Prefect in Attendance. As has already been noticed, the three *scrinia* of his department grew into four before Constantine's death, with the creation of an office dedicated to the task of arranging the emperor's timetable. The departments *ab epistulis*, the foreign secretariat, and *a libellis*, dealing with petitions and other legal matters, continued to fulfil the functions Diocletian had defined for them, but the influence of the office of the Master of the Memoranda (*magister memoriae*) gradually increased as centralization proceeded and records of all kinds became ever more important; so that in the end the Master of the Memoranda became practically second-in-command to the Master of the Offices, liaising between him and the heads of lesser departments. However, the struggle for precedence – which offered practical and financial, as well as titular, advantages – was continuous and often vicious, and it is misleading to refer back to Constantine the rigid distinctions and rankings prevailing in the later Byzantine Empire, which is often the only evidence to have survived.

The authority of the Master of the Offices also extended over three essential departments otherwise outside the control of the civil service, the Imperial Bodyguard, the frontier guard, and the *schola agentum in rebus*, the imperial secret police. Constantine has so often been accused of having turned the empire into a police state that the functions of this corps must be looked at more closely[9].

Centralization, bureaucratization and Constantine's undying suspicion, made it inevitable that the 'Men of Affairs' appointed by Diocletian to provide him with secret reports such as were formerly submitted by the hated (and now disbanded) corps of *frumentarii* should grow under his successor until its controller sometimes seemed the most powerful man in the state, more immediately awe-inspiring than even the Praetorian Prefect or the Master of the Soldiers. The secrecy surrounding some of its functions no doubt gave rise to rumours that they were more all-embracing than in fact they were; but there can be no doubt that Constantine was well-served by a large and efficient spy service. A principal officer of the Corps of Men of Affairs (*princeps*) was attached to every Vicarius' and provincial governor's office as the chief of staff, and used the opportunities this position offered both to make reports on everyone with whom it brought him into contact, especially other government employees, and efficiently to direct the activities of those of the corps' agents at work in the district. Men of Affairs controlled the imperial posting service, acted as imperial messengers, collected special donations to the treasury, and generally made themselves useful to the emperor and a nuisance to everyone else. It was commonly believed that they were the originators as well as the denunciators of most of the corruption for which the times were infamous, yet their service was counted an honourable as well as a profitable one, and there was apparently great competition to win a place in it. A successful Man of Affairs could count on imperial favour. Several were granted provincial governorships when they retired.

Precisely how many men were engaged in the civil service of the central administration it is impossible to estimate, but their total cannot have fallen short of, and probably exceeded, the strength of the army and all its supporting industries. An equal number must have worked for provincial administrations. There was, apparently, no master plan controlling the growth of the service, and many of the posts it offered were in origin occasional appointments, created to fill a proven need, or even to please a petitioner, and made permanent when they had shown their continuing worth. Under anyone with less sure an eye for administrative practicality than Constantine, such a growth would have run wild and then collapsed under its own weight, but in fact by the time he died it was so firmly rooted that in later years it was the 'mandarin' Byzantine civil service which, whether the emperor was strong or weak, kept the empire of Constantinople in being. It is no small testimony to his genius that it survived until the empire was overwhelmed by the Turks in 1453.

If, however, the growth of this administration was obscure, its goals were not. It was intended to concentrate all power into the hands of the emperor himself – and this it succeeded in doing. Constantine once said that to become emperor is a matter of destiny, but that once the power of Fate has imposed the burden of ruling on a man, it is his duty to strive to appear worthy of it[10]. In other words, once a man has power, he owes it to himself to keep and use it. In this field at least, he cannot be accused of failing to live up to his own principles. He devoted thirty years to uniting the empire under himself, and keeping all power in his own hands. Recent history had proved that the danger of fragmentation was very real, once the senior Augustus tried to share the burden with others. Severus, Bassianus, Valens, Martianus – so many of the Caesars of his own times had caused trouble. The Augustus owed it to himself, to the empire and to the Supreme God to keep what he had been given. From the moment Constantine attained supreme power until his thirtieth jubilee in 335 he strove continually to do precisely this. Then suddenly, in that year, he divided the empire between his sons and nephews. He gave command in Gaul, Spain and the Britains to Constantine II, in Italy and Africa to Constans, and the East to Constantius; he endowed Delmatius, the son of Delmatius the Censor, with supreme power on the Danube march and in Macedonia and Greece, and Hannibalianus, the son of Julius Constantius the Patrician, with similar authority in Pontus, making the one nephew a Caesar equal with his own sons, and granting the other the incredible (and ludicrous) title *rex regum*, King of Kings[11]. What made him give away what Fate had granted to him?

Ten years earlier, he had refused to share authority with either Licinius or Crispus. He had murdered Licinianus simply so that he should never become a danger. Now, in 335, he was apparently ensuring that after his death there would be either a division of power, of the kind which he had hitherto found intolerable, or that civil war would supervene.

The most credible explanation of this reversal of policy is that he was convinced that none of his sons or nephews was fit to take sole control of the vast empire when he himself died. The oldest of his sons, Constantine II, was still younger than he himself had been when he had fled from Galerius' court to his father's protection, and the youngest, Constans, was only twelve years of age when he became Caesar in 333. When Constantine divided the empire, he may well have expected to live for several more years, and hoped that he would see one of the five emerge as worthy of promotion to the rank of Augustus. He probably gave Delmatius his chance, making him Master of the Soldiers and Consul (in 333) before raising him to the purple, and fired the ambitions of Hannibalianus by giving him his own daughter Constantina in marriage and calling him King of Kings, because he doubted the ability of his own sons ever to rise to the level of excellence once set by Crispus the Victor. The truth was that he was missing his eldest son, who should have been beside him during these declining years.

He himself had been compelled to fight for power. It was precious to him, and he was probably unwilling to let any one youth simply inherit it. Nor would he trust a single designated heir to let him live out his life in peace. He divided his potential heirs by sharing the empire out among them, and so ruled them until he died. There is no record of his ever saying that if any one of them wanted supreme power after him, he would have to fight for it, but the preparation for the future he made by partitioning his estate was one of those actions which speak louder than words.

CHAPTER FIFTEEN

THE LAST YEARS

SUCCESSFUL as Constantine's policies generally were and vigorously though he pursued his twin goals of unity and peace, not even during the last seven years of his life, when his control of the empire was absolute, did he achieve either complete unity within the state or continual peace on all its frontiers.

Religion continued to furnish the most common grounds for disunity. After the Council of Nicaea, thousands, perhaps hundreds of thousands, abandoned paganism and joined the winning side. Eusebius complained dolefully of their hypocrisy[1]. The church was, however, hopelessly divided, with state catholicism itself split into the homoousian and Arian factions; and the Meletians and Donatists continuing to offer baptism and the other Christian sacraments to those who, although attracted by Christian doctrines, could not bring themselves to support the official church, either because it seemed too lax, or because they regarded its champion, Constantine, as their enemy. During these years, African Donatism spread into Western Europe, finding support partly because its ascetic teachings appealed to those whose outlook had been influenced by the pagan philosophies, but indubitably also in part because pagan opponents of the Neo-Flavians continued to find it impossible to accept the Christian emperor even after they had embraced the Christian faith.

Moreover, divisions within the Christian body were not the only threat to the commonwealth. Continuing pagans also menaced its unity. Although by the end of the reign the gods had lost many of their adherents and almost all their wealth, those who remained loyal to the cults of the pre-Constantinean state were confirmed by their losses in the opinion that it was Constantine's destiny to be remembered as the man who destroyed the empire, and they naturally continued to oppose his policies.

Constantinople: the serpent-column of Plataea as it appears today. Originally set up at Delphi to commemorate Greek victory at Plataea over the Persians in 479 B.C., it was moved to Constantinople *c.* A.D. 330, and re-erected in the Hippodrome. In later times it was revered as a symbol of the city's spirit of resistance to the Turks and, as such, was deliberately smashed by Sultan Mohammed II, the conqueror, in 1453

Photo: the Author

The Empress Helena as a saint of popular piety. In this nineteenth-century representation at Pieta, Malta, St. Helena appears as an imperious old woman, displaying the treasure she discovered at Jerusalem, the true Cross and the Holy Nails

Photo: the Author

Head of the emperor Constantine, in the Capitoline Museum, Rome

Photo: Mansell Collection

With so much to divide men, it is surprising that there was no serious rebellion between 326 and 337. There was unrest, but the army remained unequivocally loyal – and while the army kept faith, the emperor was safe from anyone except a potential assassin within his own household. By executing Crispus, Fausta, Licinianus and their friends, Constantine had eliminated the most likely sources of trouble within the palace. He replaced them with favourites, most of them low-born, all of them hated by everyone except himself and totally dependent on him not only for their fortunes but also, as events after his death showed, for their very lives. He was suspicious of everybody, but seems actually to have needed to fear no one. The efficiency of his secret police and the loyalty to himself of lesser officials and lower-ranking soldiers was so formidable that potential plotters were perhaps as frequently deterred before their plans matured as detected when they moved to put them into effect. Only one determined, though often derided, attempt was made to overthrow the administration. It was led by a man named Calocaerus or Calocerus, whom Victor identifies as the mad master of a herd of camels: 'Calocerus, the master of a herd of camels in the Island of Cyprus, insanely snatched at the vision of kingship,' he writes, 'and when he was tortured to death, as the law ordained, like a slave or bandit, he was said by the whole world to have been out of his mind'[2].

However, there are indications that this revolt was not as unimportant as Victor's story suggests. The fact that there is no official report of it arouses the suspicion that it was significant enough for Constantine to want to suppress its memory, as he had suppressed the details of earlier plots against him. Not even its date is certain. Jerome's Chronicle puts it in the year 334: 'In the Year from Abraham 2351, and Constantine's twenty-ninth, the revolution stirred up by Calocaerus in Cyprus was suppressed'[3]. The duty of quelling it was entrusted to Delmatius the son of Delmatius the Censor, who was then acting as Constantine's Master of Soldiers. Calocaerus was captured in Cyprus and executed at Tarsus in Cilicia. He was probably burned alive after torture, Constantine having banned crucifixion as the means of execution for slaves, out of respect for Christ[4]. The following year, Delmatius was raised to the purple.

According to St John Chrysostom, preaching at Constantinople some forty years after Constantine's death, there was also a revolt at about this time among the Jews, but although there was certainly unrest in Syria and Palestine, John probably exaggerated the seriousness of the trouble. The Jews were frightened by the prospect of a Christian empire and angered by the wealth and ostentation of the Christians in the Holy Land, where Christian pilgrims were frequently and outspokenly antisemitic. There may well have been isolated outbreaks of violence, but there is no evidence of a concerted Jewish rising before 352, when rebels in Palestine proclaimed a Jewish king named Patricius, who for some time successfully defied an army dispatched to dethrone him[5].

Although there was no Jewish rising, however, the Jews had good reason to hate and fear Constantine. He made no secret of his dislike for them. Although the edict of 319 forbidding Jews to stone 'converts to God' seemed reasonable to imperial jurists, as under the law only official courts were empowered to impose the death penalty, to militants among the Jews it appeared to abrogate the Divine Law, which prescribed death for apostacy. At the Council of Nicaea, Constantine personally argued against continued acceptance of the date of the Passover from the rabbis to determine the date of Easter, on the grounds that Christians should accept nothing from ungodly atheists. A coldly worded edict dated 331 grudgingly extended 'to [Jewish] priests, rulers and fathers of synagogues, and others serving there with devotion'[6] the freedom from public duties already enjoyed by the ministers of all other officially recognized cults, but two laws of 335, addressed to the Praetorian Prefect Felix, suggest that Constantine's aversion to the Jews was still obvious and was being reciprocated, while Jewish opposition to conversions continued unabated. 'It is illegal,' the first law reminded the Prefect, 'for the Jews to make difficulties for anyone who becomes a Christian from Judaism, or to do him an injury: outrages of this kind will be proportionately punished.' The other edict ruled that 'if a

Jew who has purchased a Christian, or a member of no matter what other sect soever, shall circumcise him, he shall on no account be permitted to keep in servitude the man so circumcised, but shall give him his freedom'[7].

However, despite these areas of inflammation, the empire as a whole had rarely in living memory been more tranquil. 'Bullneck'[8], as the common people irreverently nicknamed the ruler who called himself (with equal irreverence, in the opinion of some) 'the Equal of the Apostles', had so far imposed his will on the Roman world that even his continual extortions in cash and kind for the support of his armies, his household and his church did not undermine his authority. Although inevitably men grumbled, they endured him and his demands, partly from fear, partly from love of peace, and partly, in many instances, from respect, awe and even admiration of him. He had towered over the world for so long that it must have been difficult to imagine what the empire would be like without him.

One element in his policy which many found it hard either to understand or condone was his attitude towards the Goths and the Sarmatians, which to citizens proud of true Roman or Hellenic blood seemed yet another demonstration of his preference for barbarians. In 334 – just a year after a famine and plague in the Eastern provinces had proved the empire incapable of supporting the population it already had – he invited a third of a million Sarmatians to settle in the Danubian, Macedonian and Italian provinces and farm state-owned lands there. It was an act of far-sighted political expediency, by which he turned former enemies into steadfast admirers who, nearly a century later, as Eutropius recorded, still remembered him with gratitude[9]. At the time, however, it was widely misunderstood.

Rausimond's defeat in 322–3 had left the Goths shocked and disorganized. Almost ten years passed before they were again strong enough to mount a concerted attack on the lands to the south of their home pastures on the southern Steppes and the east-European plain. By 331, however, they posed so obvious a threat to the Sarmatian and Vandalic tribes of the Danube Basin that those old enemies were forced into an alliance and driven to appeal to Constantine for military aid. He promised to send an army under the Caesar Constantine II to protect them, but before the Roman forces could reach the river, the Gothic King Araric had smashed the Transdanubian Alliance and crossed into Moesia, leading his war-bands through the peaceful province on a wild career of murder, rape and arson. Like Rausimond's horde before them, however, Araric's men were no match for the legions, and when Constantine II's army approached, they withdrew northwards, back across the river. The Romans mounted a pursuit, and when they succeeded in bringing the tribesmen to battle, in Sarmatian territory on April 20, 332, cut their formations to pieces. According to the unnamed author quoted by Valesius, besides those Goths who fell in battle 'around a hundred thousand were killed by hunger and cold' in the rout ending it. 'After which, Constantine accepted hostages from among them, including King Araric's own son'[10].

What happened next is uncertain, but within two years the Sarmatians had somehow again embroiled themselves in trouble. Egged on, perhaps, by Geberic, Araric's successor, the Limigantes, a slave-tribe subject to the Sarmatians, had risen against them. Without knowing it, the Sarmatians were early victims of that flood from the East which in the fifth century was to sweep away the remnants of the Western Empire. Under intolerable pressure from the Goths and threatened by their slaves' revolt, they surrendered their tribal identity for the sake of individual survival. Some of their clan came to an understanding with the Goths and, withdrawing from the Danube Valley deep into Gothic territory, were quickly absorbed into the Gothic nation. Others trekked north and west, to the lands of the Teutonic Quadi, and found asylum there. Still others, perhaps the majority of the survivors, appealed to Constantine's charity. The Goths naturally had no objection to a peaceful Sarmatian withdrawal, so it was relatively easy for Constantine finally to pacify the Danube frontier by welcoming a third of a million Sarmatian settlers into the empire and, renewing his former treaty with the Goths, further to barbarise his inheritance (as his enemies saw it) by allowing Gothic tribesmen to settle permanently on the Danube, making them his frontier guards.

In the long run, the critics of his policy were perhaps justified. The barbarians so settled in the Danubian, Macedonian and Italian provinces in some measure prepared the way for the success of the invasions a century later. But those invasions would probably have been successful anyway, and in the short term, Constantine had achieved a great deal. Lands which had remained untilled for many years, owing to the flight of peasant farmers from the countryside with its burden of duties and taxation, were farmed again, the first permanent bridge was built across the Danube and – not least important – the empire confirmed an old alliance, with the last of all the free Greek cities, Cherson[11].

Cherson owed its freedom partly to the determination of its citizens that they should remain free, but largely to the fact that it stood at the end of the world, on the edge of the Sea of Grass, the steppelands. For eight hundred years, it had withstood the weight of Asia from the site where Sebastopol now stands, in the Crimea. From the earliest times, its population had been mixed but its institutions had been defiantly Greek, and it had looked across the Black Sea to Byzantium and the Propontis for its trade and alliances. The belligerent push southwards by the Gothic confederacy which in 331–4 involved the empire and the Danubian tribes in war also threatened the freedom and very existence of Cherson. Under the determined leadership of its First Magistrate Diogenes, the city did not wait to be attacked, but called out its citizens in arms and assailed the Goths from the rear. Chersonese intervention was perhaps not decisive, but Constantine recognized its gallantry and significance. After victory had been won, he sent rich presents to the city, promised its exports to the empire freedom from all customs dues, and recognized Chersonese independence in a new treaty confirming the existing alliance between her and the empire – a recognition which endured until the city, growing old and feeble at last, was finally absorbed into the empire during the reign of Theophilus, in 829.

Peace on the Danube had been assured, the bridge over the river was open to traffic, and the Sarmatian settlers in the empire had sown their first crops before Constantine celebrated the thirtieth anniversary of his accession in the summer of 335. As has already been noted, he made it fundamentally a Christian festival, with a Synod at Tyre and celebrations at the Holy Sepulchre in Jerusalem and at Constantinople. Not only did he fail to go to old Rome, he seems not even to have entertained the idea that such a journey was expected of him. There must have been parades, games and loyalist banquets at the old capital, but Constantine was so indifferent that he did no more than claim the consulship. Probably the most significant ceremonies at Rome that year were those accompanying the solemn translation of the bones venerated as relics of the Apostles St Peter and St Paul from the catacombs of St Sebastian, where they had been venerated since 258, to the basilicas built to honour them at the traditional sites of their martyrdoms, at the Vatican and on the Ostian Way[12]. The whole emphasis was, however, on Constantinople and the church there, now controlled by Eusebius of Nicomedia through the person of the emperor.

By this time, having recovered from the famine, Constantinople was a large and prosperous city, protected by massive fortifications and special laws granting it privileges second only to those of Rome itself. Just within the landward walls, close to the Mese and the Hadrianople Gate, was rising the most splendid of all Constantine's churches, that which he had probably already designated as his own burial place, the Church of the Holy Apostles. From the description of it given by Eusebius of Caesarea and confirmed by a sermon of St Gregory Nazianzus, it seems to have been constructed on the pattern not of the basilica but of the cross, with a large dome over the crossing of the nave and transepts. According to the enthusiastic Eusebius, '[Constantine] carried this building to a vast height, decorating it splendidly by covering it from foundations to roof with sheets of marble of various colours . . . while the dome was completely covered with finely-wrought tracery, worked in brass and gold'[13]. The cruciform Church of the Holy Apostles might well be seen as the official grave of paganism. Preaching at the imperial jubilee, Eusebius triumphantly if prematurely proclaimed the death of the old world:

> [our emperor] alone of all those who have exercised the imperial power, having been honoured by the Supreme Ruler with a reign of three *decennalia*, now celebrates this feast not, as his predecessors would have done, by glorifying hellish devils or the apparitions of fraudulent spirits, or the deceiving and lying arts of godless men, but with an act of thanksgiving . . . He does not defile his imperial palaces with blood . . . but dedicates his own imperial spirit . . .[14].

Since the dedication of Constantinople, Constantine had in fact been working openly against paganism, and in at least one edict – now unfortunately lost – had ordered the closing of the temples. Jerome's Chronicle dates this extreme step in his twenty-fifth year (330–1)[15]: a later account suggests that there may have been more than one edict between 331 and 333: 'In his twenty-sixth and twenty-seventh years, he swooped to destroy the idols and their temples, and granted what had belonged to the idols to the churches of God.'[16]

Eusebius' *Life* describes in some detail three of the suppressions effected at this time, those of the temples of Aphrodite at Alphaca and Helipolis (Baalbek) in Syria and that of the shrine of Asclepius at Aegea. All were apparently closed because they were successful, as well as rich, and provided effective opposition to the spread of the Catholic Church, the temples of Aphrodite on the excuse that they were morally offensive, the sanctuary of the God of Healing merely because 'the devil worshipped there occasionally appeared to those who passed the night in the temple and sometimes restored the sick to health'. Troops had to be called in to enforce the closure of the shrine at Alphaca ('dedicated to the foul devil who goes by the name of Venus – a school of wickedness for all the votaries of unchasteness, and such as destroy their bodies with effeminacy'), while at Heliopolis, as Eusebius admits, the cult of the goddess was still so very much alive that her temple had to be desecrated and a church built by imperial decree before even the trimmers realized the expediency of resetting their sails to the wind blowing from Constantinople[17]. Nevertheless, by Constantine's thirtieth anniversary, pagan institutions generally had been weakened to the point at which without special fostering they could not recover. When Julian tried, less than thirty years later, to restore pagan worship, he found the shrines deserted and the rites all but forgotten, even at such key centres as Delphi and Antioch. At Constantine's thirtieth jubilee, therefore, Eusebius and his friends were justified in feeling that they had something special to celebrate.

A principal topic of conversation in political circles at Constantinople that year must have been the question of the succession. The promotion of Delmatius and Hannibalianus, announced on September 25, was one of the outstanding events of the year, deserving the prominence given to it in the Paschal Chronicle: 'The sacred celebrations of Constantine's thirtieth anniversary were celebrated most splendidly at Constantinopolitean Rome on the eighth day before the kalends of August [July 25], and he appointed his son Constans *Augustus* [actually, *Caesar*, but in 333], and proclaimed Delmatius, the son of Delmatius the Censor, as *Caesar* on the eighth day before the kalends of October and, singling out Hannibalianus, endowed him with the purple *chlamys* and appointed him as king of Cappadocia'[18]. He gave Hannibalianus his daughter Constantina as his queen and sent him with the Persian royal title 'King of Kings' to rule Pontus, the diocese filling the north-east corner of the empire, sandwiched between Armenia and the Black Sea.

The year's 'splendid' ceremonies were attended not only by delegates from every province of the empire but also by ambassadors from Ethiopia, Persia and the Far East. No doubt they returned home suitably impressed, for Constantine always put on a good show and was notoriously lavish with his presents. However, it is perhaps fortunate for the emperor's reputation that there is no record of what they thought of the effeminate dress and deportment, and the succession of tinted wigs and ever-richer jewels and clothes affected by Constantine and his favourites. His nephew Julian later claimed that they were utterly ridiculous and made the court a laughing-stock – but the pagan Julian was a very narrow-minded ascetic and, in any case, was not old enough in 335 to retain any clear memory afterwards of the general public reaction to his uncle's appearance[19]. Much more significant is the fact that Eusebius felt constrained to explain away the emperor's eccentricities, claiming in his 'Sermon at Constantine's *Tricennalia*' that Constantine dressed to please and impress the people, and not for his own gratification: 'He smiles at his dress, with its embroideries of gold and flowers, and at his imperial purple and diadem, when he sees the crowds staring like children in wonderment. . . .'[20] Was it, however, merely to please the people that the emperor had just ordered a new diadem, made to a new and very fanciful design?

There can be little doubt that Constantine was pleased with himself, and did not care who saw his self-satisfaction. He had better grounds for it than most men. He had ruled longer than any emperor except Augustus himself, and achieved more of what he had set out to do. His jubilee year passed exactly as he had dreamed his years would pass: quietly, uneventfully, and as far as could be seen from Constantinople, generally happily.

In 336, an excuse for another prolonged, expensive but no doubt enjoyable party was found by marrying the Caesar Constantius to his cousin Julius Constantius' daughter. Apart from this wedding, and a brief synod at Constantinople during which Constantine refused to restore Athenasius to Alexandria, and showed himself only too plainly under the influence of the Bishops Eusebius and the Arian party, nothing of real significance happened within the imperial frontiers.

The Secretariat for Foreign Affairs, however, reported ugly developments beyond the Euphrates in Persia and Armenia. The empire was drifting into war, although all the general populace probably knew of it was that the emperor had received special envoys from King Sapor II of Persia, exchanged rich presents with them, and sent their master a typical letter, relating how he had destroyed the persecutors, so earning himself the title 'the Victor', and stuffed full of sound advice on religious affairs. Much lay behind this embassy and its reception[21]. The forty years' peace made between Galerius and the Persians was on the point of expiring. King Sapor, who had succeeded to the Persian throne weeks before his birth in 309, had an inveterate hatred of Christians and a life-long grudge against the Roman Empire. He could never forget the five provinces cut out of Western Persia as the price of peace in 297. He had sworn to win them back, and destroy Rome's faithful ally, King Tiridates of Armenia, who had been a convinced Christian since his baptism in 302 – one willing to risk even his friendship with the Romans for the sake of giving shelter to refugees from the terror under Galerius and Maximin Daia. A violently anti-Christian reaction among the still-pagan Armenian nobility had somewhat restricted the king's pro-Christian activities, just as the continuing paganism of the senatorial class at Rome had set a limit to Constantine's work in Italy, but although Sapor's agents had made the most of the situation, Tiridates had succeeded in holding on to power, and Sapor in his mid-twenties was a frustrated and dangerous man. The real task of his embassy to Constantine in 336 was to confirm that the Roman emperor would not abandon either the Mesopotamian provinces or the Armenian king, and the significance of Constantine's rambling account of how he became 'the Victor' was that it covertly warned Sapor not to go too far. When the Persian embassy returned home, both Constantine and Sapor knew that war was inevitable.

Constantine already had two Caesars in the East, Constantius and Hannibalianus, but feared that in the last resort he could rely on neither of them. The pressure on King Tiridates increased daily and, according to Eusebius, Constantine had begun secretly to prepare for a Persian campaign even before Sapor's agents reached him. He planned a war like that against Licinius, fought under the protection of the *labarum* and with the help of the bishops' prayers. 'It also deserves to be remembered,' Eusebius relates, 'that at about the time of which I am now writing [that is, the period immediately after the tricennial celebrations], the emperor, having learned of an insurrection among some barbarians in the East, realized that he was still confronted by the task of conquering this enemy, and so decided to mount an expedition against the Persians. He therefore proceeded immediately to mobilize his armies, at the same time announcing the news of his intended march to those bishops who were at his court, some of whom he decided to take with him as companions and fellow-labourers in the service of God. . . .'[22] The Persian mission came and went, and covert preparations for war became overt. In the winter of 336–7, Constantine – how wearily at the age of sixty-two, one can only guess – personally supervised the mobilization of his field army in Asia Minor. However, he could not march until after the harvest in June, and he kept Holy Week of 337 at Constantinople, with his old friends the Bishops Eusebius. No one appears to have realized how near death he was until, after the long services of Easter Sunday, April 3, he complained of feeling ill.

'At first,' Eusebius records, 'he experienced only a slight physical indisposition, but this was soon followed by actual disease.'[23] No one has preserved an account of the symptoms of Constantine's last illness, such as those which Lactantius gloatingly compiled in relating the *Deaths of the Persecutors*, so not even a tentative diagnosis of it is possible. The indications are, however, that he had felt for some months that all was not well with him, for something had moved him to order his tomb to be prepared in the Church of the Holy Apostles, commanding 'sarcophaguses to be set up in this church, like sacred pillars in honour and memory of the number of the apostles, his own being placed in the centre, with six of theirs on either side of it'[24]

Once he had publicly admitted to feeling ill, he gave up all pretence. 'He first visited the hot springs in his own city, then proceeded to those in that which bears his mother's name, where he also spent some time in the Church of the Martyrs, offering petitions and prayers to God. And being finally convinced that his life was ending, he felt that the time had come to seek purification from the sins of his past life. . . . He poured out prayers and confessions . . . kneeling on the paved floor of the church, where he now also received for the first time the imposition of hands with prayer [so formally becoming a catachumen]. After this had been done, he went on to the suburbs of Nicomedia and having summoned the bishops to meet him there, spoke the following words to them:

' "The moment I have been waiting for so long, earnestly desiring and praying that in it I might receive the salvation of God, has come at last. Now I too may have the blessing of that seal which confers immortality: now I may receive the seal of salvation. I wanted to receive it in the waters of the River Jordan, where our Saviour is said to have been baptised as an example to us. But it pleases God – who knows what is best for us – that I should receive it here. So be it, then. Let there be no further delay [or hesitation]. If it should prove to be the will of him who is Lord of Life and Death that my life here should be further prolonged and my future destiny should be to associate with the People of God and join with them in prayer as a member of his church, I shall prescribe for myself from this time forward a way of life fitting to his service." '

The meaning of this speech is not wholly obvious. Eusebius clearly intends it to be taken as a genuine record of Constantine's Dying Words, although he admits that the emperor lived for some time after making it. Some of the words used in the original Greek are very ambiguous. However, the general sense is clear: Constantine has deliberately waited until he is – or believes himself to be – on the point of death before submitting to baptism, so that he may die without the weight of sins committed after baptism on his conscience; if he should recover from his illness, he will avoid sin in future by living as an ascetic.

But what has in fact prevented him from being baptised until now? Not, this speech seems to imply, merely the fear of sinning again after baptism, but a definite impediment to baptism. The plain meaning of such phrases as 'the moment I have been waiting for so long', and 'let there be no further delay' is that the speaker has asked for baptism before, perhaps many times, and been refused it. He has not really been looking forward with joyful expectancy to the day of his death (although Eusebius the Bishop might like his readers to believe that he has): he has been asking for baptism and has been denied it in God's name by the bishops. Now the moment has come when he cannot decently be refused it any longer. Even now, however, he fears 'delay' or 'hesitation' on the bishops' part, and has to promise to reform the pattern of his life if they will grant him what he wants. . . . All of which leaves anyone familiar with moralists and their methods asking what was Constantine's besetting sin? If this record is authentic, Constantine's way of life as emperor was so morally offensive that although his friends the bishops would work with him, pray with him, spend his money, use his authority and even ride into battle with him, they would not receive him into the church, despite the obvious propagandistic value to them of the news of his conversion.

If this speech is genuine, Constantine's eccentricities had led him into behaviour that was a public scandal. But is the speech genuine? Probably not as it stands. Although Eusebius was at Constantine's deathbed, it must – however reluctantly – be admitted that it is unlikely that he recorded his dying words with enough accuracy for a minute analysis of them to be a valid exercise. He presents in the form of a set speech what was more probably a series of separate utterances, spoken in no special order, and perhaps spread over a relatively long period of time. 'Let there be no further delay', for example, is more comprehensible as a last flash of the imperial temper than as Eusebius presents it, an almost humble request set within the framework of a coherent speech. One's impression is that Eusebius has struggled to give shape to some intractable material and add dignity to a scene which was probably in fact confused and frightening. He has not recorded the facts so much as shaped a legend to please the pious, omitting everything said by anyone apart from Constantine, and possibly also editing out some of the emperor's own remarks. It was not long after Constantine's death that accusations and counter-accusations of murder and misrepresentation flew from end to end of the empire. Eusebius' friend and ally, the other Bishop Eusebius of Nicomedia, was deeply involved in the intrigue. This account of Constantine's last words is unfortunately open to the suspicion of being propaganda for the Eusebian party. At the hour of his death, no one knew quite what would happen next. In accordance with custom, a slave or a clerk from the department of the Master of the Offices probably recorded everything that was said either by him or in his presence while he was dying: it is a pity that it is Eusebius' edited account, and not the official record of the scene, which has survived.

According to that edited account, the emperor's request for baptism was immediately granted, and then, 'at the end of the ceremonies, he clothed himself in radiant imperial robes as shining as light, and reclining on a couch of the purest white, refused ever to clothe himself in purple again. He assured his soldiers that he was happy to die, then went on to put the final touches to the necessary disposition of his affairs, bequeathing an annual donation to the inhabitants of his imperial city of Rome and sharing out inheritance of the empire among his own children, just like any patrimonial estate, and, in short, arranging everything just as it pleased him'.

'All these events took place,' Eusebius continues, 'during the most important of feasts – I mean, the august and holy festival of Pentecost [that is, between Easter and Whitsun], and on the last day [Whitsunday, May 22], which one might justly call the Feast of Feasts, he was taken at about midday into the presence of his God, leaving his mortal remains to his fellow mortals, and bearing into communion with God that part of him capable of loving and comprehending Him.'

So, it seems, Constantine never was technically 'the Christian Emperor' that he has so often been called. Like Diocletian, although for different reasons, at the end of his life he laid aside the purple to devote himself to his own affairs. Characteristically, he continued to act like an arrogant autocrat – 'arranging everything just as it pleased him' – but he took off the purple robe of power, was baptised naked (as the custom then was) and put on the white robe of the newly-made Christian. It was usual for Christian converts to wear simple white garments for a week after their baptism, to signify their purification and entry into a new life. Constantine's 'radiant imperial robes', of imperial cut but not of imperial colour, were his own version of this dress. The white couch to die on was his own idea – and his adamant refusal 'ever to clothe himself in purple again' suggests that his notorious self-will had survived his regeneration.

The bitterest of all comments on Constantine's baptism was one made by his nephew Julian, in a mocking account in his *Caesars* of why Constantine never became a god[25]. Brought into the presence of all the gods to compete with other undeified emperors for a place at the divine banquet, Constantine listened to the speeches of such heroes as Alexander the Great, Trajan and Marcus Aurelius with growing concern. 'When he had first entered the contest,' Julian claims, 'he was sure enough of himself, but when he thought about what the others had done, he saw how totally insignificant his own actions were. He had indeed overthrown two tyrants, but if the truth were told, one of them [Maxentius] was an unwarlike and effeminate man, while the other [Licinius] was a poor wretch weakened by old age, and both were hated by gods and men. And as for what he had done against the barbarians, that made him look ridiculous, for he had, as it were, paid them tribute, while fixing all his attention on Pleasure, who stood some way off from the gods, near to the portals of the Moon. He was so much in love with her that he never looked at anything else and had no time at all for Victory. However, as it was his turn and he had to say something, he declared:

'I am better than these others in the following ways: than the Macedonian [Alexander], in as much as I fought against Romans, Germans and Scythians, and not against Asiatic barbarians; than Caesar and Octavian, in as much as, unlike them, I did not rise against good and courageous citizens, but attacked only the cruellest and wickedest tyrants. As for Trajan, I shall naturally take precedence before him on account of these same glorious deeds against the tyrants, and I am his equal in respect of those lands which he added to the empire and I regained – if indeed it is not better to regain than gain in the first instance. And as for this man [Marcus who had refused to speak], by not speaking up for himself, he himself yields precedence to all of us."

'Then Silenus said, "But Constantine, are you offering us these mere Gardens of Adonis as your great deeds?"

' "What do you mean," he said, "by Gardens of Adonis?"

' "Those things," Silenus said, "which women plant in pots in honour of Aphrodite's lover, scraping together some dirt to make a garden. They flourish for a little while, then fade away almost at once."

'Constantine blushed at this, realizing that this was an exact description of what he had done . . .'

There followed statements from the emperors about their ambitions. This time, Marcus was persuaded to speak, and after he had finished defending himself for having set a precedent by deifying his worthless wife, Hermes asked Constantine his greatest ambition.

' "To collect a lot of money," he said, "and spend a lot, to gratify the desires of myself and my friends."

'At this, Silenus gave a great laugh, and said, "But if you wanted to be a banker, how did you so far forget yourself as to live the life of a confectioner and hairdresser? Your hair and your appearance have never suggested anything else: what you say now about your aims condemns you . . ." '

After this, the undeified mortals were told to put themselves under the protection of their chosen deities: Alexander joined Hercules, Octavian Apollo and Marcus Aurelius Zeus and Chronos, and so on, but Constantine did not at first know where to go. He wandered about, until 'seeing Wantonness not very far off, he ran up to her. She welcomed him tenderly and embraced him, and having wrapped him in a multicoloured cloak, led him to Debauchery. And there also he found Jesus, who had set up house with her and cried out when anyone came, "Is he a seducer? Is he a murderer? Does he do sacrilegious and infamous deeds? Then let him come close, fearing nothing! I will wash him in this water, and immediately make him clean. And if he should ever do the same things again, he has only to beat his breast and slap his head, and he shall be clean again." So Constantine went joyfully to meet Jesus, after he had withdrawn from the assembly of the gods the whole gang of his sons'.

There must have been many who felt like Julian about Constantine's baptism, though few may have had the skill to express themselves so cruelly. If any dared to make sarcastic comments at the time of the old emperor's illness and death, their insults have not survived. Eusebius records only that he was sincerely mourned, especially in the army: he had been a father to his soldiers, and now they suddenly felt themselves orphaned[26]. Despite its operatic flavour, there may well be some truth in this statement. It was thirty-one years since King Crocus had proclaimed him Augustus at York, and very few men still bearing arms could remember a time when the daily official prayers of the army had not been for the health, safety and victory of the Emperor Constantine. Moreover, many of the soldiers were barbarian by birth, and owed their citizenship to Constantine's policy of making use of former enemies. To them, the news of his death must have been an unsettling and worrying blow.

Eusebius' is the only eyewitness account of Constantine's death. It is regrettable that he did not relate the circumstances in greater detail and with less pointed emphasis on their edifying aspects. A few additional facts can be elicited from later reports. Jerome's Chronicle records that the death actually occurred at a state-owned villa at Achyrion near Nicomedia and that the baptism was performed by Eusebius of Nicomedia – or as Jerome, a confirmed Consubstantialist put it, 'at the end of his life-span, being baptised by Eusebius, the Bishop of Nicomedia, he deviated into the Arian doctrine'[27].

Sozomen's *Histories* suggest that his last hours were made restless by the fear that after his death his last commands would not be obeyed:

> [after his baptism] he confirmed the division of the empire among his sons in accordance with the disposition he had previously made and granted certain privileges to old Rome and the city named after himself. Then he placed his will in the hands of the presbyter who had constantly lauded Arius [Eusebius of Caesarea, perhaps, or one of the chaplains] and who had been commended to him as a man of virtuous life by his sister Constantia on her deathbed, and commanded him – making him swear a special oath – that he would deliver it to Constantius on his arrival. For neither Constantius nor any of the other Caesars was with his dying father. . . .[28].

In his last hours, then, Constantine had decided that Constantius, although only his second surviving son, was the one most worthy of his trust. He may well have hoped that the bishops, who had supervised his education, would be influential enough to control him and honourable enough to guide him into worthy courses. How unworthy of his confidence both Constantius and the bishops were emerged very shortly after he had been laid to rest in the midst of the Twelve Apostles.

According to Julian, Constantius reached Achyrion just before his father died, when 'he was still living, but hard pressed by disease'[29]. This seems unlikely, for from other accounts it appears that for some time after the great emperor's corpse had been taken to Constantinople and laid out on a golden catafalque at the palace, court rituals were continued as though it had been still alive. Orders were issued in its name, petitions were presented to it, the Great Chamberlain's department ceremoniously called it in the morning and put it to bed at night. This may have been because no one wanted to believe that the Victor, the Father of his country, was dead, but it was more probably because widespread unrest was feared if the knowledge that the empire had no Augustus became general before the Caesars could be brought to Constantinople. The fiction may have saved a few lives at the time – although actually, Eusebius claims 'when the soldiers in the provinces received the news of the emperor's death, they all . . . swore oaths . . . to acknowledge none but his sons as the rulers of the Roman world'[30], so that there was no danger of an immediate insurrection. Over the ensuing years, however, first scores, then hundreds and finally thousands were to die because Constantine was dead.

CHAPTER SIXTEEN

MASSACRE OF THE FLAVIANS

THROUGH the summer of 337, the corpse of the great Constantine lay on its golden bed in the palace at Constantinople, and round it from day to day the mummery of the court continued, in the pretence that the dead man still ruled the world. He was, Eusebius claimed, the first emperor ever to go on ruling after his death – a fact proving the high esteem in which God held him[1]. The eye of faith may have been able to discern in these three and a half months of interregnum divine respect for the Equal of the Apostles, but, with the prize of empire dangling within reach, not everyone was content to stand staring at a corpse, holding his breath from awe.

When the news of the emperor's death was first announced, Eusebius records in his only comment on the intense political activity surrounding the body, the colonels of the bodyguard 'selected from among the men they commanded those officers whose loyalty and zeal had long been obvious to the emperor and sent them to the Caesars with the news of what had happened'[2]. The Caesar Constantius probably reached the palace within days of the temporary coffin. Trained in political awareness from infancy, he was not deceived by the temporary tranquillity of his dead father's continued reign. He knew that however reverentially the Great Chamberlain's department and the clergy treated Constantine's memory, the time must come when a new supreme ruler or rulers would be proclaimed and the normal course of imperial government resumed. When that day came, he intended to rule the world, with or without his brothers as co-equals, but without help from anyone else. For the time being, however, he was content to be at Constantinople, visibly directing affairs in accordance with his father's last commands, while his agents worked among the troops and reported to him on the activities of his potential rivals.

His propagandists did well among the legions. 'Throughout the provinces,' Eusebius says, 'as soon as the soldiers learned the news of the emperor's death, they all . . . swore . . . to recognize no one but his sons as rulers of the Roman world, and it was not long before they decided that they should no longer be called Caesars, but should all be honoured with the title Augustus'[3]. As reports of the soldiers' reactions trickled in, Constantius must have been delighted. The situation was developing precisely as he had planned. The new world would have nothing to offer the Caesar Delmatius, or any other descendent of Constantius Chlorus by Theodora, let alone any of Constantine's favourites. When at last he signed the order for his father's funeral, he and his brothers were already assured of a golden future and most of the other Neo-Flavians and their friends were doomed.

At the last moment, a hitch threatened the smooth course of events. Rome demanded the privilege of guarding the emperor's body, showing the genuineness of its respect for him by honouring him as Constantine the Divine. 'The Roman Senate and people,' Eusebius reports, 'took the news as a calamity . . . and gave themselves up to excessive grief. The baths and markets were closed, [and] public spectacles and all other recreations . . . suspended . . . They honoured him with paintings . . . showing heaven itself and the emperor resting in a heavenly mansion.'[4]

Rome's grief may have been politic rather than real, but her claim to the body was too strong easily to be ignored. The Empress Helena was already buried at Rome in a tomb which Constantine had apparently prepared for himself. He had always called himself a Roman emperor: now, at long last, the Roman people wanted to recognize him as their own. However, although in 306 Constantine had acquiesced in the cult of Constantius Chlorus the god, the world inherited by Constantius II was too Christian for it to be expedient for him to encourage worship of his father and Constantine was too closely identified with Constantinople for either the new emperor or the Arian bishops seriously to consider handing him over to the Romans. When Constantine did later appear in heaven, it was not as a Roman godling, but as an Eastern saint. In the matter of the funeral at least, Constantius decided to honour his father's own wishes, ordering that it should be at Constantinople, with entombment at the Church of the Holy Apostles.

Eusebius' description of the funeral is remarkable, in as much as it suggests that it was a purely military ceremony, without religious rituals of any kind, either pagan or Christian. It was only after the official party had left the church that Christian priests performed their own rites, although the tomb was in a building dedicated by the dead man to their God. There was, of course, no precedent for burying a Christian emperor. It looks as though, despite the delay, Constantius had still not decided by the day of the funeral how matters ought to be arranged. State and military funerals were, however, traditionally regarded as religious rites in themselves, so Eusebius' silence about religious ceremonies at Constantine's burial should perhaps be taken to indicate not that there were no such ceremonies, but that Constantine's body was entombed with the customary rites – which, because they were pagan in origin, Eusebius chose to ignore:

> His second son . . . celebrated his father's funeral in the city bearing his name. He himself led the procession, preceded by military detachments in full battle order and followed by vast crowds. The body itself was surrounded by companies of the Spearmen and units of the heavy infantry. When the procession reached the church dedicated to the Saviour's apostles, the coffin was entombed there . . . and as soon as [Constantius] and the military cortege had withdrawn, the ministers of God came forward, together with the whole congregation of the faithful, and prayerfully performed the ceremonies of divine worship. They also paid due honour to the character of the blessed prince, whose body rested on a tall, conspicuous monument, and the whole multitude joined the priests of God in offering prayers for his soul. . .[5].

Planning the Church of the Apostles, Constantine had dreamed of resting there forever in the midst of the Twelve, not merely one of them, but a symbol of, if not a substitute for, their Leader. During the months of the church's construction, his agents had been busy in Palestine collecting alleged relics of the apostles and their companions, to be laid up in the church with his body, awaiting the general resurrection. He had, however, reckoned without the degree to which his building projects had overstrained the resources of the empire. The Church of the Holy Apostles was too badly built to last so long. Before the end of Constantius' reign, and while a bishop named Macedonius was patriarch of Constantinople, the fabric began to crack and, as Socrates relates, the emperor's body had to be removed for safety:

> The church where the coffin containing the remains of the Emperor Constantine lay threatened to fall down, so that those visiting it, as well as those whose habit it was to frequent it for devotional purposes, were made very afraid. Also, Macedonius wanted to remove the emperor's bones, lest the coffin should be buried in ruins. When the people heard this, they tried to prevent it, insisting that, 'The Emperor's bones must not be disturbed!' on the grounds that such a disentombment would be the equivalent of digging up a grave. Macedonius, however, maintained that disentombment could not possibly harm the corpse, and thus two factions came into being on this question. Moreover, those who held the doctrine of consubstantiality joined the opposition, on the grounds that disentombment would be an impiety. Totally disregarding these prejudices, Macedonius had the emperor's bones transferred to the Church of Acacius the Martyr, whereupon a vast mob, made up of the two opposing parties, rushed there and set upon one another with great fury, so that there was huge loss of life: the churchyard was covered with blood, and a well there overflowed with it, so that it ran into the adjacent portico, and out into the street itself. . .[6].

This affray enraged Constantius, but by the time that it occurred the empire had grown accustomed to the scent of fresh blood around his father's corpse. The bodies of his relatives and friends had fallen around him as thickly as in some prehistoric funeral rite. Constantius has consistently been blamed for this bloodletting, and it is difficult to absolve him from responsibility for it, although he tried to represent it as a spontaneous action on the soldiers' part, they being determined that only Constantine's sons should live to rule. There can, however, be little doubt that, foreseeing that Constantine's favourites, if not actually dangerous to himself and his brothers, would restrict their freedom of action and might prove focuses of unrest, he took steps to eliminate them.

Remarkably, his purge of his father's friends did not extend to the clergy. Both Hosius of Cordoba and the Bishops Eusebius survived the change of regime. Hosius, now a very old man, still had enough courage and sense of responsibility to write mandatory letters to Constantius, though their warnings went unregarded[7]. The Bishops Eusebius were sufficiently skilled politicians actually to improve their positions during the terror. Most Catholic – that is, Consubstantialist – historians claim that they achieved this by working on Constantius through a third Eusebius, the Chief Eunuch and Master of the Sacred Bedchamber who, fortunately for them, was an Arian. His power was certainly very great: Ammianus caustically notes that Constantius had considerable influence with him[8]. Constantius' religious policy was probably shaped by his opinions. However, Philostorgus preserves a story purporting to show that Eusebius of Nicomedia took extreme steps personally to win favour with Constantius at the very beginning of his reign, putting the new emperor in his debt by providing him with the excuse he needed to kill off his potential rivals. 'As the thirty-second year of Constantine's reign drew near,' he relates,

> he began to die through the effect of poisons given to him by his brothers in Nicomedia. And just before the end came, learning of the plot, he wrote his will, demanding that vengeance be unleashed, commanding his sons to see that this was done lest evil persons should design something similar against them. He then gave the will to Eusebius, the Bishop of Nicomedia. So that the emperor's brothers, suspecting what had happened, should not find it and learn what was written there, he put the paper into the dead man's hand and covered it with his clothes. And when, suspecting him, they commanded him to reveal it to them, he handed over to them one similar to that the emperor held. Afterwards, he put what the emperor had written into Constantius'

hands. . . . And not very long afterwards, he executed them, as his father had commanded[9].

The credibility of this story has often been denied. It is usually claimed that if Philostorgus did not invent it out of whole cloth, he garbled the truth, which was that Eusebius forged an accusation against Constantine's brothers, Julius Constantius and Delmatius, to please Constantius II. There is no more evidence for this version, however, than for Philostorgus'. It is impossible to show from near-contemporary sources that Constantine ever became suspicious of his brothers' good-will towards him, although Zonaras declares that Constantius accused them of having poisoned his father[10]. The truth is now unknowable, but the probability is that there was at no time any written accusation against Julius Constantius or anyone else; Constantius II seized on a rumour and used it in his propaganda war against his supposed rivals, and Philostorgus' story reflects rather the bitterness of the later stages of the Arian controversy than the facts of life at Constantinople in the late summer of 337. Nevertheless, arrests did begin not long after Constantius took up the reins of government, when he and his brothers Constantine II and Constans were proclaimed joint *Augusti* on September 9, 337[11], and the killing did not stop until the only other surviving male descendants of Constantius Chlorus were two sons of Julius Constantius, and an infant son of Eutropia.

The family in which Constantius' murder squads operated was quite an extensive one. Constantine was survived by all his own children and most of his father's children and grandchildren[12]. On May 22, 337, there were living his three sons and two daughters; Constantine II (Flavius Claudius Constantinus), Caesar in Gaul; Constantius II (Flavius Julius Constantius), Caesar in the East; Constans (Flavius Julius Constans), Caesar in Italy, King Hannibalianus' wife Constantina, and Helena, who was then unmarried; his two half-brothers and two half-sisters: Julius Constantius the Patrician, Delmatius the Censor, Anastasia and Eutropia. His third half-brother, Hannibalianus, had died in childhood and without issue. Delmatius' two sons, the Caesars Delmatius and Hannibalianus King of Kings, were the primary targets of Constantius II's purge. Julius Constantius was Constantius II's father-in-law. He had earlier been married to Galla, the Senator Rufinus' sister, by whom he had two sons and a daughter; one of Galla's sons had died in infancy, the second, Gallus, was to become briefly, in the 350s, Constantina's second husband and Constantius' Caesar; his daughter was Constantius' wife. In 337, Julius Constantius was living with his second wife, one Basilina, the daughter of Constantine's favourite Comenius, once his praetorian prefect, and consul in 325. She had borne him one son, Julian, who with his half-brother survived the massacre, to become Constantius II's Caesar in 355, be proclaimed Augustus by the army in 360, and inherit the whole empire on Constantius' sudden death in 361. Anastasia, who had once been married to the ill-fated Caesar Bassianus, was now married to the equally ill-fated Flavius Optatus, another of Constantine's favourites, who had once taught Licinianus grammar, but had risen to be consul in 334. Eutropia's husband was yet another of Constantine's favourites, Flavius Popilius Virius Nepotianus, who had been consul in 336; he appears to have died in the massacre of the Flavians, but his son, also named Flavius Popilius Nepotianus, was the third male member of the family to outlive the year of terror. In 350, he proclaimed himself Caesar at Rome, only to be killed, dragging his mother Eutropia down with him into ignominy and death.

In 337–8, the killing began with those closest to power, Constantius' uncles and their adult children, together with the favourites Optatus and the Praetorian Prefect in Attendance, Ablavius. There were many violent deaths in 338, but theirs appeared to the historians particularly treacherous and horrible, perhaps because they revived memories of the anarchy before Diocletian seized power. Zosimus' account, for instance, could hardly be more scornful in its disapproval:

> Constantius first executed death upon Constantius his father's brother, using the soldiers to do it, then contrived a similar plot against Delmatius Caesar, so arranging matters as to destroy Optatus along with him. Then he killed Ablavius, the Prefect in

> Attendance, and as soon as these relations had been put in their places, he urged Hannibalianus after them, stirring up an outcry among the soldiers, so that sovereignty might be in the hands of none but Constantine's sons[13].

Some historians denied that Constantius actually ordered the murder of Delmatius Caesar or arranged the riot among the soldiers in the course of which he died. In defence of his memory, Eutropius claimed that 'the three sons who succeeded [Constantine] as one man rejected his brother's sons, yet when Delmatius Caesar – by nature, the most able of them and a man not unlike his uncle – was killed not long after in a military uprising, Constantius his cousin suffered at it rather than rejoiced'[14]. But it is difficult to absolve Constantius of all responsibility for even this death. Even if he did not actually order Delmatius' murder, he had promoted the view that only Constantine's sons should rule. Care was taken to blur the issue of responsibility for most of the deaths, but the execution of his aunt Anastasia's husband Optatus makes it obvious that he was determined to permit no possible rival to survive, and Ablavius' death confirms it. Ablavius' career had recently taken another step forward, with the betrothal of his daughter Olympias to the Caesar Constans. After Julius Constantius' murder, however, he was suddenly exiled to Bithynia and his property confiscated. His execution followed, some time in 338. He had come a long way since, as the child of poor parents, he had started his working life as a junior clerk in the offices of the Governor of Crete at the beginning of the century, but, skilful as he must have been at handling difficult situations, he could not survive Constantius' malevolence[15].

The executions seem to have aroused some bitter comment, but no actual opposition. Successfully weeding out potential rivals was not the same thing, however, as running the empire efficiently. If the three sons of Constantine were to retain the power suddenly thrust upon them, they had to make plans for the future. Constantine's death had not stopped the Persian conflict, and during the winter of 337–8, Sapor invaded the five trans-Euphratian provinces, laying siege to Nisibis, where he was held by a gallant defence for sixty-three days before withdrawing his forces eastwards. This was the first of three sieges of Nisibis in a war which flared up sporadically over many years, and as Augustus of the East Constantius ought to have been at least within easy posting distance of the fighting. Instead, he was in Europe, at a conference with his brothers arranged to finalise the frontiers each of them was to hold.

The meeting was held somewhere in the Danube provinces, probably in Pannonia, or possibly at Viminacium in Dacia, in the early summer of 338[10]. Already, jealousy and differences of religious policy were dividing the brothers. While Constantius had come under the influence of the Bishops Eusebius at Constantinople, Constantine II had met Athenasius in his exile at Trier and been so impressed by him that he had readily granted his petition to be permitted to return to Alexandria. Constans, too, was already learning to look askance at his old tutors, the Arians. Despite their mutual suspicion, however, the brothers quickly reached agreement. Constantius' demands were modest, and he was granted all he requested: the County of the East, with Egypt, Hannibalianus' Kingdom of Pontus, and responsibility for the future of the Armenian alliance and the conduct of the Persian Wars. Constantine II took his grandfather's first empire, in the Britains, Gaul and Spain, while Constans assumed supreme authority over the Italian, African, Danubian and Macedonian provinces, together – surprisingly – with Thrace and Constantinople, which Constantius seems quite readily to have surrendered to him. Constantius' only remaining toehold in Europe was in the church at Constantinople, where at about this time Eusebius of Nicomedia contrived to make himself archbishop on the death of the homoousian Alexander.

Immediately after the Dacian conference, Constantius tried to withdraw completely from involvement in European affairs, but the quarrel in the church and, soon, a dispute between Constantine II and Constans over precedence drew him back into Western politics, when, in 339, Constans voluntarily ceded Constantinople and its hinterland to him as a bribe to buy his support against their elder brother. Constantine II appears to have seen himself as some kind of Senior Augustus, even going so far as to write laws and make appointment in Constans' empire. In 340, he took advantage of Constans' absence from Italy to quell trouble among the Danubian tribes suddenly to invade Italy. His campaign of conquest turned into disaster, when Constans ambushed and killed him at Aquileia[17]. For the next ten years, Constans and Constantius divided the Roman world between them, in almost exactly the same way as their father had shared it with Licinus from 314 to 324. Neither Augustus remained popular for long, although Constantius contained the Persian menace from the East, and Constans won signal victories on the Danube and the Rhine, and probably at Hadrian's Wall. Despite a reputation for timidity, Constantius was always willing to fight for what he wanted, the shortness of his temper and the tenacity with which he held a grudge making up for his lack of daring. He was notorious for his boasting and his lies[18]. Constans was described by Victor as 'the minister of unspeakable depravity and a leader in avarice and contempt for the soldiers'[19]. Whatever good qualities he had seem not to have survived his acquisition of supreme power at the age of fifteen. He probably had as little time for bishops as for generals, but to many homoousian Christians he was the hero who saved the Western church from Arianism. It was his contempt for the soldiers to whom he owed his victories which killed him in 350, at the age of twenty-seven, when a freedman of his father's, an officer named Magnentius, had himself proclaimed Augustus and found such immediate support that Constans panicked and tried to hide himself away, only to be murdered by a rebel on the Spanish frontier.

Within two years of Constans' death, Constantius had put down Magnentius' and several lesser rebellions, to make himself single master of his father's empire. His rule as sole Augustus lasted ten years, until Julian was proclaimed Augustus by the army in Gaul in 360. Although he married three times, his only child, a daughter, was not born until after he had been dead three months; so that when, in November 361, he died on a march from the Persian frontier to a confrontation with the usurper, supreme power passed legitimately to Julian as the last surviving grandson of Constantius Chlorus and great-grandson of Herculius Maximianus. His wife, Constantine's daughter Helena, had died in 360 as the result of a midwife's incompetence, after his first son had died in infancy, so that when Julian himself met his death in a skirmish with the Persians in 363, the only living representative of the Neo-Flavian dynasty was the two-year-old Constantia Posthuma. A general named Jovian was proclaimed Augustus by the army, and the family of Constantius Chlorus seemed to have passed into history. Some years later, however, old memories were stirred when Constantia Posthuma married the Emperor Gratian and was hailed as Augusta at Trier; but she died childless and it was left to the myth-makers to keep alive the family name of Constantius the Pale and his bull-necked son Constantine. They did their work well. Soon, Constantine the Victor became known in some parts of the East as Saint Constantine and throughout the West as Constantine the Great.

CHAPTER SEVENTEEN

THE CONSTANTINE LEGENDS

CANONIZATION is nowadays a delicate affair, involving a sifting of behaviour and motives so thorough as usually to be fatal to the claims of any but martyrs to be named saints of the church. For the first thousand years of Christian history, however, new saints were generally made in the West, as even today they can still only be made in the East, by the general acclamation of their merits by the Faithful. Before about the year 1000, there was no special machinery of canonization. Had there been, Helena would have stood little chance, and her son Constantine none at all, of achieving recognition as saints.

Yet in fact the Roman Martyrology has an entry under the date August 18: 'At Rome, on the Via Lavicana, St Helen, Mother of Constantine the Great, the Most Pious Emperor, who, by fostering and building up the church, gave a most outstanding example to other princes'[1]; and although the cult of Constantine himself has never been universal, it was once observed at three churches in Constantinople as well as in individual parishes in Sicily, England, Calabria and Bohemia, while the modern Greek church celebrates on May 21 the combined feasts of Helena and 'the glorious sovereign, Equal of the Apostles, Crowned by God, Constantine'.

It would appear, then, that Constantine's last victory was over the bishops. He persuaded them to accept him at his own valuation. They did not even reject his claim to be 'the bishop of those outside the church' – in whatever sense they understood his equivocal phrasing of it – and later, after they had seen him lying on his white baptismal couch, waiting for death, they accepted him as a saint 'crowned by God'. Among the Armenians, as well as the Greeks, he is still remembered as not only St Constantine the Emperor, but also St Constantine the Penitent, his repentence being recalled in stories about his heroic penances before baptism, on his knees on the pavement of the basilica at Helenopolis, and his remorse after the execution of Crispus the Hero 'whom I unjustly condemned'. In the West, although called a saint only to flatter the Frankish emperors of the Dark Ages, who prided themselves that they were fashioning their reigns on his, he was for centuries held up as a model ruler, partly because of his devotion, but largely because of the generosity of his gifts to the clergy. He had bought Pope Militiades' support back in the days when, using the word 'catholic', both pope and emperor had meant the same thing; and later, when Rome might have doubted both his morality and his orthodoxy, had bound Pope Silvester to him with donations so large that Roman Christianity could not afford to repudiate him, and indeed, tried to claim that the pope, and not Bishop Eusebius of Nicomedia, had baptised him.

Oddly enough, it was among the pagans that this story first found credence. Zosimus claims that his information was that the emperor was baptised at Rome during his vicennial visit, when he was overcome by self-hatred after murdering Crispus and desperately seeking someone able to cleanse him from blood-guilt. Sopater the Neoplatonist told him that no pagan shrine offered such a service, although in fact many had done so for centuries, so he turned to the Christians to have his sins washed away[2]. In the light of Eusebius' testimony concerning his last days and death, it is unlikely that there is any grain of truth in this story. Yet before the Dark Ages, it was generally accepted among Christians that Constantine had been baptised at Rome, by Pope Silvester himself.

The earliest known Christian reference to this story occurs in a document known as the *Gesta Liberii*[3], 'The Acts of Liberius', which records that Pope Liberius (352–6) learned from a book about 'Silvester the Bishops of the Romans' that Constantine was 'cleansed from leprosy in the name of Jesus Christ' by Pope Silvester, and accepted baptism from him. The *Gesta* probably dates from the end of the fourth century. By a century later, its reference to Constantine's miraculous cure had grown into a long text entitled *The Life of St Silvester*, which circulated in the East in Greek and Syriac versions, and was known at Rome before the year 500[4].

Silvester ruled the Roman church from 314 to 335. There is very little authentic information about him, except that he attended neither the Synod of Arles nor the Council of Nicaea, but was officially informed of the decisions made at both meetings. The *Liber Pontificatis*[5] says that he was a Roman, the son of a certain Rufinus, lists the churches built at Rome during his reign, together with their treasures and endowments, and claims that he baptised Constantine, but tells the story in phrases drawn directly from the *Life of St Silvester*, so that it is not an independent witness. The *Life* – which was doubtless evoked by the need to provide the emperor with a respectable, non-Arian background when his cult was already established at Constantinople – makes up the gaps left by more orthodox and truthful chronicles.

Its unnamed author tries to give authenticity to his story by introducing it with a dedication in which he says that Eusebius omitted much deserving of preservation from his *History* and *Life of Constantine*, including twenty volumes relating the Acts of the Saints and Martyrs of the five apostolic sees, Rome, Antioch, Jerusalem, Ephesus and Alexandria: among them, perhaps the most important is this *Life of Silvester*. Having thus proved the respectability of his sources, he begins his remarkable tale in an orthodox way with an account of Silvester's childhood, naming his mother, Justa, and his school, one organized at Rome by a priest named Cyrinus. The schoolmaster was famous for his hospitality, and it was his practice of this ancient virtue which first brought Silvester into the public eye. During the Great Persecution, Cyrinus offered asylum to an Antiochene priest named Timothy, who was, however, betrayed to the Praetorian Prefect 'Tarquinius' and executed. Inspired by Cyrinus' charity, Silvester claimed Timothy's body and buried it in a cemetery known as Theona's Garden, near St Paul's tomb. This action drew the attention of the authorities to him, and he was arrested in his turn, but miraculously escaped death. Such striking divine intervention on his behalf aroused Pope Militiades' interest, and after enquiries concerning his eligibility, the pope made him a deacon and later ordained him priest. On Militiades' death, the Roman church elected him its pope.

He was, the *Life* claims, a good pope, although, like most good popes, he quarrelled with the Greek church about the liturgy. Before Constantine's march on Rome, his most notable exploits were to persuade the higher clergy to wear long-sleeved tunics instead of the short-sleeved dalmatic, which some puritanical ladies had denounced as indecent, and imprison three hundred feet underground a dragon which had been terrorizing Rome from that ancient place of execution, the Tarpeian Rock.

Then Constantine defeated Maxentius at Milvian Bridge, and assumed power at Rome. Basically a good man himself, he was led into erroneous paths by his wife, the evil-minded Fausta Maximiana. No sooner were they firmly established in the capital than she persuaded her husband to start persecuting the Christians. The campaign of terror was so violent that Silvester fled with his clergy to 'Mount Syraptim' and hid in a cave. Soon, Constantine's wickedness was punished by an attack of leprosy. He consulted doctors, magicians and pagan priests in search of a cure, but nothing helped him until one day he expressed moral revulsion at a suggestion from priests of Capitoline Jupiter that if he would bathe in the blood of new-born children, his health would be restored. His indignant repudiation of their prescription earned him divine mercy. That night, two 'gods' appeared to him in a dream and told him to seek out Silvester, who would cure him. Silvester was found, and explained that the 'gods' of the dream were not divine beings, but Saints Peter and Paul, Christ's missionaries to the world. Constantine remained unconvinced until Silvester showed him statues of the apostles, which he immediately recognized as portraits of the men in his dream. After a day of solemn fast, Silvester 'washed' him in the baths of the Lateran Palace, cleansing him both of his leprosy and his sins. While in the water, the emperor was surrounded by a wonderful, unearthly light, and emerging from it, he immediately began to plan Christian legislation, decreeing among other things that Christ should be worshipped throughout the empire, while blasphemers and those offering violence to converts should be condignly punished. He ordered that churches everywhere should become places of asylum, but that no church should be built anywhere without prior permission from the local bishop, while all bishops should be subject to the bishop of Rome 'so that priests throughout the Roman world shall have this man as their head, as magistrates have the king as theirs'.

On the day *albis depositis*, the eighth day after his baptism, on which he laid aside the white robe signifying his regeneration, Constantine went to the *confessio* of St Peter, where the saint's relics were venerated, and marked out the foundations of the Vatican basilica; the following day, he started a new palace for Silvester at the Lateran and issued an edict urging the poor to become Christians, offering special privileges to converts.

This edict aroused a storm of protest from rich, pagan senators. To reassure them, Constantine called an assembly at the Basilica of Ulpius, at which he formally announced his own conversion but ruled that no one would be compelled to adopt Christianity, although the commoners called for coercive measures against continuing pagans.

Among those shocked by these developments was Constantine's mother. She was then in Bithynia, giving her two young grandsons Constantius and Constans a long spring holiday at her home. She wrote to her son, congratulating him on abandoning idolatry, but regretting that he had not accepted her religion, Judaism, the only true faith. Constantine replied suggesting that the question of which religion was superior to all others should be settled at a public debate between leading rabbis and bishops. Welcoming this idea, Helena went to Rome and a disputation was held there on August 13, 315, between twelve rabbis on the one hand and the pope alone on the other. Silvester defended the doctrines of the Trinity and the Incarnation so brilliantly that to stop Helena and all the spectators asking for baptism forthwith, one of the rabbis performed a miracle, killing a bull by whispering the secret Name of God into its ear. When everyone was satisfied that the animal was dead, Silvester resurrected it with the Name of Christ. After that, nothing could stop the conversions, which continued until the pope died, twenty years later, by which time most of the world was Christian.

There is no Mount Syraptim near Rome, but there is a famous Mount Soractum: on several occasions, the *Life of Silvester* comes as close as this to the truth. Its author knew much of Constantine's pro-Christian legislation, and of his gift of Fausta's Lateran Palace to the popes, but he did not know that many of the edicts post-dated the death of Licinius. He knew that Helena was connected with Drepanum in Bithynia, but not that Constans was born after 320. He knew that it was Rome's senators who provided the strongest opposition both to Constantine and Christianity, but it was a major blunder to confuse Fausta's husband with her brother Maxentius, making Constantine a typical persecuting emperor at Rome before his conversion, punished by God for his sins.

The tradition that Constantine was baptised at the Lateran seemed to be confirmed (and may have been initially inspired) by his planning and endowment of a magnificent baptistery there. In the sixth-century *Liber Pontificalis*, it is described as the place

> where the Augustus Constantine was baptised, made of porphyry, entirely covered inside, at the doors, on the roof and where the water actually lies with thirty-eight pounds of purest silver; in the middle is a porphyry column bearing a gold *fiala* with a torch, weighing fifty-three pounds, of purest gold, where in the Paschal season two hundred pounds of balsam burn, supported on a branched stand. On the lip of the baptismal pool is a golden lamb, from where the water flows, weighing thirty pounds; to the right of the lamb, a Saviour in purest silver, five foot high, weighing a hundred and seventy pounds; to the left of the lamb, Blessed John the Baptist in silver, five foot high, holding a written title with the words ECCE AGNUS DEI, ECCE QUI TOLLIS PECCATA MUNDI, weighing a hundred and twenty-five pounds; also seven silver pipes from which water flows, each weighing eighty pounds, and an incense-burner of purest gold, set with forty-nine emeralds and weighing fifteen pounds[6].

The reference in the *Life of Silvester* to a papal authority over bishops matching that of kings over magistrates probably dates from the first controversies over the nature and extent of papal jurisdiction, in the years preceding the Council of Constantinople of 381. Later popes claimed more. At some time after the loss of the Western Empire to the barbarians, signalized by the abdication of the last Western emperor Romulus 'Augustulus' in 476, they began to urge their right of universal jurisdiction over the whole church, and, when the West came close to admitting it, claimed imperial sovereignty over the whole Western world, secular and religious, maintaining that this absolute power had been granted to Silvester and his successors by Constantine.

The date of the most famous statement of this claim, the *Constitution of Constantine*, containing the notorious *Donation of Constantine*[7], is still widely disputed. The earliest known manuscript of it dates from the ninth century, but there are good reasons for believing that it was actually forged in the second half of the eighth, probably in Gaul but with the connivance of Pope Hadrian II, to help in the papal struggle for domination over the Frankish Kings Pepin and Charlemagne. It describes at length the circumstances leading up to the emperor's alleged baptism and instant restoration to health, in phrases very similar to those used in the earlier *Life of Silvester*, then continues with the new revelation that Constantine first tried to reward Silvester by crowning him with his own imperial diadem, and when that was refused, presented him with a white tiara, explaining its significance in an edict reading:

> It is our desire that the pontifical dignity shall never be debased, but shall be honoured above that of terrestrial empire and our own glorious authority: we therefore bestow upon, and abandon to, our Blessed Pontiff Silvester, the Universal Pope, first our palace, as it has hitherto been called, then the city of Rome and all the provinces, places and cities in Italy and all these Hesperidean Regions. We desire that they shall be under the control, authority, and jurisdiction of Silvester and the pontiffs his successors: we decree this under the weight of imperial censures, by our sacred divine ordinance and pragmatic sanction, it being

our will that these our gifts shall remain forever in the possession of the Holy Roman Church.

To ensure that the pope will enjoy the full and free exercise of power in the vast empire of the West so presented to him, the *Constitutum* continues, the seat of imperial government will be transferred to the East, 'because it would not be right for the emperor to continue to possess anything where he has established the Kingdom of Priests and the capital of the Christian religion'.

Two of Pope Hadrian II's surviving letters suggest that both this audacious forgery and the *Life of St Silvester* were familiar to him. The earlier of them, written in May 778 to Charlemagne, is an appeal for help against the Lombards, who were then seeking to enlarge their kingdom in Italy by nibbling at the lands over which the popes had, by various means, acquired virtual sovereignty. 'Just as in the time of Blessed Silvester,' Hadrian wrote,

> the Most Pious Constantine of Blessed Memory, that great emperor, by his generosity raised up and exalted the Holy Catholic and Apostolic Church of God, granting her sovereignty in these Hesperidean regions, so now in these felicitous times, shared by Us and by You, let the Holy Church of the Blessed Apostle Peter be made to burgeon, raising her up, daily raising her ever higher. Then those races who see this happening will be moved to say: 'Lord save the king! Hear us in the day when we call upon thee! For behold now a new Most Christian Emperor, a new Constantine, has arisen, him through whom God condescended to grant all things to his church, the church of the Blessed Peter, Prince of the Apostles'. So, then, do as much as has been done by other emperors, patricians and god-fearing men, making grants to the Patrimony of the Blessed Peter and to the Holy Roman and Apostolic Church, for the good of their souls and the remission of their sins, in the districts of Tuscany, Spoleto, Benevento, Corsica and in the lands of the Sabines – grants which, as time has passed, have been taken away, ravished away, by the execrable Lombard race: let them now, during your reign, be restored to the church. Moreover, there are in our archives at the Lateran other such donations: we shall send them to you for your enlightenment. . .[8].

The second letter, written to the Empress Irene and the Emperor Constantine V during the Iconoclastic Controversy, is interesting not only because it relates yet again the story of Constantine's conversion at Rome, but also because it repeats the comparison of devout emperors with Constantine, who has obviously become for the Roman Pontiff the shining example of the true Christian ruler: coloured soot-and-whitewash, totally remote from the blood-stained, party-loving, sarcastic reality:

> Thus [if you follow papal policies], you will come to be compared with one now sleeping in the power of God, the Emperor Constantine, with Helena his mother, lights and pillars of the orthodox faith and exalted by your Holy Mother the Catholic and Spiritual Roman Church, and there will be a good hope that their pious titles will be transferred to you by God, Most Pious Ones, so that the talk throughout the whole world will be of a new Constantine and a new Helena, by whom the Holy Catholic and Apostolic Church is being renewed. . . . This is how it came about that the Most Holy and Blessed Pope Silvester first bore witness to the orthodox faith of Christians [concerning images]: once when, happily to record, the Emperor Constantine [despite his disease] was able to sleep through the night, the Blessed Apostles Peter and Paul came to him while he slept and said, 'As you have commanded that the children's blood must not be shed to heal your sickness, we have been sent by Christ to bring you help from him. Listen, therefore, to our advice, and do what we command: first, call into your presence as a friend the Blessed Silvester, who has left Rome because of your persecution and is lying hidden with his clergy in a cave on Mount Sorapeum. He will prepare a sacred bath for you in which you will wash, whereupon it will be granted to you that not only your leprosy but in fact all that troubles you will be taken away. And when this famous and good man has regenerated you, you will realize that the churches of the Romans should be everywhere restored —for he will indeed cleanse you—and you will declare your rejection of idolatry, and proclaim that the true God is to be worshipped, and arrange all your policies according to his will.' And the emperor, awakening from sleep, summoned all those courtiers with him in the palace, and told them what had been shown him in sleep, and immediately gave orders sending his servants to Mount Sorapeum, where Blessed Father Silvester

with his chaplains was filling his empty days with joy by readings from the sacred books. And when he saw the soldiers surrounding the hill, he asked why, expecting to be swept away into martyrdom, but his chaplains were inspired to say, 'Lo, now is the awaited time: now is the day of salvation!' and, coming out from the cave, they were told by the soldiers why they should go with them to the emperor. And he went, with three presbyters and two deacons as companions, and on seeing the emperor, he said, 'Peace be to thee, O Emperor, and victory, coming down upon thee from heaven!' The emperor listened with a joyful look and a peaceful mind while Blessed Silvester explained the revelation given to him in his dreams and, when he had finished speaking, enquired how he ought to reward the gods Peter and Paul who had appeared to him. The Holy Father replied that they were in no sense gods, but servants and disciples of our Lord Jesus Christ, chosen by him to convert all nations to faith in him. When the emperor heard this, he was anxious to know if their stories were related anywhere, whereupon Blessed Silvester told the deacons to bring out those they had, together with the images of the apostles. When the emperor saw these, he cried out, 'They are the men I saw in my vision! I no longer have any doubts! Prepare the bath for my salvation!' And the bath having been prepared, he was immersed in the sacred liquid, and his original health was immediately restored. And so that the blessing which he had received should not be forgotten, he began to build churches to God, decorating their pillars as a memorial with sacred images of our Lord Jesus Christ Incarnate, and all the venerable saints[9].

The search for a new Constantine, a Defender of the Faith ready to model himself on the emperor of the Silvester-legend, continued through the Middle Ages. Pope Leo III crowned Charlemagne on Christmas Day in the year 800 – both of them believing that they were restoring the lost world of the fourth century – with the nostalgic words, 'Life and victory to Charles, the Most Pious Augustus, crowned by God, the great peace-loving Emperor of the Romans'. In October 816, the newly-elected Pope Stephen IV, travelling to Rheims to confer with Charlemagne's successor on the problem of the Lombards, took with him what he believed to be Constantine's crown, and with it crowned Louis the Pious and his queen as Augustus and Augusta. A century later, when the nominal hegemony of

Europe passed to Otto the German, he in his turn was crowned by the pope as Constantine's successor; in 996, when Otto III chose the moment of the pope's death to march on Rome for his coronation, the new pontiff took the regnal name Silvester II, partly to flatter Otto's belief that he was the new Constantine – for so he announced himself – partly to remind him that after the crowning he would rule the West as the tenant of its true landlord, the pope. By this time, no one seems publicly to have doubted the validity of the *Donation* and the claims based on it. With the revival of legal studies (and the papacy) in the eleventh century, it formed one of the principal foundations of the theory of universal papal sovereignty – a theory which perhaps reached its apotheosis in the Year of Jubilee, 1300, when Pope Boniface VIII clothed himself in imperial armour, dressed his cardinals in scarlet as though they were Caesars, and appeared to the gaping crowds, declaring, 'I am emperor: I am the Augustus.' He was repeating the same message, although less colourfully, when in 1302 he wrote in the bull *Unam Sanctam*, 'It is absolutely necessary . . . for every creature to be subject to the Roman Pontiff.' Despairing of terrestrial kings, the pope had become his own New Constantine.

At this stage, some doubts were expressed, not only about papal claims, but also about the genuineness of the *Constitutum Constantini*. Early in the twelfth century, Italian scholars were severely censured for declaring it a forgery and in the thirteenth two men were burned for having the temerity to denounce it. The papacy was so strong in its defence not only because it wrote papal authority into the fundamental law of Europe, but also because the ideal of an empire united under a Christian prince was precious in itself. Protests continued to be voiced from time to time, but not until the Renaissance was it generally accepted that Constantine had given the Western church little more than he had given the churches of Nicomedia and Alexandria, and the *Constitutum*, at last admitted to have been spurious, was relegated to that limbo of good things which never were, the back of the moon. However, the legend of Constantine, the Most Pious Emperor, and his delightful mother, lived on, both in the East, where Russian Czars continued to be crowned as Caesars, reincarnations of Constantine, and in the West, where Austrian rulers wore the crown of the Holy Roman Empire, until the First World War.

The Constantine legend was essentially a parable of power and authority ideally employed in the service of religion; the Helena-cycle was a series of stories illustrating the marriage of the feminine virtues and faith. Little of the innkeeper's daughter who married a Protector, or of the imperious old woman who listened to Voices in the Holy Land, remains in her finished portrait as painted by Hakluyt in the sixteenth century:

> Helena Flavia Constantina, the heire and onely daughter of Coelus, sometime the most excellent King of Britain, by reason of her singular beauty, faith, religion, goodnesse and godly maiestie [according to the testimony of Eusebius] was famous in all the world. Amongst all the women of her time there was none either in the liberall arts more learned, or in the instruments of music more skillfull, or in the divers languages of nations more abundante than herselfe. She had a naturall quicknesse of wil, eloquence of speech, and most notable grace in all her behaviour. She was seene in the Hebrew, Greeke, and Latine tongues. . .[10].

As Hakluyt suggests, the origins of the cult of the Emperor's mother may already be traced in Eusebius' *Life of Constantine*. As well as telling the story of her founding of churches in the Holy Places, he maintains that after Constantine had named her Augusta she became very popular with the army, the men spontaneously cheering her whenever she appeared[11]. He does not record that it was she who discovered the True Cross at the Holy Sepulchre, but within twenty years of the foundation of the basilica there, Bishop Cyril of Jerusalem spoke of it in a sermon as common knowledge[12]. The *Liber Pontificalis*, however, dates the discovery in the year 310, in the middle of those thirty years of Helena's life of which nothing is known. The ruling pope was Eusebius 'a Greek by race, formerly a physician . . . In his times, the Cross of our Lord Jesus Christ was discovered on May 3, and Judas, also known as Cyriacus, was baptised'[13].

This note is interesting because it does not claim that the discovery was made by Helena, although most accounts link the date May 3, Judas-Cyriacus and the empress firmly together. May 3 is still the Feast of the Invention of the True Cross. Was there once another story of the discovery of the Cross, relating to a period before the empress' journey to the Holy Land, originally bearing the name of an otherwise obscure relic-hunter – a name which, from deference to the Augusta's memory, has been dropped from the *Liber Pontificalis*? If there was, it has disappeared without trace. Christian tradition since Cyril of Jerusalem has made Helena and the True Cross inseparable.

Socrates' version of Helena's discoveries is the least cumbered with unnecessary miracles. 'Commanded by God in dreams to do so,' he relates,

> Helena went to Jerusalem, to find what had been that city as desolate as 'a lodge in a garden of cucumbers' as the Prophet [Isaiah] said. She made a careful search for Christ's tomb, from where he arose after his burial, and with divine help found it, although only after much difficulty. A few words will suffice me to explain what caused the difficulty: after the Passion, Christians paid great devotion to Christ's tomb, but those who hated Christianity covered the spot with a mound of earth, built a temple of Aphrodite on it, and set up her statue there, so that the place would be forgotten. This device was successful for a long time – until, in fact, it became known to the emperor's mother. She had the statue thrown down, the earth removed and the site cleared, and found three crosses in the tomb. One of them was that blessed cross on which Christ had hung, the other two, those on which the thieves crucified with him had died. With them also was found the *titulum* on which Pilate had written in various languages that the Christ so crucified was the king of the Jews. The doubt as to which was the cross they sought caused the emperor's mother much distress, but she was soon relieved of her worry by Bishop Macarius of Jerusalem. He used faith to dissolve doubt, seeking and obtaining a sign from God. The sign was this: a certain woman living nearby was afflicted by illness and just then at the point of death; the bishop arranged for each of the crosses to be brought to her, believing that by the touch of the precious cross she would be healed. Nor were his hopes disappointed, for whereas after she had been touched by

> the two crosses which were not the Lord's she continued in a moribund condition, when the third, the True Cross, touched her, she was instantly healed and regained her former strength. That, then, is how the genuine cross was discovered. The emperor's mother set up a cross on the spot . . . and called it 'New Jerusalem' . . . and left there a piece of the Cross encased in silver, as a memorial for any who might wish to see it. The rest she sent to the emperor, who, convinced that any city where such a relic was preserved would be perpetually secure, secretly enclosed it in his own statue, which stands on a large porphyry column in the forum called Constantine's at Constantinople. I admit that what I have written here, I know only by hearsay, but almost all the inhabitants of Constantinople swear that it is true. Moreover, the nails with which Christ's hands were fastened to the Cross [which Constantine's mother had also found in the tomb and sent on], Constantine had made into bridle bits and a helmet, which he wore in battle. . .[14].

Telling an almost identical story, Sozomen adds details about the finding of the tomb: 'Some say that the facts were first disclosed by a Hebrew living in the East, who derived his information from documents coming down to him from his father, but it seems more credible to suppose that God revealed the facts through signs and dreams – for I do not think that information has to be derived from human sources when God has decided that something should be revealed.' He also records that Constantine made a bit from one of the nails because Zechariah had prophesied that 'that which shall be upon the bit of the horse shall be holy to the Lord Almighty'[15]. It is an explanation, whether true or not, fully consonant with Constantine's approach to religion; like building the Cross into the porphyry column, and putting the *palladium* from Troy under it, it reveals a mind at once both practical and superstitious, interested in the relics of the past not for what they are, but for the supernatural power they may be supposed to control for the benefit of whoever possesses them.

Later accounts of the Invention of the True Cross added many picturesque details. The Oriental Jew of Sozomen's account acquired the name Judas and a legend of his own. It was said of him that he was the leader of the Palestinian Jews, and that when Helena first appeared in the Holy Land he refused to identify the site of the Holy Sepulchre for her. After he had been persuaded by threats and promises to help her, the crosses were discovered in a cistern near Golgotha, and when the true cross had been identified, he declared himself converted by the miracle and was baptised as Cyriacus – so becoming the Judas-Cyriacus of the *Liber Pontificalis.* It was he who discovered the Holy Nails 'shining like gold' and took them to Constantine, who had him made a bishop. He lived in great honour until the reign of Julian, when many attempts were made to persuade him to apostatise. Boiling lead was poured into his mouth, and instantly went cold. He was roasted on an iron bedstead over a brisk fire, but the fire went out. He was thrown into a snake-pit, but whenever a snake bit him, it died. Not even boiling oil would blister him, and finally to kill him Julian himself had to strike off his head with a sword[16].

Not all the fragments of the true cross were kept at Jerusalem and Constantinople. Some were sent to Rome, to be the chief glory of the basilica of the Holy Cross in Jerusalem. The *Liber Pontificalis* records that they arrived in the reign of Pope Silvester: 'At this time, the Augustus Constantine made a basilica at the Sessorian Palace, where some of the wood from the Holy Cross of our Lord Jesus Christ was encased in gold and jewels – whence the name Jerusalem by which the church was dedicated and is known until this day. The gifts there included . . .' gold and silver dishes, a silver altar weighing two hundred and fifty pounds, and seven estates, together bringing in 1,061 *solidi* annually[17].

A rich literature has grown up around the later dispersal of these and other alleged relics of the Passion discovered by expeditions financed by later emperors and kings in imitation of Constantine's financing of Helena's pilgrimage. It is too copious to be explored here, but mention may be made of the fate of three of the Holy Nails which, because of their links with Constantine as well as their supposed origin, came to be symbols of sovereignty in Europe. One was worked into the material of the Iron Crown of the Lombards and a thousand years after Judas' discovery of it was still exerting a fascination in Northern Italy when the Visconti of Milan were intriguing for power there. Another was worked into a lance, which came to be known as Constantine's and accepted as the visible sign of authority in Central Italy. In 935, Henry I of Germany paid Rudolph II of Burgundy a good price for it as part of his preparations for an ultimately successful invasion of the Italian Peninsula. Constantine would have understood and approved. He had, it was true, dreamed up the *labarum*, not purchased it, but if that had been put to him would have argued that his own was a very special case: he was specially favoured by the Power ruling the universe; but it is up to every king to do the best he can in the circumstances in which he finds himself, and Henry had done precisely that. He would have recognized the German king as a fellow professional in the art of ruling, another pragmatic survivor.

The third nail found its way to Britain. According to William of Malmesbury, one of the gifts which Hugh the Good, Duke of the Franks, sent to King Athalstan of England, to persuade the king to give him his daughter's hand in marriage was 'the sword of Constantine the Great, on which the name of the ancient owner could be read in letters of gold; on the pommel also could be seen an iron nail fixed above three plates of gold – one of the four the Jewish party prepared for the crucifixion of our Lord's body. . . .'[18]

So Constantine's name lived on, both because his story was colourful, and because it was useful to emperors and kings, popes and patriarchs. Comprehensible as it is, however, that he became symbolic of unity and victory, authority and imperial greatness under the aegis of religion, it is nonetheless remarkable how remote the idealized image of him is from the facts of his life. All those characteristics – the quick temper, the sneering, jeering manner, the cruelty, the effeminacy, the heresy itself – for which he might have been condemned, have been forgotten. So too has the chief charge which might have been brought against him, that he interfered in ecclesiastical affairs and in doing so diverted Christian attention from spiritual concerns by offering opportunities of acquiring political influence to the bishops. His bringing the church into politics in a position subordinate to himself has had a baleful influence on the whole of subsequent Christian history. Not only did it ultimately sentence the popes to pursuit of the chimera of universal sovereignty, it also bound the Eastern patriarchs in subjection to later emperors and kings. He was the first, and not the least successful, of the caesaropapists. He actually called himself a bishop – 'the bishop of those outside' the church, bringing divine blessings not only to Christians but to all imperial subjects – and made the bishops believe that his imperial dignity gave him quasi-spiritual authority within the Christian body. As a result, his successor Justinian was able to sustain the claim that all authority, religious as well as secular, within the Byzantine state flowed from the sacred person of the emperor. Spiritually disastrous though this development was, from the imperial point of view, it was, of course, a triumph. The triumph was Constantine's. He had achieved it by successfully translating Diocletian's concepts of the roots of power, jurisdiction and stability, into terms acceptable to the Christians. In this sense, he was indeed, as he continued to call himself throughout his life, the Chief Pontiff, bridge-building not so much between heaven and earth, as between the old world and the new.

However, he built more than bridges. The world his sons inherited was not that in which he had risen to power. It was one that he had constructed for them single-handed, out of the materials assembled from the ruins of the anarchy by Diocletian, Maximian and Constantius Chlorus. For good or evil, he deserved to be remembered as Constantine the Great.

BIBLIOGRAPHY

Principal Sources

Eusebius Pamphilus, Bishop of Caesarea

HISTORY OF THE CHURCH, Berlin Corpus, vol. 9, books 9 and 10; with French translation, *Sources chrétiennes*, 55, Paris, 1958; English versions, Oulton and Lawlor, *Eusebius Ecclesiastical History*, Loeb Classical Library, 1932, Williamson, *Eusebius: the History of the Church*, Penguin L 138, 1965; see also, N. H. Baynes, *Eusebius and the Christian Empire*, in *Mélanges Bidez*, I, Brussels, 1934, pp. 13ff.

LIFE OF THE BLESSED EMPEROR CONSTANTINE (*De Vita Constantini*), Berlin Corpus, vol. 7; English version, *Library of the Nicene Fathers*, vol. 1 (with Constantine's *Oration to the Saints* and Eusebius' *Sermon for Constantine's Tricennalia*) for various views in the continuing debate over the authenticity of the *Life of Constantine*, see also: G. Pasquali, *Die Composition des Vita Constantini des Eusebius* in *Hermes*, vol. 45, 1910, pp. 396ff.; P. Battifol, *Les documents de la Vita Constantini*, in the *Bulletin d'ancienne litérature et d'archéologie chrétienne*, vol. 4, 1914, pp. 81ff.; O. Seeck, *Die Urkunden der Vita Constantini* in *Zeitschrift fuer Kirchengeschichte*, vol. 18, 1897, pp. 321ff.; N. H. Baynes, *Constantine the Great and the Christian Church*, London, 1931, pp. 40ff.; H. Gregoire, *Eusèbe n'est pas l'auteur de la Vita Constantini dans sa forme actuelle*, art. in *Byzantion*, 1938, pp. 561ff.; *La Vision de Constantin liquidée*; art. in *Byzantion*, 1939, pp. 341ff.; F. Vittinghof, *Eusebius als Verfasser der Vita Constantini*, art. in Rh Mus. 96, 1953, pp. 330ff.; A. H. M. Jones, *Notes on the Genuineness of the Constantinian Documents in Eusebius's Life of Constantine*, art. in J.E.H.5, 1955, pp. 196ff.

CHRONICLE, see Jerome

Lactantius

HOW THE PERSECUTORS DIED, *De Mortibus Persecutorum*, ed. Brandt, Vienna Corpus, vol. 19, 1890; with French translation, *Sources chrétiennes*, 39, Paris, 1954; English version, *Library of the Ante-Nicene Fathers*, vol. 7; see also, R. Pichon, *Lactance*, Paris, 1901; Borleffs, *An scripsit Lactantius libellum qui est de mortibus persecutorum*, in *Mnemosyne*, LVIII, 1930, pp. 223ff.; F. Winkelmann, *Zur Geschichte des Authentizitätsproblems D.Y.C.*, in *Klio*, 40 (1962), pp. 187ff.; DIVINE INSTITUTES: English version in *Library of the Ante-Nicene Fathers*, vol. 7.

Aurelius Victor, *De Caesaribus*, ed. Pichlmayr and Gruendal, Leipzig, 1961
Epitome de Caesaribus, ed. Pichlmayr and Gruendal, Leipzig, 1961
Valesius, *Excerpta Valesiana*, ed. J. Moreau, Leipzig, 1961
Optatus of Milevium, *De Schismate Donatistorum*, Vienna Corpus, vol. 26, 1893
Gelasius of Cyzicus, ed. Loeschke-Heinemann, Berlin Corpus, vol. 28, Leipzig, 1918
Zosimus, *Historia Nova*, fragments, ed. Mendelssohn, Leipzig, 1887
Orosius, *Historiae adversus paganos*, Vienna Corpus, col. 5, 1882
Philostorgus, fragments, Berlin Corpus, vol. 21, Leipzig, 1913, and J. Bidez, *Byzantion*, vol. X, 1935, pp. 403ff.
Socrates Scholasticus, *Ecclesiastical History*, in P.G. LXVII; English version in *Library of the Nicene Fathers*, series 2, vol. 2
Sozomen, *Ecclesiastical History* in P.G. LXVII; English version in *Library of the Nicene Fathers*, series 2, vol. 2
Theodoret, *Ecclesiastical History*, ed. Parmentie, Berlin Corpus, vol. 19, 1911
Eutropius, *Breviarum ab urbe condita*, ed. Hallidie, London, 1892; Welch and Duffield, London, 1892
Jerome, *Chronicle*, ed. Fotheringham, *The Bodleain MS of St Jerome's Version of the Chronicle of Eusebius*, Oxford, 1905
Idatius, *Fasti Hydatiani*, in Mommsen, *Monumenta Germaniae Historica auc. ant.*, vol. IX, 1892, pp. 197ff.
Panegyrics in E. Gallatier, *Panegyriques latines*, vol. 1 and 2, Paris, 1949 and 1952
R. A. B. Mynors, *XII panegyrici latini*, Oxford, 1964
Historia Augusta: formerly attributed to six chroniclers, now generally said to have been composed as an anti-Christian tract by an anonymous admirer of the Emperor Julian, see Paully-Wissowa, vol. VIII, col. 2051ff.; MS, Palatino-Vaticanus 899
Coins in *The Roman Imperial Coinage*, 6 (1967) and 7 (1966)
Laws in O. Seeck, *Regesten der Kaiser und Päpste* (1919)

Modern authorities

From the vast literature on the life and reign of Constantine, I suggest the following titles:

A. Alföldi, *The Conversion of Constantine and Pagan Rome*, Oxford, 1948
art. *Hoc signum Victor eris* in *Pisciculi für F. J. Dölger*, 1939, pp. 1ff.
N. Anastos, *The Edict of Milan*, art. in *Revue des Etudes Byzantines*, 1968, pp. 13ff.
P. Battifol, *La Paix constantinienne et le catholicisme*, Paris, 1914

N. H. Baynes, *Constantine the Great and the Christian Church*, Proceedings of the British Academy, 1929

W. W. Buckland, *Textbook of Roman Law from Augustus to Justinian*, Cambridge, 1963

V. Burch, *Myth and Constantine the Great*, London, 1927

J. Burckhardt, *The Age of Constantine the Great*, trans. Hadas, Routledge and Kegan Paul, 1949

C. E. Coleman, *Constantine the Great and Christianity*, Columbia University Publications in History, Economics and Public Law (60, 2), 1914

J. B. Firth, *Constantine the Great*, New York, 1905

W. H. Frend, *The Donatist Church*, Oxford, 1952

K. Hönn, *Konstantin der Grosse*, 1945

A. H. M. Jones, *Constantine and the Conversion of Europe*, Hodder and Stoughton, London, 1948

Later Roman Empire, three volumes maps, Blackwell, Oxford, 1964

B. J. Kidd, *A History of the Church until A.D. 461*, Oxford, 1922

P. de Labriolle, *La réaction païonne*, Paris, 1934

R. MacMullen, *Constantine*, 1969

J. Marrice, *Numismatique constantinienne 1–3*, Paris, 1908–12

A. Momigliano (ed.), *The Conflict between Paganism and Christianity in the Fourth Century*, 1963

W. Schneemelcher, *Athenasius v. Alexandrien als Theologe und Kirchenpolitiker*, art. in ZNW 43, 1950–1, pp. 242ff.

E. Schwartz, *Der Kaiser Constantin und die Christliche Kirche*, 2nd ed., 1936

O. Seeck, *Geschichte des Untergangs der Antiken Welt*, vol. 1

Regesten der Kaiser und Päpste fur die Jahre 311–476, 1919

W. Seston, *L'empire chrétien* in *Relazione X congresso internaz. scienze storiche*, 6, 1955, pp. 792ff.

E. Stein, *Histoire du bas-empire*, vol. 1, 1949

J. Vogt, *Constantinus der Grosse in Sein Jahrhundert*, 1949

art. *Constantinus der Grosse* in *Reallexikon für Antike und Christentum*, vol. 3, 1957

Cambridge Ancient History, vol. 12, 1939

Cambridge Mediaeval History, vol. 1, 1911

REFERENCES AND NOTES

CHAPTER ONE

1. *Corp. Inscrip. Lat.*, 1, 2, p. 312; *Natales Caesarum:* 'Divi Constantini, III Kal. Martii.'
2. Victor, Epitome *41*, also gives sixty-three years.
3. Eusebius Pamphilius, *De Vita Constantini*, 2, 47.
4. *Panegyricus Maximiano et Constantino*, 1.
5. Trebellius, on Gallienus, speaks of 'Duke Claudius, who later attained the *imperium*, first forefather of our Caesar Constantine'; see also, Lampridius Elegabalus, *ad Const. Aug*, *35*, where the reference is to 'Claudius, the founder of your family'; cf. O. Seeck, *Geschichte des Untergangs der Antiken Welt*, vol. 1, p. 45.
6. Trebellius on Claudius II, 13.
7. *Caesars*, 39, 26.
8. *Corp. Inscrip. Lat.*, 1, 2, 301.
9. Anon. Vales., 1, 1: the historical value of this record is, however, questionable, as the author does not mention Constantius' highest office before he became Caesar to Maximian – that of Praetorian Prefect.
10. His full name was Marcus Aurelius Valerius Maximianus Herculius; cf. Paully-Wissowa, *Real-Encyclopaedie der Altertums-Wissenschaft*, XIV², col. 2486ff.
11. 'He promoted Constantius and Galerius Maximianus, surnamed Armentarius, to be Caesars' – Victor, *Caesars*, 39. The date, March 1, is given in Eumenius' *Panegyrics before Constantius*, 3. The year may have been 293.
12. On the organization and manning of Diocletian's army, see A. H. M. Jones, *Later Roman Empire*, pp. 52–60; 607f.; *Cambridge Mediaeval History*, vol. 1, ch. 2.
13. The famous *Edictum de pretiis* is mentioned by Lactantius in *de Mortibus Persecutorum*, 7, 6, 7, and discussed in Jones, op. cit., p. 61, and F. Tenney, *Economic Survey of Ancient Rome*, v. 5, pp. 310–421.
14. Jones, op. cit., pp. 61–68.
15. Lactantius, *de Mort. Pers.*, 7, where there is a critical summary of Diocletian's reforms in general.
16. Eutropius, 10, 2.
17. Zosimus, 2, 8.
18. Orosius, 7, 5, apparently copying Jerome, *Chronicon*, under the

Year from Abraham 2322: 'Constantine was born of the concubine Helena'.

19. The true name of the author of the *Historia Augusta* remains unknown. Formerly attributed to six known fourth-century writers, it is now usually said to be an anonymous anti-Christian pamphlet, probably dating from the reign of Julian the Apostate.
20. Victor, *Epit.*, 39, 2.
21. Eumenius, *Panegyrics before Constantine*, 4; in *Panegyrici Latini*, ed. Baehrens, Leipzig, 1911.
22. Julius Firmicius, *de Astrologia*, 1, 1, 4; Anon. Vales., 2, 2, confirmed also by Stephenus Byzantianus, and Constantinus Porphyrinus.
23. The translation of 'The Life of the Blessed Emperor Constantine' most generally available is that made in the mid-nineteenth century by E. C. Richardson, and published in the Library of the Nicene Fathers, vol. 1, p. 481ff.
24. *Origo Constantini Aug.*, published in Mon. Germ. Hist. auc. ant., ix, pp. 7ff.

CHAPTER TWO

1. cf. *Cambridge Mediaeval History*, vol. 1, p. 3.
2. Praxagoras, *Apud Photium*, 63.
3. *de Mort. Pers.*, 19.
4. *de Vit. Const.*, 1, 19.
5. *Epit.*, 41; see note at chapter 15.8.
6. See also the coins: in profile, the older Constantine generally appears gross and, probably, goitrous; his appearance is not helped by the attempts of the die-makers to depict him with his eyes turned heavenwards. cf. the description in *de Mort. Pers.*, 18, where he is said to have been 'distinguished by the beauty of his figure'.
7. On Mani, see pp. 46f., Lebreton, *Les Apocryphes et le manichéisme*, in Fliche et Martin, *Histoire de l'Eglise*, vol. 2, chap. 9.
8. *de Mort. Pers.*, 24.
9. cf. Gibbon, *Decline and Fall of the Roman Empire*, vol. 1, p. 387 (Everyman ed.).
10. Praxagoras, *Apud Photium*, 63.
11. Eutropius, 9, 21–22. Mamertius, *Panegyric*, 12, describes the preparations for the British Campaign. Eumenius, Panegyric before Constantius, 12, mentions the first repulse of Maximian, and describes Carausius' fall.
12. Eutropius, 9, 23; Orosius, 7, 25.
13. Eumenius, *pro instaurandis scholis oratio*, passim.

14. *de Mort. Pers.*, 18.
15. Incerti, Panegyr. Maximiano et Constantino, 4; see also Zosimus, 2, 20.
16. Cod. Justinian, V, xxvi, 1; Cod. Theodos., IX, vii, 1; Cod. Theodos., IX, ix, 1.

CHAPTER THREE

1. Eusebius Pamphilius, *History of the Church, H.E.*, 8, 1.
2. Cod. Gregorian., XV, iii, 1.
3. On Gnosticism and Dualism, see Lebreton, *La Crise gnostique*, in Fliche et Martin, *Histoire de l'Eglise*, vol. 2, chap. 1.
4. On Plotinus, see Paully-Wissowa, *Real-Encyclopaedie etc.*, XXI^1, col. 471ff.
5. On Porphyry, see A. Harnack, *Porphyrus 'Gegen die Christen' 15 Buecher, Zeugnisse, Fragmente und Referata*, published in the Proceedings of the Berlin Academy for 1916; Labriolle, *La réaction paienne*, Paris, 1934, pp. 232f.
6. Eusebius Pamph., *H.E.*, 8, 1 and 8, 4.
7. *de Mort. Pers.*, 9.
8. On the martyrs of this time, see Fliche et Martin, op. cit., vol. 2, pp. 458ff. and the references there.
9. *de Mort. Pers.*, 11.
10. *de Vit. Const.*, 2, 50–51.
11. *de Mort. Pers.*, 12: 'a fitting and auspicious day, consecrated to the mighty Terminus, the seventh day before the Kalends of March'.
12. Eusebius Pamph., *H.E.*, 8, 6.
13. *de Mort. Pers.*, 12.
14. Constantine, *Oratio ad sanctorum coelum*, 25; cf. Eusebius Pamph., *H.E.*, 8, 2.
15. cf. Eusebius Pamph., *H.E.*, 8, 13.
16. Eusebius Pamph., *H.E.*, 8, 13; cf. *de Mort. Pers.*, 17 and Eutropius, 9, 27.
17. *de Mort. Pers.*, 18; Eusebius Pamph., *H.E.*, 8, 13; Idatius, *Chronicon*, under Diocletian IX et Maximian VIII.
18. See chap. 2, n. 1.
19. *de Mort. Pers.*, 19.
20. Art. *Daia* in Paully-Wissowa, IV^2, col. 1896.
21. *de Mort. Pers.*, 21; Idatius, *Chronicon*, under Dioc. IX, Maximian VIII; character in Anon Vales., 49; see also, Paully—Wissowa, IIA^2, col. 2002, art. *Severus (15)*.
22. *de Mort. Pers.*, 24; Zosimus, 2, 8; Eumenius, *Panegyr. Constantino*, 7, 7; Anon. Vales., 2, 4.

23. Anon. Vales., 2, 4; cf. Idatius, *Chronicon*, Constantio VI, Maximin., VI.
24. Victor, *Ep.*, 41.
25. Eumenius, *Paneg.*, 7, 8.
26. Eusebius Pamphil., *H.E.*, 8, 13.
27. *de Mort. Pers.*, 24.
28. Zosimus, 2, 9.
29. *de Mort. Pers.*, 24–5.
30. Optatianus, *Carm.*, 8, 19f.
31. Eusebius Pamphilius, *H.E.*, 8, 13.

CHAPTER FOUR

1. Art. *Maxentius* in Paully-Wissowa, XIV², cols. 2147ff.; Mamertini, *Paneg. Maximiano Herculio dictus.*, 14.
2. Eutropius, 10, 2.
3. Anon. Vales., 2, 4; cf. Lactantius, 26.
4. *de Mort. Pers.*, 26.
5. Eutropius, 10, 2, Zonarus, 12, 33. The attempt to recall Diocletian may have been made after Severus' invasion of Italy.
6. For the evidence of th coins, see Cohen, 80; Maurice, 1, 172, II, i.
7. *de Mort. Pers.*, 26.
8. The evidence is in *de Mort. Pers.*, 26; Anon. Vales., 2, 4; Socrates Scholasticus, *H.E.*, 1, 2; Zosimus, 2, 10; Eutropius, 10, 2 maintains that Severus was killed during the fighting.
9. Eumenius, *Paneg. Constantino*, 12.
10. *Paneg. Maximiano et Constantino*, 1.
11. ibid., 2: 'To you, Constantine, who have acquired the title of emperor from your father-in-law.'
12. *de Mort. Pers.*, 22.
13. Zosimus, 2, 12; Victor *Caes.*, 40; *Ep.* 40; cf. Paully-Wissowa, I², col. 1445.
14. The Spanish revolt against Maxentius is known only from the evidence of coins minted at Tarraco, where *solidi* were struck in Constantine's fourth year—that is, before 25 July 310.
15. *de Mort. Pers.*, 28; cf. Eutropius, 10, 3.
16. *de Mort. Pers.*, 29.
17. Eusebius Pamphilus, *H.E.*, 8, 14.
18. All the authorities stress Licinius' ignorance and avarice: cf. especially Victor's *Caes.* and *Ep.* When he became emperor, he was aged about forty-five.
19. Some accounts place it in the year 307, but it is difficult to see how all the events from Galerius' defeat to the appointment of

Licinius could have been crowded into the months of the autumn of a single year.

20. *de Mort. Pers.*, 29.
21. *de Mort. Pers.*, 32, and coins in Eckhel, 8, pp. 52 and 72.

CHAPTER FIVE

1. Eusebius Pamphilus, *de Vita Const.*, 1, 25.
2. ibid., 1, 25.
3. Eumenius, *Gratiarum actio Constantino*, 13, proclaimed to celebrate the fifth anniversary of Constantine's accession, after July 25, 310.
4. ibid., *passim*.
5. Maurice, *Numismatique constantinienne*, ii (1911), xxff.; but see Alföldi, *The Conversion of Constantine and Pagan Rome*, pp. 40f., 54, and the references there.
6. Baynes, *The Divine Institutes* in *Byzantine Studies*, Univ. of London, 1955, pp. 352ff.
7. *Incerti. Paneg. Const. Aug.*, 21, 3 and 7.
8. Anon. Vales., 4, 10; Zosimus, 2, 10, 2; Victor, *Ep.*, 40, 3.
9. *Sol invicto comiti Augusti nostri*: actually 'The Unconquered Sun, comrade of our Augustus' – making the emperor superior to the sun-god. The last issue in this series was not made until after the defeat of Licinius and shortly before the Christian Council of Nicaea.
10. Eumenius, *Paneg. Constantino*, 14.
11. *Chronicon*, at A.2325 (A.D. 309–310).
12. *de Mort. Pers.*, 29–30.
13. *de Mort. Pers.*, 30.
14. Eusebius Pamphilus, *H.E.*, 8, 14.
15. Victor, *Caesars*, 40, 19; cf. Zosimus, 2, 14.
16. Eutropius, 10, 4.
17. Constantine, *ad Sanctorum. Coe. Or.*, 25.
18. *de Mort. Pers.*, 33–5; Eusebius Pamphilus, *H.E.*, 8, 16.
19. Eusebius Pamphilus, *H.E.*, 8, 17.
20. *de Mort. Pers.*, 35.
21. *de Mort. Pers.*, 36.
22. *de Mort. Pers.*, 43.
23. Eusebius Pamphilus, *H.E.*, 9, 1.
24. Mansi, *Sacrorum conciliorum . . . collectio*, Graz, 1960 vol. 2, col. 21–2.
25. Mansi, *Sacrorum conciliorum . . . collectio*, Graz, 1960, vol. 2, col. 513ff. and 539ff.

26. *de Mort. Pers.*, 35.
27. Zosimus, 2, 15–16.

CHAPTER SIX

1. Constantine, *Oration to the Saints*, 25.
2. On religious syncretism and the tendency to monotheism in Roman religion, see C. Bailey, *Phases in the Religion of Ancient Rome*, O.U.P., 1932, pp. 256–9.
3. Socrates Scholasticus, *H.E.*, 1, 2.
4. Sozomen, *H.E.*, 1, (3 and) 4.
5. The *labarum* as it was in later years is described in Eusebius, *de Vita Const.*, 1, 30–31; see also art. *Labarum* in Paully-Wissowa, XII[1], col. 240ff.
6. *de Mort. Pers.*, 48.
7. *de Vita Const.*, 1, 28–30.
8. Eusebius Pamphilus, *H.E.*, 9, 9.
9. *Incert. Paneg. Constantino*, 16.
10. *de Mort. Pers.*, 44; cf. Zosimus, 2, 15–15; Eutropius, 10, 4; Nazarenius, *Paneg. Constantino*, 6–14; 21 7.
11. Eumenius, *Paneg. Constantino*, 12, 8 and O; Nazarenius, *Paneg. Const.*, 4, 25; cf. O. Seeck, *Geschichte des Undergangs der Antiken Welt*, vol. 1, pp. 117ff.
12. Eutropius, 10, 4.
13. Eusebius Pamphilus, *H.E.*, 9, 9.
14. Maxentius' superstition is discussed in Paully-Wissowa, art. *Maxentius*, XIV[2], cols. 241ff.
15. Eusebius Pamphilus, *H.E.*, 9, 9, quoting *Exodus*, 15, 4–5.
16. cf. *de Mort. Pers.*, 44.
17. *de Vita Const.*, 1, 40; 2, 55, and Constantine's letters and edicts, *passim*.
18. Eusebius Pamphilus, *H.E.*, 9, 9.
19. *V.* art. *Hosius* in *The New Catholic Encyclopaedia*, Magraw-Hill, 1966 and the bibliography there.
20. Eusebius Pamphilus, *H.E.*, 10, 5.
21. Eusebius Pamphilus, *H.E.*, 10, 6.
22. The Palace was already in Pope Melitiades' hands in October 313, when the Synod of Rome was held, according to the *Liber Pontificalis*, '*in domum Faustae in Latrano*'.
23. *de Vita Const.*, 1, 43.
24. On appointments of pagans to offices in Constantine's Rome, see Alföldi, op. cit., chap. 7, *Constantine with Rome*.
25. Zosimus, 2, 17; Victor, *Caes.*, 40, 25.
26. Dessau, *Inscrip. Lat. Select.*, 694; cf. *de Vita Const.*, 2, 12. On the meaning of the inscription, see Alföldi, op. cit., 72; V. Schultze,

Zeitschrift für Kirchengeschichte, vii, p. 350; O. Seeck, op. cit., vol. 1, p. 495.

CHAPTER SEVEN

1. *Incert. Paneg. Constantino*, 11.
2. Zosimus, 2, 17.
3. Eusebius Pamph., *H.E.*, 9, 9.
4. Eusebius Pamph., *H.E.*, 1, 8.
5. Eusebius Pamph., *H.E.*, 9, 9.
6. O. Seeck, op. cit., vol. 1, pp. 148, 503.
7. Eusebius Pamph., *H.E.*, 9, 9.
8. On the Edict of Milan, see M. Anastos, art. *The Edict of Milan*, in *Revue des Etudes Byzantines*, 1967, pp. 13ff.; Alföldi, op. cit., *passim.*
9. *de Mort. Pers.*, 48.
10. Eusebius Pamph., *H.E.*, 10, 5.
11. Eusebius Pamph., *H.E.*, 10, 5 and 7.
12. Anon. Vales., 5, 14–15.
13. Zosimus, 2, 18; *de Mort. Pers.*, 46, probably in fact not Campus Serenus, but Campus Ergenus, cf. H. Gregoire, *Byzantion*, 13, 1938, p. 585.
14. *de Mort. Pers.*, 46.
15. *de Vita Const.*, 4, 20.
16. *de Mort. Pers.*, 49.
17. *Paneg.*, 9, 20–21; Zosimus, 2, 17; Anon. Vales., 5, 13.
18. *de Mort. Pers.*, 50–51.
19. Zosimus, 2, 18–20; Eutropius, 10, 5; Anon. Vales., 5, 14–15; Victor, *Ep.*, 41.
20. Eutropius, 10, 5.
21. On Valens, see Clinton, *Fasti Romani*, vol. 1, at 314, cols. 2 and 3; Anon. Vales, 5, 17–18; Zosimus, 2, 19–20.
22. Sirmium had been Marcus Aurelius' capital of choice, and had frequently been used by the Illyrian emperors as their headquarters in the continual struggle to control the Danube Valley.
23. Eusebius Pamph., *H.E.*, 1, 48.
24. On Vettius Rufinus, see Paully-Wissowa, IA[1], col. 1186, art. *Rufinus 15.*
25. The general law, however, remained that a man should be tried in the province where his offence was committed, whether it was his home town or not: Cod. Theod. IX, i, 1. It was only the aristocratic *honestiores* who were forbidden trial in their own cities.
26. Idatius, *Chronicon*, under the consulship of Gallicanus and

Septimus Bassus (A.D. 317); Zosimus, 2, 20; cf. Eusebius Pamph., *de Vita Const.*, 4, 40.

27. Peace and tranquillity were Constantine's constant themes throughout the years of his sole rule; cf. his role in the Arian Controversy, chapter ten, and especially his letters to the bishops, pp. 192, 202, 242.

CHAPTER EIGHT

Not all the problems of the chronology of Donatist origins have been completely resolved, and some of the dates given in this chapter are open to question. However, if perfect solutions to all the problems were found, it is doubtful if they would significantly alter our evaluation of Constantine's attitude towards Christianity and role in African events from 312 to 322.

1. On Donatus, see *Reallexikon für Antike und Christentum*, vol. IV, cols. 128ff. Accounts of the Donatist Controversy may be found in W. H. C. Frend, *The Donatist Church*, Oxford, 1952. H. von Soden, *Urkunde zur Entstehungsgeschichte d. Donatismus*, Bonn, 1913; P. Monceau, *Histoire littéraire de l'Afrique chrétienne*, vol. 4; cf. Eusebius Pamph., *H.E.*, 10; Augustine of Hippo, *de Baptismo*, 4 and the writings of Optatus of Milevium.
2. Mansi, *Sacrorum Conciliorum Nova et Amplissima Collectio*, vol. 1, cols. 1247–8, Graz, 1960; Jones, *Constantine and the Christian Church*, Hodder and Stoughton, London, 1948, chapters on Donatism.
3. Optatus, *de Schism. Donat.*, 1, 19, in *Corpus Script. Eccles. Lat.*, vol. 26; Augustine, *Ad. Cath. Ep.*, 18, 46.
4. Constantine, to Anulinus, Eusebius Pamph., *H.E.*, 10, 7.
5. Eusebius Pamph., *H.E.*, 10, 6.
6. Optatus, *de Schism. Donat.*, 1, 22.
7. Optatus, *de Schism. Donat.*, 1, 22.
8. Eusebius Pamph., *H.E.*, 10, 5.
9. Optatus, *de Schism. Donat.*, 1, 23; Mansi, op. cit., vol. 2, cols. 433ff.
10. cf. Constantine's letter to the Proconsul Aelianus, *Optatus*, app. 3; cf. Mansi, 2, col. 466.
11. Eusebius Pamph., *H.E.*, 10, 5.
12. The documents in the case against Felix of Aptunga are preserved in appendix I to Optatus, *de Schism. Donat.* '*Acta Purgationis Felicis*'.
13. Hefele, *Histoire des Conciles*, vol. 1, pp. 275ff.; Mansi, op. cit., vol. 2, cols. 463ff.
14. On Ingentius, see Augustine, *Epistles*, 88, 4; *contra Cresconium*, 3, 70 and 81.

15. Constantine's letter to the Bishops at Arles is preserved in Optatus, App. 5.
16. Optatus, *de Schism. Donat.*, 1, 26.
17. Optatus, *de Schism. Donat.*, 1, 26.
18. Optatus, App. 7, the letter *Perseverare.*
19. Augustine, *contra Cresconium*, 3, 71.
20. cf. *Passio Donati*, in P.L.8, 252–8.
21. *Cod. Theod.*, IX, xxxiv, 1.
22. *Cod. Theod.*, IX, xxxiv, 3.
23. Optatus, App. 1: *Gesta apud Zenophilum.*
24. Constantine, *Quod fides* in Optatus, App. 9.
25. *Cod. Theod.*, I, xxvii, 1.
26. *Cod. Theod.*, VI, i, 1 (cf. *Cod. Just.*, I, ix, 3).
27. *Cod. Theod.*, VI, i, 3.

CHAPTER NINE

1. References at chapter seven, n. 26.
2. *Anon. cont. Dionis*, 15, 1, in *F.H.G.*, iv, 199.
3. Eusebius Pamph., *H.E.*, 10, 8; *de Vita Const.*, 2, 3.
4. *Cod. Theod.*, IX, xvi, 3.
5. *Cod. Theod.*, IX, xvi, 2 and 1.
6. *Cod. Theod.*, IX, xl, 2.
7. *Cod. Theod.*, I, xxvii, 1 – extended to the clergy generally in laws dated April 8, 321 (*Cod. Theod.*, IV, vii, 1) and June 8, 323 (*Cod. Just.*, I, xiii, 1).
8. *Cod. Theod.*, IX, xii, 1.
9. *Cod. Theod.*, VII, xvi, 1.
10. *Cod. Theod.*, IX, iii, 1.
11. *Cod. Just.*, III, xii, 3.
12. *Cod. Theod.*, II, viii, 1.
13. *de Vita Const.*, 1, 52.
14. Eusebius Pamph., *H.E.*, 10, 8 – which summarizes Licinius' anti-Christian legislation.
15. *de Vita Const.*, 2, 13–19.
15. *de Vita Const.*, 1, 31.
17. *de Vita Const.*, 2, 5.
18. cf. Nazarenius, *Paneg. Constantino*, 3.
19. Victor, *Caesars*, 41, 7.
20. cf. Nazarenius' panegyric, and laws (e.g. *Cod. Theod.*, I, xx, 21) dated from Serdica in 321.
21. The birth of Crispus' son is mentioned in a law preserved in the Theodosian Code, *Cod. Theod.*, IX, xxxviii, 1. His name and fate remain uncertain.
22. cf. Starr, *Roman Imperial Navy*, Heffer, Cambridge, 1960, p. 197.

23. Zosimus, 2, 22–8; cf. Anon. Vales., 5, 28.
24. Zosimus, 2, 21.
25. The issue matched and was countered by similar issues praising Licinius, 'Victorious Everywhere', 'the Unconquered Jovian Augustus', 'the Best of Princes'.
26. *de Vita. Const.*, 2, 16.
27. Anon. Vales, 5, 28; Victor, *Ep.*, 41, 6; Zosimus, 2, 25.
28. Anon. Vales, 5, 28.
29. *de Vita Const.*, 2, 12.
30. Zosimus, 2, 28; Eutropius, 10, 6; Anon. Vales., 5, 28.
31. Jerome, *Chronicon,* at Anno 2339 (A.D. 323–4) – the chronicles all agree that the Roman senate was used to legitimise this murder – just as it was used to cover Constantine's assumption of the title 'Maximus' – see Zosimus, 2, 28; Victor, *Ep.*, 41, 7; *de Vita Const.*, 2, 19.
32. *Cod. Theod.*, XVI, xv, 1 and 2.
33. *de Vita Const.*, 2, 20.
34. Socrates Scholasticus, *H.E.*, 1, 4; Zonarus, 13, 1.

CHAPTER TEN

1. *de Vita Const.*, 2, 56.
2. *de Vita Const.*, 2, 24–42.
3. *de Vita Const.*, 2, 46.
4. On the Meletian Schism, see Sozomen, *H.E.*, 1, *passim.* Many elements of the story – e.g. the two imprisonments of Peter of Alexandria – have been denied by scholars. But the basic fact, that the Great Persecution led to schism in Egypt, is incontrovertible.
5. Mansi, op. cit., vol. 2, cols. 407ff.
6. On the life of Arius, see the ancient authorities collected in Lebreton and Zeiller, *Histoire de l'Eglise,* vol. 2, part 2, chapter 1, p. 69; *Reallexikon für Antike und Christentum,* vol. 1, art. *Arius.*
7. On Lucian of Antioch, see Fliche et Martin (eds.), *Histoire de l'Eglise*, vol. 2, pp. 350ff., *l'Eglise d'Antioche à la fin du III siècle.*
8. Epiphanius, *Haeres.*, 69, 3; Athenasius, *Contra Arianos*, 1, 8; cf. Socrates, *H.E.*, i, 5 and 2, 25.
9. Constantine, to Arius and Alexander, on *Proverbs 8, 22: De Vita Const.*, 2, 64–72. The authenticity of this letter has been denied.
10. Philostorgus, *H.E.*, 1, 7; Eusebius Pamph., *de Vita Const.*, 3, 6.
11. Pitra, *Analecta Sacra*, vol. 4, p. 224.
12. *de Vita Const.*, 3, 10.
13. cf. *Reallexikon für Antike und Christentum*, art. *Arius*; J. H. Newman, Card., *Arians of the Fourth Century*; H. A. Gwatkin, *Studies in Arianism.*

14. Philostorgus, *H.E.*, 1, 9.
15. Eusebius' letter is preserved by Socrates Scholasticus, in *H.E.*, 1, 8.
16. Mansi, op. cit., vol. 2, cols. 666ff.
17. *de Vita Const.*, 3, 15.
18. Socrates Scholasticus, *H.E.*, 1, 9; Gelasius of Cyzica, *H.E.*, 2, 37.
19. *Cod. Theod.*, XV, xii, 1; cf. *de Vita Const.*, 4, 25; Socrates, *H.E.*, 1, 18; Sozomen, *H.E.*, 1, 8. However, gladiators were not finally suppressed until the reign of Honorius, in A.D. 404.

CHAPTER ELEVEN

1. *Carm.*, 4, 1ff.; cf. also *Carm.*, 18, 32ff., where he writes of Byzantium as 'the Sister Rome', *Roma Soror.*
2. Victor, *Ep.*, 41.
3. *Cod. Theod.*, I, ix, 4.
4. Eutropius, 10, 6.
5. Victor, *Caesars*, 41, 11.
6. Victor, *Ep.*, 41, 11.
7. Philostorgus, *H.E.*, 2, 4.
8. Zosimus, 2, 29.
9. Apollinaris Sidonius, *Epist.*, 5, 8.
10. *Cod. Theod.*, IX, xxiv, 1.
11. *Cod. Just.*, IX, ix, 30.
12. *Cod. Just.*, V, xxvi, 1.
13. *Cod. Theod.*, IX, viii, 1.
14. *Cod. Theod.*, VII, 20, 2.
15. Zosimus, II, 29.
16. cf. Benedictus Canonicus, *Mirabilia Urbis Romae*, trs. F. M. Nichols, 'The Marvels of Rome', London, 1889; reprinted in Holt, E. G., *A Documentary History of Art*, vol. 1, p. 70 (Doubleday, N.Y., 1957).
17. John Chrysostom, *Ep. ad Philipp.*, 4, 15, 5.

CHAPTER TWELVE

1. *Cod. Theod.*, XIII, v, 7.
2. Sozomen, *H.E.*, 2, 3.
3. Eagles indicated the site for the city: saints and angels defended it: see Baynes, *The Supernatural Defenders of Constantinople*, in *Byzantine Studies*, pp. 248ff.
4. William of Malmesbury, *Chronicle*, London, 1847, pp. 372–3.
5. Anon. Vales, 5, 29.
6. Zosimus, 2, 30–33, 35.
7. cf. Alföldi, op. cit., pp. 111 and 116.
8. Anon. Vales., 5, 29. On the new classes at Constantinople, see

F. Stein, *Geschichte des Spätromischen Reiches*, 1, p. 194; Jones, *Later Roman Empire*, vol. 1, pp. 83f.

9. Lactantius, *Divine Institutes*, 7; discussed in Marni, *La fondazione di CP in uno passo del Chronicon Paschale*, in *Atto dello VII Congresso Int. di Stud. Byz.* (Rome, 1953), pp. 416ff.
10. Lactantius, *Divine Institutes*, 7.
11. Chron. Pas. 285; under the consulship of Gallianus and Symmachus; cf. E. Gren, *Zu den Legenden von der Gründung KP* in *Serta Kazaroviana* I, pp. 151–7.
12. The ceremonies of the consecration and dedication of Constantinople are discussed in D. Lathoud art. in *Echos d'Orient*, xxiii (1924), pp. 289ff.
13. Sozomen, *H.E.*, 2, 3.
14. *Corpus Inscript. Lat.*, xi, 5283.
15. *Cod. Theod.*, I, xiii, 7.
16. Philostorgus, *H.E.*, 1, 2, 9.
17. The significance of this statue and its inscription are discussed in Alfoldi, op. cit., p. 59; see also his references, p. 131. A slightly different view is taken here.
18. See city plan, p. 227.
19. Sozomen, *H.E.*, 2, 3.
20. *de Vita Const.*, 3, 47.
21. *de Vita Const.*, 3, 52.
22. Socrates, *H.E.*, 1, 16.
23. The case is discussed by Burckhardt, op. cit., p. 353.
24. Eunapius, *Aedes*,. 41.
25. Burckhardt, *The Age of Constantine the Great*, p. 350, trs. Hadas, Routledge and Kegan Paul, 1949.
26. Socrates Scholasticus, *H.E.*, 1, 16.
27. Jerome, *Chronicon*, Anno 2346, Constantine's 24th.
28. *The Alexandrian Chronicle*, p. 285; cf. Gibbon, *Decline and Fall of the Roman Empire*, vol. 2, chap. 18 (Everyman Edition, pp. 87–8).

CHAPTER THIRTEEN

1. Eunapius, *Aedes.*, 37, 45; Zosimus, 2, 40.
2. *Reallexikon für Antike und Christentum*, vol. 1, art. *Athenasius.*
3. Constantine, *Epist. on the Heretics*, preserved in *de Vita Const.*, 2, 64–5.
4. *de Vita Const.*, 3, 66.
5. Theodoret, *H.E.*, 1, 20; Gelasius of Cyzica, *H.E.*, 3 *app.*; Athenasius, *Apol. contra Arianos*, 7.
6. Socrates Scholasticus, *H.E.*, 1, 25—the date of this letter is disputed; it was written one November 27, but the year could be any from 327 to 334.

7. Socrates Scholasticus, *H.E.*, 1, 26; Sozomen, *H.E.*, 2, 27.
8. Gelasius of Cyzica, *H.E.*, 3, 16. It has been suggested that this letter was addressed not, in fact, to Alexander of Alexandria, but to Alexander of Byzantium, in the year 335.
9. *de Vita Const.*, 3, 59–69; Philostorgus, *H.E.*, 3, 15; Theodoret, 1, 21.
10. *de Vita Const.*, 3, 60.
11. *de Vita Const.*, 3, 61.
12. Socrates Scholasticus, *H.E.*, 1, 36; Sozomen, *H.E.*, 2, 33.
13. *de Vita Const.*, 4, 18–20.
14. Socrates Scholasticus, *H.E.*, 1, 27.
15. In a letter preserved in Athenasius, *Apologia contra Arianos*, 64.
16. Athenasius, *Apologia contra Arianos*, 61–2.
17. Socrates Scholasticus, *H.E.*, 1, 9; Gelasius of Cyzicas, *H.E.*, 3, 19 preserves Constantine's letter to Arius.
18. On Delmatius the Censor, see Paully-Wissowa, IV², col. 2455.
19. Theodoret, *H.E.*, 1, 28; the principal documents are preserved in Athenasius, *Apol. Contra Arianos*, 64–8; see also British Museum Papyrus 1913.
20. Athenasius, *Apol. contra Arianos*, 70.
21. Theodoret, *H.E.*, 1, 26.
22. *de Vita Const.*, 4, 42.
23. H. I. Bell, *Jews and Christians in Egypt*, pp. 53ff. (London, 1924).
24. Socrates Scholasticus, *H.E.*, 1, 32–3; Athenasius, *Apolog. contra Arianos*, 8.
25. *de Vita Const.*, 4, 43–5.
26. Socrates Scholasticus, *H.E.*, 1, 34; Sozomen, *H.E.*, 2, 28; Athenasius tells the story in *Apol. contra Arianos*, 86.
27. Athenasius, *Apol. contra Arianos*, 9, cf. 87.
28. Athenasius, *de Synodis*, 21.
29. Sozomen, *H.E.*, 2, 31.
30. Athenasius, *Epist. de Morte Arii*, in *Epist. ad Episcopos Aegypti et Libyae*, 19.

CHAPTER FOURTEEN

1. Eutropius, 10, 6–7.
2. Victor, *Epit.*, 41.
3. *de Vita Const.*, 4, 24.
4. On the solidus, see Paully-Wissowa, IIIA, cols. 920ff.; Jones, *Later Roman Empire*, vol. 1, pp. 107–9, 439–48.
5. On inflation in the age of Constantine, see Jones, op. cit., 26ff., 108f. and on the *iugum*, Jones, op. cit., pp. 438–43.
6. Jones, op. cit., pp. 52–60, 97ff., 607f.

7. The court-room exchange is preserved in Optatus, App. I: *Gesta apud Zenophilum.*
8. On the Constantinean Civil Service, see *Cambridge Mediaeval History*, vol. 1, chapter 2; Jones, op. cit., pp. 100–4, 367–71.
9. Jones, op. cit., pp. 103f.
10. Burckhardt, *The Age of Constantine the Great*, p. 336.
11. Anon. Vales., 6, 35; cf. Zosimus, 2, 39.

CHAPTER FIFTEEN

1. *de Vita Const.*, 4, 54.
2. Victor, *Caesars*, 41, 11.
3. Jerome, under Anno 2351, Constantine's 29th.
4. Sozomen, *H.E.*, 1, 8.
5. The rising was suppressed by Gallus, the son of Julius Constantius, then acting as Caesar to Constantius II: Jerome, under Anno 2368; Socrates, *H.E.*, 2, 33.
6. *Cod. Theod.*, VI, i, 4.
7. *Cod. Thoed.*, VI, i, 5.
8. 'Bull-necked for ten years,' the popular word ran, 'for the next twelve a brigand and for the last ten, the newest recruit to the cause of rash extravagances.'
9. Eutropius, 10, 6.
10. Anon. Vales, 6, 31.
11. The history of Cherson is outlined in Pauly-Wissowa, III², cols. 2242ff.
12. cf. *Liber Pontificalis*, ed. Duchesne, vol. 1, pp. 172ff.
13. *de Vita Const.*, 4, 58–9.
14. Eusebius Pamph., *Sermon for Constantine's Tricennalia*, in the *Library of the Nicene Fathers*, vol. 1, pp. 581ff, chap. 2.
15. 331 was the year of the Christian Ablavius' consulship, when his influence over the emperor reached new heights. It was also a year when Constantine felt the shortage of money very acutely, owing to a famine in the East, as well as the cost of imperial building programmes. It may well be that it also saw the first overt steps against the pagan temples and their treasuries. The worship of Constantine's own imperial image had long been forbidden: *de Vita Const.*, 4, 16.
16. Libanius, the Emperor Julian's friend, described the sack of the temples in his Orations (30, 6), but explicitly claimed that 'Constantine changed nothing at all with regard to the legal cults' —*pro templis*, 6.
17. *de Vista Const.*, 3, 54–8.
18. *Paschal Chronicle*, p. 286. Idatius' chronicle fixes the date of

Delmatius promotion: XIV Kal. Oct., September 25. See also Athenasius, Apol. contra Arianos, 1.

19. Julian, on Constantine, see p. 296, where Julian compares his uncle to a confectioner with the mind and ambitions of a banker.
20. Eusebius Pamph., *Sermon for Constantine's Tricennalia*, 5.
21. For the long history of Rome's troubles with Persia, see the *Cambridge Ancient History*, vol. 12, chap. 9 and *Cambridge Mediaeval History*, vol. 1, chap. 3.
22. *de Vita Const.*, 4, 56.
23. *de Vita Const.*, 4, 61.
24. *de Vita Const.*, 4, 60.
25. For the Greek text and an English translation see W. Cave-Wright, *Julian*, vol. 2: *Caesars*, Heinemann, 1913.
26. *de Vita Const.*, 4, 65.
27. Jerome, under Anno 2353, Constantine's 31st. Cf. Victor, *Epitome*: 'When he had lived sixty-three years, ruling for half of them – thirteen as sole emperor – he was consumed by disease. The body was buried in Byzantine Constantinople.'
28. Sozomen, *H.E.*, 2, 34.
29. Julian, *Or.*, 1, 16.
30. *de Vita Const.*, 4, 68.

CHAPTER SIXTEEN

1. *de Vita Const.*, 4, 67.
2. *de Vita Const.*, 4, 68.
3. *de Vita Const.*, 4, 68. Cf. the Paschal Chronicle, where the division of the empire is described.
4. *de Vita Const.*, 4, 69.
5. *de Vita Const.*, 4, 70–1.
6. Socrates Scholasticus, *H.E.*, 1, 38.
7. Athenasius, *Hist. Ar.*, 44. In extreme old age, Hosius was finally persuaded by Constantius II to set his name to the Arian creed known as the 'Blasphemy of Sirmium'. He died that same year, A.D. 357.
8. Ammianus, 18, 4, 3. Eusebius of Nicomedia finally achieved the chief ambition of the Arian founding fathers when in 340 he became Bishop of Constantinople. He died in 342. His Collucianist Eusebius of Caesarea had died in 340.
9. Philostorgus, *H.E.*, 2, 16.
10. In contrast, Julian the Apostate, who himself narrowly escaped death in the massacres, put the blame squarely on Constantius' shoulders – so also did such different witnesses as Zosimus (2, 40) and Athenasius.
11. Date fixed by Idatius: V.Id.Sept.

12. See the genealogical tables, pp. 346-8.
13. Zosimus, 2, 40.
14. Eutropius, 10, 9.
15. On Ablavius, see Paully-Wissowa, 1[1], col. 103, art. *Ablabius.*
16. Julian, *Or.*, 1, 19.
17. Victor, *Caesars*, 41, 22.
17. Victor, *Caesars*, 41, 22; Eutropius, 10, 9; Zosimus, 2, 41.
18. Ammianus, 16, 8, 10; 21, 16, 18.
19. Victor, *Caesars*, 41, 23.

CHAPTER SEVENTEEN

1. *Martyrologium Romanum*, Rome, 1922, p. 195.
2. Zosimus, 2, 29.
3. *Liber Pontificalis*, ed. Duchesne, vol. 1, pp. CXIVff.
4. *Liber Pontificalis*, ed. Duchesne, vol. 1, pp. CVIIff.
5. *Liber Pontificalis*, ed. Duchesne, vol. 1, pp. CIX–CXVIII.
6. *Liber Pontificalis*, ed. Duchesne, vol. 1, p. 174.
7. For an English translation of the *Donation*, see, R. D. G. Laffan, *Select Documents of European History 800–1492*, London, 1930. H. Bettenson, *Documents of the Christian Church*, Oxford, 1943.
8. Cf. E. Amann, *L'époque carolingienne*, p. 60ff, in Fliche et Martin, *Histoire de l'église*, vol. 6.
9. E. Amann, *op. cit.*, pp. 116ff. Text in Mansi, vol. 12, col. 1055ff.
10. Hakluyt. *Voyages*, vol. 2.
11. *De Vita Const.*, 3, 47.
12. *Catacheses*, 4, 10; 10, 19; 13, 4.
13. *Liber Pontificalis*, ed. Duchesne, vol. 1, p. 167.
14. Socrates Scholasticus, *H.E.*, 1, 17.
15. Sozomen, *H.E.*, 2, 1.
16. *Liber Pontificalis*, ed. Duchesne, vol. 1, pp. CVIIIff.
17. *Liber Pontificalis*, ed. Duchesne, vol. 1, p. 179.
18. J. A. Giles, *William of Malmesbury's Chronicle*, London 1847, *in loc.*

THE NEO-FLAVIANS

?

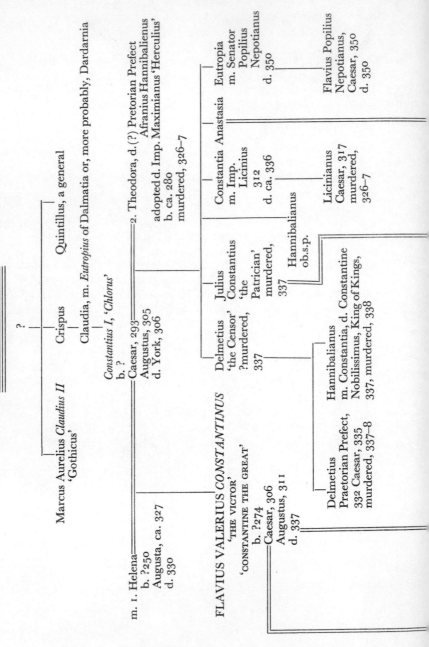

Marcus Aurelius *Claudius II* 'Gothicus'

Crispus

Quintillus, a general

Claudia, m. *Eutropius* of Dalmatia or, more probably, Dardarnia

Constantius I, *'Chlorus'*
b. ?
Caesar, 293
Augustus, 305
d. York, 306

m. 1. Helena
b. ?250
Augusta, ca. 327
d. 330

2. Theodora, d. (?) Pretorian Prefect Afranius Hannibalienus
adopted d. Imp. Maximianus 'Herculius'
b. ca. 280
murdered, 326–7

FLAVIUS VALERIUS *CONSTANTINUS*
'THE VICTOR'
'CONSTANTINE THE GREAT'
b. ?274
Caesar, 306
Augustus, 311
d. 337

Delmetius
'the Censor'
?murdered, 337

Julius Constantius
'the Patrician'
murdered, 337

Hannibalianus
ob.s.p.

Constantia
m. Imp. Licinius 312
d. ca. 336

Anastasia

Eutropia
m. Senator Popilius Nepotianus
d. 350

Delmetius
Praetorian Prefect, 332 Caesar, 335
murdered, 337–8

Hannibalianus
m. Constantia, d. Constantine
Nobilissimus, King of Kings,
337, murdered, 338

Licinianus
Caesar, 317
murdered, 326–7

Flavius Popilius Nepotianus,
Caesar, 350
d. 350

m.2. Basilina, d. Comenius

JULIANUS 'the Apostate'
Caesar, 335
Augustus, 360, d. 362

m.1. Galla, sister Senator Rufinus

ob.s.p. a son,

GALLUS,
Caesar, 351
murdered, 353

a daughter
m. Constantius II

m. 1. Bassianus Caesar, executed 314
2. Flavius Optatus, Consul, 334 murdered, 337–8

m. 1. Minervina

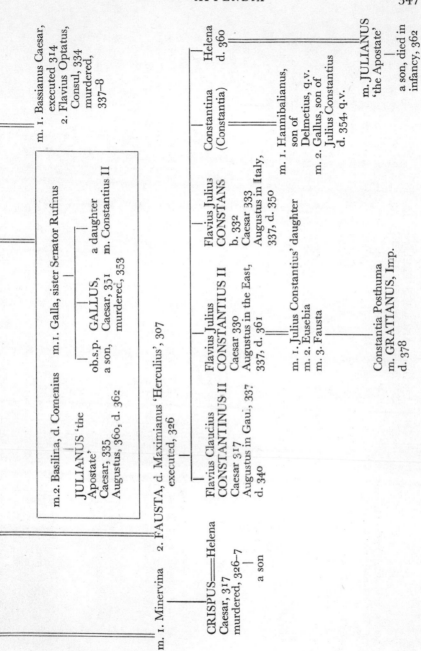

CRISPUS——Helena
Caesar, 317
murdered, 326–7

a son

2. FAUSTA, d. Maximianus 'Herculius', 307
executed, 326

Flavius Claudius
CONSTANTINUS II
Caesar 317
Augustus in Gaul, 337
d. 340

Flavius Julius
CONSTANTIUS II
Caesar 330
Augustus in the East, 337, d. 361

m. 1. Julius Constantius' daughter
m. 2. Eusebia
m. 3. Fausta

Constantia Posthuma
m. GRATIANUS, Imp.
d. 378

Flavius Julius
CONSTANS
b. 332
Caesar 333
Augustus in Italy, 337, d. 350

Constantina
(Constantia)

m. 1. Hannibalianus, son of Delmetius, q.v.
m. 2. Gallus, son of Julius Constantius d. 354, q.v.

Helena
d. 360

m. JULIANUS
'the Apostate'

a son, died in infancy, 362

THE JOVIANS AND HERCULIANS

Diocles, Praetorian Prefect to Numerius
took power, 284 as

DIOCLETIAN 'JOVIUS'
abdicated, 305
died, 313–6

appointed:
GALERIUS, Caesar 293, m. Valeria, daughter of Diocletian
Augustus, 305
d. 311

SEVERUS, Caesar, 305
d. 309

LICINIUS, Caesar, 310, Augustus, 311–24
m. Constantia, daughter of Constantius Chlorus 'the Herculian'

MAXIMIN DAZA, Caesar 305
d. 313

LICINIUS' son, Licinius 'LICINIANUS'
was Jovian Caesar, 317–26

Maximian, Praetorian Prefect in the West
associated with Diocletian, Caesar, 286
Augustus, 293

MAXIMIAN 'HERCULIUS'

appointed:
CONSTANTIUS CHLORUS, m. Theodora, adopted daughter of Maximian,
Caesar, 293, Augustus 305, died 306

CONSTANTINE, married Fausta, daughter of Maximian
self-styled Augustus at York, 306 Caesar, 306
Augustus, 311–337
CONSTANTINE'S son
CRISPUS was Herculian Caesar, 317–326
BASSIANUS was Herculian Caesar in 313
LICINIUS named VALENS Herculian Caesar in 314
and *M. Martianus* Herculian Augustus in 323

MAXENTIUS, married Galerius' daughter
self-styled Augustus at Rome
305–12

The ultimate triumph of the Flavians is reflected in the inscription from the Temple to their Genius, cut at Hispellum in Umbria some time between 333 and 337, to—
'The Emperor Caesar Flavius Constantinus, Maximus, Germanicus, Sarmarticus, Gothicus, the Victor, the Triumphant, the Augustus—
and Flavius Constantinus, and Flavius Constantius, and Flavius Constans . . .'

(Dessau, *Inscrip. Lat.* ser. 1, no. 705)

INDEX